The
Literature
of Fact

The
Literature
of Fact

READINGS FOR WRITERS

W. Ross Winterowd

Lucy Hawk

Geoffrey R. Winterowd

Prentice Hall, Englewood Cliffs, New Jersey 07632

LIBRARY OF CONGRESS
Library of Congress Cataloging-in-Publication Data

The Literature of Fact : readings for writers / [edited by] W. Ross
Winterowd, Lucy Hawk, Geoffrey R. Winterowd.
     p.   cm.
  Includes index.
  ISBN 0-13-537622-X
  1. College readers. 2. English language--Rhetoric.
I. Winterowd, W. Ross. II. Hawk, Lucy.   . III. Winterowd,
Geoffrey R.
PE1417.L637 1988
808'.0427--dc19   87-33402
                                                  CIP

© 1988 by Prentice-Hall, Inc.
A Division of Simon & Schuster
Englewood Cliffs, New Jersey 07632

Printed in the United States of America

10 9 8 7 6 5 4 3 2 1

Cover design: Ben Santora
Manufacturing buyer: Ray Keating

ISBN 0-13-537622-X

PRENTICE-HALL INTERNATIONAL (UK) LIMITED, *London*
PRENTICE-HALL OF AUSTRALIA PTY. LIMITED, *Sydney*
PRENTICE-HALL CANADA INC., *Toronto*
PRENTICE-HALL HISPANOAMERICANA, S.A., *Mexico*
PRENTICE-HALL OF INDIA PRIVATE LIMITED, *New Delhi*
PRENTICE-HALL OF JAPAN, INC., *Tokyo*
SIMON & SCHUSTER ASIA PTE. LTD., *Singapore*
EDITORA PRENTICE-HALL DO BRASIL, LTDA., *Rio de Janeiro*

Contents

2

Biography   59

3

The New Journalism   101

4

The Lyric in Prose   163

_____ **PART TWO   FIELDS** _____

5

History   215

6

The Social Sciences 259

7

The Sciences 291

Preface

"The literature of fact" is not original with us. It is the title of a course John McPhee teaches at Princeton, of a collection of English Institute essays edited by Angus Fletcher, and of a scholarly study by Ronald Weber; doubtless it appears frequently in other milieus. It hardly denotes a new genre, for after all, Thucydides had, we presume, essentially the same purposes as Barbara Tuchman; the works of Charles Lamb and Lewis Thomas are very much in the same genre; and Norman Mailer followed illustrious ancestors, notably Defoe, in writing a nonfiction novel, *The Executioner's Song*. In the eighteenth century, Addison and Steele were as "new" in their journalism as are Tom Wolfe or Hunter Thompson.

Although "the literature of fact" is not a revolutionary departure from tradition, it is nonetheless a genre that, within the last two decades, has become increasingly prominent and popular. In 1965, Truman Capote's masterful *In Cold Blood* was published in book form—the first of the contemporary nonfiction novels (although some give that honor to *Picture*, Lillian Ross's 1952 account of the making of *The Red Badge of Courage*). In 1970, Tom Wolfe proclaimed a new genre with the title of his collection of pieces by, among others, Gay Talese, Truman Capote, Terry Southern, Norman Mailer, George Plimpton, Joan Didion, Hunter Thompson, and Garry Wills: *The New Journalism*. With such practitioners as Lewis Thomas, Joan Didion, F. Gonzalez-Crussi, and Loren Eiseley, the personal essay (in this volume, we call it "the lyric in prose") has taken on new life.

In short, we would not argue that our age has invented a literature outside the historical forces of tradition and the individual talent, but we do feel that the body of writings we call *The Literature of Fact* are, at present, especially appropriate for college readers, both students and their teachers.

What criteria set *The Literature of Fact* apart from other referential texts? To answer this question, we refer to Kenneth Burke, who tells us that in reading we are controlled by either *the psychology of information* or *the psychology of form*. When we read strictly for information, we have wrung a text dry as soon as we can learn no more from it, but when we read on the basis of the psychology of form—appreciating texture; structure; universal patterns of experience, such as climax and repetition—we do not drain the text but can return to it again and again, as we do to music. In short, there is a difference between reading for utilitarian and for esthetic purposes.

Perhaps this is why the literature of fact is so appealing: it satisfies both our interest in the factual and our hunger for significant form. We can think of the Coleridgean metaphor of a frost-covered windowpane. We can see through the pane to the outside world, but we can also contemplate the frost patterns as objects of delight. But, of course, a pane of glass, regardless of how spotless, is nonetheless a pane of glass, reflecting and diffusing. Even when not frost-covered, it presents a visual experience for anyone who is interested in looking. Whether the pane of glass is "there" or not depends on the intention (and attention) of the viewer.

In his introduction to *The New Journalism*, Tom Wolfe argues that what makes this journalism new is the writers' use of the novelist's techniques: setting scenes, getting into characters' minds, but primarily supplying rich detail, resulting in a novelistic texture rather than a journalistic leanness. In other words, the new journalists are good story-tellers. This holds true for the nonfiction novelists, historians, biographers, and autobiographers that we include in this volume. As for writers in the nonnarrative modes—those who deal with subjects in the social, biological, and exact sciences—our interest in them as producers of literature (as opposed to professional treatises) centers on their ability to make the specialized accessible to general readers in an elegant way. A good example is *Gorillas in the Mist*, a naturalist study. Readers need no specialized background to follow the discussion and are pleased, we think, by the elegance of the exposition.

Our point is that referential writing from all fields can be viewed from the perspectives that we usually apply to fictional narratives and to lyrics. And that is probably why the literature of fact is an increasingly popular genre.

I once heard a wise person say, "When you read historical fiction, you get the worst of both worlds: bad history and bad fiction." When a historian views his or her craft as producing literature, you get the best of both worlds: good history and good narrative. In the literature of fact, you satisfy both the longing for what Theodore Roethke, in his poem "The Longing," called "the imperishable quiet at the heart of form" and the hunger for knowledge of the world.

The first section of this book introduces genres of the literature of fact: autobiography, biography, the new journalism, and what we call the lyric in prose (more conventionally, the personal essay). The second section, "Fields of Study," meets the needs of courses aimed at what is commonly termed "writing across the curriculum," with selections concerning history, social science, biological science, exact science, and the arts.

This organization invites students to consider problems of content and form in relation to readers who constitute a group that might be called "the educated public."

*The
Literature
of Fact*

Introduction

The Literature of Fact

Tentatively, we can divide the world of writings into literature and nonliterature, although to be sure, the categories are not watertight, and the definitions blur toward the center of the spectrum between the two poles of literature and nonliterature.

However, if we think about purposes for reading, the term *literature of fact* will become clear. On the one hand, we read for the pleasure of the story, for the mood the poem conveys, for the excitement of wondering "Who done it?" In other words, we read for the experience the text provides, not for information. (In this discussion, *text* means anything in writing, not just "textbook.") On the other hand, we sometimes read for practical, utilitarian purposes: to learn about a subject, to discover how something works, to find out how to do something, to keep up with the news and ideas of our time.

Let us say, then, that texts we read for the experience they provide are literature, and texts we read for the information they contain are nonliterature. (By this definition, you as reader determine what is literature and what is not.) Some texts, however, seem to have the properties of both categories of writing: they inform us about the world around us (in the jargon, they are "referential"), yet they satisfy our longing for the reading experience: telling a good story, using language elegantly, creating a mood, giving us a sense of perfect structure. In other words, some texts seem to have the properties (or potentials) of both good literature and good nonliterature, and this is what we call the literature of fact.

It comes from all fields: history, the sciences and social sciences, journalism, the humanities. It can deal with any subject, but in ways that are understandable to nonspecialists. One physicist writing only for other physicists is not producing what we, in this volume, call the literature of fact. From the standpoint of scholars in botany, a technical paper by a botanist may be brilliantly executed, but we would not include it in our definition. The literature of fact, like other literature, appeals to a general audience, not only to a group of specialists.

The Organization and Purpose of This Book

The first section, "Genres," is organized according to types of writing, not according to subject matter fields: personal narrative, biography, the new journalism, and what we call the lyric in prose (that is, the personal essay). The second section, "Fields of Study," contains essays on history, social science, the sciences, and the arts, all of them written for the general, educated reading public, not for specialists in their fields.

We think the readings in this collection will interest you. The subject matter the selections cover is timely and interesting, and the viewpoints and voices of the authors are contemporary.

As you read these selections, you will be gaining knowledge about, and a sense of contemporary writing and thinking; you will begin to understand the concerns of some of the thinkers of our age, and you will learn how they express themselves. So *The Literature of Fact* will be a valuable part of your general education.

More immediately (although not more practically), the book will give you ideas to discuss and write about, and it will give you models you can adapt to your own purposes. From reading the selections, you will begin to pick up the tone and methods of contemporary professionals. In other words, the book will help you become a more effective and versatile writer. The questions for discussion that follow each selection and the suggestions for writing at the end of each chapter will aid you in making the most effective use of the book.

Our goal has been to create an interesting book that will help writers become better writers.

C H A P T E R

1

Personal Narrative

No matter how impersonal the prose might seem, all writing is personal in one way or another because the author expresses his or her own opinions, attitudes, personality, and knowledge. Because most writing is not spur-of-the-moment, writers often spend a great deal of time with their own thoughts before starting to create the text.

How much more personal, then, is writing about events in one's own life! Yet personal narrative is rarely about the author alone. Just as a geographical location has no meaning without its relation to other localities, writers define themselves as entities that interact with people and events. Maxine Hong Kingston and Eudora Welty, in writing about their parents, try to discover their own beginnings. John Wideman, who set out to write about his brother, a prisoner convicted of murder, tells us, "Another book could be constructed about a writer who goes to prison to interview his brother but comes away with his own story." *Brothers and Keepers*, from which a selection appears in this chapter, is just that story. Willie Morris and Jack Henry Abbott write of their experiences with institutions in opposition to the individual: the university and the prison.

As you read the selections in this chapter, be aware of how the authors interact with the world around them and the importance of that interaction in the personal narratives.

The genres of personal narrative are not watertight categories but overlap and blend into one another. For example, the *diary* and the *journal* are day-by-day accounts of events, written more or less on the spot; but the diary is usually not intended as a public document whereas the journal is meant to be published in some way.

Autobiography—from the Greek *auto-*, "self"; *bios-*, "mode of life"; and *graphein*, "to write"—is a chronological account, but not a series of relatively independent entries. The autobiographer looks back on his or her life, or on a period of that life, and recounts events, impressions, significances. The autobiographer is very like the novelist, but works with his or her personal history, with the facts of existence rather than fictions, attempting to capture in the narrative the texture of the past. An example is Eudora Welty's *One Writer's Beginnings*, from which an excerpt appears in this chapter.

The *memoir* is a kind of autobiography, but is generally associated with historical events. (Presidents of the United States write their memoirs after they leave office.) A memoir usually does not cover the author's whole life, but only that portion with historical significance. The selection from *North Toward Home*, by Willie Morris, is a good example of memoir writing.

Like novels, epic poems, and other fictions, personal narrative tells stories; but like history, the stories are factual. We read history for more than the facts, however; historical writing deals not only with events but with concepts and values, as do the forms of personal narrative.

In *One Writer's Beginnings*, Eudora Welty describes the theme of her own writing, and although she is talking about fiction, she might well be referring to personal narrative:

> It is our inward journey that leads us through time—forward or back, seldom in a straight line, most often spiraling. Each of us moving, changing, with respect to others. As we discover, we remember; remembering, we discover; and most intensely do we experience this when our separate journeys converge.[1]

In this chapter, you will find seven representative selections of personal narrative. You are encouraged to view these readings as prompts and models for your own "inward journeys" through time.

---

[1]Eudora Welty, *One Writer's Beginnings* (New York: Warner Books, 1985), p. 112.

WILLIE MORRIS

Willie Morris was born in Jackson, Mississippi, in 1934. He received his baccalaureate degree from the University of Texas in 1956 and then completed another B.A. and an M.A. at Oxford on a Rhodes Scholarship. From 1960 to 1962, he was editor-in-chief of the Texas Observer *in Austin, and from 1963 through 1967, he was editor of* Harper's *magazine, but he resigned from the magazine in an editorial dispute he characterized as "the money men against the literary men."*

*Although he has written a novel (*The Last of the Southern Girls, *1973), two autobiographical narratives (*North Toward Home, *1967 and* Good Old Boy, *1971), and short stories, he is primarily known as a superb journalist. In the following selection from his memoirs—*North Toward Home, *first published in 1967—we read the account of a young journalist, still in college, facing political pressures and ethical questions that are typical of those encountered by responsible writers everywhere.*

A great irony. . . .

A great irony occasionally besets an American state university, for it allows and at its best encourages one to develop his critical capacities, his imagination, his values; at the same time, in its institutional aspects, a university under pressure can become increasingly wary of the very intent and direction of the ideals it has helped spawn. It is too easy, too much a righteous judgment, to call this attitude hypocrisy, for actually it is a kind of schizophrenia. This involves more than a gap between preaching and practicing; it involves the splitting of a university's soul. There can be something brutal about a university's teaching its young people to be alive, aware, critical, independent, and free, and then, when a threatening turn is taken, to reject by its actual behavior the substance of everything it claims for itself. Then ideals and critical capacities exist in a vacuum. They are sometimes ignored, and in extreme instances victimized. And the greater society suffers as well.

For a year I had been reading heavily in politics, history, and the journalism of the great editors. I took to my heart the memorable statement in Joseph Pulitzer's will, now reprinted every day on the editorial pages of the *St. Louis Post-Dispatch*, and which I subsequently tacked to the wall in my office next to my typewriter, as I have in every office where I have worked: "that it will always fight for progress and reform, never tolerate injustice or corruption, always fight demagogues of all parties, never belong to any party, always oppose privileged classes and public plunderers, never lack sympathy for the poor, always remain devoted to the public welfare, never be satisfied merely with printing news, always be drastically independent, never be afraid to attack wrong, whether by predatory plutocracy or predatory poverty."

I read the journalism of H. L. Mencken, Lincoln Steffens, William Allen White, S. S. McClure, Bernard DeVoto, Hodding Carter, Ralph McGill, and Brann the Iconoclast. I read the files of *The Daily Texan* itself, learning of different and more alive times—the great editorials of Horace Busby, who brought sanity and courage to the campus during the Rainey disaster of the 1940s, D. B. Hardeman, Ronnie Dugger, and others. The political climate of the state had become more pointed to me, and in long and sometimes agonizing talks with the brightest and most perceptive student leaders I had thought out the huge responsibility of the largest and most prominent student newspaper in the South in a period when the integration issue was coming alive; my experience with my hometown Citizens Council had helped me judge the extent of my own personal change, and showed the sad barbarism of intransigence. I was suffused with the ideals of freedom of expression and the open marketplace. I had the most emphatic belief that this freedom should be used to positive purposes, that freedom is as freedom does, that the pages of this newspaper should reflect the great diversity of the place I had come to know, that the University of Texas was too much a part of its state and of the rest of the world to avoid editorials on significant questions beyond the campus, and that the campus itself—as so many others then—was bogged down in dullness, complacency, and the corporate mentality. My deficits, as I fully realized later, were a self-righteousness, a lack of subtlety in polemic, and an especially underdeveloped awareness of the diplomatic approach.

President Kennedy, Theodore Sorensen later wrote, liked to improvise on the passage from Ecclesiastes: "A time to weep and a time to laugh, a time to mourn and a time to dance, a time to fish and a time to cut bait." I did not know as much about bait-cutting then as I would later. But I wanted the paper which would briefly be mine to be a living thing, distinctive and meaningful, in both its own tradition and the tradition of hard-hitting, outspoken American journalism. The University of Texas itself had taught me to place a high value on these qualities; the necessity of the free marketplace of ideas was apparently high on its list of formal priorities. It was in the books in its libraries, the valedictions of its deans, administrators, commencement speakers, even on the buildings and statues around its campus. You cannot make gestures of support for all these things and expect them to have no context. They either apply to a particular setting or they do not apply at all. They are either watered down to appease the distrusts of a power faction or they are not. But uphold these ideas long enough, frequently enough, and with such inspiration, and some young people are not only going to believe in them, they are going to believe in them with the fervor of the young, and even arrange their lives and their sense of honor by them.

So it was that I came out fighting hard, and the reactions were no sooner than immediate. I erred, first of all, into editorializing occasionally about state politics, particularly its twin deities, oil and gas. I suppose the authorities had not expected a gentle-natured Southern boy to overreach into areas ruled by hidden divinities; a student editor in Texas could blaspheme the Holy Spirit and the Apostle Paul, but irreverence stopped at the wellhead. We were going against a set of scandals and money frauds that had rocked Governor Shivers' administration. We were seeking intelligence and good will on integration and lauding most Texans for their tolerant attitude. Occasionally we chided John Foster Dulles' view of the rest of the world. Against the reactions from the school administration we categorically defended student press freedom and our right to comment as we wished on controversial state and national issues. We were committing the crime of being vigorous and outspoken, naïvely idealistic and exuberantly but not radically liberal in a state that at that time had little patience with either, on a campus where exuberance was reserved for the minor furies, and in a decade which encouraged little essential ebullience in the young.

There began a series of summonses to President Logan Wilson's office, much like a grade-school student who had been caught throwing spitballs in class being called to the principal; I was immediately reminded of my tribulations with my fourth-grade teacher, the evangelical Miss Abbott. Wilson's personal secretary would telephone and say, "Mr. Morris, the President would like to confer with you. Could we see you at three?" Ushered into the offices of the principal, who ruled over an academic domain stretching from El Paso to Galveston, I would wait in the outer chamber for an appropriate five minutes and admire there the lush carpet six inches deep; then the President was ready to see me. I would be offered menthol cigarettes and dealt with soothingly, charmingly, and with the condescension befitting the occasion. These biting editorials had to stop, though for a while the issue was not presented quite that frontally. There were meetings with the corps of deans, especially the one who had been a captain in the Navy and who believed that when an order is given, people should hop-to; anyone to the political left of Eisenhower, he once told me, was stupid if not downright treacherous. At first he was baffled, but this gave way to rage; there was no bemusement in these quarters. The slight liquid film that glazed his eyes as I came into his office suggested that he was keeping himself under control with some difficulty; his apparent preference was to assign me to the brig. A good part of the time I was scared, and Logan Wilson must have been equally miserable; he was beginning to get caught in a vicious crossfire. The political appointees who ran the University were beginning to use the old and tested dogmatisms. And in the end more people than President Wilson and I were to be involved.

Finally the Regents erupted. At a meeting with several student leaders, including good friends of mine who were president and vice-president of the student body, they declared that the student paper should not discuss controversial state and national topics, and that college students were not interested in these things anyway. *The Daily Texan*, they said, had especially gone too far astray in commenting on a piece of natural gas legislature. There, now, was the rub! A little later they handed down a censorship edict. This was based, they said, not on principle but on legal considerations. They cited the rider on state appropriations bills, which stipulated that no state money "shall be used for influencing the outcome of any election or the passage or defeat of any legislative measure." Then they advanced one step further, a major step as it turned out, and announced that "editorial preoccupation with state and national political controversy" would be prohibited.

My friends and I on the *Texan* did some painful soul-searching after that announcement. Should we give in and avoid an agonizing fight? Was a fight worth it? The next morning, as I remember it, I drove out to Lyndon

Johnson's lakes, to the one my beauty queen and I liked so much; I sat around under a scrub oak for a time reading some Thomas Jefferson. Then I came back to town and talked with Bergen, our managing editor, a shy, deceptive little man with an abundance of courage, and we decided in thirty minutes what Tom Jefferson likely would have recommended all along.

That began one of the greatest controversies in the history of American college journalism. Bergen and I stayed up all night in the editor's office, planning and writing editorials under the new censorship arrangement. We submitted critical editorials the next day, attacking the implications of the Regents' order, along with a guest editorial from *The New York Times* on the natural gas legislation* and several paragraphs from Thomas Jefferson on press freedom. All were rejected. The Jefferson quotes had been included in a personal column, and when he was censored there was thunder in the heavens, fire in the sky was reported over Monticello, and a thirty-minute moratorium on bourbon was declared in Charlottesville. But the student majority on the publications board outvoted the faculty representatives, and all the editorials were printed in toto in the next issue.

We kept right on going. We authorized a brilliant young law student, the "attorney general" for the student government, to examine the legal consequences of the Regents' order. He counselled with some of the state's most respected lawyers and legal scholars and refuted the applicability of the appropriations rider. The Regents' interpretation of this rider, he argued, had "terrifying implications" and could be used in the same way to stifle legitimate comment among students, faculty, and quasi-independent corporations housed on the campus like the alumni organization, the student government, and the law review.

In retrospect a number of things stand out clearly. One Regent saying, "The *Texan* has gone out of bounds in discussing issues pertaining to oil and gas because 66 percent of Texas tax money comes from oil and gas." And another adding, "We're just trying to hold Willie to a college yell." ("There are our young barbarians, all at play!") . . . A journalism professor coming up to me the day after the controversy began and whispering, "I just want to shake your hand. I'm proud to know you." . . . My parents phoning long-distance from Mississippi and asking, "Son, you in trouble? They won't kick you out of school so close to graduation, will they?" . . . At one of the interminable meetings of the publications board, one faculty representative saying to me, "You know what you are? You're a *propagandist*," a gripping judgment coming from an associate professor of advertising . . . And I recall one afternoon soon after the Regents' action when I telephoned J. Frank Dobie, the indomitable and lovable old *pater familias* of Texas writers, who had lost his own teaching job at the University in the 1940s, and asked if he would consider

*This was the Fulbright-Harris bill that Eisenhower later vetoed for the exertion of "improper influences" on the Senate.

writing to the letters column commenting on our troubles. "Hell," he said, "I been workin' on one all mornin'." The Board of Regents, Dobie's letter said, "are as much concerned with free intellectual enterprise as a razorback sow would be with Keats' 'Ode on a Grecian Urn' "—a well-known statement now despite the fact that this phrase, and many another colorful one, were deleted after I had gone home to sleep and the paper was going to press.

One day one of the few outspoken old souls on the faculty in that period, an English professor who had never ceased to fight the political appointees with scorn and satire even in the 1940s, stood up in a faculty meeting and asked what the student newspaper's troubles *meant* in terms of the entire university. "We should discuss this matter," he said, waving his walking cane at his colleagues, "and deplore a contemptuous, cynical attitude toward what the student body or what an elected student leader may say." He spoke of the "dignity of the student" as a "new citizen"; a university's funds, he said, "should not be meant to *stifle* discussion but to encourage it." There was no further discussion, however, from the faculty. I wrote a lead-editorial on his speech and entitled it "Whispers in a Sleepy Lagoon." The night of its publication, as I sat at my desk eating a cold hamburger and drinking my fourth cup of black coffee, one of the administrative deans telephoned. "You published that editorial," he said, "but do you know that professor is runnin' around on his wife?" I had barely slept in a week, and at this point the fatigue had robbed me of any semblance of cynicism or humor. "Why you old bastard!" was all I could say, and hung up the telephone.

Looking back on it now, I had forgotten what a nasty time it was, how it sapped the patience of all of us on both sides, and the sad indignity with which many decent but weak men had to try to enforce official demands that I think they would have preferred in their hearts to ignore. One grew to be sympathetic, if not respectful, of some of these men, stripped as they were of power and sometimes, I believe, ashamed.

Finally, after more troubles, after we ran blank spaces and editorials entitled "Let's Water the Pansies," or "Don't Walk on the Grass" and held to our prerogatives to publish what we wished, there was a loosening up. There were no further official orders, and we remained free. But I was obsessed with the fear that in winning the battle we had lost the war, and that we had fought back wrongly and badly—and that the fight had not been worth it.

Yet I do not believe it was coincidence that in May of that year the Regents and the administration sought to impose in the general faculty a sweeping set of restrictions on the involvement of University of Texas faculty members in politics and political issues. One of the administration's spokesmen described these restrictions as the drawing of "a little circle" around political responsibilities. "That little circle," one young professor, the philosopher John Silber, said, "happens to comprise 90 percent of my political concerns." The issue was resoundingly defeated. For whom was the bell trying to toll? I believed then there was a connection there; the contempt for an independent student voice trying to engage itself in important issues in that age of McCarthy and silence was reflected in an effort to do lasting damage to a state university's most basic civil liberties. Perhaps if the student newspaper had not chosen to meet the whole question head-on and in public, the controlling political faction would have thought anything easy and possible. Perhaps we won something more than a battle after all.

People would tell me long afterward that this sort of thing could never happen again in the later climate of the University of Texas, that everything became much better, that academic freedom, and freedom of expression, had been won, and were old issues now. I am convinced this is true. The 1960s were not the 1950s, and at our state universities these issues would become, not more straightforward, but more complex, involving considerations of the very quality of the mass society. In 1956 the issue was a direct one, and it became bigger than *The Daily Texan*, bigger than the Board of Regents, bigger than the University itself—and it could never be old-fashioned.

I have often asked myself in the years that followed, would I do all this again? I would be less than honest if I answered that question simply.

At the time, as I understood later, the tone, style, and content of public discourse meant much more to me than the practical considerations of how one arranges complicated matters in feasible, flexible terms. There could have been more subtle and practical ways of dealing with the problem that confronted us. For this kind of personal diplomacy I was too immature and too impressionable.

Yet I was twenty years old; the real antagonists were in the seats of power. To my credit I knew who the enemy was. It would be an unwarranted personal renunciation for me to say retrospectively that the indignation I felt in 1956 was unjustified. It is legitimate to assume that editors of student papers at any university have a right to arouse the authorities, and within the laws of libel to bring them down on him. It is right to be able to carry on an aggressive campaign against an ethic they consider sterile and contemptuous. The attempt to censor *The Daily Texan* in 1956 involved not a displacement of dissent, but the running roughshod over it by real power, and the more sophisticated kind of criticism that served as its forum—the kind of wealth which still encourages the idea in America that anything can be bought, including culture. A friend of mine in the state legislature would say to me a few years later, perhaps Texas can never become a truly civilized place until its great natural resources are gone.

For three years I had written my column, "The Round-Up," and in my "30" piece that spring, the last one I wrote, I said, with too many genuflections to Thomas Wolfe:

The University of Texas, I fear, has travelled all too swiftly toward beautiful buildings and sterling reputations. Its leaders, in submitting to those who relish the corporate purse, have too often, and even without reluctance, betrayed the corporation of ideas . . . It has existed at the whim of those forces which would readily crush its heart, its soul, and its mind.

The quick Texas rich, who apply the values of fast money to the values of higher education, have dealt foolishly and cruelly with the prerogatives of the spirit . . . As a result, our University condones the tyranny of the majority, and it encourages in its students sedate complacency to the national and regional arbiter.

It must lead, not follow . . . it must insist that society and the race can be made better. It must strive to show our people, our uneducated and our quick rich, that our civilization is doomed when the material can coerce the human spirit.

I believe that our University is lost, and that being lost has been silent and afraid, but that someday its destiny shall be fulfilled more courageously, more magnificently, and more humbly than we have ever imagined. It is in the bright promise of this vision that I close.

At graduation at the end of that year the air was heavy with the scents of the berry trees; most of the students were long since gone, and the campus was more lovely and still than I had ever seen it before. The chimes on the Tower rang with stirring processionals to the Class of 1956, and proud country parents stood in diffident little groups watching their children march past. I received my diploma, and before a packed audience walked out the wrong door of the auditorium. At the reception afterward a journalism professor said, "I told my wife, there goes Morris, lost again," and the mother of one of my classmates walked up to me and said, "Why, you look too *innocent* to have caused all that newspaper trouble." The next day I left the campus, my '47 Plymouth loaded with books and the paraphernalia of four years, and drove all night one final time to the place I had come from.

Questions for Discussion

1. One editor titled this selection "Irreverence Stops at the Wellhead." Explain why that title is appropriate.

2. Knowing what you do about Morris, why is this incident important to his life? (In answering this question, you might refer back to the headnote that introduces the selection.)

3. The subject of the essay is an event that took place in the 1950s. Is the essay still relevant? Explain.

4. The passage was written a little more than a decade after the incident took place, and the author had had time to reflect on the events. What is the author's attitude toward his actions as a student editor?

5. What ethical and legal questions does the essay raise? Explain your stand on these issues.

6. Do you think Morris's handling of events was immature and ill-considered or mature and rational? How would you have responded to the pressures and counterpressures?

7. Explain what Morris intends in the following passage (from page 7):

   President Kennedy, Theodore Sorensen later wrote, liked to improvise on the passage from Ecclesiastes: "A time to weep and a time to laugh, a time to mourn and a time to dance, a time to fish and a time to cut bait." I did not know as much about bait-cutting then as I would later.

8. Point out and explain one metaphor or simile you think is particularly effective.

RICHARD RODRIGUEZ

In his autobiography, **Hunger** of **Memory,** *Richard Rodriguez tells of alienation from his native Mexican culture and his absorption into Anglo society. His family moved from Mexico to California, and Richard was born in San Francisco in 1944. He attended Catholic parochial schools and graduated from Stanford University with a B.A. In 1969 he received his M.A. from Columbia University. He has done graduate work at the University of California at Berkeley and at the Warburg Institute in London.*

Mr. Secrets

I am writing about those very things my mother has asked me not to reveal. Shortly after I published my first autobiographical essay seven years ago, my mother wrote me a letter pleading with me never again to write about our family life. "Write about something else in the future. Our family life is private." And besides: "Why do you need to tell the *gringos* about how 'divided' you feel from the family?"

I sit at my desk now, surrounded by versions of paragraphs and pages of this book, considering that question.

When I decided to compose this intellectual autobiography, a New York editor told me that I would embark on a lonely journey. Over the noise of voices and dishes in an East Side restaurant, he said, "There will be times when you will think the entire world has forgotten you. Some mornings you will yearn for a phone call or a letter to assure you that you still are connected to the world." There *have* been mornings when I've dreaded the isolation this writing requires. Mornings spent listless in silence and in fear of confronting the blank sheet of paper. There have been times I've rushed away from my papers to answer the phone; gladly gotten up from my chair, hearing the mailman outside. Times I have been frustrated by the slowness of words, the way even a single paragraph never seemed done.

I had known a writer's loneliness before, working on my dissertation in the British Museum. But that experience did not prepare me for the task of writing these pages where my own life is the subject. Many days I feared I had stopped living by committing myself to remember the past. I feared that my absorption with events in my past amounted to an immature refusal to live in the present. Adulthood seemed consumed by memory. I would tell myself otherwise. I would tell myself that the act of remembering is an act of the present. (In writing this autobiography, I am actually describing the man I have become—the man in the present.)

Times when the money ran out, I left writing for temporary jobs. Once I had a job for over six months. I resumed something like a conventional social life. But then I have turned away, come back to my San Francisco apartment to closet myself in the silence I both need and fear.

I stay away from late night parties. (To be clearheaded in the morning.) I disconnect my phone for much of the day. I must avoid complex relationships—a troublesome lover or a troubled friend. The person who knows me best scolds me for escaping from life. (*Am I evading adulthood?*) People I know get promotions at jobs. Friends move away. Friends get married. Friends divorce. One friend tells me she is pregnant. Then she has a baby. Then the baby has the formed face of a child. Can walk. Talk. And still I sit at this desk laying my words like jigsaw pieces, a fellow with ladies in housecoats and old men in slippers who watch TV. Neighbors in my apartment house rush off to work about nine. I hear their steps on the stairs. (They will be back at six o'clock.) Somewhere planes are flying. The door slams behind them.

"Why?" My mother's question hangs in the still air of memory.

The loneliness I have felt many mornings, however, has not made me forget that I am engaged in a highly public activity. I sit here in silence writing this small volume of words, and it seems to me the most public thing I ever have done. My mother's letter has served to remind me: I am making my personal life public. Probably I will never try to explain my motives to my mother and father. My mother's question will go unanswered to her face. Like everything else on the pages, my reasons for writing will be revealed instead to public readers I expect never to meet.

I

It is to those whom my mother refers to as the *gringos* that I write. The *gringos*. The expression reminds me that she and my father have not followed their children all the way down the path to full Americanization. They were changed—became more easy in public, less withdrawn and uncertain—by the public success of their children. But something remained unchanged in their lives. With excessive care they continue today to note the difference between private and public life. And their private society remains only their family. No matter how friendly they are in public, no matter how firm their smiles, my parents never forget when they are in public. My mother must use a high-pitched tone of voice when she addresses people who are not relatives. It is a tone of voice I have all my life heard her use away from the house. Coming home from grammar school with new friends, I would hear it, its reminder: My new intimates were strangers to her. Like my sisters and brother, over the years, I've grown used to hearing that voice. Expected to hear it. Though I suspect that voice has played deep in my soul, sounding a lyre, to recall my "betrayal," my movement away from our family's intimate past. It is the voice I hear even now when my mother addresses her son or daughter-in-law. (They remain public people to her.) She speaks to them, sounding the way she does when talking over the fence to a neighbor.

It was, in fact, the lady next door to my parents—a librarian—who first mentioned seeing my essay seven years ago. My mother was embarrassed because she hadn't any idea what the lady was talking about. But she had heard enough to go to a library with my father to find the article. They read what I wrote. And then she wrote her letter.

It is addressed to me in Spanish, but the body of the letter is in English. Almost mechanically she speaks of her pride at the start. ("Your dad and I are very proud of the brilliant manner you have to express yourself.") Then the matter of most concern comes to the fore. "Your dad and I have only one objection to what you write. You say too much about the family . . . Why do you have to do that? . . . Why do you need to tell the *gringos*? . . . Why do you think we're so separated as a family? Do you really think this, Richard?"

A new paragraph changes the tone. Soft, maternal. Worried for me she adds, "Do not punish yourself for having to give up our culture in order to 'make it' as you say. Think of all the wonderful achievements you have obtained. You should be proud. Learn Spanish better. Practice it with your dad and me. Don't worry so much. Don't get the idea that I am mad at you either."

"Just keep one thing in mind. Writing is one thing, the family is another. I don't want *tus hermanos* hurt by your writings. And what do you think the cousins will say when they read where you talk about how the aunts were maids? Especially I don't want the *gringos* knowing about our private affairs. Why should they? Please give this some thought. Please write about something else in the future. Do me this favor."

Please.

To the adult I am today, my mother needs to say what she would never have needed to say to her child: the boy who faithfully kept family secrets. When my fourth-grade teacher made our class write a paper about a typical evening at home, it never occurred to me actually to do so. "Describe what you do with your family," she told us. And automatically I produced a fictionalized account. I wrote that I had six brothers and sisters; I described watching my mother get dressed up in a red-sequined dress before she went with my father to a party; I even related how the imaginary baby sitter ("a high school student") taught my brother and sisters and me to make popcorn and how, later, I fell asleep before my parents returned. The nun who read what I wrote would have known that what I had written was completely imagined. But she never said anything about my contrivance. And I never expected her to either. I never thought she *really* wanted me to write about my family life. In any case, I would have been unable to do so.

I was very much the son of parents who regarded the most innocuous piece of information about the family to be secret. Although I had, by that time, grown easy in public, I felt that my family life was strictly private, not to be revealed to unfamiliar ears or eyes. Around the age of ten, I was held by surprise listening to my best friend tell me one day that he "hated" his father. In a furious whisper he said that when he attempted to kiss his father before going to bed, his father had laughed: "Don't you think you're getting too old for that sort of thing, son?" I was intrigued not so much by the incident as by the fact that the boy would relate it to *me*.

In those years I was exposed to the sliding glass-door informality of middle-class California family life. Ringing the doorbell of a friend's house, I would hear someone inside yell out, "Come on in, Richie; door's not locked." And in I would go to discover my friend's family undisturbed by my presence. The father was in the kitchen in his underwear. The mother was in her bathrobe. Voices gathered in familiarity. A parent scolded a child in front of me; voices quarreled, then laughed; the mother told me something about her son after he had stepped out of the room and she was sure he couldn't overhear; the father would speak to his children and to me in the same tone of voice. I was one of the family, the parents of several good friends would assure me. (Richie.)

My mother sometimes invited my grammar school friends to stay for dinner or even to stay overnight. But my parents never treated such visitors as part of the family, never told them they were. When a school friend ate at our table, my father spoke less than usual. (Stray, distant words.) My mother was careful to use her "visitor's voice." Sometimes, listening to her, I would feel annoyed because she wouldn't be more herself. Sometimes I'd feel embarrassed that I couldn't give to a friend at my house what I freely accepted at his.

I remained, nevertheless, my parents' child. At school, in sixth grade, my teacher suggested that I start keeping a diary. ("You should write down your personal experiences and reflections.") But I shied away from the idea. It was the one suggestion that the scholarship boy couldn't follow. I would not have wanted to write about the minor daily events of my life; I would never have been able to write about what most deeply, daily, concerned me during those years: I was growing away from my parents. Even if I could have been certain that no one would find my diary, even if I could have destroyed each page after I had written it, I would have felt uncomfortable writing about my home life. There seemed to me something intrinsically public about written words.

Writing, at any rate, was a skill I didn't regard highly. It was a grammar school skill I acquired with comparative ease. I do not remember struggling to write the way I struggled to learn how to read. The nuns would praise student papers for being neat—the handwritten letters easy for others to read; they promised that my writing style would improve as I read more and more. But that wasn't the reason I became a reader. Reading was for me the key to "knowledge"; I swallowed facts and dates and names and themes. Writing, by contrast, was an activity I thought of as a kind of report, evidence of learning. I wrote down what I heard teachers say. I wrote down things from my books. I wrote down all I knew when I was examined at the end of the school year. Writing was performed after the fact; it was not the exciting experience of learning itself. In eighth grade I read several hundred books, the titles of which I still can recall. But I cannot remember a single essay I wrote. I only remember that the most frequent kind of essay I wrote was the book report.

In high school there were more "creative" writing assignments. English teachers assigned the composition of short stories and poems. One sophomore story I wrote was a romance set in the Civil War South. I remember that it earned me a good enough grade, but my teacher suggested with quiet tact that next time I try writing about "something you know more about—something closer to home." Home? I wrote a short story about an old man who lived all by himself in a house down the block. That was as close as my writing ever got to my house. Still, I won prizes. When teachers suggested I contribute articles to the school literary magazine, I did so. And when I was asked to join the school newspaper, I said yes. I did not feel any great pride in my writings, however. (My mother was the one who collected my prize-winning essays in a box she kept in her closet.) Though I remember seeing my by-line in print for the first time, and dwelling on the printing press letters with fascination: RICHARD RODRÍGUEZ. The letters furnished evidence of a vast public identity writing made possible.

When I was a freshman in college, I began typing all my assignments. My writing speed decreased. Writing became a struggle. In high school I had been able to handwrite ten- and twenty-page papers in little more than an hour—and I never revised what I wrote. A college essay took me several nights to prepare. Suddenly everything I wrote seemed in need of revision. I became a self-conscious writer. A stylist. The change, I suspect, was the result of seeing my words ordered by the even, impersonal, anonymous typewriter print. As arranged by a machine, the words that I typed no longer seemed mine. I was able to see them with a new appreciation for how my reader would see them.

From grammar school to graduate school I could always name my reader. I wrote for my teacher, I could consult him or her before writing, and after, I suppose that I knew other readers could make sense of what I wrote—that, therefore, I addressed a general reader. But I didn't think very much about it. Only toward the end of my schooling and only because political issues pressed upon me did I write, and have published in magazines, essays intended for readers I never expected to meet. Now I am struck by the opportunity. I write today for a reader who exists in my mind only phantasmagorically. Someone with a face erased; someone of no particular race or sex or age or weather. A gray presence. Unknown, unfamiliar. All that I know about him is that he has had a long education and that his society, like mine, is often public (*un gringo*). . . .

I write very slowly because I write under the obligation to make myself clear to someone who knows nothing about me. It is a lonely adventure. Each morning I make my way along a narrowing precipice of written words. I hear an echoing voice—my own resembling another's. Silent! The reader's voice silently trails every word I put down. I reread my words, and again it is the reader's voice I hear in my mind, sounding my prose.

When I wrote my first autobiographical essay, it was no coincidence that, from the first page, I expected to publish what I wrote. I didn't consciously determine the issue. Somehow I knew, however, that my words were meant for a public reader. Only because of that reader did the words come to the page. The reader became my excuse, my reason for writing.

It had taken me a long time to come to this address. There are remarkable children who very early are able to write publicly about their personal lives. Some children confide to a diary those things—like the first shuddering of sexual desire—too private to tell a parent or brother. The youthful writer addresses a stranger, the Other, with "Dear Diary" and tries to give public expression to what is intensely, privately felt. In so doing, he attempts to evade the guilt of repression. And the embarrassment of solitary feeling. For by rendering feelings in words that a stranger can understand—words that belong to the public, this Other—the young diarist no longer need feel all alone or eccentric. His feelings are capable of public intelligibility. In turn, the act of revelation helps the writer better understand his own feelings. Such is the benefit of language: By finding public words to describe one's feelings, one can describe oneself to oneself. One names what was previously only darkly felt.

I have come to think of myself as engaged in writing graffiti. Encouraged by physical isolation to reveal what is most personal; determined at the same time to have my words seen by strangers. I have come to understand better why works of literature—while never intimate, never individually addressed to the reader—are so often among the most personal statements we hear in our lives. Writing, I have come to value written words as never before. One can use *spoken* words to reveal one's personal self to strangers. But *written* words heighten the feeling of privacy. They permit the most thorough and careful exploration. (In the silent room, I prey upon that which is most private. Behind the closed door, I am least reticent about giving those memories expression.) The writer is freed from the obligation of finding an auditor in public. (As I use words that someone far from home can understand, I create my listener. I imagine her listening.)

My teachers gave me a great deal more than I knew when they taught me to write public English. I was unable then to use the skill for deeply personal purposes. I insisted upon writing impersonal essays. And I wrote always with a specific reader in mind. Nevertheless, the skill of public writing was gradually developed by the many classroom papers I had to compose. Today I *can* address an anonymous reader. And this seems to me important to say. Somehow the inclination to write about my private life in public is related to the ability to do so. It is not enough to say that my mother and father do not want to write their autobiographies. It needs also to be said that they are unable to write to a public reader. They lack the skill. Though both of them can write in Spanish and English, they write in a hesistant manner. Their syntax is uncertain. Their vocabulary limited. They write well enough to communicate "news" to relatives in letters. And they can handle written transactions in institutional America. But the man who sits in his chair so many hours, and the woman at the ironing board—"keeping busy because I don't want to get old"—will never be able to believe that any description of their personal lives could be understood by a stranger far from home.

Questions for Discussion

1. What did you learn about Rodriguez's composing process (and perhaps your own) from reading "Mr. Secrets"?
2. Explain why, in the view of this author, it is important to be able to write for an anonymous reader. As Rodriguez says, "Today I *can* address an anonymous reader. And this seems to me important to say. Somehow the inclination to write about my private life is related to the ability to do so" (p. 21).

3. What are the connotations of the word *gringo*? What attitudes does Rodriguez convey through its use in the context of "Mr. Secrets"?
4. Why does the author's mother use a "visitor's voice"?
5. Explain why Rodriguez was unable to keep a diary and why he invented fictions to write about his home life.
6. Briefly explain the *gist* of this selection.

JACK HENRY ABBOTT

Jack Henry Abbott was in prison when he wrote In the Belly of the Beast, *a work that gained the interest of Norman Mailer, one of America's preeminent literary persons. Mailer advocated Abbott's release, and early in 1981 he was paroled. On July 18, 1981, Abbott argued with an aspiring playwright, twenty-two-year-old Richard Adan, and stabbed him to death. Abbott is now in custody, awaiting the outcome of prosecution for murder. Between the time of the stabbing and the time when Abbott was once again taken into custody,* In the Belly of the Beast *earned $100,000 in royalties.*

State-Raised Convict

I was born January 21, 1944, on a military base in Oscoda, Michigan. I was in and out of foster homes almost from the moment of my birth. My formal education: I never completed the sixth grade. At age nine I began serving long stints in juvenile detention quarters. At age twelve I was sent to the Utah State Industrial School for Boys. I was "paroled" once for about sixty days, then returned there. At age eighteen I was released as an adult. Five or six months later I was sent to the Utah State Penitentiary for the crime of "issuing a check against insufficient funds." I went in with an indeterminate sentence of up to five years. About three years later, having never been released, I killed one inmate and wounded another in a fight in the center hall. I was tried for capital offense under the old convict statute that requires either *mandatory* death if malice *aforethought* is found, or a sentence of from three to twenty years. I received the latter sentence. An "indeterminate term" is what justifies the concept of *parole*. Your good behavior determines how long you stay in prison. The law merely sets a minimum and a maximum—the underlying assumption being that *no one* serves the maximum. A wrong assumption in my case. At age twenty-six I escaped for about six weeks.

I am at this moment thirty-seven years old. Since age twelve I have been free the sum total of nine and a half months. I have served many terms in solitary. In only three terms I have served over ten years there. I would estimate that I have served a good fourteen or fifteen years in solitary. The only serious crime I have ever committed in free society was bank robbery during the time I was a fugitive.

It was a big red-brick building with two wings. It stood about four stories high. It was constructed by the U.S. Army back when the state was still a territory. It was one of several buildings that had served as disciplinary barracks for the military. These barracks had long ago passed into the hands of the state and were part of a juvenile penal institution.

In the basement of the big red-brick building were rows of solitary confinement cells. The basement was entered from outside the building only.

I am about twelve or thirteen years old. It is winter. I am marching in a long double-file of boys. We are marching to the mess hall. There is a guard watching as we march toward him. There is a guard walking behind us as we march.

My testes shrink and the blood is rushing and my eyes burn, ache. My heart is pounding and I am trying hard to breathe slowly, to control myself.

I keep glancing at the guards: in front and behind the line.

The fields beyond are plowed and covered with an icy blanket of snow. I do not know how far beyond those fields my freedom lies.

Suddenly my confederate at the front of the line whirls and slugs the boy behind him. The front guard, like an attack dog, is on them both—beating them into submission. Seconds later the guard at the back rushes forward, brushing me as he passes.

I break away from the line, and run *for my life*. I stretch my legs as far as I can, and as quickly as I can, but the legs of a boy four feet six inches tall cannot stretch very far.

The fields are before me, a still flatland of ice and snow, and the huge clods of frozen, plowed earth are to me formidable obstacles. The sky is baby-blue, almost white. The air is clear.

I haven't covered fifty yards when I hear the pursuit begin: "You! Stop!" I immediately know I will be caught, but I continue to run.

I do not feel the blow of his fist. I'm in midair for a moment, and then I'm rolling in frozen clods of soil. I am pulled to my feet; one of my arms is twisted behind my back; my lungs are burning with the cold air; my nostrils are flared. I am already trying to steel myself for the punishment to come.

The other inmates stand in a long straight line, flanked by guards, and I am dragged past them. I do not respect them, because they will not run—will not try to escape. My legs are too short to keep up with the guard, who is effortlessly holding my arm twisted high up behind my back, so I stumble along, humiliated. I try hard to be dignified.

I see the door to the basement of the red-brick building, and we are approaching it in good time. A snowflake hits my eye and melts. It is beginning, softly, to snow.

At the top of the stairs to the basement, I am flung down against a high black-steel door. I stand beside it at attention as the guard takes out a huge ring of keys and bangs on the door. We are seen through a window. The door yawns open and an old guard appears, gazing at me maliciously.

We enter. We are standing at the top of a number of wide concrete steps that descend to the floor of the basement. I am thrown down the stairs, and I lie on the floor, waiting. My nose is bleeding and my ears are ringing from blows to my skull.

"Get up!"

Immediately I am knocked down again.

"Strip!"

I stand, shakily, and shed my clothing. His hands are pulling my hair, but I dare not move.

"Turn around!"

I turn.

"Bend over!"

I bend over. He inspects my anus and my private parts, and I watch, anxiously, hoping with all my might be does not hurt me there.

He orders me to follow him.

We enter a passageway between rows of heavy steel doors. The passage is narrow; it is only four or five feet wide and is dimly lighted. As soon as we enter, I can smell nervous sweat and feel body warmth in the air.

We stop at one of the doors. He unlocks it. I enter. Nothing is said. He closes and locks the door, and I can hear his steps as he walks down the dark passageway.

In the cell, there is a barred window with an ancient, heavy mesh-steel screen. It is level with the ground outside. The existing window-panes are caked with decades of soil, and the screen prevents cleaning them. Through the broken ones I peer, running free again in my mind across the fields.

A sheet of thick plywood, on iron legs bolted to the floor, is my bed. An old-fashioned toilet bowl is in the corner, beside a sink with cold running water. A dim light burns in a dull yellow glow behind the thick iron screening attached to the wall.

The walls are covered with names and dates—some of the dates go back twenty years. They were scratched into the wall. There are ragged hearts pierced with arrows and *pachuco* crosses everywhere. Everywhere are the words: "mom," "love," "god"—the walls sweat and are clammy and cold.

Because I am allowed only my undershorts, I move about to keep warm.

When my light was turned out at night, I would weep uncontrollably. Sixty days in solitary was a long, long time in those days for me.

When the guard's key would hit the lock on my door to signal the serving of a "meal," if I were not standing at attention in the far corner of the cell, facing it, the guard would attack me with a ring of keys on a heavy chain.

I was fed one-third of a regular meal three times a day. Only one day a week I was taken from my cell and ordered to shower while the guard stood in the shower-room doorway and timed me for three minutes.

Locked in our cells, we could not see one another, and if we were caught shouting cell-to-cell, we were beaten. We tapped out messages, but if they heard our taps, we were beaten—the entire row of cells, one child at a time.

I served five years in the big red-brick building, and altogether, two or three in solitary confinement. When I walked out, I was considered an adult, subject to adult laws.

I served so long because I could not adjust to the institution and tried to escape over twenty times. I had been there for the juvenile "crime" of "failure to adjust to foster homes."

. . . He who is state-raised—reared by the state from an early age after he is taken from what the state calls a "broken home"—learns over and over and all the days of his life that people in society can do anything to him and not be punished by the law. Do anything to him with the full force of the state behind them.

As a child, he must march in lock-step to his meals in a huge mess hall. He can own only three shirts and two pair of trousers and one pair of shoes.

People in society come to him through the state and injure him. Everyone in society he comes in contact with is in some capacity employed by the state. He learns to avoid people in society. He evades them at every step.

In *any* state in America someone who is state-raised can be shot down and killed like a dog by anyone, who has no "criminal record," with full impunity. I do not exaggerate this at all. It is a fact so ordinary in the minds of state-raised prisoners that it is a matter of common sense. If a prisoner were to show a skeptical attitude toward things of this nature, the rest of us would conclude that he is losing his mind. He is questioning what is self-evident to us; a practical fact of life.

. . . My mind keeps turning toward one of the main aspects of prison that separates ordinary prisoners who, at some point in their lives, serve a few years and get out never to return—or if they do, it is for another short period and never again—and the convict who is "state-raised," i.e., the prisoner who grows up from boyhood to manhood in penal institutions.

I have referred to it as a form of instability (mental, emotional, etc.). There is no doubt (let us say there is *little* doubt) that this instability is *caused* by a lifetime of incarceration. Long stretches of, say, from ages ten to seventeen or eighteen, and then from seventeen or eighteen to ages thirty and forty.

You hear a lot about "arrested adolescence" nowadays, and I believe this concept touches the nub of the instability of prisoners like myself.

Every society gives its men and women the prerogatives of men and women, of *adults*. Men are given their dues. After a certain age you are regarded as a man by society. You are referred to as "sir"; no one interferes in your affairs, claps your hands or ignores you. Society is solicitous in general and serves you. You are shown respect. Gradually your judgment is tempered because gradually you see that it has real effects; it impinges on the society, the world. Your experience mellows your emotions because you are free to move about anywhere, work and play at anything. You can pursue any object of love, pleasure, danger, profit, etc. You are taught by the very terms of your social existence, by the objects that come and go from your intentions, the natures of your own emotions—and you learn about yourself, your tastes, your strengths and weaknessess. You, in other words, mature emotionally.

It is not so for the state-raised convict. As a boy in reform school, he is punished for being a little boy. In prison, he is punished for trying to be a man in the sense described above. He is treated as an adolescent in prison. Just as an adolescent is denied the keys to the family car for *any* disobedience, *any* mischief, I am subjected to the hole for *any* disobedience, *any* mischief. I will go to the hole for murder as well as for stealing a packet of sugar. I will get out of the hole in either case, and the length of time I serve for either offense is no different. My object is *solely* to avoid leaving evidence that will leave me open to prosecution out there in the world beyond these walls where a semblance of democracy is practiced.

Prison regimes have prisoners making extreme decisions regarding moderate questions, decisions that only fit the logical choice of either-or. No contradiction is allowed openly. You are not allowed to change. You are only allowed to submit; "agreement" does not exist (it implies equality). You are the rebellious adolescent who must obey and submit to the judgment of "grownups"—"tyrants" they are called when we speak of men.

A prisoner who is not state-raised tolerates the situation because of his social maturity prior to incarceration. He knows things are different outside prison. But the state-raised convict has no conception of any difference. He lacks experience and, hence, maturity. His judgment is untempered, rash, his emotions are impulsive, raw, unmellowed.

There are emotions—a whole spectrum of them—that I know of only through words, through reading and my immature imagination. I can *imagine* I feel those emotions (know, therefore, what they are), but *I do not*. At age thirty-seven I am barely a precocious child. My passions are those of a boy.

Questions for Discussion

1. The passage begins with a factual recitation of the author's criminal record, then goes to a description of the juvenile penal institution, and ends with an analysis of the author's own personality. How does each section reinforce the others?

2. Why would Abbott use only two paragraphs to recount his whole life but devote several pages to describing the red-brick building and what took place inside it?

3. Prison is meant, in part at least, to reform criminals. The system has obviously failed in Abbott's case. Why?

4. Why does Abbott switch from past tense to historical present when he begins the narrative about his attempted escape from the Utah State Industrial School for Boys (page 24)?

   I *am* about twelve or thirteen years old. It *is* winter. I *am* marching in a long double-file of boys. We *are* marching to the mess hall.

   Is the switch effective?

5. The "big red-brick building" is, of course, an actual structure in Ogden, Utah, but in the selection from *In the Belly of the Beast*, the building becomes a symbol. Explain this symbolism.

6. The selection ends thus: "At age thirty-seven I am barely a precocious child. My passions are those of a boy." Explain what Abbott means.

7. Abbott's style is not elaborate. Its sentences are relatively short and uncomplicated; the passage is not highly metaphorical. Here is a typical passage (page 25):

   We enter. We are standing at the top of a number of wide concrete steps that descend to the floor of the basement. I am thrown down the stairs, and I lie on the floor, waiting. My nose is bleeding and my ears are ringing from blows to my skull.

   In your opinion, is the style of the passage effective? Explain.

JOHN EDGAR WIDEMAN

---

*Born in 1941 in Washington, D.C., John Edgar Wideman completed his undergraduate education at the University of Pennsylvania in 1963. Winning a Rhodes Scholarship, he went on to Oxford, where he completed a Ph.B. in 1966. Wideman has taught at Howard University, the University of Pennsylvania and the University of Wyoming. He has published novels (*Glance Away, *1967;* Hurry Home, *1970;* The Lynchers, *1973), short stories, poetry, and articles.*

John Edgar's brother Robby was convicted of murder and sentenced to life imprisonment in Pennsylvania. Brothers and Keepers *is the story of the crime that Robby committed and the relationship between the two brothers as they try to understand their tragedy. "The business of making a book together was new for both of us. Difficult. Awkward," Wideman tells us. But the book was made, and it is a fascinating piece of writing, as the following selection will indicate.*

The business of making a book together. . . .

The business of making a book together was new for both of us. Difficult. Awkward. Another book could be constructed about a writer who goes to a prison to interview his brother but comes away with his own story. The conversations with his brother would provide a stage for dramatizing the writer's tortured relationship to other people, himself, his craft. The writer's motives, the issue of exploitation, the inevitable conflict between his role as detached observer and his responsibility as a brother would be at the center of such a book. When I stopped hearing Robby and listened to myself listening, that kind of book shouldered its way into my consciousness. I didn't like the feeling. That book compromised the intimacy I wanted to achieve with my brother. It was as obtrusive as the Wearever pen in my hand, the little yellow sheets of Yard Count paper begged from the pad of the guard in charge of overseeing the visiting lounge. The borrowed pen and paper (I was not permitted into the lounge with my own) were necessary props. I couldn't rely on memory to get my brother's story down and the keepers had refused my request to use a tape recorder, so there I was. Jimmy Olson, cub reporter, poised on the edge of my seat, pen and paper at ready, asking to be treated as a brother.

We were both rookies. Neither of us had learned very much about sharing our feelings with other family members. At home it had been assumed that each family member possessed deep, powerful feelings and that very little or nothing at all needed to be said about these feelings because we all were stuck with them and talk wouldn't change them. Your particular feelings were a private matter and family was a protective fence around everybody's privacy. Inside the perimeter of the fence each family member resided in his or her own quarters. What transpired in each dwelling was mainly the business of its inhabitant as long as nothing generated within an individual unit threatened the peace or safety of the whole. None of us knew how traditional West African families were organized or what values the circular shape of their villages embodied, but the living arrangements we had worked out among ourselves resembled the ancient African patterns. You were granted emotional privacy, independence, and space to commune with your feelings. You were encouraged to deal with as much as you could on your own, yet you never felt alone. The high wall of the family, the collective, communal reality of other souls, other huts like yours eliminated some of the dread, the isolation experienced when you turned inside and tried to make sense out of the chaos of your individual feelings. No matter how grown you thought you were or how far you believed you'd strayed, you knew you could cry *Mama* in the depths of the night and somebody would tend to you. Arms would wrap round you, a soft soothing voice lend its support. If not a flesh-and-blood mother then a mother in the form of song or story or a surrogate, Aunt Geral, Aunt Martha, drawn from the network of family numbers.

Privacy was a bridge between you and the rest of the family. But you had to learn to control the traffic. You had to keep it uncluttered, resist the temptation to cry wolf. Privacy in our family was a birthright, a union card granted with family membership. The card said you're one of us but also certified your separateness, your obligation to keep much of what defined your separateness to yourself.

An almost aesthetic consideration's involved. Okay, let's live to-gether. Let's each build a hut and for security we'll arrange the individual dwellings in a circle and then build an outer ring to enclose the whole village. Now your hut is your own business, but let's in general agree on certain outward forms. Since we all benefit from the larger pattern, let's compromise, conform to some degree on the materials, the shape of each unit. Because symmetry and harmony please the eye. Let's adopt a style, one that won't crimp anybody's individuality, one that will buttress and enhance each member's image of what a living place should be.

So Robby and I faced each other in the prison visiting lounge as familiar strangers, linked by blood and time. But how do you begin talking about blood, about time? He's been inside his privacy and I've been inside mine, and neither of us in thirty-odd years had felt the need to exchange more than social calls. We shared the common history, values, and style developed within the tall stockade of family, and that was enough to make us care about each other, enough to insure a profound depth of mutual regard, but the feelings were undifferentiated. They'd seldom been tested specifically, concretely. His privacy and mine had been exclusive, sanctioned by family traditions. Don't get too close. Don't ask too many questions or give too many answers. Don't pry. Don't let what's inside slop out on the people around you.

The stories I'd sent to Robby were an attempt to reveal what I thought about certain matters crucial to us both. Our shared roots and destinies. I wanted him to know what I'd been thinking and how that thinking was drawing me closer to him. I was banging on the door of his privacy. I believed I'd shed some of my own.

We were ready to talk. It was easy to begin. Impossible. We were neophytes, rookies. I was a double rookie. A beginner at this kind of intimacy, a beginner at trying to record it. My double awkwardness kept getting in the way. I'd hidden the borrowed pen by dropping my hand below the level of the table where we sat. Now when in hell would be the right moment to raise it? To use it? I had to depend on my brother's instincts, his generosity. I had to listen, listen.

Luckily there was catching up to do. He asked me about my kids, about his son, Omar, about the new nieces and nephews he'd never seen. That helped. Reminded us we were brothers. We got on with it. Conditions in the prisons. Robby's state of mind. The atmosphere behind the prison walls had been particularly tense for over a year. A group of new, younger guards had instituted a get-tough policy. More strip searches, cell shakedowns, strict enforcement of penny-ante rules and regulations. Grown men treated like children by other grown men. Inmates yanked out of line and punished because a button is undone or hair uncombed. What politicians demanded in the free world was being acted out inside the prison. A crusade, a war on crime waged by a gang of gung-ho guards against men who were already certified casualties, prisoners of war. The walking wounded being beaten and shot up again because they're easy targets. Robby's closest friends, including Cecil and Mike, are in the hole. Others who were considered potential troublemakers had been transferred to harsher prisons. Robby was warned by a guard. We ain't caught you in the shit yet, but we will. We know what you're thinking and we'll catch you in it. Or put you in it. Got your buddies and we'll get you.

The previous summer, 1980, a prisoner, Leon Patterson, had been asphyxiated in his cell. He was an asthma sufferer, a convicted murderer who depended on medication to survive the most severe attacks of his illness. On a hot August afternoon when the pollution index had reached its highest count of the summer, Patterson was locked in his cell in a cellblock without windows and little air. At four o'clock, two hours after he'd been confined to the range, he began to call for help. Other prisoners raised the traditional distress signal, rattling tin cups against the bars of their cells. Patterson's cries for help became screams, and his fellow inmates beat on the bars and shouted with him. Over an hour passed before any guards arrived. They carted away Patterson's limp body. He never revived and was pronounced dead at 10:45 that evening. His death epitomized the polarization in the prison. Patterson was seen as one more victim of the guards' inhumanity. A series of incidents followed in the ensuing year, hunger strikes, melees between guards and prisoners, culminating in a near massacre when the dog days of August hung once more over the prison.

One of the favorite tactics of the militant guards was grabbing a man from the line as the prisoners moved single-file through an archway dividing the recreation yard from the main cell blocks. No reason was given or needed. It was a simple show of force, a reminder of the guards' absolute power, their right to treat the inmates any way they chose, and do it with impunity. A sit-down strike in the prison auditorium followed one of the more violent attacks on an inmate. The prisoner who had resisted an arbitrary seizure and strip search was smacked in the face. He punched back and the guards jumped him, knocked him to the ground with their fists and sticks. The incident took place in plain view of over a hundred prisoners and it was the last straw. The victim had been provoked, assaulted, and surely would be punished for attempting to protect himself, for doing what any man would and should do in similar circumstances. The prisoner would suffer again. In addition to the physical beating they'd administered, the guards would attack the man's record. He'd be written up. A kangaroo court would take away his *good time*, thereby lengthening the period he'd have to wait before becoming eligible for probation or parole. Finally, on the basis of the guards' testimony he'd probably get a sixty-day sojourn in the hole. The prisoners realized it was time to take a stand. What had happened to one could happen to any of them. They rushed into the auditorium and locked themselves in. The prisoners held out till armed state troopers and prison guards in riot gear surrounded the building. Given the mood of that past year and the unmistakable threat in the new warden's voice as he repeated through a loudspeaker his refusal to meet with the prisoners and discuss their grievances, everybody inside the building knew that the authorities meant business, that the forces of law and order would love nothing better than an excuse to turn the auditorium into a shooting gallery. The strike was broken. The men filed out. A point was driven home again. Prisoners have no rights the keepers are bound to respect.

That was how the summer had gone. Summer was bad enough in the penitentiary in the best of times. Warm weather stirred the prisoners' blood. The siren call of the streets intensified. Circus time. The street blooming again after the long, cold winter. People outdoors. On their stoops. On the corners. In bright summer clothes or hardly any clothes at all. The free-world sounds and sights more real as the weather heats up. Confinement a torture. Each cell a hotbox. The keepers take advantage of every excuse to keep you out of the yard, to deprive you of the simple pleasure of a breeze, the blue sky. Why? So that the pleasant weather can be used as a tool, a boon to be withheld. So punishment has a sharper edge. By a perverse turn of the screw something good becomes something bad. Summer a bitch at best, but this past summer as the young turks among the guards ran roughshod over the prisoners, the prison had come close to blowing, to exploding like a piece of rotten fruit in the sun. And if the lid blew, my brother knew he'd be one of the first to die. During any large-scale uprising, in the first violent, chaotic seconds no board of inquiry would ever be able to reconstruct, scores would be settled. A bullet in the back of the brain would get rid of troublemakers, remove potential leaders, uncontrollable prisoners the guards hated and feared. You were supremely eligible for a bullet if the guards couldn't press your button. If they hadn't learned how to manipulate you, if you couldn't be bought or sold, if you weren't into drug and sex games, if you weren't cowed or depraved, then you were a threat.

Robby understood that he was sentenced to die. That all sentences were death sentences. If he didn't buckle under, the guards would do everything in their power to kill him. If he succumbed to the pressure to surrender dignity, self-respect, control over his own mind and body, then he'd become a beast, and what was good in him would die. The death sentence was unambiguous. The question for him became: How long could he survive in spite of the death sentence? Nothing he did would guarantee his safety. A disturbance in a cell block halfway across the prison could provide an excuse for shooting him and dumping him with the other victims. Anytime he was ordered to go with guards out of sight of other prisoners, his escorts could claim he attacked them, or attempted to escape. Since the flimsiest pretext would make murdering him acceptable, he had no means of protecting himself. Yet to maintain sanity, to minimize their opportunities to destroy him, he had to be constantly vigilant. He had to discipline himself to avoid confrontations, he had to weigh in terms of life and death every decision he made; he had to listen and obey his keepers' orders, but he also had to determine in certain threatening situations whether it was better to say no and keep himself out of a trap or take his chances that this particular summons was not the one inviting him to his doom. Of course to say no perpetuated his reputation as one who couldn't be controlled, a bad guy, a guy you never turn your back on, one of the prisoners out to get the guards. That rap made you more dangerous in the keepers' eyes and therefore increased the likelihood they'd be frightened into striking first. Saying no put you in no less jeopardy than going along with the program. Because the program was contrived to kill you. Directly or indirectly, you knew where you were headed. What you didn't know was the schedule. Tomorrow. Next week. A month. A minute. When would one of them get itchy, get beyond waiting a second longer? Would there be a plan, a contrived incident, a conspiracy they'd talk about and set up as they drank coffee in the guards' room or would it be the hair-trigger impulse of one of them who held a grudge, harbored an antipathy so elemental, so irrational that it could express itself only in a burst of pure, unrestrained violence?

If you're Robby and have the will to survive, these are the possibilities you must constantly entertain. Vigilance is the price of survival. Beneath the vigilance, however, is a gnawing awareness boiling in the pit of your stomach. You can be as vigilant as you're able, you can keep fighting the good fight to survive, and still your fate is out of your hands. If they decide to come for you in the morning, that's it. Your ass is grass and those minutes, and hours, days and years you painfully stitched together to put off the final reckoning won't matter at all. So the choice, difficult beyond words, to say yes or say no is made in light of the knowledge that in the end neither your yes nor your no matters. Your life is not in your hands.

Questions for Discussion

1. The passage discusses two major ideas: brothers getting to know one another in order to write a book and the constant vigilance that is necessary in prison. How are the two parts linked? How are both related to the author's purpose in the selection?

2. From what you have read here, would you be led to believe that prison is a good place to reflect on one's life? (What is the etymology of *penitentiary* and its related terms *penitence* and *penitent*? You can find the answer to this question in a standard desk dictionary. Do you find any irony in the history of the word's meaning?)

3. The opening paragraph raises some major issues regarding the author's intentions and his role in writing about his brother. Are these issues relevant only to the situation John Wideman recounts, or do they have wider significance? Explain.

4. The author's brother was given a sentence of life imprisonment. Yet Wideman writes, "Robby understood that he was sentenced to die." What does this statement mean? How literal is it?

5. The first paragraph in this selection talks about some of the dangers and difficulties of writing. How do Wideman's attitudes and ideas on that subject compare with those of Richard Rodriguez?

6. Compare and contrast Wideman's home and family life with those of Richard Rodriguez. (See "Comparison" and "Contrast" in the Glossary.) Both families were minorities, one ethnic and one racial. Do they have anything in common that relates to their minority status?

7. In what ways do Wideman and Abbott agree about prisons and prisoners? In what ways do they differ?

8. Compare Wideman's style with Abbott's. Think of diction or word choice, sentence structure, imagery, and figurative language. Which style do you prefer? Why?

MAXINE HONG KINGSTON

In 1940, Maxine Hong was born in Stockton, California, daughter of parents who immigrated from China in the 1930s and, eventually, started a laundry in Stockton—a classic story, almost a cliché, of Chinese in the United States. Maxine took a degree in English at the University of California at Berkeley and studied for an advanced degree in education. In 1962, she married Earll [sic] Kingston and in 1967 moved to Honolulu, where she taught at the Mid-Pacific Institute, a private coeducational high school, until 1977 when she was named visiting assistant professor of creative writing at the University of Hawaii.

Woman Warrior—which has been called variously an autobiography, a novel, and a memoir—was a great critical success, winner of the National Book Critics' Circle Award for nonfiction in 1976.

"Ghosts" appear throughout the book: members of the white majority and the Americanized part of Maxine also. In the following selection from Woman Warrior, *the metaphor of ghosts is, as you will see, very important.*

Shaman

When I last visited my parents, I had trouble falling asleep, too big for the hills and valleys scooped in the mattress by child-bodies. I heard my mother come in. I stopped moving. What did she want? Eyes shut, I pictured my mother, her white hair frizzy in the dark-and-light doorway, my hair white now too, Mother. I could hear her move furniture about. Then she dragged a third quilt, the thick, homemade Chinese kind, across me. After that I lost track of her location. I spied from beneath my eyelids and had to hold back a jump. She had pulled up a chair and was sitting by the bed next to my head. I could see her strong hands in her lap, not working fourteen pairs of needles. She is very proud of her hands, which can make anything and stay pink and soft while my father's became like carved wood. Her palm lines do not branch into head, heart, and life lines like other people's but crease with just one atavistic fold. That night she was a sad bear; a great sheep in a wool shawl. She recently took to wearing shawls and granny glasses, American fashions. What did she want, sitting there so large next to my head? I could feel her stare—her eyes two lights warm on my graying hair, then on the creases at the sides of my mouth, my thin neck, my thin cheeks, my thin arms. I felt her sight warm each of my bony elbows, and I flopped about in my fake sleep to hide them from her criticism. She sent light at full brightness beaming through my eyelids, her eyes at my eyes, and I had to open them.

"What's the matter, Mama? Why are you sitting there?"

She reached over and switched on a lamp she had placed on the floor beside her. "I swallowed that LSD pill you left on the kitchen counter," she announced.

"That wasn't LSD, Mama. It was just a cold pill. I have a cold."

"You're always catching colds when you come home. You must be eating too much *yin*. Let me get you another quilt."

"No, no more quilts. You shouldn't take pills that aren't prescribed for you. 'Don't eat pills you find on the curb,' you always told us."

"You children never tell me what you're really up to. How else am I going to find out what you're really up to?" As if her head hurt, she closed her eyes behind the gold wire rims. "Aiaa," she sighed, "how can I bear to have you leave me again?"

How can I bear to leave her again? She would close up this room, open temporarily for me, and wander about cleaning and cleaning the

From *The Woman Warrior: Memoirs of a Childhood Among Ghosts*, by Maxine Hong Kingston. Copyright © 1975, 1976 by Maxine Hong Kingston. Reprinted by permission of Alfred A. Knopf, Inc.

shrunken house, so tidy since our leaving. Each chair has its place now. And the sinks in the bedrooms work, their alcoves no longer stuffed with laundry right up to the ceiling. My mother has put the clothes and shoes into boxes, stored against hard times. The sinks had been built of gray marble for the old Chinese men who boarded here before we came. I used to picture modest little old men washing in the mornings and dressing before they shuffled out of these bedrooms. I would have to leave and go again into the world out there which has no marble ledges for my clothes, no quilts made from our own ducks and turkeys, no ghosts of neat little old men.

The lamp gave off the sort of light that comes from a television, which made the high ceiling disappear and then suddenly drop back into place. I could feel that clamping down and see how my mother had pulled the blinds down so low that the bare rollers were showing. No passer-by would detect a daughter in this house. My mother would sometimes be a large animal, barely real in the dark; then she would become a mother again. I could see the wrinkles around her big eyes, and I could see her cheeks sunken without her top teeth.

"I'll be back again soon," I said. "You know that I come back. I think of you when I'm not here."

"Yes, I know you. I know you now. I've always known you. You're the one with the charming words. You have never come back. 'I'll be back on Turkey-day,' you said. Huh."

I shut my teeth together, vocal cords cut, they hurt so. I would not speak words to give her pain. All her children gnash their teeth.

"The last time I saw you, you were still young," she said. "Now you're old."

"It's only been a year since I visited you."

"That's the year you turned old. Look at you, hair gone gray, and you haven't even fattened up yet. I know how the Chinese talk about us. 'They're so poor,' they say, 'they can't afford to fatten up any of their daughters.' 'Years in America,' they say, 'and they don't eat.' Oh, the shame of it—a whole family of skinny children. And your father—he's so skinny, he's disappearing."

"Don't worry about him, Mama. Doctors are saying that skinny people live longer. Papa's going to live a long time."

"So! I knew I didn't have too many years left. Do you know how I got all this fat? Eating your leftovers. Aiaa, I'm getting so old. Soon you will have no more mother."

"Mama, you've been saying that all my life."

"This time it's true. I'm almost eighty."

"I thought you were only seventy-six."

"My papers are wrong. I'm eighty."

"But I thought your papers are wrong, and you're seventy-two, seventy-three in Chinese years."

"My papers are wrong, and I'm eighty, eighty-one in Chinese years. Seventy. Eighty. What do numbers matter? I'm dropping dead any day now. The aunt down the street was resting on her porch steps, dinner all cooked, waiting for her husband and son to come home and eat it. She closed her eyes for a moment and died. Isn't that a wonderful way to go?"

"But our family lives to be ninety-nine."

"That's your father's family. My mother and father died very young. My youngest sister was an orphan at ten. Our parents were not even fifty."

"Then you should feel grateful you've lived so many extra years."

"I was so sure you were going to be an orphan too. In fact, I'm amazed you've lived to have white hair. Why don't you dye it?"

"Hair color doesn't measure age, Mother. White is just another pigment, like black and brown."

"You're always listening to Teacher Ghosts, those Scientist Ghosts, Doctor Ghosts."

"I have to make a living."

"I never do call you Oldest Daughter. Have you noticed that? I always tell people, 'This is my Biggest Daughter.' "

"Is it true then that Oldest Daughter and Oldest Son died in China? Didn't you tell me when I was ten that she'd have been twenty; when I was twenty, she'd be thirty?" Is that why you've denied me my title?

"No, you must have been dreaming. You must have been making up stories. You are all the children there are."

(Who was that story about—the one where the parents are throwing money at the children, but the children don't pick it up because they're crying too hard? They're writhing on the floor covered with coins. Their parents are going out the door for America, hurling handfuls of change behind them.)

She leaned forward, eyes brimming with what she was about to say: "I work so hard," she said. She was doing her stare—at what? My feet began rubbing together as if to tear each other's skin off. She started talking again, "The tomato vines prickle my hands; I can feel their little stubble hairs right through my gloves. My feet squish-squish in the rotten tomatoes, squish-squish in the tomato mud the feet ahead of me have sucked. And do you know the best way to stop the itch from the tomato hairs? You break open a fresh tomato and wash yourself with it. You cool your face in tomato juice. Oh, but it's the potatoes

that will ruin my hands. I'll get rheumatism washing potatoes, squat-
ting over potatoes."

She had taken off the Ace bandages around her legs for the night.
The varicose veins stood out.

"Mama, why don't you stop working? You don't have to work
anymore. Do you? Do you really have to work like that? Scabbing in the
tomato fields?" Her black hair seems filleted with the band of white at
its roots. She dyed her hair so that the farmers would hire her. She
would walk to Skid Row and stand in line with the hobos, the winos,
the junkies, and the Mexicans until the farm buses came and the
farmers picked out the workers they wanted. "You have the house," I
said. "For food you have Social Security. And urban renewal must have
given you something. It was good in a way when they tore down the
laundry. Really, Mama, it was. Otherwise Papa would never have retired.
You ought to retire too."

"Do you think your father wanted to stop work? Look at his eyes;
the brown is going out of his eyes. He has stopped talking. When I go to
work, he eats leftovers. He doesn't cook new food," she said, confessing,
me maddened at confessions. "Those Urban Renewal Ghosts gave us
moving money. It took us seventeen years to get our customers. How
could we start all over on moving money, as if we two old people had
another seventeen years in us? Aa"—she flipped something aside with
her hand—"White Ghosts can't tell Chinese age."

I closed my eyes and breathed evenly, but she could tell I wasn't
asleep.

"This is terrible ghost country, where a human being works her
life away," she said. "Even the ghosts work, no time for acrobatics. I
have not stopped working since the day the ship landed. I was on my
feet the moment the babies were out. In China I never even had to hang
up my own clothes. I shouldn't have left, but your father couldn't have
supported you without me. I'm the one with the big muscles."

"If you hadn't left, there wouldn't have been a me for you two to
support. Mama, I'm really sleepy. Do you mind letting me sleep?" I do
not believe in old age. I do not believe in getting tired.

"I didn't need muscles in China. I was small in China." She was.
The silk dresses she gave me are tiny. You would not think the same
person wore them. This mother can carry a hundred pounds of Texas
rice up- and downstairs. She could work at the laundry from 6:30 a.m.
until midnight, shifting a baby from an ironing table to a shelf between
packages, to the display window, where the ghosts tapped on the glass.
"I put you babies in the clean places at the laundry, as far away from the
germs that fumed out of the ghosts' clothes as I could. Aa, their socks

and handkerchiefs choked me. I cough now because of those seventeen years of breathing dust. Tubercular handkerchiefs. Lepers' socks." I thought she had wanted to show off my baby sister in the display window.

In the midnight unsteadiness we were back at the laundry, and my mother was sitting on an orange crate sorting dirty clothes into mountains—a sheet mountain, a white shirt mountain, a dark shirt mountain, a work-pants mountain, a long underwear mountain, a short underwear mountain, a little hill of socks pinned together in pairs, a little hill of handkerchiefs pinned to tags. Surrounding her were candles she burned in daylight, clean yellow diamonds, footlights that ringed her, mysterious masked mother, nose and mouth veiled with a cowboy handkerchief. Before undoing the bundles, my mother would light a tall new candle, which was a luxury, and the pie pans full of old wax and wicks that sometimes sputtered blue, a noise I thought was the germs getting seared.

"No tickee, no washee, mama-san?" a ghost would say, so embarrassing.

"Noisy Red-Mouth Ghost," she'd write on its package, naming it, marking its clothes with its name.

Back in the bedroom I said, "The candles must have helped. It was a good idea of yours to use candles."

"They didn't do much good. All I have to do is think about dust sifting out of clothes or peat dirt blowing across a field or chick mash falling from a scoop, and I start coughing." She coughed deeply. "See what I mean? I have worked too much. Human beings don't work like this in China. Time goes slower there. Here we have to hurry, feed the hungry children before we're too old to work. I feel like a mother cat hunting for its kittens. She has to find them fast because in a few hours she will forget how to count or that she had any kittens at all. I can't sleep in this country because it doesn't shut down for the night. Factories, canneries, restaurants—always somebody somewhere working through the night. It never gets done all at once here. Time was different in China. One year lasted as long as my total time here; one evening so long, you could visit your women friends, drink tea, and play cards at each house, and it would still be twilight. It even got boring, nothing to do but fan ourselves. Here midnight comes and the floor's not swept, the ironing's not ready, the money's not made. I would still be young if we lived in China."

"Time is the same from place to place," I said unfeelingly. "There is only the eternal present, and biology. The reason you feel time pushing is that you had six children after you were forty-five and you worried about raising us. You shouldn't worry anymore, though, Mama. You should feel good you had so many babies around you in middle age. Not many mothers have that. Wasn't it like prolonging youth? Now wasn't it? You mustn't worry now. All of us have grown up. And you can stop working."

"I can't stop working. When I stop working, I hurt. My head, my back, my legs hurt. I get dizzy. I can't stop."

"I'm like that too, Mama. I work all the time. Don't worry about me starving. I won't starve. I know how to work. I work all the time. I know how to kill food, how to skin and pluck it. I know how to keep warm by sweeping and mopping. I know how to work when things get bad."

"It's a good thing I taught you children to look after yourselves. We're not going back to China for sure now."

"You've been saying that since nineteen forty-nine."

"Now it's final. We got a letter from the villagers yesterday. They asked if it was all right with us that they took over the land. The last uncles have been killed so your father is the only person left to say it is all right, you see. He has written saying they can have it. So. We have no more China to go home to."

It must be all over then. My mother and father have stoked each other's indignation for almost forty years telling stories about land quarrels among the uncles, the in-laws, the grandparents. Episodes from their various points of view came weekly in the mail, until the uncles were executed kneeling on broken glass by people who had still other plans for the land. How simply it ended—my father writing his permission. Permission asked, permission given twenty-five years after the Revolution.

"We belong to the planet now, Mama. Does it make sense to you that if we're no longer attached to one piece of land, we belong to the planet? Wherever we happen to be standing, why, that spot belongs to us as much as any other spot." Can we spend the fare money on furniture and cars? Will American flowers smell good now?

"I don't want to go back anyway," she said. "I've gotten used to eating. And the Communists are much too mischievous. You should see the ones I meet in the fields. They bring sacks under their clothes to steal grapes and tomatoes from the growers. They come with trucks on Sundays. And they're killing each other in San Francisco." One of the old men caught his visitor, another old fellow, stealing his bantam; the owner spotted its black feet sticking out of his guest's sweater. We woke up one morning to find a hole in the ground where our loquat tree had stood. Later we saw a new loquat tree most similar to ours in a Chinese neighbor's yard. We knew a family who had a sign in their vegetable patch: "Since this is not a Communist garden but cabbages grown by private enterprise, please do not steal from my garden." It was dated and signed in good handwriting.

"The new immigrants aren't Communists, Mother. They're fugitives from the real Communists."

"They're Chinese, and Chinese are mischievous. No, I'm too old to keep up with them. They'd be too clever for me. I've lost my cunning, having grown accustomed to food, you see. There's only one thing that I really want anymore. I want you here, not wandering like a ghost from Romany. I want every one of you living here together. When you're all home, all six of you with your children and husbands and wives, there are twenty or thirty people in this house. Then I'm happy. And your father is happy. Whichever room I walk into overflows with my relatives, grandsons, sons-in-law. I can't turn around without touching somebody. That's the way a house should be." Her eyes are big, inconsolable. A spider headache spreads out in fine branches over my skull. She is etching spider legs into the icy bone. She pries open my head and my fists and crams into them responsibility for time, responsibility for intervening oceans.

The gods pay her and my father back for leaving their parents. My grandmother wrote letters pleading for them to come home, and they ignored her. Now they know how she felt.

"When I'm away from here," I had to tell her, "I don't get sick. I don't go to the hospital every holiday. I don't get pneumonia, no dark spots on my x-rays. My chest doesn't hurt when I breathe. I can breathe. And I don't get headaches at 3:00. I don't have to take medicines or go to doctors. Elsewhere I don't have to lock my doors and keep checking the locks. I don't stand at the windows and watch for movements and see them in the dark."

"What do you mean you don't lock your doors?"

"I do. I do. But not the way I do here. I don't hear ghost sounds. I don't stay awake listening to walking in the kitchen. I don't hear the doors and windows unhinging."

"It was probably just a Wino Ghost or a Hobo Ghost looking for a place to sleep."

"I don't want to hear Wino Ghosts and Hobo Ghosts. I've found some places in this country that are ghost-free. And I think I belong there, where I don't catch colds or use my hospitalization insurance. Here I'm sick so often, I can barely work. I can't help it, Mama."

She yawned. "It's better, then, for you to stay away. The weather in California must not agree with you. You can come for visits." She got up and turned off the light. "Of course, you must go, Little Dog."

A weight lifted from me. The quilts must be filling with air. The world is somehow lighter. She has not called me that endearment for years—a name to fool the gods. I am really a Dragon, as she is a Dragon, both of us born in dragon years. I am practically a first daughter of a first daughter.

"Good night, Little Dog."

"Good night, Mother."

She sends me on my way, working always and now old, dreaming the dreams about shrinking babies and the sky covered with airplanes and a Chinatown bigger than the ones here.

Questions for Discussion

1. In this selection, white people are called "ghosts." What reasons, other than skin color, might the Chinese people have for using this term? Why is the metaphor important?

2. Almost all of the ideas in this passage are expressed in dialogue. Explain why this method makes it either easier or more difficult to get the gist of the passage. Do you feel there are some thoughts left unsaid? If so, do you have an idea of what they are? Explain.

3. The passage deals with the theme of separation from family, society, and homeland. What are the mother's attitudes toward these alienations? The daughter's attitudes?

4. Many people find *Woman Warrior* difficult to read and understand. Explain why this should be so?

5. In what ways are the minority experiences of Richard Rodriguez, John Edgar Wideman, and Maxine Hong Kingston similar? Different?

6. In one sentence, state the thesis, or main idea, of this selection.

EUDORA WELTY

On Pinehurst Street in Jackson, Mississippi, stands the home of one of America's most respected writers, Eudora Welty. She was born in 1909 in Jackson, took a bachelor's degree at the University of Wisconsin, and attended Columbia University for a year (1930–1931). She has worked for newspapers and radio stations in Mississippi and was briefly a member of the New York Times *book review staff.*

*Since publishing her first collection of stories in 1941 (*A Curtain of Green*), Eudora Welty has regularly produced short stories and novels and has been honored with the Pulitzer Prize, among other awards.*

One Writer's Beginnings *is interesting for a variety of reasons. It is a self-portrait of a sensitive writer and keen observer and also a vivid depiction of a bygone era. In the selection that follows, the author takes us for a ride on a train—an experience few of us will ever have, but one that is very much a part of our national history as a symbol of both progress and romance.*

Finding a Voice

I never saw until after he was dead a small keepsake book given to my father in his early childhood. On one page was a message of one sentence written to him by his mother on April 15, 1886. The date is the day of her death. "My dearest Webbie: I want you to be a good boy and to meet me in heaven. Your loving Mother." Webb was his middle name—her maiden name. She always called him by it. He was seven years old, her only child.

He had other messages in his little book to keep and read over to himself. "May your life, though short, be pleasant / As a warm and melting day" is from "Dr. Armstrong," and as it follows his mother's message may have been entered on the same day. Another entry reads: "Dear Webbie, If God send thee a cross, take it up willingly and follow Him. If it be light, slight it not. If it be heavy, murmur not. After the cross is the crown. Your aunt, Nina Welty." This is dated earlier—he was then three years old. The cover of the little book is red and embossed with baby ducklings falling out of a basket entwined with morning glories. It is very rubbed and worn. It had been given him to keep and he had kept it; he had brought it among his possessions to Mississippi when he married; my mother had put it away. . . .

I think now, in looking back on these summer trips—this one and a number later, made in the car and on the train—that another element in them must have been influencing my mind. The trips were wholes unto themselves. They were stories. Not only in form, but in their taking on direction, movement, development, change. They changed something in my life: each trip made its particular revelation, though I could not have found words for it. But with the passage of time, I could look back on them and see them bringing me news, discoveries, premonitions, promises—I still can; they still do. When I did begin to write, the short story was a shape that had already formed itself and stood waiting in the back of my mind. Nor is it surprising to me that when I made my first attempt at a novel, I entered its world—that of the mysterious Yazoo-Mississippi Delta—as a child riding there on a train: "From the warm windowsill the endless fields glowed like a hearth in firelight, and Laura, looking out, leaning on her elbows with her head between her hands, felt what an arriver in a land feels—that slow hard pounding in the breast."

Excerpted by permission of the publishers from *One Writer's Beginnings* by Eudora Welty, Cambridge, MA: Harvard University Press. Copyright © 1983, 1984 by Eudora Welty.

The events in our lives happen in a sequence in time, but in their significance to ourselves they find their own order, a timetable not necessarily—perhaps not possibly—chronological. The time as we know it subjectively is often the chronology that stories and novels follow: it is the continuous thread of revelation. . . .

I had the window seat. Beside me, my father checked the progress of our train by moving his finger down the timetable and springing open his pocket watch. He explained to me what the position of the arms of the semaphore meant; before we were to pass through a switch we would watch the signal lights change. Along our track, the mileposts could be read; he read them. Right on time by Daddy's watch, the next town sprang into view, and just as quickly was gone.

Side by side and separately, we each lost ourselves in the experience of not missing anything, of seeing everything, of knowing each time what the blows of the whistle meant. But of course it was not the same experience: what was new to me, not older than ten, was a landmark to him. My father knew our way mile by mile; by day or by night, he knew where we were. Everything that changed under our eyes, in the flying countryside, was the known world to him, the imagination to me. Each in our own way, we hungered for all of this: my father and I were in no other respect or situation so congenial.

In Daddy's leather grip was his traveler's drinking cup, collapsible; a lid to fit over it had a ring to carry it by; it traveled in a round leather box. This treasure would be brought out at my request, for me to bear to the water cooler at the end of the Pullman car, fill to the brim, and bear back to my seat, to drink water over its smooth lip. The taste of silver could almost be relied on to shock your teeth.

After dinner in the sparkling dining car, my father and I walked back to the open-air observation platform at the end of the train and sat on the folding chairs placed at the railing. We watched the sparks we made fly behind us into the night. Fast as our speed was, it gave us time enough to see the rose-red cinders turn to ash, each one, and disappear from sight. Sometimes a house far back in the empty hills showed a light no bigger than a star. The sleeping countryside seemed itself to open a way through for our passage, then close again behind us.

The swaying porter would be making ready our berths for the night, pulling the shade down just so, drawing the green fishnet hammock across the window so the clothes you took off could ride along beside you, turning down the tight-made bed, standing up the two snowy pillows as high as they were wide, switching on the eye of the reading lamp, starting the tiny electric fan—you suddenly saw its blades turn into gauze and heard its insect murmur; and drawing across it all the pair of thick green theaterlike curtains—billowing, smelling of cigar smoke—between which you would crawl or dive headfirst to button them together with yourself inside, to be seen no more that night.

When you lay enclosed and enwrapped, your head on a pillow parallel to the track, the rhythm of the rail clicks pressed closer to your body as if it might be your heart beating, but the sound of the engine seemed to come from farther away than when it carried you in daylight. The whistle was almost too far away to be heard, its sound wavering back from the engine over the roofs of the cars. What you listened for was the different sound that ran under you when your own car crossed on a trestle, then another sound on an iron bridge; a low or a high bridge—each had its pitch, or drumbeat, for your car.

Riding in the sleeper rhythmically lulled me and waked me. From time to time, waked suddenly, I raised my window shade and looked out at my own strip of the night. Sometimes there was unexpected moonlight out there. Sometimes the perfect shadow of our train, with our car, with me invisibly included, ran deep below, crossing a river with us by the light of the moon. Sometimes the encroaching walls of mountains woke me by clapping at my ears. The tunnels made the train's passage resound like the "loud" pedal of a piano, a roar that seemed to last as long as a giant's temper tantrum.

But my father put it all into the frame of regularity, predictability, that was his fatherly gift in the course of our journey. I saw it going by, the outside world, in a flash. I dreamed over what I could see as it passed, as well as over what I couldn't. Part of the dream was what lay beyond, where the path wandered off through the pasture, the red clay road climbed and went over the hill or made a turn and was hidden in trees, or toward a river whose bridge I could see but whose name I'd never know. A house back at its distance at night showing a light from an open doorway, the morning faces of the children who stopped still in what they were doing, perhaps picking blackberries or wild plums, and watched us go by—I never saw with the thought of their continuing to be there just the same after we were out of sight. For now, and for a long while to come, I was proceeding in fantasy.

I learned much later—after he was dead, in fact, the time when we so often learn fundamental things about our parents—how well indeed he knew the journey, and how he happened to do so. He fell in love with my mother, and she with him, in West Virginia when she was a teacher in the mountain schools near her home and he was a young man from Ohio who'd gone over to West Virginia to work in the office of a lumber construction company. When they decided to marry, they saw it as part of the adventure of starting a new life to go to a place far away and new to both of them, and that turned out to be Jackson, Mississippi. From rural Ohio and rural West Virginia, that must have seemed, in 1904, as far away as Bangkok might possibly seem to young people today. My father went down and got a job in a new insurance company being formed in Jackson. This was the Lamar Life. He was promoted almost at once, made secretary and one of the directors, and he was to stay with the company for the rest of his life. He set about first thing finding a house in Jackson, then a town of six or eight thousand people, for them to live in until they could build a house of their own. So during the engagement, he went the thousand miles to see her when he could afford it. The rest of the time—every day, sometimes twice a day—the two of them sent letters back and forth by this same train.

Their letters had all been kept by that great keeper, my mother; they were in one of the trunks in the attic—the trunk that used to go on the train with us to West Virginia and Ohio on summer trips. I didn't in the end feel like a trespasser when I came to open the letters: they brought my parents before me for the first time as young, as inexperienced, consumed with the strength of their hopes and desires, as *living* on these letters. I would have known my mother's voice in her letters anywhere. But I wouldn't have so quickly known my father's. Annihilating those miles between them—the miles I came along to travel with him, that first time on the train—those miles he knew nearly altogether by heart, he wrote more often than only once a day, and mailed his letters directly onto the mail car—letters that are so ardent, so direct and tender in expression, so urgent, that they seemed to bare, along with his love, the rest of his whole life to me.

On the train I saw that world passing my window. It was when I came to see it was *I* who was passing that my self-centered childhood was over. But it was not until I began to write, as I seriously did only when I reached my twenties, that I found the world out there revealing, because (as with my father now) *memory* had become attached to seeing, love had added itself to discovery, and because I recognized in my own continuing longing to keep going, the need I carried inside myself to know—the apprehension, first, and then the passion, to connect myself to it. Through travel I first became aware of the outside world; it was through travel that I found my own introspective way into becoming a part of it.

This is, of course, simply saying that the outside world is the vital component of my inner life. My work, in the terms in which I see it, is as dearly matched to the world as its secret sharer. My imagination takes its strength and guides its direction from what I see and hear and learn and feel and remember of my living world. But I was to learn slowly that both these worlds, outer and inner, were different from what they seemed to me in the beginning. . . .

It seems to me, writing of my parents now in my seventies, that I see continuities in their lives that weren't visible to me when they were living. Even at the times that have left me my most vivid memories of them, there were connections between them that escaped me. Could it be because I can better see their lives—or any lives I know—today because I'm a fiction writer? See them not as fiction, certainly—see them, perhaps, as even greater mysteries than I knew. Writing fiction has developed in me an abiding respect for the unknown in a human lifetime and a sense of where to look for the threads, how to follow, how to connect, find in the thick of the tangle what clear line persists. The strands are all there: to the memory nothing is ever really lost.

The little keepsake book given to my father so long ago, of which I never heard a word spoken by anybody, has grown in eloquence to me. The messages that were meant to "go with him"—and which did—the farewell from his mother on the day of her death; and the doctor's following words that the child's own life would be short; the admonition from his Aunt Penina to bear his cross and murmur not—made a sum that he had been left to ponder over from the time he had learned to read. It seems to me that my father's choosing life insurance as his work, and indeed he exhausted his life for it, must have always had a deeper reason behind it than his conviction, strong as it was, in which he joined the majority in the twenties, that success in business was the solution to most of the problems of living—security of the family, their ongoing comfort and welfare, and especially the certainty of education for the children. This was partly why the past had no interest for him. He saw life in terms of the future, and he worked to provide that future for his children.

Right along with the energetic practice of optimism, and deeper than this, was an abiding awareness of mortality itself—most of all the mortality of a parent. This care, this caution, that ruled his life in the family, and in the business he chose and succeeded in expanding so far, began very possibly when he was seven years old, when his mother, asking him with perhaps literally her last words to be a good boy and meet her in heaven, died and left him alone.

Strangely enough, what Ned Andrews had extolled too, in all his rhetoric, was the future works of man and the leaving of the past behind. No two characters could have been wider apart than those of Ned Andrews and Christian Welty, or more different in their self-expression. They never knew each other, and the only thing they had in common was my mother's love. Who knows but that this ambition for the betterment of mankind in the attainable future was the quality in them both that she loved first? She would have responded to the ardency of their beliefs. I'm not sure she succeeded in having faith in their predictions. Neither got to live their lives out; the hurt she felt in this was part of her love for both.

My father of course liberally insured his own life for the future provision of his family, and had cause to believe that all was safe ahead. Then the Great Depression arrived. And in 1931 a disease that up to then even he had never heard of, leukemia, caused his death in a matter of weeks, at the age of fifty-two.

Questions for Discussion

1. Why do the train rides Welty took with her father have such emotional resonance for her?

2. Welty makes an analogy between a trip and the short story. What similarities does she see? Is this analogy effective? Explain.

3. What discoveries does the author make when traveling with her father?

4. Certain objects take on great importance in Welty's narrative—for example, her father's keepsake book, his collapsible cup, and the rail car's berth. What purpose does this attention to detail serve? What do these objects symbolize for the author?

5. This selection deals with what the author learns about her parents and herself. Do you feel that writers inevitably learn something of themselves as they write about others? How so?

6. *One Writer's Beginnings*, from which this selection was taken, consists of three lectures Eudora Welty delivered at Harvard University in 1983. If you had attended those lectures, would you have had trouble following Ms. Welty's thoughts? What does she do to make her narrative appealing and understandable to listeners?

JOAN DIDION

One of America's most popular and respected writers, Joan Didion was born in Sacramento, California, in 1934. She took her bachelor's degree at the University of California at Berkeley. From 1956 to 1963, she was associate feature editor for Vogue. *In 1964, she married John Gregory Dunne, the prominent American writer whose best-known work is* True Confessions.

Didion is known for her novels The Book of Common Prayer *and* Play It as It Lays, *the latter about Las Vegas, the movie industry, and the freeway society of Southern California. Her essays have been collected in* The White Album *and* Slouching Towards Bethlehem, *from which "On Going Home" is taken.*

Understanding the title Slouching Towards Bethlehem *helps one grasp the full significance of "On Going Home." The title comes from a poem by William Butler Yeats, "The Second Coming," portraying a chaotic future in which not Christ, but a "rough beast" will slouch toward Bethlehem to be born. Yeats says,*

> *Things fall apart; the center cannot hold;*
> *Mere anarchy is loosed up the world. . . .*

Didion's essay gives one a sense of her belief that "things fall apart."

On Going Home

I am home for my daughter's first birthday. By "home" I do not mean the house in Los Angeles where my husband and I and the baby live, but the place where my family is, in the Central Valley of California. It is a vital although troublesome distinction. My husband likes my family but is uneasy in their house, because once there I fall into their ways, which are difficult, oblique, deliberately inarticulate, not my husband's ways. We live in dusty houses ("D-U-S-T," he once wrote with his finger on surfaces all over the house, but no one noticed it) filled with mementos quite without value to him (what could the Canton dessert plates mean to him? how could he have known about the assay scales, why should he care if he did know?) and we appear to talk exclusively about people we know who have been committed to mental hospitals, about people we know who have been booked on drunk-driving charges, and about property, particularly about property, land, price per acre and C-2 zoning and assessments and freeway access. My brother does not understand my husband's inability to perceive the advantage in the rather common real-estate transaction known as "sale-leaseback," and my husband in turn does not understand why so many of the people he hears about in my father's house have recently been committed to mental hospitals or booked on drunk-driving charges. Nor does he understand that when we talk about sale-leasebacks and right-of-way condemnations we are talking in code about things we like best, the yellow fields and the cottonwoods and the rivers rising and falling and the mountain roads closing when the heavy snow comes in. We miss each other's points, have another drink and regard the fire. My brother refers to my husband, in his presence, as "Joan's husband." Marriage is the classic betrayal.

Or perhaps it is not any more. Sometimes I think that those of us who are now in our thirties were born into the last generation to carry the burden of "home," to find in family life the source of all tension and drama. I had by all objective accounts a "normal" and a "happy" family situation, and yet I was almost thirty years old before I could talk to my family on the telephone without crying after I had hung up. We did not fight. Nothing was wrong. And yet some nameless anxiety colored the emotional charges between me and the place that I came from. The question of whether or not you could go home again was a very real part of the sentimental and largely literary baggage with which we left home in the fifties; I suspect that it is irrelevant to the children born of the fragmentation after World War II. A few weeks ago in a San Francisco bar I saw a pretty young girl on crystal take off her clothes and dance for the cash prize in an "amateur-topless" contest. There was no particular sense of moment about this, none of the effect of romantic degradation, of "dark journey," for which my generation strived so assiduously. What sense could that girl possibly make of, say, *Long Day's Journey into Night?* Who is beside the point?

That I am trapped in this particular irrelevancy is never more apparent to me than when I am home. Paralyzed by the neurotic lassitude engendered by meeting one's past at every turn, around every corner, inside every cupboard, I go aimlessly from room to room. I decide to meet it head-on and clean out a drawer, and I spread the contents on the bed. A bathing suit I wore the summer I was seventeen. A letter of rejection from *The Nation*, an aerial photograph of the site for a shopping center my father did not build in 1954. Three teacups hand-painted with cabbage roses and signed "E.M.," my grandmother's initials. There is no final solution for letters of rejection from *The Nation* and teacups hand-painted in 1900. Nor is there any answer to snapshots of one's grandfather as a young man on skis, surveying around Donner Pass in the year 1910. I smooth out the snapshot and look into his face, and do not see my own. I close the drawer, and have another cup of coffee with my mother. We get along very well, veterans of a guerrilla war we never understood.

Days pass. I see no one. I come to dread my husband's evening call, not only because he is full of news of what by now seems to me our remote life in Los Angeles, people he has seen, letters which require attention, but because he asks what I have been doing, suggests uneasily that I get out, drive to San Francisco or Berkeley. Instead I drive across the river to a family graveyard. It has been vandalized since my last visit and the monuments are broken, overturned in the dry grass. Because I once saw a rattlesnake in the grass I stay in the car and listen to a country-and-Western station. Later I drive with my father to a ranch he has in the foothills. The man who runs his cattle on it asks us to the roundup, a week from Sunday, and although I know that I will be in Los Angeles I say, in the oblique way my family talks, that I will come. Once home I mention the broken monuments in the graveyard. My mother shrugs.

I go to visit my great-aunts. A few of them think now that I am my cousin, or their daughter who died young. We recall an anecdote about a relative last seen in 1948, and they ask if I still like living in New York City. I have lived in Los Angeles for three years, but I say that I do. The baby is offered a horehound drop, and I am slipped a dollar bill "to buy a treat." Questions trail off, answers are abandoned, the baby plays with the dust motes in a shaft of afternoon sun.

It is time for the baby's birthday party: a white cake, strawberry-marshmallow ice cream, a bottle of champagne saved from another party. In the evening, after she has gone to sleep, I kneel beside the crib and touch her face, where it is pressed against the slats, with mine. She is an open and trusting child, unprepared for and unaccustomed to the ambushes of family life, and perhaps it is just as well that I can offer her little of that life. I would like to give her more. I would like to promise her that she will grow up with a sense of her cousins and of rivers and of her great-grandmother's teacups, would like to pledge her a picnic on a river with fried chicken and her hair uncombed, would like to give her *home* for her birthday, but we live differently now and I can promise her nothing like that. I give her a xylophone and a sundress from Madeira, and promise to tell her a funny story.

Questions for Discussion

1. Characterize Didion's relationship with her parents. Refer to specific passages in the selection to explain your characterization.

2. It has been written of Didion that she "has passed beyond optimism and pessimism to a far country of quiet anguish, where the landscape resembles the flat, featureless sunbaked Central Valley of her California childhood." Do you think this describes "On Going Home"? Indicate passages in the text to back up your answer.

3. What does Didion mean by *home*, beyond the idea that it is one's parents' house? Why can't she promise her daughter "home"?

4. How is "On Going Home" structured? How is its content put together? Why would Didion probably be forced to change her principle of structure if she were to write a book about "going home"?

5. You might be interested in reading other works by Joan Didion (mentioned in the headnote to this selection). You would find that virtually all of her work is as pessimistic as "On Going Home." Is such a bleak outlook on life justified? Explain.

—————————   SUGGESTIONS FOR WRITING   —————————

1.   John Wideman writes, "We shared the common history, values, and style developed within the tall stockade of family, and that was enough to make us care about each other, enough to insure a profound depth of mutual regard, but the feelings were undifferentiated. They'd seldom been tested specifically, concretely."

Can you think of a time when you and a close relative or friend shared a major event? Write a personal narrative about that event, explaining what you learned about your relative or friend through the experience.

2.   Primary and secondary public schools have often been facetiously (or not so facetiously) compared with prisons. Using whatever tone you wish (humorous, serious, ironic, sarcastic), write about your life in school and explain how school, as an institution, influenced you.

3.   Some of the general subjects the authors in this chapter deal with are academic freedom (Morris), parents (Welty), institutions and institutional life (Abbott), sibling relationships (Wideman), being an outsider or a member of a minority group (Rodriguez and Kingston), and the problem of "going home again" (Didion).

Choose one of these subjects as the topic for a personal narrative and consciously try to imitate one of the authors. Thus, you might use Abbott's staccato prose in an essay about some institution you have been associated with or Welty's attention to detail in a discussion of your parents (or other close relative), or you might develop a symbol such as Kingston's "ghosts" to stand for a group to which you have not gained admission.

Indeed, as you write your personal narrative, you can use appropriate devices you have found in any of the selections in the chapter.

4.   Choose an event in your life that is just beginning and that will come to its conclusion within two weeks or so: a project you have started and must complete; some event, such as the wedding of a family member or friend; preparation for a major test; a physical training program or diet; a period of sacrifice, such as Lent; a health crisis of your own or of a friend or family member—any episode in your life that is meaningful to you. Keep a journal of that event.

Remember that a journal records on-the-spot impressions and thoughts and that it is specific and concrete.

5.   Describe a possession that you feel reflects your personality. Tell how you obtained the object and what makes it seem special to you.

6.   Write a description of a place that holds a special significance for you.

7.   Abbott, Robby Wideman, Rodriguez, and Willie Morris possess individual values that are counter to a system—school, family, prison, government. Write a personal narrative about a situation in which you found, or find, yourself in conflict with some institution.

8.   The world does not encourage people to be different; many people are challenged and threatened by our complex society. Some cannot adapt or conform. Kingston, Rodriguez, Robby Wideman, and Abbott all cannot, or will not, accept the constraints placed on them by their various cultures.

Write on one of the following topics concerning nonconformity: (a) Choose one author's circumstances and defend or oppose the stance taken by that author. (b) Ghostwrite a portion of an autobiography of a bag lady, hobo, or some other character who is definitely not a part of mainstream society. Your autobiography should explain why that person either chose or was forced into that particular way of life.

9.   Write a character sketch of Jack Henry Abbott or Joan Didion, using details from the selections of which they are the authors to support your interpretation. What sort of person is your subject? Is he or she like anyone else you know? Does anything about your subject puzzle you? Do you like or dislike your subject?

10.   Describe three things in your life that always upset you. If you could change these situations, how would you do it?

11.   Summarize the mother's attitude toward work in the selection by Maxine Hong Kingston and, compare and contrast it with your own attitude toward work.

C H A P T E R
2

Biography

Is there really a sharp dividing line between fact and fiction in narrative writing (such as biography)? We might say that the biographer merely records what is, whereas the novelist invents or makes up that which never was. However, in the words of critic Robert Scholes, "All writing, all composition, is construction. We do not imitate the world, we construct versions of it."[1] Scholes is saying that all narratives—biographies *and* novels, for instance—are fictions.

In a good biography, as in a good novel, characters come to life and exist in their full human complexity. We experience their use of language through direct quotations:

> "I look down the tracks and see you coming—and out of every haze & mist your darling rumpled trousers are hurrying to me. . . ."
> —Zelda in a letter to Scott Fitzgerald, from *Zelda*, by Nancy Milford

[1]Robert Scholes, *Structural Fabulation: An Essay on the Fiction of the Future* (Notre Dame: University of Notre Dame Press, 1976), p. 7.

"Always there echoes and re-echoes in my ears—Duty, Honor, Country. Today marks my final roll call with you. But I want you to know that when I cross the river my last conscious thoughts will be of the Corps; and the Corps; and the Corps. I bid you farewell."
>—Douglas MacArthur speaking to the cadets at West Point,
>from *American Caesar*, by William Manchester

We see the characters in action, doing things.

The girl [Thomas More's young wife] rebelled! She answered her husband's insistence with tears, and sometimes she beat her head against the floor. The husband, unable to do anything with her, suggested a visit to her father in the country. Off they went, the bride delighted to go home.
>—From *Thomas More*, by Richard Marius

Furthermore, the actions in the narratives take place in scenes, not merely against a blank, white background.

On Monday, in a chill rain, the twenty-five hundred men of the corps formed on the plain—MacArthur's old room, 1123, provided an excellent view of the scene—and, facing the Hudson, saluted as six cannon roared in salute, the smoke mingling with the mists on the bluffs overlooking the river.
>—From *American Caesar*,
>by William Manchester

Whether fiction or biography, the characters have motives—reasons for doing what they do. The novelist, of course, can know everything there is to know about his or her characters, having created them, and therefore can see into their minds, read their innermost thoughts, and be certain about motives:

Isabel had no hidden motive in wishing her cousin not to take her home; it simply seemed to her that for some days past she had consumed an inordinate quantity of his time, and the independent spirit of the American girl who ends by regarding perpetual assistance as a sort of derogations to her sanity had made her decide that for these few hours she must suffice to herself.
>—From *The Portrait of a Lady*, by Henry James

The biographer, however, can only speculate and draw conclusions on the basis of available evidence:

Why did he [Thomas More] marry her [Alice Middleton] so soon after Jane's [his first wife's] death? Her [first] husband had left her considerable property when he died, and both More and his father saw marriage as an economic union— as did nearly everyone in that time. People did not marry for love; as the colloquy of Erasmus shows, they hoped to love each other only after they had lived together for a time.

    Still, his haste seems almost indecent, and his biographers have puzzled over it; at times they seem embarrassed by it.

—From *Thomas More*, by Richard Marius

In short, then, the biographer uses most of the techniques of the novelist. The main difference between a biography and a novel—between *Zelda*, by Nancy Milford, and *The Portrait of a Lady*, by Henry James—is simply that we can verify the materials that went into a biography: we can check the documents (letters, diaries, legal papers) from which the biographer draws his or her "facts"; we can visit the scenes of the action; we can sometimes get eyewitness accounts—and so on. Because of this, we take *Thomas More*, by Richard Marius, to be biography and *The Great Gatsby*, by F. Scott Fitzgerald, to be fiction.

Many scholars feel that biography in English really began in the sixteenth century when William Roper wrote his *Life of Sir Thomas More* and George Cavendish wrote *Life of Wolsey*. Before this time, accounts of lives were didactic (to teach the readers a lesson) or commemorative, to praise the subject. In their biographies, Roper and Cavendish, for the first time, attempted to give well-rounded and truthful accounts of their subjects' lives.

In the eighteenth century, biography reached maturity. With *Lives of the Poets*, Samuel Johnson raised biography to the level of art and established veracity—truth to the facts as the writer saw them—as the criterion for biography. Johnson himself was the subject of one of the most famous of all biographies, that of James Boswell, whose *Life of Samuel Johnson* gives readers a vivid account of its subject as a living, breathing human being.

The selections in this chapter provide a sample of modern biography, but one twentieth-century development is worth mentioning: the biography that can be classified as *documentary fiction*. In this sort of text, the author uses the biographical facts of a character's life as the framework for a narrative, but writes from the standpoint of a novelist, sometimes inventing characters and events and assuming the novelist's omniscient ability to see into the minds of characters. The leading practitioner of this form is Irving Stone, who has written fictional biographies of Vincent van Gogh, Tom Paine, Heinrich Schliemann, Leonardo da Vinci, and other historical figures.

In the seventeenth century, the English poet John Dryden defined biography as "the history of particular men's lives," but a good biography is much more; it gives readers a grasp of the times in which the subjects lived, of the ideas that concerned them, of their morals and manners and characteristic life-styles. Biography gives readers an understanding of people, events, and ideas.

JANE HOWARD

---

*Writer, teacher, lecturer, Jane Howard (born 1935) is a graduate of the
University of Michigan. She has been a reporter and then an editor for
Life magazine. She lives in New York City and Sag Harbor, Long Island.
Her other books are* Please Touch, A Different Woman, *and* Families.

    *Margaret Mead was the first child ever born at West Park Hospital
in Philadelphia when she came into the world on December 16, 1901.
Her father, Edward Sherwood Mead, taught at the Wharton School of
Commerce of the University of Pennsylvania, and her mother, Emily Fogg
Mead, was a cultured woman who arranged a fellowship at Bryn Mawr
College so she could continue her studies while she reared a family.*

    *In 1919, Margaret entered DePauw University, but after a year
transferred to Barnard, in New York City. It was at Barnard and then
Columbia, where she completed her doctorate, that her intellectual and
professional life gained its direction under the influence of two noted
scholars, Ruth Benedict, author of* Patterns of Culture, *and Franz Boas,
one of the founding fathers of anthropology.*

    *In 1925, at the age of twenty-four, Margaret Mead set out on her
first field trip—to Samoa, where she studied the life-styles and society of
the Islanders. Her report of this study,* Coming of Age in Samoa,
*portrayed Samoan society as almost Edenic, life without the conflicts,
tensions, and inhibitions of the "civilized" West. The book was a great
success, the sort of volume that would gain the attention of intellectuals,
not just professional anthropologists; it was Margaret Mead's first major
step on the road to fame (though not fortune).*

    Book followed book: Growing Up in New Guinea *(1930),* Sex and
Temperament in Three Primitive Societies *(1935),* And Keep Your Powder
Dry *(1942),* Male and Female *(1949),* The School in American Culture
(1951), Cultural Patterns and Technical Change *(1954)—and many more.*

    *Margaret Mead had three husbands, each an anthropologist: Luther
Cressman, Reo Fortune, and Gregory Bateson, by whom she had a
daughter.*

    Mead died on November 15, 1978.

    *In the selection that follows, we see Margaret Mead at the peak of
her career: an internationally renowned and respected anthropologist and
intellectual, consulted by governments and heads of government, on the
faculty of Columbia University and a curator at the American Museum
of Natural History, surrounded by admiring young scholars and students.*

Teaching Me Something

TRUTH, KNOWLEDGE, VISION
—*inscription outside American Museum of Natural History*

IN LUMINE TUO VIDEBIMUS LUMEN
(In thy light shall we see light)
—*motto of Columbia University*

Whatever else Margaret Mead was doing, and wherever she happened to be, she never stopped teaching. Whether her subject matter was the rag content of paper used for field notes or the lettuce used for a salad, she could no more help instructing anyone around her than she could help breathing. Colleges and faculties and classrooms were far from the only places to find students.

She would have agreed with C. S. Lewis that "the ripest are kindest to the raw"; her eye was always out for young talent to nurse along, as she had been guided in her own youth by Franz Boas and Ruth Benedict, but nobody was too old to benefit from her instruction, formal or impromptu. Her Dublin colleague Feichin O'Doherty, the priest and psychologist, said that knowing her had allowed him to give immeasurably more to his students, "because of her clarification of my thought. She made luminous what I had seen before, but simply."

The cartoon picture of light bulbs symbolizing ideas keeps recurring in tales of Mead the teacher. Electricity lingered in rooms where her classes had met, it is said, for an hour after the class was over. Ken Heyman, whom Mead discovered in a Columbia classroom and took along to photograph several field trips, told a less metaphorical story about Mead and illumination. Visiting a primitive Bali village with her in 1957, he pointed out to her, with a laugh, some light bulbs the inhabitants had hung up: what use, he asked Mead, could these people possibly have for light bulbs?

"Just because in your society people only use them for light," she replied, "doesn't mean they aren't beautiful objects." Mead, Heyman said, "taught me how to look at things. She was remarkable with her eyes: we'd communicate almost extrasensorily, with just a nod or a look. She'd sit where the women sat, and although she was very unattractive, she could communicate so well with her eyes that even before they heard her speak, they'd be involved with her. She did something curious with her chubby little hands, too. She would sit with her palms up, as if to say, 'I come empty-handed, I carry no weapons, I am here to receive; show me.' It's quite uncomfortable to sit that way, but I saw her do it often, especially when she was talking to children."

"I am here to receive; show me," could have been Mead's motto wherever she went. In Australia, Marjorie Bull took her to visit a friend's quadriplegic nineteen-year-old daughter, who had hoped to be an anthropologist and still, despite her disabilities, was studying the subject. "In anthropology," Mead told the young woman, "we want to know what life is like from every point of view." She was everybody's teacher, but everybody was hers, too. When she assigned papers to her classes, she would implore them to *"teach me something!"* and when they obliged, she was delighted. When Mead invited Heyman to accompany her on the Bali trip, the young photographer was awed. "I didn't know how to talk to a genius then. I didn't even know how to talk to a friend. I was just a kid out of college, where I'd flunked courses. I knew so little of Asia that I barely liked Chinese food, when suddenly there I was washing in a Dutch bathtub in Indonesia that turned out to be a family's whole supply of drinking water for a week. Another time, when Margaret was given a piece of rotten awful pork with flies on it, I said, 'You're not going to eat *that*, are you?' and she said, 'You bet I am, and so are you.' But she drew the line somewhere. When a chief offered me his daughter, she said, 'Now, Ken!' "

Three kinds of students, Mead once said, were attracted to her classes: those who wanted her name on their records, those who wanted to hear her, and those who were seriously interested in anthropology. The last category, streaming through her classrooms and seminars, gave her many of the people who became her TAs—teaching assistants—at Columbia, and who helped to staff her turret office at the American Museum of Natural History. Her large lecture course, she said, was "designed to catch mavericks—people who don't know what they're looking for." Some students referred to these lecture courses as "Tuesday night at the movies"; one called them "immense travelogues, carelessly designed."

Mead could be and was lured away for terms of a week or a semester or a year as a guest professor at Emory, at Yale, at Fordham, at New York University, and at any number of other colleges and universities, but her chief allegiance was to Columbia. There she had taught her first course in 1940 at the Extension, which evolved into the School of General Studies, and held appointments more years than not for the rest of her life. In the spring term of 1966, typically, she gave three courses: G4172x, Cultures of the Pacific; G8272y, Methods and Problems in Anthropology; and G9352y, Seminar in Culture and Personality, a course for graduate students only. "I am sorry to have to limit my teaching to one semester next year," she wrote to her department chairman, Marvin Harris, on November 24, 1964, "but the exigencies of field work make it necessary, as conditions in New Guinea are so uncertain. I hope that the usual arrangements for my assistant can be maintained so that there will be a continuity in my work with graduate students while I am absent from New York."

Columbia never paid her more than a modest salary or promoted her beyond the rank of adjunct professor, but the university and its satellite Teachers' College suited her for other reasons. One was that the American Museum of Natural History, her career's official headquarters, was only a short cab ride away. The museum appeared to underrate her too; she was not made a full Curator of Ethnology there until 1964, but she was sent under its auspices to a lot of places she wanted to go, and allowed to carry on a good many extracuratorial duties in her tower overlooking Seventy-seventh Street and Columbus Avenue. Much of the business of the Research in Contemporary Cultures project just after the war, most of the affairs of the Institute for Intercultural Studies, and arrangements with Mead's various publishers were conducted from that office.

The museum gave her a headquarters for what one of her publishers called her "*apparat*—a system of aides who read her galley proofs and assisted her in all kinds of ways," and to whom she would make motherly phone calls at two in the morning to make sure they had got home safely, and again four hours later to remind them, as one *apparat* member recalled, "which nine things we were supposed to do first when we got to the office." The more Mead's enterprises sprawled beyond routine museum duties, the more she relied on these research assistants. "My needs are far greater for research assistants than they are for salary," she wrote in 1957 to the Menninger Foundation, where she was to speak. She asked that part of her lecture fee "be handled as a research grant, either through the American Museum of Natural History or the Institute for Intercultural Studies." For her *apparat* Mead sought women under thirty, a *New York Post* article reported, "with serious career intentions somewhere in the behavioral science field . . . intelligence at the Ph.D. candidate level . . . physical strength (the arrangements at the museum make the job physically exacting and there is a flight of stairs to be climbed) . . . height (a girl over five-foot-five has an easier time in this office)," and professional typing.

These young women constituted yet another of the *ad hoc* sororities Mead depended on all her life. The bond of these alumnae is strong: in the employ of "MM," as most of them called her, they read her galleys, designed her travel logistics, filed her papers according to her intricate color-coding system, and answered the hundreds of letters she got every week. When she made a serious new friend, as she claimed to do every two or three months, the new name was added to her Christmas card list. Later employees also kept on hand a supply of her queen-sized pantyhose, picked up her pants suits at the dry cleaners and her Dexedrine prescriptions from the pharmacy, and massaged her back, according to the instructions of her Chilean psychic healer, when she fell ill. ("If she'd been a man," said one employee, "I'd have had grounds for a lawsuit.") Most of them liked what they did. One spoke of her strong desire "to spare Dr. Mead any awareness of how much effort it took to make her life run smoothly. I wanted everything to seem to flow."

This museum office, where the decibel level was often fearsome, was Mead's most-used classroom, and an almost entirely female domain. She taught and mothered these young women who oddly, considering their youth, mothered her in turn. But few of them stayed around for longer than a couple of years. They weren't supposed to. "She kept hiring graduate students without minding the constant turnover," said Bridget McCarthy, who worked in the museum in the early 1960s, became Mead's first bibliographer, and later directed the Oregon School of Arts and Crafts. "She didn't want people who'd last. Temporary people, she said, helped her keep up with the times, and as soon as they were ready to go on to other, better things, she would urge them out.

"People who had imaginative ways to cope would flourish in that office," said McCarthy. "She was convinced that there always *is* a way, it's just a matter of figuring out what it is. She was very impressed, for instance, the day I came to work in a rainstorm wearing plastic bags over my shoes. You couldn't work in that office if you were going to make excuses. Why should an intelligent, educated, bright, white middle-class American have to make excuses? I'm not an anthropologist by any means," McCarthy said, "but I'll always be scheming the way Margaret Mead taught me to. I've often thought what a big influence she and Rhoda Métraux had on me. They taught me that the point is not so much to perpetuate yourself as to solve a problem and fill a need."

Ingenious employees and Mead's serious students got her meticulous attention. "Her comments on papers," said one of her graduate students, "were extraordinarily detailed. You felt when she was talking about someone else's paper that she was talking about yours as well." Students with personal problems were stunned when she would phone to ask how they were doing. She always made time to see them, and was especially attentive to students in the last stages of graduate school. She phoned a woman student preparing for the oral defense of her dissertation to remind her to wear a pretty dress. When Vincent Crapanzano was preparing in 1967 for his orals at Columbia Mead urged him to be sure and bring a map with him.

"I think," he replied, "that everyone knows where Morocco is." That, said Mead, was not the point. "Look," she told him, "there'll come a question you won't know how to answer, and the minute that happens, just get up and point out whatever you want to on the map, and they'll be so impressed they won't notice your confusion." But not everyone was so singled out, Timothy Asch said, or so charmed by Mead. "Oftentimes during Ph.D. orals she would turn on kids who didn't know their stuff. She'd sell them down the drain and expect them to come back, which some of them didn't. But what wonderful help she gave some of us! To potential employers she would say, 'I *know* you've got the money; I know all about that big grant you got last year from the government,' and force them to part with it for our sakes."

Questions for Discussion

1. What is the gist or main point of this selection?
2. How do the details of the narrative relate to that gist? (Are any of the details irrelevant?) For example, does the story about Vincent Crapanzano help establish the main point of the selection? How so?
3. So far as you can determine, what sort of person was Margaret Mead? On what do you base your opinion? What evidence can you point to?
4. What is Jane Howard's attitude toward Margaret Mead? On what do you base your opinion?
5. Reciprocity seems to have been a guiding principle in Mead's life. What instances from this passage show this to be so? Do you find this to be so in her dealings with institutions as well as human beings?
6. What characteristics in Mead's personality would be useful for an anthropologist?
7. Mead was quoted as saying, "In anthropology, we want to know what life is like from every point of view." Do you think that biography is seeing what a particular individual's life is like from every point of view? Explain.
8. What is the method of arrangement of the selection? What would be the main topics in an outline of the selection?

WILLIAM MANCHESTER

William Manchester, born in 1922, holds a bachelor's degree from the University of Massachusetts and a master's from the University of Missouri. After spending the first part of his career as a reporter and foreign correspondent, he became managing editor of the publications division of Wesleyan University and has been associated with that school since 1968, as faculty member, writer-in-residence, and adjunct professor of history. He has written novels, biographies, and histories—for instance, The Arms of Krupp, which was widely reviewed and admired.

After the assassination of President John F. Kennedy, the Kennedy family asked Manchester to write the official account of the events concerning the president's death. Manchester did massive research and negotiated lucrative contracts for publication with Look magazine and Harper & Row. However, the Kennedy family began having second thoughts about publishing the book, and ultimately Jacqueline Kennedy filed suit to stop publication altogether, either in the serial form in Look or in the Harper & Row edition. The controversy was settled out of court, with Harper & Row agreeing to revise some of the passages that dealt with Jacqueline Kennedy.

General Douglas MacArthur, the subject of Manchester's American Caesar, was one of America's great military heroes, leading allied forces in the Pacific in World War II, accepting the Japanese surrender on the deck of the battleship Missouri, and then becoming high commissioner of Japan after the war.

It has been said that MacArthur was the intellect and force that prepared Japan for its highly successful role in the postwar era. Under MacArthur, the Japanese adopted a new constitution and rebuilt their industrial economy.

When war broke out in Korea, MacArthur became commander there, but confronted President Harry Truman in a policy dispute, and Truman relieved MacArthur of command.

In the selection that follows, we see MacArthur in his last days, bidding farewell to West Point, his beloved alma mater, and visiting with comrades in arms in his suite in the Waldorf Towers in New York.

Taps

From *American Caesar: Douglas MacArthur 1880–1964*

His last and most memorable good-bye was to West Point. Addressing the corps of cadets, he took as his text the academy's motto: "Duty, Honor, Country." Interestingly, he warned them never to dispute "controversial issues" with their civilian leaders: "These great national problems are not for your professional or military solution." Then, speaking without a note, striding back and forth, he closed with a passage that no one who was on the plain that noon will ever forget: "The shadows are lengthening for me. The twilight is here. My days of old have vanished, tone and tint; they have gone glimmering through the dreams of things that were. Their memory is one of wondrous beauty, watered by tears, and coaxed and caressed by the smiles of yesterday. I listen vainly, but with thirsty ear, for the witching melody of faint bugles blowing reveille, of far drums beating the long roll. In my dreams I hear again the crash of guns, the rattle of musketry, the strange, mournful mutter of the battlefield. But in the evening of my memory, I always come back to West Point. Always there echoes and re-echoes in my ears—Duty, Honor, Country. Today marks my final roll call with you. But I want you to know that when I cross the river my last conscious thoughts will be of the Corps; and the Corps; and the Corps. I bid you farewell."

He had not, of course, spoken extemporaneously. No one could improvise such rhetoric. The awed cadets thought that he was coining the phrases as he trod the platform before them, but what they had actually witnessed was the last performance of a consummate actor who always wrote his own lines beforehand, honed and polished them, and committed them to memory. Lou Sullivan recalls him pacing like a brooding hawk through his ten-room apartment, puffing a corncob as he rehearsed, his slippers flapping on the rugs and his long robe streaming behind him. In a way these scenes were more spectacular than the final production. An Oriental butler stood by with a glass of water, and the striding General was surrounded by evocations of the Far East: paintings, vases, urns, and other gifts from the Japanese. "In the vast splendor," recalls William A. Ganoe, who renewed their acquaintance there after an interval of thirty-nine years, "I had the feeling that I had barged into a palace."

Except on MacArthur's birthdays, when his former officers gathered to honor him, not many others saw him. Hoover and James A. Farley, Waldorf neighbors, were always welcome; Red Blaik would bring diagrams of new plays; and West Point Superintendent James B. Lampert would escort delegations of first classmen to assure the General that the academy hadn't changed and to hear his prophecies on the future of their profession. Strangers, however, were turned away by elaborate security precautions. Elevator operators wouldn't take them above the thirty-fifth floor unless they could produce credentials; those who had them were met upstairs by Sullivan and, when his bodyguard duties ended after thirty months and he was transferred elsewhere, hotel security men replaced him. No one could phone the suite unless switchboard operators had been given their names. Even then, Jean took all calls, making very sure that the General wanted to speak to the caller before handing him the phone.

Sullivan continued to visit him one or two times a week, and often he would spend the evening with the General and Jean, the three of them watching television. In the beginning his bodyguard had thought MacArthur cold and austere, but later he concluded that this was largely reticence; a MacArthur friend, he found, was a cherished friend. As they watched televised baseball—the General would always recite a player's batting average before the man reached the plate—the old soldier would cover Sullivan's hand with his own from time to time and say gently, "How are you doing, Sully?" He gave the bodyguard pipes and a .32-caliber Smith and Wesson, and showed him the derringer he himself carried whenever he left the apartment; like Eisenhower during his years as president of Columbia, MacArthur never ventured into Manhattan unarmed. Once Sullivan revealed that he planned to enter a Randall's Island track meet. MacArthur fired him up with a pep talk, ending: "Don't come back unless you're a winner." Inspired, the bodyguard broke the track's hammer-throw record and, though he was the oldest man there, he was voted the meet's outstanding athlete. He recalls: "I think the General could talk *any*body into *any*thing."

Neither MacArthur nor his wife had expected to end their lives in a New York hotel. During the Tokyo years she had dreamed of retiring to a little white house in the South; the house he had then had in mind was the same color but somewhat larger. ("I should have lived here," he had wistfully told Kennedy.) But the Waldorf was centrally located, within a short distance of both Saint Bartholomew's Episcopal Church—she and Arthur joined the congregation there—and First Army headquarters at 90 Church Street, where, in a four-room corner suite which had been cleared for him, the General read the cable traffic each morning. Fifth Avenue's smart shops were just two blocks away from the Waldorf; Jean could find endless displays of the clothes and jewelry she loved: matched pearls, head-hugging caps (she felt that anything larger overpowered her), and black opera pumps in her rare size, $5^{1/2}$ AAA. Black had become her favorite shade, but now, to keep abreast of the mid-century trend toward pale colors, she added dresses of gray, white, and a mauve-pink. Her husband also became something of a clotheshorse. Debonair in a homburg and herringbone suits, he often visited at the menswear department of Saks Fifth Avenue. The manager was ecstatic: "What a figure to work with! Wonderful! A tailor's dream!"

One of his acquisitions at Saks was a dinner jacket, for Broadway's theaters had been one of the MacArthurs' incentives in settling down here. They saw *Oklahoma!*, the Hollywood Ice Review, and the rodeo in Madison Square Garden; Ethel Merman and Judy Garland entertained them backstage; when they tired of plays and musical comedies, there were concerts, lectures, the New York City Ballet, and, of course, the movies at Radio City, where their favorite stars were John Wayne and Ward Bond. Ever the athlete manqué, MacArthur never missed a fight. At Yankee Stadium, the Polo Grounds, and Ebbets Field, he usually sat in the owners' boxes. No matter how far behind his team was, he always remained to the bitter end, an intent, fragile old man with thin white hair, eyes gleaming and fist clenched, demanding a comeback against all odds. In time he came to know many of the players personally. The one he admired most, and liked most, was Jackie Robinson.

Ah Cheu never accompanied the MacArthurs on their outings. One room in the suite was hers, and she became something of a recluse there. Arthur no longer needed her; he was at school, or taking piano lessons, or visiting the Statue of Liberty with Sully and his son Bobby—roaming the homeland which he was learning to know and love at last. Like the General, Jean had assumed that he would attend West Point. Shortly after they had unpacked at the Waldorf, they took the boy up the Hudson. He watched a parade and tried on a cadet's shako. It didn't fit then; it never would; he wasn't meant for a military career. Instead he attended Columbia, graduating in 1961. The old soldier insisted that he approved because, he told Bunker, "my mother put too much pressure on me. Being number one is the loneliest job in the world, and I wouldn't wish it on any son of mine." Apparently being a MacArthur was too much; after his father's death Arthur moved to the other side of Manhattan and took an assumed name. His identity thus concealed, he lived for his music, a fugitive from his father's relentless love.

"People grow old only by deserting their ideals," MacArthur had written, paraphrasing another writer. "Years may wrinkle the skin, but to give up interest wrinkles the soul. . . . You are as young as your faith, as old as your doubt; as young as your self-confidence, as old as your fear; as young as your hope, as old as your despair. In the central place of every heart there is a recording chamber; so long as it receives messages of beauty, hope, cheer and courage, so long are you young. When . . . your heart is covered with the snows of pessimism and the ice of cynicism, then and then only are you grown old—and then, indeed, as the ballad says, you just fade away."

He remained confident, hopeful, undespairing, optimistic, and free of doubt to the end, but on January 26, 1964, the day he turned eighty-four it was clear that at long last he was ready to depart this life. He had just finished his 213,000-word memoirs; a soiled spot on the back of one chair marked the place where he had rested his head while covering pad after pad of fourteen-inch yellow ruled paper with his angular Victorian scrawl. To a writer, the manuscript is astonishing. There are almost no erasures or deletions; the prose flowed from him in an even, immutable stream. Soldiers' memoirs are generally dull. MacArthur's, which appeared after his death, are vivid and controversial—controversial, both in substance and in style, because certain passages seemed to have been lifted from earlier books by Whitney and Willoughby. It is difficult to see the General as a plagiarist, and in fact there may be other explanations. They may all have been drawing on a common source, notes made in the past, or it is possible that the General wrote those paragraphs shortly after his dismissal, holding them for future publication, and that his officers took them from him. At all events, the rest of the text was certainly his, and it testified as nothing else could that his mind was penetrating and lucid to the end. But his body was failing fast. Dr. Egeberg believes that he might have survived for years had he sought medical attention earlier. He disliked physicians as such, however, perhaps because they reminded him of infirmities he preferred to ignore. The Army eleven, arriving in early December to discuss last week's Navy game with him, had been shocked to find him shrunken in height and weight and jaundiced. So were the officers who filed in, wearing all their ribbons as they always did because he liked that, to congratulate him for having reached another birthday. Some of them sensed that this would be his last, and so, it developed, did he.

They stiffened at attention as he entered the living room. He began, as always, with a ringing: "Comrades at arms!" Then, putting them at ease, he said, in much the same words of previous years, "You probably don't realize how much I look forward to these gatherings, bringing back vivid memories of the experiences we shared. These are milestones in my life, as it were, and I look forward to each one hopefully, and accept it gratefully." This time, however, he said he wanted to depart from custom and tell them a story about a Scotsman who was riding a crowded train from London to Edinburgh. "At the first stop," he said, "he worked his way over the knees of the others in the compartment, and they saw him run into the station and get back on board just as the train was pulling out. At the next stop he did the same thing, and when he just barely caught the train on the third stop, one of the passengers said 'Jock, why are you running into the station at every stop? We have conveniences on the train. Stay aboard.' And Jock looked up and around the group and said, 'I'll tell you. I'm a very sick man. Yesterday I went to see my doctor and the doctor told me that my days were few. He said: "Jock, if you want to see your old Scotland again, you'd better start right out and go up there—and, mind you, even though you start now, you

may not get there." So I'm buying my ticket from station to station.' "
Everyone started to laugh and stopped when they saw that the General's face
was grave.

By March 1 his weight was down to 140 pounds. He was suffering from
nausea, constant headache, and what he described as "abdominal complaints." The yellowish pigmentation of his skin and eyes was deepening; a
physician diagnosed his jaundice as "moderately severe." Informed of this by
the surgeon general, President Johnson phoned the Waldorf that evening and
told the General that an air-force transport would pick him up at La Guardia
Field in the morning to fly him to the Walter Reed Medical Center in
Washington. Superintendent Lampert and a group of other officers rode to the
airport to see him and Jean off. MacArthur, walking shakily to the plane,
said: "I've looked that old scoundrel death in the face many times. This time
I think he has me on the ropes. But I'm going to do the very best I can."

On March 6 army doctors performed exploratory surgery to find the
obstruction in his biliary system. They feared malignancy, but there was
none. Liver damage and several gallstones were discovered, however, and the
gallbladder was removed. His condition was described as "satisfactory." Nevertheless he was weak; blood transfusions began, and Jean and Arthur settled
into a three-room suite at the hospital for a long vigil. Two more major
operations followed, to remove a duct and intestinal obstruction with perfo-
ration and to relieve esophageal bleeding. In critical condition, he clung to
life for four incredible weeks regaling physicians, nurses, and orderlies with
reminiscences until the night of Friday, April 3, when he sank into a peaceful
coma. He died at 2:39 P.M. Sunday from acute kidney and liver failure.

At 5:07 P.M. a twelve-car autocade left Walter Reed for New York—
there was a touching scene between Jean and a nurse, both red-eyed, consol-
ing each other—and a police escort led the hearse and the rest of the
cavalcade through the dark evening to Manhattan's Seventh Regiment Armory at Park Avenue and Sixty-sixth Street. By 10:47 P.M., when the coffin
was carried into the armory's Clark Room, the tributes had begun to pour in.
President Johnson ordered nineteen-gun salutes fired on American military
posts around the world, and flags flown at half-staff until the burial Saturday
in Norfolk.

The plain, gray steel, government-issue casket rested on a catafalque
between four flickering candles; it was half open, the bottom half covered
with the Stars and Stripes. The General's own flag, five white stars on a field
of red, stood alongside. He wore twin circlets of stars, but no ribbons on his
breast; his instructions on that point had been explicit. Also at his direction,
he was dressed in his most faded suntans, worn and washed to softness.
Smoothing this uniform, he had once told Mydans: "I suppose, in a way, this
has become part of my soul. It is a symbol of my life. Whatever I've done

that really matters, I've done wearing it. When the time comes, it will be in these that I journey forth. What greater honor could come to an American, and a soldier?"

The setting was appropriate: five men, representing the five services, stood around the catafalque at parade rest. The armory had been built in 1880, the year of the General's birth, and the Clark Room had an air of old-fashioned elegance. The ceiling was lofty, the paneling was of polished oak; one wall was dominated by a massive fireplace which was all but obscured Monday afternoon by masses of fragrant flowers. Some of them came from MacArthur's first wife, who told reporters that her years with him had been "the happiest of my life." That, too, seemed fitting; he had always relished superlatives. What was inapt was the appearance, in the Scripps-Howard and Hearst papers, of the Lucas and Considine interviews, now ten years old and unreflective of his later convictions. Whitney called them "fictional non-sense," and Lucas called Whitney a liar. *Life* said: "Worse than a specter at a feast is a loud-mouthed gossip at a funeral." The *Saturday Review* said: "They demanded for him the highest honors but they saw to it that he was deprived of a decent burial. Who are 'they'? Only superficially are 'they' the scoop-hungry newsmen. More basically 'they' are the extremist supporters who never really understood him." Max Ascoli wrote in the *Reporter*: "Throughout his life, he had the gift or the curse of being a storm center. May his soul rest in peace, for here on earth his memory will never know peace."

MacArthur would have gloried in his funeral. He had drawn up plans for it, of course—he planned everything—but his instructions, from the GI casket to the ribbonless blouse, had been uncharacteristically modest, intended, perhaps, to be conspicuous in their simplicity. President Kennedy, now four months in his own grave, had persuaded him of the need for "a suitable national tribute," with West Point's cadets playing a prominent part. Told of it, the General had smiled and said: "By George, I'd like to see that."

On Monday, in a chill rain, the twenty-five hundred men of the corps formed on the plain—MacArthur's old room, 1123, provided an excellent view of the scene—and, facing the Hudson, saluted as six cannon roared in salute, the smoke mingling with the mists on the bluffs overlooking the river. Lambert told them: "The gallant battle which he waged in his last days symbolized to all of us the very principles to which he dedicated his living." Later in the day, first classmen, their sleeves streaked with chevrons of authority, appeared at the armory, one of them taking his station by the five-star flag, which he would carry in the coming parade. On Tuesday thirty-five thousand New Yorkers, standing three abreast outside the brass-studded doors in a line that stretched north past Seventy-second Street, waited to pass by the bier, and at 8:00 A.M. Wednesday, as a bugle signaled ruffles and flourishes, the senior cadet commanded the procession, now ready to move: "For-ward *march!*"

Flags stirred in a rising breeze, but the rain, still heavy, drenched them. The first units in the four-block-long order of march were the West Point band, a battalion of cadets, and an honor guard of generals and admirals. Then came the caisson, drawn by six Fort Myer horses and carrying the coffin, now fully closed and flag draped. Following it were the five-star standard; a riderless, caparisoned horse with reversed boots in its stirrups, the symbol of a fallen warrior since the days of Genghis Khan; and massed colors and marchers. Watched by millions on television, they proceeded down Park Avenue, Fifty-seventh Street, Broadway, and Seventh Avenue to Pennsylvania Station. At 9:15 A.M. the funeral train pulled out, stopping briefly at Trenton and slowing at Odenton and Aberdeen in Maryland for military delegations to pay their respects. Bobby and Ethel Kennedy were aboard as official mourners. Informed that Johnson was waiting to meet them in Union Station, Bobby whispered to Blaik: "Wait until he lays an eye on me and you'll see ice."

The President, however, went straight to Jean and Arthur and embraced them. There was an embarrassing moment of confusion as they left for the Capitol, with Johnson's and Kennedy's chauffeurs jockeying for position and the President's Secret Service men finally leaping in front of the Kennedy car ("I wish they'd been that alert in Dallas," Bobby said), but the President seemed too moved to have eyes for anyone except the General's widow and son. In the great rotunda, his face clenched with emotion, he placed a wreath of red, white, and blue flowers at the foot of the coffin. It lay in state there until the following afternoon, when the procession re-formed and took it to Washington National Airport. A government plane flew it to the naval air station in Norfolk, the third city in which the body lay in state for public mourners. On Saturday, after services in Saint Paul's Episcopal Church—the congregation included Yoshida, who had boarded the first flight from Tokyo when he learned of MacArthur's death—it was entombed in Norfolk's 114-year-old courthouse, which was then dedicated as a memorial to the General. There he lies now, in a cool crypt beneath the silent calm of sepulchral stone.

Questions for Discussion

1. What is your own impression of General Douglas MacArthur? How would you characterize him? (Refer to the text for evidence to support your opinion.)

2. What is William Manchester's attitude toward General Douglas MacArthur? (Refer to the text for evidence to support your opinion.)

3. What was MacArthur's purpose in his farewell speech at West Point? What did he do to accomplish that purpose?

4. MacArthur characteristically used striking metaphors to convey his meanings and feelings. Discuss the metaphors in the passage from MacArthur's writing that begins, "People grow old only by deserting their ideals." What are their literal meanings? Are the metaphors effective?

5. The story of the Scotchman that MacArthur told is a parable (a brief story that illustrates a moral or religious principle). What is the meaning of the parable? Why would MacArthur convey his meaning in such a way rather than stating it directly?

6. In a biography, as in other stories, *scene* can be very important, reinforcing the mood and the meaning. (In a film, for example, thunder, lightning, and wind on a dark night prepare the audience for events that are to happen.) What is the effect of the scene Manchester portrays in the narrative of the funeral?

7. What is the *symbolic* value of the clothes MacArthur chose for his burial?

8. The title *American Caesar* implies that MacArthur is larger than life. What parts of this selection show MacArthur as larger than life?

9. The selection opens with MacArthur's "Duty, Honor, and Country" speech at West Point. In what way is this theme repeated in the conclusion?

10. The passage mentions that neither MacArthur nor his wife had intended to retire to a hotel. In this reading, what clues do you find that explain why they did spend their final days in the Waldorf Astoria? What does this tell you about the man himself?

11. What is the significance of the title *American Caesar?*

12. Neither Dwight David Eisenhower nor Douglas MacArthur would go out without a gun when they were living in Manhattan. Should all people carry guns to protect themselves?

NANCY MILFORD

Nancy Winston Milford, born in 1938, was educated at the University of Michigan, where she took her B.A., and Columbia University, where she completed the M.A. and Ph.D. She is married to Kenneth Milford and has three children.

F. Scott Fitzgerald's novels—The Beautiful and Damned, This Side of Paradise, The Great Gatsby, Tender Is the Night, The Last Tycoon—*and his short stories characterized the era known as the "Jazz Age" and the "Roaring Twenties," the period immediately following World War I when Prohibition gave bootleggers the opportunity to make fortunes selling bathtub gin, when flappers danced the Charleston in skirts that at the time were shockingly short, when the stock market soared and the boom economy was destined to go on forever. Mah-Jongg was the favorite game, and Emile Coué had the nation repeating, "Day by day in every way I am getting better and better."*

Scott and Zelda Fitzgerald quickly became symbols of the Jazz Age, and they still are. Nancy Milford's biography of Zelda is not only about a tragic woman who spent much of her adult life in and out of mental institutions, struggling with schizophrenia and severe depression, but also about a symbol of a period in American history. Of Milford's biography of Zelda Sayre Fitzgerald, Christopher Lehmann-Haupt said, " The cumulative effect is profound and at times overwhelmingly moving."

In the selection that follows, Milford tells of the months following the wedding of Zelda and Scott.

The Twenties

Zelda and Scott put their first wedding present, a Tiffany chocolate set, on the dresser in their Biltmore suite 2109, and beside it a wilting Easter lily, which remained in place throughout their honeymoon. One of the first things that Zelda did as the wife of F. Scott Fitzgerald was to go shopping with a friend of Scott's from St. Paul, Marie Hersey. Zelda's trousseau had been put together in Montgomery with only the sketchiest notion of the fashionable requirements of cosmopolitan life. Somewhat painfully Scott saw Zelda for the first time against the background of the restrained chic of the East, and as he later wrote: ". . . no sooner does a man marry his reproachless ideal than he becomes intensely self-conscious about her." Zelda had organdy dresses with great flounces and ruffles, and a glorious pair of velvet lounging pants, but very little that was appropriate for New York. Scott felt she needed the tactful guidance of Miss Hersey's taste, and together they bought her a smart Patou suit. Zelda said it felt strange to be charging things to Scott.

Zelda seemed to be amenable to the shopping lesson, but her resentment was simply hidden. She wrote later: "It was the first garment bought after the marriage ceremony and again the moths have unsymmetrically eaten the nap off the seat of the skirt. This makes fifteen years it has been stored in trunks because of our principle of not throwing away things that have never been used. We are glad—oh, so relieved, to find it devastated at last."

But in the spring of 1920 the Fitzgeralds were just beginning; they were young and happy, *This Side of Paradise* was becoming a brilliant success, and for the moment the angels were on their side. Zelda called Scott her "King of the Roses," and themselves "The Goofos," and ordered fresh spinach and champagne for midnight snacks at the Biltmore. Those days in New York were gaudy ones, and Zelda caught the spirit of the city when she wrote about it later,

> Vincent Youmans wrote the music for those twilights just after the war. They were wonderful. They hung above the city like an indigo wash. . . . Through the gloom, the whole world went to tea. Girls in short amorphous capes and long flowing skirts and hats like straw bathtubs waited for taxis in front of the Plaza Grill; girls in long satin coats and colored shoes and hats like straw manhole covers tapped the tune of a cataract on the dance floors of the Lorraine and the St. Regis. Under the sombre ironic

parrots of the Biltmore a halo of golden bobs disintegrated into black lace and shoulder bouquets. . . . It was just a lot of youngness: Lillian Lorraine would be drunk as the cosmos on top of the New Amsterdam by midnight, and football teams breaking training would scare the waiters with drunkenness in the fall. The world was full of parents taking care of people.

But there were no overseeing parents in Scott and Zelda's world to protect them, and in 1920 they would have scoffed at the idea of needing any, for no young couple rode the crest of good fortune with more flair than they. Scott undressed at the *Scandals*, Zelda, completely sober, dived into the fountain at Union Square, and when they moved from the Biltmore to the Commodore they celebrated by spinning around in the revolving doors for half an hour. As she wrote in *Save Me the Waltz*, "No power on earth could make her do anything, she thought frightened, any more, except herself."

Dorothy Parker never forgot meeting Zelda for the first time—astride the hood of a taxi with Scott perched upon the roof. "Robert Sherwood brought Scott and Zelda to me right after their marriage. I had met Scott before. He told me he was going to marry the most beautiful girl in Alabama *and* Georgia!" Mrs. Parker thought that even then their behavior was calculated to shock. "But they did both look as though they had just stepped out of the sun; their youth was striking. *Everyone* wanted to meet him. *This Side of Paradise* may not seem like much now, but in 1920 it was considered an experimental novel; it cut new ground." Within eight months the novel had sold 33,000 copies, but its sales alone were not what counted; it was reviewed and talked about everywhere. Scott was suddenly "the arch type of what New York wanted." He wrote later, "I who knew less of New York than any reporter of six months' standing and less of its society than any hallroom boy in a Ritz stag line, was pushed into the position not only of spokesman for the time but of the typical product of that same moment." And it was not Scott alone, but Zelda, too, who was caught up in the swirl of publicity, and not knowing what New York expected of them they "found it rather confusing," Scott wrote. "Within a few months after our embarkation on the Metropolitan venture we scarcely knew any more who we were and we hadn't a notion what we were."

Scott was the first of his group of Princeton friends living in New York to marry. Edmund Wilson was a hard-working journalist and co-editor with John Peale Bishop of *Vanity Fair*. Each of these men had made fine starts in the literary world, with Scott having the most commercially successful career. They were all quite naturally curious about his bride. Alexander McKaig, who was another Princeton classmate and frient of Scott's, came to know the Fitzgeralds intimately during the first year of their marriage. He, Wilson, and Bishop, sometimes with Ludlow Fowler and Townsend Martin, met frequently for dinner parties and conversation. McKaig had a job in advertising and wrote on weekends and in the evening. Boyish looking with a snub nose and dark curling hair, he appeared more cherubic than he was. He kept a diary in which he made frequent entries concerning his life and the lives of his friends. Although it is a perceptive record, it is also an envious one. Nine days after Scott and Zelda's marriage McKaig made the following entry: "Called on Scott Fitz and his bride. Latter temperamental small town, Southern Belle. Chews gum—shows knees. I do not think marriage can succeed. Both drinking heavily. Think they will be divorced in 3 years. Scott write something big—then die in a garret at 32."

Dorothy Parker's impressions of Zelda were similar: "I never thought she was beautiful. She was very blond with a candy box face and a little bow mouth, very much on a small scale and there was something petulant about her. If she didn't like something she sulked; I didn't find that an attractive trait."

Lawton Campbell remembers being invited some time later to lunch with the Fitzgeralds; he was working and had only one hour to spare.

> When I entered, the room was bedlam. Breakfast dishes were all about, the bed unmade, books and papers scattered here and there, trays filled with cigarette butts, liquor glasses from the night before. Everything was untidy and helter-skelter. Scott was dressing and Zelda was luxuriating in the bath-tub. With the door partly open, she carried on a steady flow of conversation.
>
> "Scott," she called out, "tell Lawton 'bout . . . tell Lawton what I said when . . . Now . . . tell Lawton what I did . . ."
>
> Before Scott could comply, she would proceed to tell me herself about last night's wild adventure. Scott would cue her and then laugh at her vivid description. . . . Going back to the kitchens at the old Waldorf. Dancing on the kitchen tables, wearing the chef's headgear. Finally, a crash and being escorted out by the house detectives. This badinage went on until Zelda appeared at the bathroom door, buttoning up her dress. I looked at my watch. It was five minutes of two. My lunch hour had gone.

When the Fitzgeralds moved into the Commodore, McKaig visited them there. Scott and Zelda were propped up on their bed, smoking. McKaig sat on a pillow on the floor eating sandwiches delivered from a delicatessen. They talked until dawn. Their own conversation ran playfully to theories, as Zelda wrote in *Save Me the Waltz*,

> that the Longacre Pharmacies carried the best gin in town; that anchovies sobered you up; that you could tell wood alcohol by the smell. Everybody knew where to find the blank verse in Cabell and how to get seats for the Yale game. . . . People met people they knew in hotel lobbies smelling of orchids and plush and detective stories, and asked each other where they'd been since last time. . . . "We're having some people," everybody said to

everybody else, "and we want you to join us," and they said, "We'll telephone."

All over New York people telephoned. They telephoned from one hotel to another to people on other parties that they couldn't get there—that they were engaged. It was always tea-time or late at night. . . . New York is a good place to be on the up-grade.

To their own surprise and delight, Scott and Zelda discovered that they were being heralded as models in the cult of youth. Scott was asked to lecture before audiences that were ready to adore him as their spokesman. A literary gossip column reported, "We watched him wave his cigarette at an audience one night not long ago, and capture them by nervous young ramblings, until he had the room (mostly 'flappers') swaying with delight. Then the auto-graph hunters! This admiration embarrassed him much—but after we had escaped into the outer darkness he acknowledged, with a grin, that he rather liked it." Still he and Zelda were safe, Scott thought, "apart from all that," and if the city bewitched them by offering fresh roles for them, they played them because "We felt like small children in a great bright unexplored barn."

In May they decided to buy a car. Scott was not getting to his writing in the city, and they thought that if they took a house in the country for the summer the peace and quiet would be conducive to work. For a part of Scott was aware that the sense of tranquillity he had once observed in Edmund Wilson's New York apartment, where "life was mellow and safe, a finer distillation of all that I had come to love at Princeton," would elude him forever if he did not soon make an effort to secure it for himself.

Swimming was a necessity for Zelda and as long as they found a place close to water she could be happy. A car would facilitate their search. Leon Ruth, an old Montgomery friend of Zelda's, was in New York studying at Columbia and it was his advice the Fitzgeralds sought when they went car hunting. Ruth recalled: "Neither of them could drive much. Scott used to borrow my car in Montgomery when he was courting Zelda, so I knew fairly well the limits of his ability. As I remember it we went down to the Battery and it was a choice between a new sedan and a second-hand Marmon sports coupé. Of course, they couldn't resist the Marmon. Well, we bought it and I drove them up to 125th Street. I showed Scott how to shift on the way and both of them knew something about steering. Then they put me out and struck off."

Eventually, in Westport, Connecticut, a short distance from the Sound, they found the Wakeman cottage, a gray-shingled house surrounded by coun-tryside. It seemed a perfect retreat and they took it. Zelda wrote Ludlow Fowler:

We have a house with a room for you and a ruined automobile because I drove it over a fire-plug and completely deintestined it . . . and much health and fresh-air which is all very nice and picturesque, although I'm still partial to Coney Island—And as soon as we get a servant and some sheets from Mamma you really must come out and recuperate and try to enjoy the home you helped so much to get organized. Only, by the time you *do* come I'll probably have grown so fat like this [sketch of a circle with arms and legs and head] that you won't be able to recognize me. I s'pose I'll have to wear a [a measure of music with the words "Red, red rose" written beneath it] to disclose my identity—or condition—At present, I *think* it's the home-cooking of Mrs. M—-but, of course, one never knows. . . . But it's a deep secret and you MUST keep very quiet and not laugh too hard and be VERY sympathetic—

As it turned out, she was not pregnant. Within a few weeks they arranged with the Japanese Reliable Servant Agency to hire a houseboy and began to invite their friends for weekend visits. It was going to be a relaxed and productive summer with guests coming out only on Saturday or Sunday. They joined one of the quieter bathing clubs; Zelda was to spend her time swimming and reading; Scott was fiddling with an idea for a new novel, *The Flight of the Rocket*. It would be about Anthony Patch and his wife, Gloria Gilbert: "How he and his beautiful young wife are wrecked on the shoals of dissipation. . . ."

After McKaig's first visit to Westport he wrote: "Fitz & Zelda fighting like mad—say themselves marriage can't succeed." By the fourth of July their partying had become as time-consuming in Westport as it had been in New York. McKaig noted that Scott spent $43 for liquor in one day and then left McKaig to pay for the food for dinner.

During one of their carnival nights in Westport, Zelda sounded the fire alarm. Within a few minutes three fire engines and a score of cars came into the Compo Beach area. There was no fire and no one could be found who knew anything about the alarm. Angrily the fire chief traced the call to the Wakeman house, but Scott and Zelda claimed they knew nothing about it. According to a newspaper report which Zelda clipped for her scrapbook, a member of the Fitzgerald family suggested to the chief that perhaps someone had come into their house during their absence and sent in an alarm. The article said that everyone was greatly worked up over the false alarm and that there was a statute which dealt with people who sent in false alarms for the fun of it. The Fitzgeralds were brought before court the following week, but because the evidence was only circumstantial no blame could be fastened to them. Scott gallantly said that he would bear the costs of the department's run.

George Jean Nathan, who with Mencken edited *The Smart Set*, which had first published Scott, began to visit them frequently during the summer. An urbane and witty bachelor, Nathan quickly took to Zelda and began a flirtation that consisted of teasing Scott and writing gay notes to Zelda facetiously signed "Yours, for the Empire, A Prisoner of Zelda." Zelda was delighted by the attention of a man whom Scott clearly admired and respected. Soon each of Nathan's letters to Westport was addressed to Zelda alone; they ran along the following lines:

> Dear Blonde: Why call me a polygamist when my passion for you is at once so obvious and so single? Particularly when I am lit. Is it possible that Southern Gals are losing their old perspicacity?
>   I am very sorry to hear that your husband is neglectful of his duties to you in the way of chewing gum. That is the way husbands get after five months of marriage.

During one of his weekends in Westport he had discovered her diaries. "They interested me so greatly that in my capacity as a magazine editor I later made her an offer for them. When I informed her husband, he said that he could not permit me to publish them since he had gained a lot of inspiration from them and wanted to use parts of them in his own novels and short stories, as for example 'The Jelly Bean.'" Zelda apparently offered no resistance to this rather high-handed refusal of Nathan's offer, and the diaries remained Scott's literary property rather than hers.

By the end of the summer the friendship between Nathan and the Fitzgeralds had cooled considerably and they did not see him for a while. Zelda was not always discreet in her show of affection and something had occurred to arouse Scott's jealousy. The balance in their marriage was undergoing a subtle shift. During their courtship Zelda had consistently held the upper hand, and held it somewhat imperiously. Now Scott found that he did not entirely trust Zelda and was vexed by her flirtatiousness; the rift with Nathan was not serious because neither Nathan nor Zelda was serious, but the flirtation had irritated Scott.

Their differences began to surface. Zelda discovered that Scott was a fearful man and that he invented stories to cover himself. As there was not a particle of fear within Zelda she found it hard to fathom Scott's sudden attacks of jitters. Zelda was finicky about her food and Scott was not. Scott could not fall asleep unless his bedroom was hermetically sealed; Zelda could not bear sleeping without a window open. Zelda did not have the vaguest notion about sewing on shirt buttons when they came off, or seeing that shirts went to the laundry. She simply let everything pile up in the recesses of a closet while Scott fumed about a lack of fresh laundry, for he was accustomed to changing twice a day if he felt like it. Minor though these differences were, they broke the spell of the honeymoon. What remained were the long talks throughout the night, those joint monologues like shared dreams which brought with them a closeness so binding that it was to last a lifetime.

By mid-July Zelda seemed both restless and homesick. The tug of the South soon became irresistible and impulsively Scott suggested that they take an automobile trip to Montgomery. He later wrote amusingly about the trials of their trip in a three-part article called "The Cruise of the Rolling Junk." A rolling junk was exactly what their Marmon turned out to be; it was, to put it gently, past its prime. The decision to travel was Scott's and he came about it quite casually—if one can believe the article.

> Zelda was up. This was obvious, for in a moment she came into my room singing aloud. Now when Zelda sings soft I like to listen, but when she sings loud I sing loud too in self-protection. So we began to sing a song about biscuits. The song related how down in Alabama all the good people ate biscuits for breakfast, which made them very beautiful and pleasant and happy, while up in Connecticut all the people ate bacon and eggs and toast, which made them very cross and bored and miserable—especially if they happened to have been brought up on biscuits.

The song over, Zelda complained that even if there were biscuits in Connecticut there weren't any peaches to go with them. Overwhelmed by the logic of her complaint, Scott suggested that they drive to Alabama, where there were both biscuits and peaches. Two months earlier Zelda had received the following telegram from a group of her Southern beaus.

HURRY BACK TO MONTGOMERY AS TOWN IS SHOT TO PIECES SINCE YOU LEFT. NO PEP. NO FUN. NO ONE TO GIVE THE GOSSIPERS A SOURCE OF CONVERSATION. THE COUNTRY CLUB IS INTENDING FIRING THEIR CHAPERONE AS THERE IS NO FURTHER NEED FOR HER. KNITTING PARTIES PREVAIL. JAIL CONVERTED INTO SEWING ROOM. FOR THE SAKE OF SAVING DEAR OLD MONTGOMERY PEP UP AND HURRY BACK!

Now she would have a chance to show off her famous husband and to broadcast the things they had done together in New York. No one in Montgomery could match their exploits, and because she felt more at home in the South than she yet did in New York or Connecticut, it would be not only a triumphant return but a welcome respite.

The trip itself was a series of minor catastrophes: there were blowouts, lost wheels, and broken axles. Zelda, who was to navigate, had no idea how to read a map. Her white knickerbocker suit (which had been made to match Scott's) was considered shocking enough in Virginia almost to keep them out of a good hotel. The manager eventually relented and Zelda compromised at the next stop by putting a skirt on over the outfit. At last they reached Alabama. "Suddenly Zelda was crying, crying because things were the same and yet were not the same. It was for her faithlessness that she wept and for the faithlessness of time."

They stayed for less than two weeks and returned by train, having sold their battered Marmon to the first susceptible buyer.

Questions for Discussion

1. As briefly as possible, state the gist or main point of the selection.
2. What sort of people were Zelda and Scott Fitzgerald? In your discussion of this question, refer to evidence in the text.
3. What was Nancy Milford's attitude toward the Fitzgeralds? On what do you base your opinion?
4. What was the attitude of friends and acquaintances toward Zelda—such people as Dorothy Parker, Alexander McKaig, Lawton Campbell, and George Jean Nathan? How does Milford present those attitudes? Is the method effective?
5. Here is the first sentence of the selection: "Zelda and Scott put their first wedding present, a Tiffany chocolate set, on the dresser in their Biltmore suite 2109, and beside it a wilting Easter lily, which remained in place throughout their honeymoon." Why did Milford choose to start with the information about the wedding present and the lily? What is their meaning?
6. What does Zelda mean in the passage of her writing quoted on pages 79 and 80? What point is she trying to convey? How is she trying to convey it?
7. What couple today are as symbolic of their time as were Scott and Zelda of theirs? By discussing this couple, give a characterization of our own times.

RICHARD MARIUS

---

*A Tennessean, Richard Marius was born in 1933. He completed his
B.S. degree at the University of Tennessee and then went on to take
a Bachelor of Divinity degree at Southern Baptist Theological
Seminary. After completing an M.A. and, in 1962, a Ph.D. at Yale, he
went on to become a professor of history at the University of
Tennessee. He is currently director of expository writing at Harvard
University.*

Among his writings are a novel, The Coming Rain *(1969), and*
Luther *(1974), a biography.*

*Sir Thomas More was born in 1478 and received a classical
education in the household of Cardinal Morton and at Oxford. At
the Inns of Court, he studied to become a lawyer and was so
successful in that profession that he came to the notice of King
Henry VIII, entering that monarch's service in 1518 and ultimately
becoming lord chancellor in 1529 after the fall of Cardinal Wolsey,
who had been Henry's chief deputy.*

*In 1532 More resigned from the king's service, claiming ill
health, but as a devout Catholic, he had come to disagree with the
king's policies, including Henry's divorce from Catherine of Aragon.*

*The crisis came when Henry demanded that More subscribe to
the Act of Supremacy, which would make the king head of the
church in England. When More refused, Henry charged him with
treason and had him imprisoned in the Tower of London. A royal
tribunal found More guilty, and he was beheaded in 1534.*

*In the selection that follows, we see More grappling with the
problem of the desires of the flesh versus the spiritual duties of a
Christian.*

Priesthood or Marriage?

There is much to suggest that the years between 1501 and his marriage in 1504 or 1505 marked a spiritual crisis for Thomas More. In his 1539 letter Erasmus wrote that More thought of being ordained but that he could not shake off his desire for a wife, that he decided he would become a good husband rather than a bad priest. Stapleton said that More thought of becoming a Franciscan friar.

Roper tells us that before his marriage More "gave himself to prayer and devotion in the Charterhouse of London, religiously living there without vow about four years." Erasmus, who detested monks, makes no mention of this stay, but he does say that More engaged in vigils, fasting, and prayer there. Most modern scholars, puzzled at the thought that the monks of the Charterhouse might have taken in boarders, think that More may have lived in the neighborhood and shared in the daily services of the monastery. We do not know.

More always venerated the Carthusians. Erasmus wrote as if monks were nearly always hypocrites, and he spent much of his energy trying to keep from being sent back to the monastery where he had taken vows as a youth. More mocked the bad monk, but he spoke as if he longed for the monastery all his life, and he would always recall the Carthusians and remember that some monks were saintly.

The Carthusians were grave and devout and spent much time in prayer, solitude, and silence. Their stern boast was that their order had never been reformed because it had never fallen into corruption. When the Reformation came, no monastic order showed itself more willing to suffer agony and cruel death for the old faith. Even if he did not live within their sprawling compound, More's daily sharing of their rituals left him deeply stirred by their austere piety. He was of their temper, and he certainly believed that theirs was the surest way to heaven.

His decision to marry must have been agonizing. Today it is hard even for devout Catholics to understand how completely the cult of virginity captivated the church of the Middle Ages. From the beginning, Christians prized virginity above matrimony. A deep sexual asceticism runs through much of the New Testament. It is remarkable that Jesus, called a rabbi and springing from a Judaism that considered men hardly men unless they were married, should have remained, apparently, without a wife. He commended those who had made themselves eunuchs for the kingdom of heaven. Two centuries later, Origen of Alexandria took this praise of eunuchs literally and castrated himself so he might serve God without the temptation of lust. Later interpreters were not so literal, but they thought these strange words of Jesus meant that priests should abstain from sex and make themselves figurative eunuchs. Paul was hostile to women in general though not always in particular. Given the uncertainty of the times and the supposed near return of Jesus, he thought it better for everyone to remain single like himself, though he conceded that it was better to marry than to burn. To the Corinthians he allowed marriage as a substitute for fornication, but he suggested that husband and wife might agree to abstain from sexual intercourse during special periods of devotion.

Paul's combination of antipathy and grudging acceptance remained the view of the church. Marriage was permitted, and in time matrimony became a sacrament, but virginity was thought far superior. Augustine wrote that marriage was once commanded of the people of God because it was necessary to propagate the holy race; now, he said, it was only a remedy for human weakness and a consolation for human frailty. Even before Augustine an early pope wrote that marriage for priests was a pollution that they could not allow themselves; he implied that it was a pollution for the laity, too, but to them it was permitted because they were lesser beings. Marriage gave men and women carnal pleasure of a sort thought revolting by theologians who had rarely if ever experienced it. Jerome, the translator of the Vulgate and a contemporary of St. Augustine's, said that anyone who loved his wife too much might be damned, and he advised sexual intercourse without passion and only for the procreation of children. The church always held that the only justification for marriage was the production of children, and many church fathers cautioned husbands not to lust after their wives and not to use them as whores.

As the centuries passed, fantastic stories of heroic saints proliferated, and nearly all of them included tales of startling virginity or amazing abstinence by married people. More read the stories and repeated some of their miracle tales in one of his polemical religious works against heresy in which he defended with all his might the veneration of saints. In *The Golden Legend*, a medieval collection of stories he knew well, we find the tale in which the apostle Thomas appears in the room where a young man has taken his bride to consummate their union. Thomas tells the young couple that purity is the queen of all the virtues, the one that leads to eternal salvation. "Virginity is the sister of the angels," he says, and he makes clear that "pollution," by which he means any kind of sexual intercourse, in marriage or out of it, leads directly to hell. So the couple abstains; the bride becomes a martyr, the husband a bishop.

All this is nonsense to us, and we must realize that in every age, popular piety—of which *The Golden Legend* is an example—is more extreme than the formal theology of the church. Still, many devout Christians did believe that sexuality was a slide into hell, and More seems to have been one of them.

His inner anxiety over the desires of the body could hardly have been relieved by a series of public lectures he gave on *The City of God* by Augustine of Hippo soon after finishing his legal studies. Augustine was always his favorite saint, the writer who more than anyone else influenced the shaping of his mind. He knew Augustine almost by heart, and *The City of God* is more often quoted in his works than anything else in the Augustinian corpus. More spoke in the church of St. Lawrence Jewry, probably at the suggestion of William Grocyn, the rector. These lectures brought More into public notice for the first time, and they made a great impression. Erasmus mentioned them, and so did Roper; all the other sixteenth-century biographers did the same.

We have no idea what More said, but we know Augustine and *The City of God*. Augustine towered over the Latin Middle Ages. He defended the church against infidels, pagans, and heretics, and he was the first major theologian to teach that secular government should force people to be good Christians. He wrote Bible commentaries, and he tried to make paradoxical doctrines like the trinity and predestination seem plausible to the educated citizens of the dying Roman Empire. He believed that all sensuality was evil. He wrote against Julian of Eclanum:

> What sober-minded man would not prefer to take food, dry or moist, without any stinging carnal pleasure, if he could, as the air he draws in and lets out into the surrounding air by inhaling and exhaling?

In 1519, when Erasmus described More's abstemious nature, he probably—without quite knowing it himself—gave us a man whose views on sensual pleasure were much like St. Augustine's; it was not that the pleasures of the senses were harmful merely when they were taken in excess; they were a sign of wickedness merely by their being, and the Christian should limit indulgence in them as much as possible.

The worst of the sensual sins, according to Augustine, was sexuality. As a Christian who believed in the doctrine of creation, he had to believe that marriage and childbearing accomplished a divine purpose since society required a steady supply of new life to take the place of the old that died. But since sexual intercourse was almost impossible to isolate from intense sensual pleasure, he could not view sexuality without a certain loathing, and at times he came very close to saying that sexual intercourse is a sign of our depravity. He had had a mistress when he was young. When he became a Christian, he put her away, although he had had a son by her, Adeodatus, whose name means "gift of God." His primary view of Christian salvation was that it was redemption from sensuality, which, if indulged in unchecked, would lead the soul directly to hell. He never ceased to exhort Christians to chastity, by which he meant abstention from sexual intercourse, and even when he praised marriage, he took care to say that virginity or abstinence was a higher state. Always, in his view, the man who succumbed to the sensuality of marriage was inferior to the person to whom God gave the gift of surmounting passion.

Absorbed as he was in Augustine's work, More would have been saturated with the teaching that those who fall to sensuality will continue their plummeting into hell itself. That he lectured on Augustine at this time would indicate that he was seriously contemplating entry into the priesthood. It was quite common for young men knowledgeable in the law to study theology and become clerics. Many of More's friends were clerics; John Colet, whom he deeply revered, was learned and puritanical and thought that even the vergers who took care of church buildings should be restrained from sexual intercourse by vows of chastity. Colet's devotion to virginity would certainly have communicated itself to the younger man who admired him so much. In the normal course of things, More might have been expected to be ordained. Instead he married.

Stapleton says that More feared "even with the help of his practices of penance that he would not be able to conquer the temptations of the flesh that come to a man in the vigour and ardour of his youth," and so "he made up his mind to marry. Of this he would often speak in after life with great sorrow and regret, for he used to say that it was much easier to be chaste in the single than in the married state."

In a work he did about the time that he made his decision to marry, we can find evidence of the brooding his choice inspired in him. This was a translation of a biography of Pico della Mirandola done by Pico's nephew, Giovanni Francesco. More presented his little work as a New Year's gift to Joyce Lee, the daughter of an old family friend, who had just entered the convent of the Poor Clares, whose house was not far from the Tower. The Clares lived withdrawn from the world in a life of extreme simplicity, prohibited by the rules of their order from receiving any material gift; so More gave Joyce Lee a spiritual present.

In his translation More made a few minor changes from the Latin original, but they are insignificant. The importance of his effort is that he thought enough of Pico and the book about him to make the translation and to give it to a woman friend who had entered a religious vocation.

Stapleton says that early in his life More made Pico his ideal because Pico had been a learned and devout layman. Obviously much in Pico's life would have appealed to More. Pico was an extraordinarily learned Italian, deeply devout, abstemious, noble, diligent, and prolific with his pen. One of his most important beliefs was that human beings have free will and can choose whether they will rise toward God or sink toward the beasts. He mocked astrologers for their determinism because he found the dignity of man to lie in the soul's capacity for choice and in its ability to ascend to God through the great chain of being that knits creation together.

More would have seen Pico as an example of the Christian life he might live himself—warmhearted lay piety, at home in a cultured world. But when Pico died, aged thirty, in 1494, he was a disciple of Girolamo Savonarola, then preaching sternly against the vanity of art and other forms of idle worldliness and predicting the imminent end of the world. After Pico died, so Giovanni Francesco said, Pico appeared to Savonarola in a dream, his body suffused with fire. He was in purgatory, and the fire was his punishment for refusing a religious vocation and remaining a layman. More faithfully translated the story; it must have given him somber reflections.

Gloomier yet would have been the recollection that, though a layman, Pico remained unmarried. He fled both marriage and worldly business in the proud palaces of stately lords, More's translation says. In jest Pico said that if he had to choose one over the other, he would take marriage, thinking there was less jeopardy in that than in service to princes.

Pico's poetry is deeply melancholy, as if it might be presumptuous to suggest that anyone might enjoy the sensual world; in that respect it is in rebellion against the sensual nature of poetry of the later Middle Ages in which versifiers endlessly propounded the delights of color and growing things and the bliss of earthly love. More translated Pico's verse with great skill and with much greater feeling than he discovered in himself when he wrote poetry of his own. His own sensuality was always half tamed at best, but his melancholic temperament brought him easily to the melancholy of Pico, who had managed to raise gloom to a pious art. Here are some lines, in More's translation:

> This wretched life, the trust and confidence
> Of whose continuance maketh us bold to sin,
> Thou perceivest well by experience
> Since that hour, in which it did begin,

It holdeth on the course and will not lin [wait]
But fast it runneth on and passen shall
As doth a dream or shadow on the wall.

Consider well that every night and day
While that we busily provide and care
For our disport, revel, mirth and play
For pleasant melody and dainty fare
Death stealeth on full slyly and unware [unperceived].
He lieth at hand and shall us enterprise [grasp]
We know not how soon or in what mannerwise.

These are Pico's thoughts, faithfully rendered by More, and they are More's thoughts, too. But either shortly before or shortly after he wrote them, he married.

The wife he chose was Jane Colt, the eldest daughter of a family friend who lived in the country. Roper tells us that More continued his attendance at the Charterhouse monastery "until he resorted to the house of one Master Colt, a gentleman of Essex, that had oft invited him there." John Colt was a prosperous man who had three daughters, and Thomas More would naturally impress a father with daughters to wed. Roper's "until" is significant; it looks as if More's stay at the Charterhouse came to an end as a direct consequence of the persistent invitations of Master John Colt to come to the country and meet his daughters. Probably John More urged his son to go ahead. However that may be, More went and met the young women, "whose honest conversation and virtuous education provoked him there specially to set his affection." Roper's sentence is a little confusing; it sounds as if More gave his affection to all three of them. Maybe he did. For a young, passionate man accustomed to four years of relative isolation in the company of Carthusian monks, the sudden proximity of available young women must have been a shock, and Roper suggests that More's clerical aspirations caved in before the general "affection" stirred up in him by this meeting.

Roper says that More liked the second daughter better than he did Jane, the eldest. But he thought it would be a shame for the firstborn not to be married first; so he resolved to fancy the eldest and framed his desire toward her. Little by little he succeeded, and they were married.

We must suppose that Roper got this tale from More himself. There is no reason to think that Margaret, More's eldest daughter and Roper's wife, was ignorant of it. In that light the story is rather cruel, though Roper told the tale to illustrate the kindness of his father-in-law, and that is probably why More told it himself. Here again he seems to be a man on a stage he has made, acting out a part he has chosen before the world.

The story may also represent something else—the feeling in More that the first reason for having a wife was sexual necessity. Then almost any wife would do, and once the wedding was over, a strong and resolute man with virtue on his mind could shape his wife's character according to his own tastes.

Erasmus, writing of More years before Roper put pen to paper, supports this view. He said that More married a young girl, untrained and having no experience but the country, so he could make of her what he wanted. He had her instructed in literature and trained in all kinds of music. Erasmus may even tell us something in addition to what this letter reveals. In his colloquy called "Marriage," he tells of a young man who married a girl of seventeen who had never spent any time outside the country home of her parents. Her very simplicity impressed the youth because he imagined that he could train her to match his own taste. He taught her literature and music, and when they had been to a sermon, he made her repeat the words of the preacher to see if she had understood them and remembered them.

The girl rebelled! She answered her husband's insistence with tears, and sometimes she beat her head against the floor. The husband, unable to do anything with her, suggested a visit to her father in the country. Off they went, the bride delighted to go home. Once there, the husband left her with her mother and her sisters and went hunting with the father. He asked the question: What could he do to make his wife obey? The father counseled a good beating. The husband demurred. He would prefer that the father use his skill or his authority; he did not want to beat his wife into submission.

The father did his part; he drew his daughter aside, and he reminded her of how ugly she was, how crude, how often he had feared that he could not find her a husband. With much effort he had found the girl a man who would delight even a beautiful and talented woman, a man who would scarcely think her fit to be a servant if he were not so kind. She was rebelling against this princely fellow. The father then seemed ready to beat her; he may have drawn back his hand as if to strike her. The daughter went down on her knees and begged forgiveness. She also fell on her knees before her young husband and begged him to forgive her, too. Ever afterwards she was a perfect wife, doing everything her husband wanted, no matter how lowly it might be. In a few years they loved each other, and the girl congratulated herself for her good luck in marrying such a man.

Modern scholars note the similarity between the opening of this colloquy, published in 1523, and the description by Erasmus in 1519 of More's marriage to Jane. They assume that the story of this husband

and his weeping young wife is a true account of the relation between Thomas More and his first wife. They may be right; if More told Roper how he came to marry Jane in the first place, he might well have told Erasmus how he made her a good wife. But the artistic imagination always decorates reality, and perhaps it is an error to read the little dialogue by Erasmus as literal history.

The attitude of the husband in the colloquy is indeed like that of Thomas More toward women in general. They are most virtuous when they are submissive to the authority of a good man. The husband in the colloquy shows the relentless drive for improvement that we find always in More, a man who could not bear to waste a minute. Even his pleasures were intended to instruct, and we may be driven to reflect that in this aspect he often sounds rather like an eighteenth-century Methodist born out of his time.

Poor Jane must have taken an emotional beating in her marriage even if her husband did forgo his legal right to beat her with his fists. She died in 1511 after bearing him four children—Margaret, Elizabeth, Cecily, and John. She was twenty-three. More loved her in his way. In the epitaph he composed for the tomb that was never to hold his bones, she was his "dear little wife."

He married again within a month. His second wife, Alice Middleton, widow of a London merchant, was already in full maturity, six years older than he. By all accounts she was quarrelsome, petty, ignorant, and even stupid, and there is nothing to suggest that she was sexually attractive. Harpsfield calls her "aged, blunt, and rude," implying that she was so when she married More. More made her the target of many unkind jokes, though in his epitaph he praised her.

Why did he marry her, and why so soon after Jane's death? Her husband had left her considerable property when he died, and both More and his father saw marriage as an economic union—as did nearly everybody in that time. People did not marry for love; as the colloquy of Erasmus shows, they hoped to love each other only after they had lived together for a time.

Still, his haste seems almost indecent, and his biographers have puzzled over it; at times they seem embarrassed by it. They usually explain it by More's desire to have a mother for his children, and this must have been part of his decision. Dame Alice brought a daughter with her—also named Alice—so she had some experience with children, and, as we have seen, More praised her for giving loving attention to his offspring. She was, by our standards, probably more manager than mother, for she took over the household, and More wrote her as one might write to a good steward. She apparently had a sharp eye for accounts, ridding the house of parasitic guests who stayed too long. Andrea Ammonio, friend to both More and Erasmus, fled the premises after some kind of encounter with her, and he wrote ungallantly to Erasmus of the "hooked beak of the harpy." If More sought a good manager, he found one.

He may have had another motive in marrying Alice—the continuation of his lifelong struggle against sexuality and desire. We have noted his observation that it was harder to remain chaste as a married man than as a single person. He must have had in mind the ability of married men to satisfy their sexual longings whenever they wanted, and he took to heart the consensus of the church fathers who held that sex for pleasure alone—even with one's wife—was a sin. Early Christians, responding to their general horror of sex, frequently took vows to abstain from sexual intercourse even if they were married. Sexual intercourse after menopause was a questionable act. And it is just possible that More married his second wife with this early Christian abstinence in mind. The doctors of the church had debated the validity of any second marriage, and the debate had gone on for centuries, finally settling to a grudging consensus that second marriages were valid for Christians though not signs of valiant faith.

Menopause at that time, as now, came when women were about forty-five, but many women reached it earlier, and Dame Alice may have already passed through menopause when More married her. At the very least she was near the end of her childbearing time. Had More married a younger woman, a person of his temperament might have justified habitual sexual relations with her by the hope of fathering other children. But sexual intercourse with a woman after menopause could only be for the sexual pleasure that the church fathers had condemned so vehemently. In Augustine's eyes, using a wife merely for pleasure was to make her a whore. It is quite unlikely that a man of More's devout and ascetic disposition would have indulged in sexual intercourse with a woman who could not give birth. His four children by Jane Colt were born one after another about as quickly as human biology permits, seeming to testify to his own regular sexual activity for as long as his marriage to her lasted. He married Dame Alice when he was only thirty-three—not far beyond the height of his sexual powers, and if he then began to abstain completely from sex, we may understand a little better the hair shirt, the whips, the vigils, and his later horror at the Protestant approval of clerical marriage.

His marriage with Dame Alice, then, was probably a quiet and unobtrusive way of living a life of sexual abstinence while he remained in the world to do his duty to his children, to his father, and to society at large. He always believed that the natural man sought pleasure for the body but that the true Christian sought pain and punishment in this life for sins that had to be punished somewhere, either in this world or in the world to come. His marriage to Dame Alice may have been a continuing penance.

He may also have used Dame Alice to cancel a revived longing for priesthood or the monastic life. As he himself later pointed out, a man could become a priest after his first wife died, but a second marriage closed the sacrament of ordination to him forever. Paul had written that a "bishop" could be the husband of one wife; the church interpreted this text to mean "no more than one." A man who had been married twice was, by canon law, a "bigamist," even if his first wife had very properly died and left her husband a widower; no bigamist could be a priest.

More loved his children, and his sense of responsibility for them was enormous, but they might have been provided for had he chosen the priestly vocation when Jane died. Her family was well-to-do, and it is unlikely that More would have married her without receiving a substantial dowry, which he might have returned on condition that it be used for the support of his children. John More was also prosperous enough to help his grandchildren should his son have chosen to be ordained—though the elder More would have been irate at the thought. The lure of priesthood in such circumstances must have become once again beguiling, and More's later ruminations as to why he could not be a priest—ruminations that in context seem gratuitous—may reveal this prospect suddenly presented a second time by the death of his wife in 1511. His quick marriage to Alice Middleton may well have been a way of slamming a door that had suddenly flown open years after he thought he had shut it forever with his marriage to the young Jane Colt.

Whatever may have been the cause of the union, it is clear that after 1511 his two marriages, his children, his growing household, and his offices fixed him irrevocably on the public stage. He might retain the wounds left over from his decision to forsake the priesthood, and from time to time these old wounds might cause an ache in his bones. But he was to be a public man, and he set about to make himself a public career.

Questions for Discussion

1. How could the suppositions about More's attitudes and his marriages be made to seem more credible? After all, the direct evidence is now slim. Can you think of any ways in which an author might be more convincing in his or her presentation of the life of a figure from a remote historical era?

2. If Richard Marius's interpretation is accurate, what seems to have been the position of women in sixteenth-century society? On what do you base your opinion?

3. What are your reactions to the methods proposed for making a wife behave in the sixteenth century?

4. Compare and contrast attitudes held toward women by Sir Thomas More and his contemporaries with those held by people today.

5. What is the gist of the selection?

6. As a biographer, in what ways is Marius similar to Jane Howard, William Manchester, and Nancy Milford? What techniques do they share? And how is Marius different from the others?

—————————— SUGGESTIONS FOR WRITING ——————————

1. "Three kinds of students," Mead once said, "were attracted to her classes: those who wanted her name on their records, those who wanted to hear her, and those who were seriously interested in anthropology."

What kinds of students are in your classes?

In answering that question, choose one example of each type and develop a "sketch" of the person. What does he or she look like? Wear? How does he or she talk? What are his or her apparent motives?

2. Characterize one of your teachers. In developing this piece of writing, you might think about Jane Howard's "portrait" of Margaret Mead.

Howard chooses a theme: Margaret Mead's relationship with students. She then develops this theme in some detail—with specific examples, such as the story about Ken Heyman and the one about Vincent Crapanzano, as well as Mead's use of and relationship with her aides.

Furthermore, Howard includes carefully chosen details: for example, "Later employees also kept on hand a supply of her queen-sized pantyhose. . . ."

3. Have you known an "imperial" person, such as Douglas MacArthur—not necessarily a general or a president, but someone who might well have been a Caesar? Perhaps this person is one of your teachers, a relative, an acquaintance, a boss.

Write a biographical sketch of this person, focusing on a brief period in that individual's life.

4. Zelda Fitzgerald was and is a symbol of the Roaring Twenties, the Jazz Age. Do you know anyone who is a symbol of some era or institution? For example, a businessperson you know might be, for you, a symbol of free enterprise; or perhaps your brother or sister is symbolic of the Punk era.

Write a biographical sketch of a person you think is a symbol of a time, a place, or an institution.

5. Write a sketch about a rock or movie star who is the object of intense adulation by fans. Explain why the person elicits such a strong response. Give your own reactions to such idolatry of entertainers, rather than of heroes.

6. Write your own farewell speech—bidding adieu to that which was important in your life.

7.   MacArthur said that people grow old only by deserting their ideals. But we frequently hear that someone is too idealistic. Present your own opinion and reasoning about idealism. *Caution*: In this essay, you must be specific; don't merely generalize about idealism.

8.   Read a biography of a satanic character, such as the Marquis de Sade, Adolf Hitler, Jack the Ripper, Count Vlad (the original of Dracula), Genghis Khan, the Roman emperor Caligula, Idi Amin, Pol Pot, Stalin. Does the biographer enable you to understand the dementia of the subject? What techniques does the biographer use to give you access to this strange, hellish world?

9.   Read a biography of a saintly person, such as Mother Teresa, Albert Schweitzer, Mahatma Gandhi, or Saint Francis of Assisi. Explain the power these saintly characters seem to possess. Does the biographer enable you to understand such a subject? What techniques does the biographer use to give you access to this world of saintliness?

3

The New Journalism

INTRODUCTION

For the past couple of decades, readers have been hearing about New Journalists such as Tom Wolfe (whose book *The Right Stuff* was made into a movie), Hunter S. Thompson (the basis for the character Duke in *Doonesbury*), and John McPhee (among whose works is, believe it or not, a long and fascinating book about Florida oranges).

What is the New Journalism? What can writers learn from this contemporary genre?

New Journalists use the techniques of prose fiction (novels, short stories) to make their reports of actual events vivid and understandable. As Tom Wolfe points out, New Journalists do *not* give us the facts and nothing but the facts; they give us *both* the facts *and* their own attitudes toward those facts; New Journalists, like novelists, do more than report; they tell stories.[1] Therefore, in the New Journalism, you will find much background detail: what places look like, how subjects dress and talk, what people do. The reports of these writers are likely to use much

[1]Tom Wolfe, *The New Journalism* (New York: Harper & Row, 1973), pp. 3–52.

dialogue. And most important, the New Journalists do not attempt to maintain the cold objectivity of standard journalism but, rather, express their own personalities and opinions in their pieces. In short, New Journalism is writing that presents dramatic detail; like the fiction you enjoy reading, the New Journalism is specific, not general. For example, John McPhee introduces us to a Pennsylvania State game warden:

> Alt, who is in his thirties, was wearing a visored khaki cap with a blue-and-gold keystone on the forehead, and a khaki cardigan under a khaki jump suit. A lithe and light-bodied man with tinted glasses and a blond mustache, he looked like a lieutenant in the Ardennes Forest.

In the introduction to Chapter 1 we found that specific detail is the fuel that makes personal narrative function: the shapes, colors, sounds, and smells of places; the accents, gestures, and dress of people; all of the details that make for the vividness of life. Such is the case with New Journalism.

In personal narrative, however, the focus is on the writer; readers are interested in what they can learn about the teller of the tale. In New Journalism, the focus shifts toward the subject matter, but the writer is still very much with us as a personality.

As you read the selections that follow, notice how the writers use detail and how they interject themselves into their reports.

New Journalism holds a mirror up to the times we live in. It not only tells the reader how other people live but how the reader lives as well. It helps explain the forces that shape our society.

In *Dispatches*, his book about the Vietnam War, Michael Herr superbly characterizes the new journalism. He says that traditional journalism is "uni-prose": "The press got all the facts (more or less), it got too many of them. But it never found a way to report meaningfully about death, which of course was really what it was all about. . . . Conventional journalism could no more reveal this war than conventional firepower could win it. . . ."[2] As a New Journalist, Herr attempted to report what experiencing a war means to the people who are in it.

The New Journalism attempts to report "what it was all about."

[2]Michael Herr, *Dispatches* (New York: Avon, 1978), pp. 226–232.

TOM WOLFE

---

*Born in Richmond, Virginia, on March 2, 1931, Tom Wolfe attended
Washington and Lee University and took a doctorate in American
Studies at Yale. He eschewed an academic career for journalism, working
for the New York* Herald Tribune, *the Washington* Post, *and* New York
Magazine. *With such books as* The Kandy-Kolored Tangerine-Flake
Streamline Baby *and* The Electric Kool-Aid Acid Test, *Wolfe established
himself as a leading cultural critic and journalist.* The Right Stuff, *which
was made into a movie, is a brilliant study of America's first astronauts.*

*Tom Wolfe and New Journalism are virtually synonymous, and his
book* The New Journalism, *published in 1973, became the bible of the
movement. In that volume, Wolfe included selections by Rex Reed, Gay
Talese, Richard Goldstein, Michael Herr, Truman Capote, Joe Eszterhas,
Terry Southern, Hunter S. Thompson, Norman Mailer, Nicholas Tomalin,
Barbara L. Goldsmith, Joe McGinnis, George Plimpton, James Mills, John
Gregory Dunne, John Sack, Joan Didion, "Adam Smith," Robert
Christgau, Gary Wills, and himself.*

*Wolfe characterizes his own style as "wowie!" And frequently it is
kandy-kolored and electric, as you will see at times in this selection.*

*As you read this essay, pay attention to devices of style. Note also
how Wolfe structures his essay, putting scenes together one after another
to form a total impression but sustaining no narrative line and not
following any particular logical sequence. The effect is very much like
montage in film.*

Las Vegas (What?) Las Vegas
(Can't hear you! Too noisy)
Las Vegas!!!

Hernia, hernia, hernia, hernia, hernia, hernia, hernia, hernia, hernia, hernia, hernia, hernia, hernia, HERNia; hernia, HERNia, hernia, hernia, hernia, hernia, HERNia, HERNia, HERNia, hernia, hernia, hernia, hernia, hernia, hernia, hernia, eight is the point, the point is eight; hernia, hernia, HERNia; hernia, hernia, hernia, hernia, all right, hernia, hernia, hernia, hernia, hard eight, hernia, hernia, hernia, HERNia, hernia, hernia, hernia, HERNia, hernia, hernia, hernia, HERNia, hernia, hernia, hernia, hernia.

"What is all this *hernia hernia* stuff?"

This was Raymond talking to the wavy-haired fellow with the stick, the dealer, at the craps table about 3:45 Sunday morning. The stickman had no idea what this big wiseacre was talking about, but he resented the tone. He gave Raymond that patient arch of the eyebrows known as a Red Hook brush-off, which is supposed to convey some such thought as, I am a very tough but cool guy, as you can tell by the way I carry my eyeballs low in the pouches, and if this wasn't such a high-class joint we would take wiseacres like you out back and beat you into jellied madrilene.

At this point, however, Raymond was immune to subtle looks.

The stickman tried to get the game going again, but every time he would start up his singsong, by easing the words out through the nose, which seems to be the style among craps dealers in Las Vegas—"All right, a new shooter . . . eight is the point, the point is eight" and so on—Raymond would start droning along with him in exactly the same tone of voice, "Hernia, hernia, hernia; hernia, HERNia, HERNia, hernia; hernia, hernia, hernia."

Everybody at the craps table was staring in consternation to think that anybody would try to needle a tough, hip, elite *soldat* like a Las Vegas craps dealer. The gold-lamé odalisques of Los Angeles were staring. The Western sports, fifty-eight-year-old men who wear Texas string ties, were staring. The old babes at the slot machines, holding Dixie Cups full of nickles, were staring at the craps tables, but cranking away the whole time.

Raymond, who is thirty-four years old and works as an engineer in Phoenix, is big but not terrifying. He has the sort of thatchwork hair that grows so low all along the forehead there is no logical place to part it, but he tries anyway. He has a huge, prognathous jaw, but it is as smooth, soft and round as a melon, so that Raymond's total effect is that of an Episcopal divinity student.

The guards were wonderful. They were dressed in cowboy uniforms like Bruce Cabot in *Sundown* and they wore sheriff's stars.

"Mister, is there something we can do for you?"

"The expression is 'Sir,' " said Raymond. "You said 'Mister.' The expression is 'Sir.' How's your old Cosa Nostra?"

Amazingly, the casino guards were easing Raymond out peaceably, without putting a hand on him. I had never seen the fellow before, but possibly because I had been following his progress for the last five minutes, he turned to me and said, "Hey, do you have a car? This wild stuff is starting again."

The gist of it was that he had left his car somewhere and he wanted to ride up the Strip to the Stardust, one of the big hotel-casinos. I am describing this big goof Raymond not because he is a typical Las Vegas tourist, although he has some typical symptoms, but because he is a good example of the marvelous impact Las Vegas has on the senses. Raymond's senses were at a high pitch of excitation, the only trouble being that he was going off his nut. He had been up since Thursday afternoon, and it was now about 3:45 A.M. Sunday. He had an envelope full of pep pills—amphetamine—in his left coat pocket and an envelope full of Equanils —meprobamate—in his right pocket, or were the Equanils in the left and the pep pills in the right? He could tell by looking, but he wasn't going to look anymore. He didn't care to see how many were left.

He had been rolling up and down the incredible electric-sign gauntlet of Las Vegas' Strip, U.S. Route 91, where the neon and the par lamps— bubbling, spiraling, rocketing, and exploding in sunbursts ten stories high out in the middle of the desert—celebrate one-story casinos. He had been gambling and drinking and eating now and again at the buffet tables the casinos keep heaped with food day and night, but mostly hopping himself up with good old amphetamine, cooling himself down with meprobamate, then hooking down more alcohol, until now, after sixty hours, he was slipping into the symptoms of toxic schizophrenia.

He was also enjoying what the prophets of hallucinogen call "consciousness expansion." The man was psychedelic. He was beginning to isolate the components of Las Vegas' unique bombardment of the senses. He was quite right about this *hernia hernia* stuff. Every casino in Las Vegas is, among the other things, a room full of craps tables with dealers who keep up a running singsong that sounds as though they are saying "hernia, hernia, hernia, hernia, hernia" and so on. There they are day and night, easing a running commentary through their nostrils. What they have to say contains next to no useful instruction. Its underlying message is, We are the initiates, riding the crest of chance. That the accumulated sound comes out "hernia" is merely an unfortunate phonetic coincidence. Actually, it is part of something rare and rather grand: a combination of baroque stimuli that brings to mind the bronze gongs, no larger than a blue plate, that Louis XIV, his ruff collars larded with the lint of the foul Old City of Byzantium, personally hunted out in the bazaars of Asia Minor to provide exotic acoustics for his new palace outside Paris.

The sounds of the craps dealer will be in, let's say, the middle register. In the lower register will be the sound of the old babes at the slot machines. Men play the slots too, of course, but one of the indelible images of Las Vegas is that of the old babes at the row upon row of slot machines. There they are at six o'clock Sunday morning no less than at three o'clock Tuesday afternoon. Some of them pack their old hummocky shanks into Capri pants, but many of them just put on the old print dress, the same one day after day, and the old hob-heeled shoes, looking like they might be going out to buy eggs in Tupelo, Mississippi. They have a Dixie Cup full of nickels or dimes in the left hand and an Iron Boy work glove on the right hand to keep the callouses from getting sore. Every time they pull the handle, the machine makes a sound much like the sound a cash register makes before the bell rings, then the slot pictures start clattering up from left to right, the oranges, lemons, plums, cherries, bells, bars, buckaroos—the figure of a cowboy riding a bucking bronco. The whole sound keeps churning up over and over again in eccentric series all over the place, like one of those random-sound radio symphonies by John Cage. You can hear it any hour of the day or night all over Las Vegas. You can walk down Fremont Street at dawn and hear it without even walking in a door, that and the spins of the wheels of fortune, a boring and not very popular sort of simplified roulette, as the tabs flap to a stop. As an overtone, or at times simply as a loud sound, comes the babble of the casino crowds, with an occasional shriek from the craps tables, or, anywhere from 4 P.M. to 6 A.M., the sound of brass instruments, or electrified string instruments from the cocktail-lounge shows.

The crowd and band sounds are not very extraordinary, of course. But Las Vegas' Muzak is. Muzak pervades Las Vegas from the time you walk into the airport upon landing to the last time you leave the casinos. It is piped out to the swimming pool. It is in the drugstores. It is as if there were a communal fear that someone, somewhere in Las Vegas, was going to be left with a totally vacant minute on his hands.

Las Vegas has succeeded in wiring an entire city with this electronic stimulation, day and night, out in the middle of the desert. In the automobile I rented, the radio could not be turned off, no matter which dial you went after. I drove for days in a happy burble of Action Checkpoint News, "Monkey No. 9," "Donna, Donna, the Prima Donna," and picking-and-singing jingles for the Frontier Bank and the Fremont Hotel.

One can see the magnitude of the achievement. Las Vegas takes what in other American towns is but a quixotic inflammation of the senses for some poor salary mule in the brief interval between the flagstone rambler and the automatic elevator downtown and magnifies it, foliates it, embellishes it into an institution.

For example, Las Vegas is the only town in the world whose skyline is made up neither of buildings, like New York, nor of trees, like Wilbraham, Massachusetts, but signs. One can look at Las Vegas from a mile away on Route 91 and see no buildings, no trees, only signs. But such signs! They tower. They revolve, they oscillate, they soar in shapes before which the existing vocabulary of art history is helpless. I can only attempt to supply names—Boomerang Modern, Palette Curvilinear, Flash Gordon Ming-Alert Spiral, McDonald's Hamburger Parabola, Mint Casino Elliptical, Miami Beach Kidney. Las Vegas' sign makers work so far out beyond the frontiers of conventional studio art that they have no names themselves for the forms they create. Vaughan Cannon, one of those tall, blond Westerners, the builders of places like Las Vegas and Los Angeles, whose eyes seem to have been bleached by the sun, is in the back shop of the Young Electric Sign Company out on East Charleston Boulevard with Herman Boernge, one of his designers, looking at the model they have prepared for the Lucky Strike Casino sign, and Cannon points to where the sign's two great curving faces meet to form a narrow vertical face and says:

"Well, here we are again—what do we call that?"

"I don't know," says Boernge. "It's sort of a nose effect. Call it a nose."

Okay, a nose, but it rises sixteen stories high above a two-story building. In Las Vegas no farseeing entrepreneur buys a sign to fit a building he owns. He rebuilds the building to support the biggest sign he can get up the money for and, if necessary, changes the name. The Lucky Strike Casino today is the Lucky Casino, which fits better when recorded in sixteen stories of flaming peach and incandescent yellow in the middle of the Mojave Desert. In the Young Electric Sign Co. era signs have become the architecture of Las Vegas, and the most whimsical, Yale-seminar-frenzied devices of the two late geniuses of Baroque Modern, Frank Lloyd Wright and Eero Saarinen, seem rather stuffy business, like a jest at a faculty meeting, compared to it. Men like Boernge, Kermit Wayne, Ben Mitchem and Jack Larsen, formerly an artist for Walt Disney, are the designer-sculptor geniuses of Las Vegas, but their motifs have been carried faithfully throughout the town by lesser men, for gasoline stations, motels, funeral parlors, churches, public buildings, flophouses and sauna baths.

Then there is a stimulus that is both visual and sexual—the Las Vegas buttocks décolletage. This is a form of sexually provocative dress seen more and more in the United States, but avoided like Broadway message-embroidered ("Kiss Me, I'm Cold") underwear in the fashion pages, so that the euphemisms have not been established and I have no choice but clinical terms. To achieve buttocks décolletage a woman wears bikini-style shorts that cut across the round fatty masses of the buttocks rather than cupping them from below, so that the outer-lower edges of these fatty masses, or "cheeks," are exposed. I am in the cocktail lounge of the Hacienda Hotel, talking to managing director Dick Taylor about the great success his place has had in attracting family and tour groups, and all around me the waitresses are bobbing on their high heels, bare legs and décolletage-bare backsides, set off by pelvis-length lingerie of an uncertain denomination. I stare, but I am new here. At the White Cross Rexall drugstore on the Strip a pregnant brunette walks in off the street wearing black shorts with buttocks décolletage aft and illusion-of-cloth nylon lingerie hanging fore, and not even the old mom's-pie pensioners up near the door are staring. They just crank away at the slot machines. On the streets of Las Vegas, not only the show girls, of which the town has about two hundred fifty, bona fide, in residence, but girls of every sort, including, especially, Las Vegas' little high-school buds, who adorn what locals seeking roots in the sand call "our city of churches and schools," have taken up the chic of wearing buttocks décolletage step-ins under flesh-tight slacks, with the outline of the undergarment showing through fashionably. Others go them one better. They achieve the effect of having been dipped once, briefly, in Helenca stretch nylon. More and more they look like those wonderful old girls out of Flash Gordon who were wrapped just once over in Baghdad pantaloons of clear polyethelene with only Flash Gordon between them and the insane red-eyed assaults of the minions of Ming. It is as if all the hip young suburban gals of America named Lana, Deborah and Sandra, who gather wherever the arc lights shine and the studs steady their coiffures in the plate-glass reflection, have convened in Las Vegas with their bouffant hair above and anatomically stretch-pant-swathed little bottoms below, here on the new American frontier. But exactly!

None of it would have been possible, however, without one of those historic combinations of nature and art that creates an epoch. In this case, the Mojave Desert plus the father of Las Vegas, the late Benjamin "Bugsy" Siegel.

Bugsy was an inspired man. Back in 1944 the city fathers of Las Vegas, their Protestant rectitude alloyed only by the giddy prospect of gambling revenues, were considering the sort of ordinance that would have preserved the town with a kind of Colonial Williamsburg dinkiness in the motif of the Wild West. All new buildings would have to have at least the façade of the sort of place where piano players used to wear garters on their sleeves in Virginia City around 1880. In Las Vegas in 1944, it should be noted, there was nothing more stimulating in the entire town than a Fremont Street bar where the composer of "Deep in the Heart of Texas" held forth and the regulars downed fifteen-cent beer.

Bugsy pulled into Las Vegas in 1945 with several million dollars that, after his assassination, was traced back in the general direction of gangster-financiers. Siegel put up a hotel-casino such as Las Vegas had never seen and called it the Flamingo—all Miami Modern, and the hell with piano players with garters and whatever that was all about. Everybody drove out Route 91 just to gape. Such shapes! Boomerang Modern supports, Palette Curvilinear bars, Hot Shoppe Cantilever roofs and a scalloped swimming pool. Such colors! All the new electrochemical pastels of the Florida littoral: tangerine, broiling magenta, livid pink, incarnadine, fuchsia demure, Congo ruby, methyl green, viridine, aquamarine, phenosafranine, incandescent orange, scarlet-fever purple, cyanic blue, tessellated bronze, hospital-fruit-basket orange. And such signs! Two cylinders rose at either end of the Flamingo—eight stories high and covered from top to bottom with neon rings in the shape of bubbles that fizzed all eight stories up into the desert sky all night long like an illuminated whisky-soda tumbler filled to the brim with pink champagne.

The business history of the Flamingo, on the other hand, was not such a smashing success. For one thing, the gambling operation was losing money at a rate that rather gloriously refuted all the recorded odds of the gaming science. Siegel's backers apparently suspected that he was playing both ends against the middle in collusion with professional gamblers who hung out at the Flamingo as though they had liens on it. What with one thing and another, someone decided by the night of June 20, 1947, that Benny Siegel, lord of the Flamingo, had had it. He was shot to death in Los Angeles.

Yet Siegel's aesthetic, psychological and cultural insights, like Cézanne's, Freud's and Max Weber's, could not die. The Siegel vision and the Siegel aesthetic were already sweeping Las Vegas like gold fever. And there were builders of the West equal to the opportunity. All over Las Vegas the incredible electric pastels were repeated. Overnight the Baroque Modern forms made Las Vegas one of the few architecturally unified cities of the world—the style was Late American Rich—and without the bother and bad humor of a City Council ordinance. No enterprise was too small, too pedestrian or too solemn for The Look. The Supersonic Carwash, the Mercury Jetaway, Gas Vegas Village and Terrible Herbst gasoline stations, the Par-a-Dice Motel, the Palm Mortuary, the Orbit Inn, the Desert Moon, the Blue Onion Drive-In—on it went, like Wildwood, New Jersey, entering Heaven.

The atmosphere of the six-mile-long Strip of hotel-casinos grips even those segments of the population who rarely go near it. Barely twenty-five-hundred feet off the Strip, over by the Convention Center, stands Landmark Towers, a shaft thirty stories high, full of apartments, supporting a huge circular structure shaped like a space observation platform, which was to

have contained the restaurant and casino. Somewhere along the way Landmark Towers went bankrupt, probably at that point in the last of the many
crises when the construction workers *still* insisted on spending half the day
flat on their bellies with their heads, tongues and eyeballs hanging over the
edge of the tower, looking down into the swimming pool of the Playboy
Apartments below, which has a "nudes only" section for show girls whose
work calls for a tan all over.

Elsewhere, Las Vegas' beautiful little high-school buds in their
buttocks-décolletage stretch pants are back on the foam-rubber upholstery of
luxury broughams peeling off the entire chick ensemble long enough to
establish the highest venereal-disease rate among high-school students anywhere north of the yaws-rotting shanty jungles of the Eighth Parallel. The
Negroes who have done much of the construction work in Las Vegas'
sixteen-year boom are off in their ghetto on the west side of town, and some
of them are smoking marijuana, eating peyote buttons and taking horse
(heroin), which they get from Tijuana, I mean it's simple, baby, right through
the mails, and old Raymond, the Phoenix engineer, does not have the high
life to himself.

I am on the third floor of the Clark County Courthouse talking to
Sheriff Captain Ray Gubser, another of these strong, pale-eyed Western-
builder types, who is obligingly explaining to me law enforcement on the
Strip, where the problem is not so much the drunks, crooks or roughhousers,
but these nuts on pills who don't want to ever go to bed, and they have
hallucinations and try to bring down the casinos like Samson. The county
has two padded cells for them. They cool down after three or four days and
they turn out to be somebody's earnest breadwinner back in Denver or
Minneapolis, loaded with the right credentials and pouring soul and apolo-
giae all over the county cops before finally pulling out of never-never land for
good by plane. Captain Gubser is telling me about life and eccentric times in
Las Vegas, but I am distracted. The captain's office has windows out on the
corridor. Coming down the corridor is a covey of girls, skipping and screaming, giggling along, their heads exploding in platinum-and-neon-yellow bouf-
fants or beehives or raspberry-silk scarves, their eyes appliquéd in black like
mail-order decals, their breasts aimed up under their jerseys at the angle of
anti-aircraft automatic weapons, and, as they swing around the corner toward
the elevator, their glutei maximi are bobbing up and down with their pumps
in the inevitable buttocks décolletage pressed out against black, beige and
incarnadine stretch pants. This is part of the latest shipment of show girls to
Las Vegas, seventy in all, for the "Lido de Paris" revue at the Stardust, to be
entitled *Bravo!*, replacing the old show, entitled *Voilà*. The girls are in the
county courthouse getting their working papers, and fifteen days from now
these little glutei maximi and ack-ack breasts with stars pasted on the tips

will be swinging out over the slack jaws and cocked-up noses of patrons sitting at stageside at the Stardust. I am still listening to Gubser, but somehow it is a courthouse where mere words are beaten back like old atonal Arturo Toscanini trying to sing along with the NBC Symphony. There he would be, flapping his little toy arms like Tony Galento shadowboxing with fate, bawling away in the face of union musicians who drowned him without a bubble. I sat in on three trials in the courthouse, and it was wonderful, because the courtrooms are all blond-wood modern and look like sets for TV panel discussions on marriage and the teen-ager. What the judge has to say is no less formal and no more fatuous than what judges say everywhere, but inside of forty seconds it is all meaningless because the atmosphere is precisely like a news broadcast over Las Vegas' finest radio station, KORK. The newscast, as it is called, begins with a series of electronic wheeps out on that far edge of sound where only quadrupeds can hear. A voice then announces that this is Action Checkpoint News. "The news—all the news—flows first through Action Checkpoint!—then reaches You! at the speed of Sound!" More electronic wheeps, beeps and lulus, and then an item: "Cuban Premier Fidel Castro nearly drowned yesterday." Urp! Wheep! Lulu! No news a KORK announcer has ever brought to Las Vegas at the speed of sound, or could possibly bring, short of word of the annihilation of Los Angeles, could conceivably compete within the brain with the giddiness of this electronic jollification.

The wheeps, beeps, freeps, electronic lulus, Boomerang Modern and Flash Gordon sunbursts soar on through the night over the billowing hernia-hernia sounds and the old babes at the slots—until it is 7:30 A.M. and I am watching five men at a green-topped card table playing poker. They are sliding their Bee-brand cards into their hands and squinting at the pips with a set to the lips like Conrad Veidt in a tunic collar studying a code message from S.S. headquarters. Big Sid Wyman, the old Big-Time gambler from St. Louis, is there, with his eyes looking like two poached eggs engraved with a road map of West Virginia after all night at the poker table. Sixty-year-old Chicago Tommy Hargan is there with his topknot of white hair pulled back over his little pink skull and a mountain of chips in front of his old caved-in sternum. Sixty-two-year-old Dallas Maxie Welch is there, fat and phlegmatic as an Indian Ocean potentate. Two Los Angeles biggies are there exhaling smoke from candela-green cigars into the gloom. It looks like the perfect vignette of every Big Time back room, "athletic club," snooker house and floating poker game in the history of the guys-and-dolls lumpen-bourgeoisie. But what is all this? Off to the side, at a rostrum, sits a flawless little creature with bouffant hair and Stridex-pure skin who looks like she is polished each morning with a rotary buffer. Before her on the rostrum is a globe of coffee on a hot coil. Her sole job is to keep the poker players warmed up with coffee. Meantime, numberless uniformed lackeys are cocked and aimed about the edges to bring the five Big Timers whatever else they might desire, cigarettes, drinks, napkins, eyeglass-cleaning tissues, plug-in telephones. All around the poker table, at a respectful distance of ten feet, is a fence with the most delicate golden pickets. Upon it, even at this narcoleptic hour, lean men and women in their best clothes watch the combat of the titans. The scene is the charmed circle of the casino of the Dunes Hotel. As everyone there knows, or believes, these fabulous men are playing for table stakes of fifteen or twenty thousand dollars. One hundred dollars rides on a chip. Mandibles gape at the progress of the battle. And now Sidney Wyman, who is also a vice-president of the Dunes, is at a small escritoire just inside the golden fence signing a stack of vouchers for such sums as $4500, all printed in the heavy Mondrianesque digits of a Burroughs business check-making machine. It is as if America's guys-and-dolls gamblers have somehow been tapped upon the shoulders, knighted, initiated into a new aristocracy.

Las Vegas has become, just as Bugsy Siegel dreamed, the American Monte Carlo—without any of the inevitable upperclass baggage of the Riviera casinos. At Monte Carlo there is still the plush mustiness of the 19th century noble lions—of Baron Bleichroden, a big winner at roulette who always said, "My dear friends, it is so easy on Black." Of Lord Jersey, who won seventeen maximum bets in a row—on black, as a matter of fact—nodded to the croupier, and said, "Much obliged, old sport, old sport," took his winnings to England, retired to the country and never gambled again in his life. Or of the old Duc de Dinc who said he could win only in the high-toned Club Privé, and who won very heavily one night, saw two Englishmen gaping at his good fortune, threw them every mille-franc note he had in his hands and said, "Here. Englishmen without money are altogether odious." Thousands of Europeans from the lower orders now have the money to go to the Riviera, but they remain under the century-old status pall of the aristocracy. At Monte Carlo there are still Wrong Forks, Deficient Accents, Poor Tailoring, Gauche Displays, Nouveau Richness, Cultural Aridity—concepts unknown in Las Vegas. For the grand debut of Monte Carlo as a resort in 1879 the architect Charles Garnier designed an opera house for the Place du Casino; and Sarah Bernhardt read a symbolic poem. For the debut of Las Vegas as a resort in 1946 Bugsy Siegel hired Abbott and Costello, and there, in a way, you have it all.

I am in the office of Major A. Riddle—Major is his name—the president of the Dunes Hotel. He combs his hair straight back and wears a heavy gold band on his little finger with a diamond sunk into it. As everywhere else in Las Vegas, someone has turned on the air conditioning to the point where it will be remembered, all right, as Las Vegas-style air conditioning. Riddle has an appointment to see a doctor at 4:30 about a crimp in his neck.

His secretary, Maude McBride, has her head down and is rubbing the back of her neck. Lee Fisher, the P.R. man, and I are turning ours from time to time to keep the pivots from freezing up. Riddle is telling me about "the French war" and moving his neck gingerly. The Stardust bought and imported a version of the Lido de Paris spectacular, and the sight of all those sequined giblets pooning around on flamingo legs inflamed the tourists. The Tropicana fought back with the Folies Bergère, the New Frontier installed "Paree Ooh La La," the Hacienda reached for the puppets "Les Poupées de Paris," and the Silver Slipper called in Lili St. Cyr, the stripper, which was going French after a fashion. So the Dunes has bought up the third and last of the great Paris girlie shows, the Casino de Paris. Lee Fisher says, "And we're going to do things they *can't* top. In this town you've got to move ahead in quantum jumps."

Quantum? But exactly! The beauty of the Dunes' Casino de Paris show is that it will be beyond art, beyond dance, beyond spectacle, even beyond the titillations of the winking crotch. The Casino de Paris will be a behemoth piece of American calculus, like Project Mercury.

"This show alone will cost us two and a half million a year to operate and one and a half million to produce," Major A. Riddle is saying. "The costumes alone will be fantastic. There'll be more than five hundred costumes and—well, they'll be fantastic.

"And this machine—by the time we get through expanding the stage, this machine will cost us $250,000."

"Machine?"

"Yes. Sean Kenny is doing the staging. The whole set moves electronically right in front of your eyes. He used to work with this fellow Lloyd Wright."

"Frank Lloyd Wright?"

"Yes. Kenny did the staging for *Blitz*. Did you see it? Fantastic. Well, it's all done electronically. They built this machine for us in Glasgow, Scotland, and it's being shipped here right now. It moves all over the place and creates smoke and special effects. We'll have everything. You can stage a bombardment with it. You'll think the whole theatre is blowing up.

"You'll have to program it. They had to use the same mechanism that's in the Skybolt Missile to build it. It's called a 'Celson' or something like that. That's how complicated this thing is. They have to have the same thing as the Skybolt Missile."

As Riddle speaks, one gets a wonderful picture of sex riding the crest of the future. Whole tableaux of bare-bottomed Cosmonaughties will be hurtling around the Casino de Paris Room of the Dunes Hotel at fantastic speed in elliptical orbits, a flash of the sequined giblets here, a blur of the black-rimmed decal eyes there, a wink of the crotch here and there, until, with one vast Project Climax for our times, Sean Kenny, who used to work with this fellow, Frank Lloyd Wright, presses the red button and the whole yahooing harem, shrieking ooh-la-la amid the din, exits in a mushroom cloud.

The allure is most irresistible not to the young but the old. No one in Las Vegas will admit it—it is not the modern, glamorous notion—but Las Vegas is a resort for old people. In those last years, before the tissue deteriorates and the wires of the cerebral cortex hang in the skull like a clump of dried seaweed, they are seeking liberation.

At eight o'clock Sunday morning it is another almost boringly sunny day in the desert, and Clara and Abby, both about sixty, and their husbands, Earl, sixty-three, and Ernest, sixty-four, come squinting out of the Mint Casino onto Fremont Street.

"I don't know what's wrong with me," Abby says. "Those last three drinks, I couldn't even feel them. It was just like drinking fizz. You know what I mean?"

"Hey," says Ernest, "how about that place back 'ere? We ain't been back 'ere. Come on."

The others are standing there on the corner, squinting and looking doubtful. Abby and Clara have both entered old babehood. They have that fleshy, humped-over shape across the back of the shoulders. Their torsos are hunched up into fat little loaves supported by bony, atrophied leg stems sticking up into their hummocky hips. Their hair has been fried and dyed into improbable designs.

"You know what I mean? After a while it just gives me gas," says Abby. "I don't even feel it."

"Did you see me over there?" says Earl. "I was just going along, nice and easy, not too much, just riding along real nice. You know? And then, boy, I don't know what happened to me. First thing I know I'm laying down fifty dollars. . . ."

Abby lets out a great belch. Clara giggles.

"Gives me gas," Abby says mechanically.

"Hey, how about that place back 'ere?" says Ernest.

" . . . Just nice and easy as you please . . . "

"Aw, come on. . . . "

And there at eight o'clock Sunday morning stand four old parties from Albuquerque, New Mexico, up all night, squinting at the sun, belching from a surfeit of tall drinks at eight o'clock Sunday morning, and—marvelous!— there is no one around to snigger at what an old babe with decaying haunches looks like in Capri pants with her heels jacked up on decorated wedgies.

"Where do we *come* from?" Clara said to me, speaking for the first time since I approached them on Fremont Street. "He wants to know where we come from. I think it's past your bedtime, sweets."

"Climb the stairs and go to bed," said Abby.

Laughter all around.

"Climb the stairs" was Abby's finest line. At present there are almost no stairs to climb in Las Vegas. Avalon homes are soon to go up, advertising "Two-Story Homes!" as though this were an incredibly lavish and exotic concept. As I talked to Clara, Abby, Earl and Ernest, it came out that "climb the stairs" was a phrase they brought along to Albuquerque with them from Marshalltown, Iowa, those many years ago, along with a lot of other baggage, such as the entire cupboard of Protestant taboos against drinking, lusting, gambling, staying out late, getting up late, loafing, idling, lollygagging around the streets and wearing Capri pants—all designed to deny a person short-term pleasures so he will center his energies on bigger, long-term goals.

"We was in 'ere"—the Mint—"a couple of hours ago, and that old boy was playing the guitar, you know. 'Walk right in, set right down,' and I kept hearing an old song I haven't heard for twenty years. It has this little boy and his folks keep telling him it's late and he has to go to bed. He keeps saying, 'Don't make me go to bed and I'll be good.' Am I *good*, Earl? Am I *good*?"

The liberated cortex in all its glory is none other than the old babes at the slot machines. Some of them are tourists whose husbands said, *Here is fifty bucks, go play the slot machines*, while they themselves went off to more complex pleasures. But most of these old babes are part of the permanent landscape of Las Vegas. In they go to the Golden Nugget or the Mint, with their Social Security check or their pension check from the Ohio telephone company, cash it at the casino cashier's, pull out the Dixie Cup and the Iron Boy work glove, disappear down a row of slots and get on with it. I remember particularly talking to another Abby—a widow, sixty-two years old, built short and up from the bottom like a fire hydrant. After living alone for twelve years in Canton, Ohio, she had moved out to Las Vegas to live with her daughter and her husband, who worked for the Army.

"They were wonderful about it," she said. "Perfect hypocrites. She kept saying, you know, 'Mother, we'd be delighted to have you, only we don't think you'll *like* it. It's practically a fron*tier* town,' she says. 'It's so ga*rish*,' she says. So I said, I told her, 'Well, if you'd rather I didn't come. . . .' 'Oh, no!' she says. I wish I could have heard what her husband was saying. He calls me 'Mother.' 'Mo*ther*,' he says. Well, once I was here, they figured, well, I *might* make a good baby-sitter and dishwasher and duster and mopper. The children are nasty little things. So one day I was in town for something or other and I just played a slot machine. It's fun—I can't describe it to you. I suppose I lose. I lose a little. And *they* have fits about it. 'For God's sake, Grandmother,' and so forth. They always say '*Grand*mother' when I am supposed to 'act my age' or crawl through a crack in the floor. Well, I'll tell you, the slot machines are a *whole lot* better than sitting in that little house all day. They kind of get you; I can't explain it."

The childlike megalomania of gambling is, of course, from the same cloth as the megalomania of the town. And, as the children of the liberated cortex, the old guys and babes are running up and down the Strip around the clock like everybody else. It is not by chance that much of the entertainment in Las Vegas, especially the second-stringers who perform in the cocktail lounges, will recall for an aging man what was glamorous twenty-five years ago when he had neither the money nor the freedom of spirit to indulge himself in it. In the big theatre-dining room at the Desert Inn, The Painted Desert Room, Eddie Fisher's act is on and he is saying cozily to a florid guy at a table right next to the stage, "Manny, you know you shouldn'a sat this close—you know you're in for it now, Manny, baby," while Manny beams with fright. But in the cocktail lounge, where the idea is chiefly just to keep the razzle-dazzle going, there is Hugh Farr, one of the stars of another era in the West, composer of two of the five Western songs the Library of Congress has taped for posterity, "Cool Water" and "Tumbling Tumbleweed," when he played the violin for the Sons of the Pioneers. And now around the eyes he looks like an aging Chinese savant, but he is wearing a white tuxedo and powder-blue leather boots and playing his sad old Western violin with an electric cord plugged in it for a group called The Country Gentlemen. And there is Ben Blue, looking like a waxwork exhibit of vaudeville, doffing his straw skimmer to reveal the sculptural qualities of his skull. And down at the Flamingo cocktail lounge—Ella Fitzgerald is in the main room—there is Harry James, looking old and pudgy in one of those toy Italian-style show-biz suits. And the Ink Spots are at the New Frontier and Louis Prima is at the Sahara, and the old parties are seeing it all, roaring through the dawn into the next day, until the sun seems like a par lamp fading in and out. The casinos, the bars, the liquor stores are open every minute of every day, like a sempiternal wading pool for the childhood ego " . . . Don't make me go to bed. . . . "

Finally the casualties start piling up. I am in the manager's office of a hotel on the Strip. A man and his wife, each about sixty, are in there, raging. Someone got into their room and stole seventy dollars from her purse, and they want the hotel to make it up to them. The man pops up and down from a chair and ricochets back and forth across the room, flailing his great pig's-knuckle elbows about.

"What kind of security you call that? Walk right in the god-dern room and just help themselves. And where do you think I found your security man? Back around the corner reading a god-dern detective magazine!"

He had scored a point there, but he was wearing a striped polo shirt with a hip Hollywood solid-color collar, and she had on Capri pants, and hooked across their wrinkly old faces they both had rimless, wraparound French sunglasses of the sort young-punk heroes in *nouvelle vague* movies wear, and it was impossible to give any earnest contemplation to a word they said. They seemed to have the great shiny popeyes of a praying mantis.

"Listen, Mister," she is saying, "I don't care about the seventy bucks. I'd lose seventy bucks at your craps table and I wouldn't think nothing of it. I'd play seventy bucks just like that, and it wouldn't mean nothing. I wouldn't regret it. But when they can just walk in—and you don't give a damn—for Christ's sake!"

They are both zeroing in on the manager with their great insect corneas. The manager is a cool number in a white-on-white shirt and silver tie.

"This happened three days ago. Why didn't you tell us about it then?"

"Well, I was gonna be a nice guy about it. Seventy dollars," he said, as if it would be difficult for the brain to grasp a sum much smaller. "But then I found your man back there reading a god-dern detective magazine. *True Detectives* it was. Had a picture on the front of some floozie with one leg up on a chair and her garter showing. Looked like a god-derned athlete's-foot ad. Boy, I went into a slow burn. But when I am burned up, I am *burned up!* You get me, Mister? There he was, reading the god-derned *True Detectives.*"

"Any decent hotel would have insurance," she says.

The manager says, "I don't know a hotel in the world that offers insurance against theft."

"Hold on, Mister," he says, "are you calling my wife a liar? You just get smart, and I'm gonna pop you one! I'll pop you one right now if you call my wife a liar."

At this point the manager lowers his head to one side and looks up at the old guy from under his eyebrows with a version of the Red Hook brushoff, and the old guy begins to cool off.

But others are beyond cooling off. Hornette Reilly, a buttery hipped whore from New York City, is lying in bed with a bald-headed guy from some place who has skin like oatmeal. He is asleep or passed out or something. Hornette is relating all this to the doctor over the Princess telephone by the bed.

"Look," she says, "I'm breaking up. I can't tell you how much I've drunk. About a bottle of brandy since four o'clock, I'm not kidding. I'm in bed with a guy. Right this minute. I'm talking on the telephone to you and this slob is lying here like an animal. He's all fat and his skin looks like oatmeal—what's happening to me? I'm going to take some more pills. I'm not kidding, I'm breaking up. I'm going to kill myself. You've got to put me in Rose de Lima. I'm breaking up, and I don't even know what's happening to me."

"So naturally you want to go to Rose de Lima."

"Well, yeah."

"You can come by the office, but I'm not sending you to Rose de Lima."

"Doctor, I'm not kidding."

"I don't doubt that you're sick, old girl, but I'm not sending you to Rose de Lima to sober up."

The girls do not want to go to the County Hospital. They want to go to Rose de Lima, where the psychiatric cases receive milieu therapy. The patients dress in street clothes, socialize and play games with the staff, eat well and relax in the sun, all paid for by the State. One of the folk heroines of the Las Vegas floozies, apparently, is the call girl who last year was spending Monday through Friday at Rose de Lima and "turning out," as they call it, Saturdays and Sundays on the Strip, to the tune of $200 to $300 a weekend. She looks upon herself not as a whore, or even a call girl, but as a lady of assignation. When some guy comes to the Strip and unveils the little art-nouveau curves in his psyche and calls for two girls to perform arts upon one another, this one consents to be the passive member of the team only. A Rose de Lima girl, she draws the line.

At the County Hospital the psychiatric ward is latched, bolted, wired up and jammed with patients who are edging along the walls in the inner hall, the only place they have to take a walk other than the courtyard.

A big brunette with the remnants of a beehive hairdo and decal eyes and an obvious pregnancy is the liveliest of the lot. She is making eyes at everyone who walks in. She also nods gaily toward vacant places along the wall.

"Mrs. _____ is refusing medication," a nurse tells one of the psychiatrists. "She won't even open her mouth."

Presently the woman, in a white hospital tunic, is led up the hall. She looks about fifty, but she has extraordinary lines on her face.

"Welcome home," says Dr. _____.

"This is not my home," she says.

"Well, as I told you before, it has to be for the time being."

"Listen, you didn't analyze me."

"Oh, yes. Two psychiatrists examined you—all over again."

"You mean that time in jail."

"Exactly."

"You can't tell anything from that. I was excited. I had been out on the Strip, and then all that stupid—"

Three-fourths of the 640 patients who clustered into the ward last year were casualties of the Strip or the Strip milieu of Las Vegas, the psychiatrist tells me. He is a bright and energetic man in a shawl-collared black silk suit with brass buttons.

"I'm not even her doctor," he says. "I don't know her case. There's nothing I can do for her."

Here, securely out of sight, in this little warren, are all those who have taken the loop-the-loop and could not stand the centripety. Some, like Raymond, who has been rocketing for days on pills and liquor, who has gone without sleep to the point of anoxia, might pull out of the toxic reaction in two or three days, or eight or ten. Others have conflicts to add to the chemical wackiness. A man who has thrown all his cash to the flabby homunculus who sits at every craps table stuffing the take down an almost hidden chute so it won't pile up in front of the customers' eyes; a man who has sold the family car for next to nothing at a car lot advertising "Cash for your car—*right now*" and then thrown that to the homunculus, too, but also still has the family waiting guiltlessly, guilelessly back home; well, he has troubles.

". . . After I came here and began doing personal studies," the doctor is saying, "I recognized extreme aggressiveness continually. It's not merely what Las Vegas can do to a person, it's the type of person it attracts. Gambling is a very aggressive pastime, and Las Vegas attracts aggressive people. They have an amazing capacity to louse up a normal situation."

The girl, probably a looker in more favorable moments, is pressed face into the wall, cutting glances at the doctor. The nurse tells her something and she puts her face in her hands, convulsing but not making a sound. She retreats to her room, and then the sounds come shrieking out. The doctor rushes back. Other patients are sticking their heads out of their rooms along the hall.

"The young girl?" a quiet guy says to a nurse. "The young girl," he says to somebody in the room.

But the big brunette just keeps rolling her decal eyes.

Out in the courtyard—all bare sand—the light is a kind of light-bulb twilight. An old babe is rocking herself back and forth on a straight chair and putting one hand out in front from time to time and pulling it in toward her bosom.

It seems clear enough to me. "A slot machine?" I say to the nurse, but she says there is no telling.

". . . and yet the same aggressive types are necessary to build a frontier town, and Las Vegas is a frontier town, certainly by any psychological standard," Dr. _____ is saying. "They'll undertake anything and they'll accomplish it. The building here has been incredible. They don't seem to care what they're up against, so they do it."

I go out to the parking lot in back of the County Hospital and it doesn't take a second; as soon as I turn on the motor I'm swinging again with Action Checkpoint News, "Monkey No. 9," "Donna, Donna, the Prima Donna," and friendly picking and swinging for the Fremont Hotel and Frontier Federal. Me and my big white car are sailing down the strip and the Boomerang Modern, Palette Curvilinear, Flash Gordon Ming-Alert Spiral, McDonald's Hamburger Parabola, Mint Casino Elliptical and Miami Beach Kidney sunbursts are exploding in the Young Electric Sign Company's Grand Gallery for all the sun kings. At the airport there was that bad interval between the rental-car stall and the terminal entrance, but once through the automatic door the Muzak came bubbling up with "Song of India." On the upper level around the ramps the slots were cranking away. They are placed like "traps," a word Las Vegas picked up from golf. And an old guy is walking up the ramp, just off the plane from Denver, with a huge plastic bag of clothes slung over the left shoulder and a two-suiter suitcase in his right hand. He has to put the suitcase down on the floor and jostle the plastic bag all up around his neck to keep it from falling, but he manages to dig into his pocket for a couple of coins and get going on the slot machines. All seems right, but walking out to my plane I sense that something is missing. Then I recall sitting in the cocktail lounge of the Dunes at 3 P.M. with Jack Heskett, district manager of the Federal Sign and Signal Corporation, and Marty Steinman, the sales manager, and Ted Blaney, a designer. They are telling me about the sign they are building for the Dunes to put up at the airport. It will will be five thousand square feet of free-standing sign, done in flaming-lake red on burning-desert gold. The d—the D—alone in the word Dunes, written in Cyrillic modern, will be practically two stories high. An inset plexiglas display, the largest revolving, trivision plexiglas sign in the world, will turn and show first the Dunes, with its twenty-two-story addition, then the seahorse swimming pool, then the new golf course. The scimitar curves of the sign will soar to a huge roaring diamond at the very top. "You'll be able to see it from an airplane fifteen miles away," says Jack Heskett. "Fifty miles," says Lee Fisher. And it will be sixty-five feet up in the air—because the thing was, somebody was out at the airport and they noticed there was only one display to be topped. That was that shaft about sixty feet high with the lit-up globe and the beacon lights, which is to say, the control tower. Hell, you can only see that forty miles away. But exactly!

Questions for Discussion

1. Is the first paragraph in this essay effective? Explain your answer.
2. As briefly as possible, state Wolfe's main point in this essay. (It might help you to know that the essay on Las Vegas comes from "The New Culture-Makers," a section of *The Kandy-Kolored Tangerine-Flake Streamline Baby*.)
3. What is Wolfe's attitude toward Las Vegas? How do you know?
4. The essay is full of sense images: sights and sounds. What are some of the most vivid? Why are these images important to the point of the essay? Could Wolfe have accomplished his purpose if he had written less imagistically?
5. If you find the section on "the old babes at the slot machines" offensive, explain why. When the essay was first published in *Esquire* in the

1960s, why would it not have been as likely to offend as it is today? Explain.

6. In what ways is this essay different from the conventional journalism you find in newspapers and news magazines?

7. Explain why it would be justified to claim that one of the main theses comes at the end of the essay with "But exactly" as a response to the statement that the Dunes sign will be larger than the airport control tower.

8. Wolfe gives us various scenes of Las Vegas. Discuss which scenes seem to capture the city's atmosphere best for you and explain what details you find especially effective.

9. What *foreshadows* the second-to-last scene, which takes place in the mental ward of a hospital?

10. Wolfe writes that Raymond, the character who hears "Hernia," was beginning to isolate the components of Las Vegas's "unique bombardment of the senses." Find passages that bombard your senses and that, thus, make Wolfe's point more effective.

(DR.) HUNTER S. THOMPSON
(alias Raoul Duke alias Sebastian Owl)

*You have probably already been introduced to Hunter Thompson, for
he is the original of the character Duke in the comic strip
Doonesbury. Born in 1939, the son of a Louisville, Kentucky
insurance agent, Thompson attended public schools in Louisville. He
has been Caribbean correspondent for the* New York Herald Tribune,
South American correspondent for the National Observer, *and
national affairs editor for* Rolling Stone. *From 1956 to 1958, he
served in the U.S. Air Force.*

*One could never accuse Thompson of small-minded consistency.
An anarchist, he is a member of the American Civil Liberties Union*
and *the National Rifle Association, as well as the Overseas Press
Club.*

Published in 1966, Hell's Angels, *from which this selection is
taken, was Thompson's first book. Among his other books in which
you might be interested are* Fear and Loathing in Las Vegas, Fear and
Loathing on the Campaign Trail 1972, *and* The Great Shark Hunt.

*In reading this selection try to answer this question: How
would you describe the author's attitude toward his subject? As you
will see, Thompson's reaction to the Hell's Angels is complex.*

Roll 'em boys

On the morning of the Monterey Run, Labor Day 1964, Terry the Tramp woke up naked and hurting all over. The night before he'd been stomped and chain-whipped outside an Oakland bar by nine Diablos, a rival East Bay cycle club. "I'd hit one of their members earlier," he explained, "and they didn't appreciate it. I was with two other Angels, but they left a little bit before me, and as soon as they were gone, these bastard Diablos jumped me outside the bar. They messed me up pretty good, so we spent half the night lookin for em."

The search was futile, and just before dawn Terry went back to Scraggs' small house in San Leandro, where he was living with his wife and two children. Scraggs, a thirty-seven-year-old ex-pug who once fought Bobo Olson, was the oldest Angel then riding, with a wife and two children of his own. But when Terry came down from Sacramento that summer to look for a job in the Bay Area, Scraggs offered bed and board. The two wives got along; the kids meshed, and Terry found a job on the assembly line at a nearby General Motors plant—in itself a tribute to whatever human flexibility remains at the shop level in the American labor movement, for Terry at a glance looks hopelessly unemployable, like a cross between Joe Palooka and the Wandering Jew.

He is six feet two inches tall, 210 pounds heavy, with massive arms, a full beard, shoulder-length black hair and a wild, jabbering demeanor not calculated to soothe the soul of any personnel specialist. Beyond that, in his twenty-seven years he has piled up a tall and ugly police record: a multitude of arrests, from petty theft and battery, to rape, narcotics offenses and public cunnilingus—and all this without a single felony conviction, being officially guilty of nothing more than what any spirited citizen might commit in some drunk or violent moment of animal weakness.

"Yeah, but that rap sheet's all bullshit," he insists. "Most of those charges are phony. I've never thought of myself as a criminal. I don't work at it; I'm not greedy enough. Everything I do is natural, because I need to." And then after a moment: "But I guess I'm pushin my luck, even if I'm not a criminal. Pretty soon they'll nail me for one of these goddamn things, and then it's goodbye, Terry, for a whole lot of years. I think it's about time I cut out, went East, maybe to New York, or Australia. You know, I had a card in Actor's Equity once, I lived in Hollywood. Hell, I can make it anywhere, even if I am a fuck-up."

On another Saturday he might have slept until two or three in the afternoon, then gone out again, with a dozen or so of the brethren, to find the Diablos and whip them down to jelly. But a Labor Day Run is the biggest event on the Hell's Angels calendar; it is the annual gathering of the whole outlaw clan, a massive three-day drunk that nearly always results in some wild, free-swinging action and another rude shock for the squares. No Angel would miss it for any reason except jail or crippling injury. The Labor Day Run is the outlaws' answer to New Year's Eve; it is a time for sharing the wine jug, pummeling old friends, random fornication and general full-dress madness. Depending on the weather and how many long-distance calls are made the week before, anywhere from two hundred to a thousand outlaws will show up, half of them already drunk by the time they get there.

By nine o'clock that morning both Terry and Scraggs were on their feet. Vengeance on the Diablos could wait. Today, the run. Terry lit a cigarette, examined the bumps and welts on his body, then pulled on a pair of crusty Levis, heavy black boots, no underwear and a red sweatshirt smelling of old wine and human grease. Scraggs drank a beer while his wife heated water for instant coffee. The children had been put with relatives the night before. The sun was hot outside. Across the Bay, San Francisco was still covered in a late-lifting fog. The bikes were gassed and polished. All that remained was the gathering of any loose money or marijuana that might be lying around, lashing the sleeping bags to the bikes and donning the infamous "colors." . . .

Terry and Scraggs left the house about ten, taking it easy on the two-mile run through downtown Oakland, keeping the engine noise down, aware of the stares from passing motorists and people on street corners, observing stop signs and speed limits, then suddenly accelerating a half block from the house of Tommy, vice-president of the local chapter, where the others were waiting. Tommy was living on a quiet, deteriorating residential street in East Oakland . . . an old neighborhood with small, once-white frame houses sitting close to each other on tiny lots and sparse front lawns worn down by generations of newsboys delivering the *Oakland Tribune*. Now, on this holiday morning, his neighbors were out on front porches or at living-room windows, watching the awful show build up. By eleven about thirty Hell's Angels were there, half blocking the narrow street, shouting, drinking beer, brushing green dye on their beards, gunning their engines, adjusting their costumes and knocking each other around to get the feel of things. The girls stood quietly in a group, wearing tight slacks, kerchiefs and sleeveless blouses or sweaters with boots and dark glasses, uplift bras, bright lipstick and the wary expressions of half-bright souls turned mean and nervous from too much bitter wisdom in too few years. Like the Angels, the girls were mainly in their twenties—although some were obvious teen-agers and a few were aging whores looking forward to a healthy outdoor weekend.

In any gathering of Hell's Angels, from five to a possible hundred and fifty, there is no doubt who is running the show: Ralph "Sonny" Barger, the Maximum Leader, a six-foot, 170-pound warehouseman from East Oakland, the coolest head in the lot, and a tough, quick-thinking dealer when any action starts. By turns he is a fanatic, a philosopher, a brawler, a shrewd compromiser and a final arbitrator. To the Oakland Angels he is Ralph. Everybody else calls him Sonny . . . although when the party gets wild and loose he answers to names such as Prez, Papa and Daddy. Barger's word goes unquestioned, although many of the others could take him in two minutes if it ever came to a fight. But it never does. He rarely raises his voice—except in a rumble with outsiders. Any dissenters in the ranks are handled quietly at the regular Friday-night meetings, or they simply fade out of the picture and change their life patterns so as never again to cross paths with any group of Angels.

If the gathering at Tommy's was a little disorganized, it was because Sonny was serving time in the Santa Rita Rehabilitation Center, for possession of marijuana. With Sonny in jail, the others were keeping the action to a minimum—even though Tommy, in his quiet, disaffiliated sort of way, was running the show pretty well. At twenty-six he was a year younger than Barger: blond, clean-shaven, with a wife and two children, making $180 a week as a construction worker. He knew he was only filling in for the Prez, but he also knew that the Oakland Angels had to make a tough, full-strength appearance at the Labor Day Run. Anything less would forfeit the spiritual leadership back to southern California, to the San Bernardino (or Berdoo) chapter—the founding fathers, as it were—who started the whole thing in 1950 and issued all new charters for nearly fifteen years. But mounting police pressure in the south was causing many Angels to seek refuge in the Bay Area. By 1965, Oakland was on its way to becoming the capital of the Hell's Angels' world.

Prior to their ear-splitting departure, there was a lot of talk about the Diablos and what manner of lunacy or strange drug had caused them to commit such a sure-fatal error as an attack on a lone Angel. Yet this was a routine beef, postponed‡ and forgotten as they moved onto the freeway for an easy two-hour run to Monterey. By noon it was so

---

‡Within a month the Diablos had disbanded—terrorized by a series of stompings, beatings and chain-whippings; the Angels hunted them down one by one and did them in. "Things like that don't happen very often," Terry explained later. "Other clubs don't usually mess with us, because when they do, that's the end of them."

hot that many of the riders had taken off their shirts and opened their black vests, so the colors flapped out behind them like capes and the on-coming traffic could view their naked chests, for good or ill. The southbound lanes were crowded with taxpayers heading out for a Labor Day weekend that suddenly seemed tinged with horror as the Angel band swept past . . . this animal crowd on big wheels, going somewhere public, all noise and hair and bust-out raping instincts . . . the temptation for many a motorist was to swing hard left, with no warning, and crush these arrogant scorpions.

At San Jose, an hour south of Oakland, the formation was stopped by two state Highway Patrolmen, causing a traffic jam for forty-five minutes at the junction of 17 and 101. Some people stopped their cars entirely, just to watch. Others slowed to ten or fifteen miles an hour. As traffic piled up, there were vapor locks, boil-overs and minor collisions.

"They wrote tickets for everybody they could," said Terry. "Things like seats too low, bars too high, no mirror, no hand hold for the passenger—and like always they checked us for old warrants, citations we never paid and every other goddamm thing they could think of. But the traffic was really piling up, with people staring at us and all, and finally, by God, a Highway Patrol captain showed up and chewed those bastards good for 'creating a hazard' or whatever he called it. We had a big laugh, then we took off again."

> We get treated good here (in Monterey). Most other places we get thrown out of town.
> —Frenchy from Berdoo talking to a reporter not many hours before the Angels were thrown out of town

Between San Jose and the turnoff to Monterey, 101 rolls gracefully through the rich farming foothills of the Santa Cruz Mountains. The Hell's Angels, riding two abreast in each lane, seemed out of place in little towns like Coyote and Gilroy. People ran out of taverns and dry-goods stores to stare at these fabled big-city Huns. Local cops waited nervously at intersections, hoping the Angels would pass quietly and not cause trouble. It was almost as if some far-ranging band of Viet Cong guerrillas had appeared, trotting fast in a tight formation down the middle of Main Street, bound for some bloody rendezvous that nobody in town even cared to know about as long as the dirty buggers kept moving.

The Angels try to avoid trouble on the road. Even a minor arrest in a country town at the start of a holiday weekend can mean three days in jail, missing the party, and a maximum fine when they finally come to court. They know, too, that in addition to the original charge—usually a traffic violation or disorderly conduct—they will probably be accused of resisting arrest, which can mean thirty days, a jail haircut and another fine of $150 or so. Now, after many a painful lesson, they approach small towns the same way a traveling salesman from Chicago approaches a known speed trap in Alabama. The idea, after all, is to reach the destination—not to lock horns with hayseed cops along the way.

The destination this time was a big tavern called Nick's, a noisy place on a main drag called Del Monte, near Cannery Row in downtown Monterey. "We went right through the middle of town," recalls Terry, "through the traffic and everything. Most of the guys knew Nick's but not me because I was in jail the other time. We didn't make it till about three because we had to wait in a gas station on 101 for some of the guys running late. By the time we got there I guess we had about forty or fifty bikes. Berdoo was already in with about seventy-five, and people kept coming all night. By the next morning there were about three hundred from all over."

The stated purpose of the gathering was the collection of funds to send the body of a former Angel back to his mother in North Carolina. Kenneth "Country" Beamer, vice-president of the San Bernardino chapter, had been snuffed by a truck a few days earlier in a desert hamlet called Jacumba, near San Diego. Country had died in the best outlaw tradition: homeless, stone broke, and owning nothing in this world but the clothes on his back and a big bright Harley. As the others saw it, the least they could do was send his remains back to the Carolinas, to whatever family or memory of a home might be there. "It was the thing to do," Terry said.

The recent demise of a buddy lent the '64 affair a tone of solemnity that not even the police could scoff at. It was the sort of gesture that cops find irresistible: final honors for a fallen comrade, with a collection for the mother and a bit of the uniformed pageantry to make the show real. In deference to all this, the Monterey police had let it be known that they would receive the Angels in a spirit of armed truce.

It was the first time in years that the outlaws had been faced with even a semblance of civic hospitality—and it turned out to be the last, for when the sun came up on that bright Pacific Saturday the infamous Monterey rape was less than twenty-four hours away from making nationwide headlines. The Hell's Angels would soon be known and feared throughout the land. Their blood, booze and semen-flecked image would be familiar to readers of *The New York Times*, *Newsweek*, *The Nation*, *Time*, *True*, *Esquire* and the *Saturday Evening Post*. Within six months small towns from coast to coast would be arming themselves at the slightest rumor of a Hell's Angels "invasion." All three major television networks would be seeking them out with cameras and they would be denounced in the U.S. Senate by George Murphy, the former tap dancer. Weird as it seems, as this gang of costumed hoodlums converged on Monterey that morning they were on the verge of "making it big," as the showbiz people say, and they would owe most of their success to a curious rape mania that rides on the shoulder of American journalism like some jeering, masturbating raven. Nothing grabs an editor's eye like a good rape. "We really blew their minds this time," as one of the Angels explained it. According to the newspapers, at least twenty of these dirty hopheads snatched two teen-age girls, aged fourteen and fifteen, away from their terrified dates, and carried them off to the sand dunes to be "repeatedly assaulted."

REPEATEDLY . . . ASSAULTED

AGED 14 AND 15 . . .

STINKING, HAIRY THUGS

A deputy sheriff summoned by one of the erstwhile dates said he "arrived at the beach and saw a huge bonfire surrounded by cyclists of both sexes. Then the two sobbing, near-hysterical girls staggered out of the darkness, begging for help. One was completely nude and the other had on only a torn sweater."

Here, sweet Jesus, was an image flat guaranteed to boil the public blood and foam the brain of every man with female flesh for kin. Two innocent young girls, American citizens, carried off to the dunes and ravaged like Arab whores. One of the dates told police they tried to rescue the girls but couldn't reach them in the mobscene that erupted once the victims were stripped of their clothing. Out there in the sand, in the blue moonlight, in a circle of leering hoodlums . . . they were penetrated again and again.

The next morning Terry the Tramp was one of four Angels arrested for forcible rape, which carries a penalty of one to fifty years in the penitentiary. He denied all knowledge of the crime, as did Mother Miles, Mouldy Marvin and Crazy Cross—but several hours later, with bond set at a lowly $1,100 each, they were lodged in the Monterey County Jail in Salinas . . . out there in Steinbeck country, the hot lettuce valley, owned in the main by smart second-generation hillbillies who got out of Appalachia while the getting was good, and who now pay other, less-smart hillbillies to supervise the work of Mexican *braceros*, whose natural fitness for stoop labor has been explained by the ubiquitous Senator Murphy: "They're built low to the ground," he said, "so it's easier for them to stoop."

Indeed. And since Senator Murphy has also called the Hell's Angels "the lowest form of animals," it presumably follows that they are better constructed for the mindless rape of any prostrate woman they might come across as they scurry about from one place to another, with their dorks carried low like water wands. Which is not far from the truth, but for different reasons than California's ex-lightfoot senator might have us believe.

Nobody knew, of course, as they gathered that Saturday at Nick's, that the Angels were about to make a publicity breakthrough, by means of rape, on the scale of the Beatles or Bob Dylan. At dusk, with an orange sun falling fast into the ocean just a mile or so away, the main event of the evening was so wholly unplanned that the principal characters—or victims—attracted little attention in the noisy crowd that jammed Nick's barroom and spilled out to the darkening street.

Terry says he noticed the girls and their "dates" only as part of the overall scene. "The main reason I remember them is I wondered what that white pregnant girl was doing with a bunch of suede dudes. But I figured it was her business, and I wasn't hurtin for pussy anyway. I had my old lady with me—we're separated now, but then we were doin okay and she wouldn't have none of me hustlin anything else while she was around. Besides, hell, when you're seein old friends you haven't seen in a year or two, you don't have time to pay attention to strangers."

The only thing Terry and all the other Angels agree on—in relation to the "victims," first appearance—is that "they sure as hell didn't look no fourteen and fifteen, man; those girls looked every bit of twenty." (Police later confirmed the girls' ages, but all other information about them—including their names—was withheld in accordance with California's policy of denying press access to rape victims.)

"I can't even say if those girls were pretty or not," Terry went on. "I just don't remember. All I can say for sure is that we didn't have no trouble at Nick's. The cops were there, but only to keep people away. It was the same old story as every place else we go: traffic piling up on the street outside, local bad-asses prowling around, young girls looking for kicks, and a bunch of Nick's regular customers just digging the party. The cops did right by staying around. Everywhere we go there's some local hoods who want to find out how tough we are. If the cops weren't there we'd end up having to hurt somebody. Hell, nobody wants trouble on a run. All we want to do is to have some fun and relax."

It is said, however, that the Hell's Angels have some offbeat ideas about fun and relaxation. If they are, after all, "the lowest form of animals," not even Senator Murphy could expect them to gather together in a drunken mass for any such elevated pastimes as ping pong, shuffleboard and whist. Their picnics have long been noted for certain beastly forms of entertainment, and any young girl who shows up at a

Hell's Angels bonfire camp at two o'clock in the morning is presumed, by the outlaws, to be in a condition of heat. So it was only natural that the two girls attracted more attention when they arrived at the beach than they had earlier in the convivial bedlam at Nick's.

One aspect of the case overlooked in most newspaper accounts had to do with elementary logistics. How did these two young girls happen to be on a deserted midnight beach with several hundred drunken motorcycle thugs? Were they kidnapped from Nick's? And if so, what were they doing there in the first place, aged fourteen and fifteen, circulating all evening in a bar jammed wall to wall with the state's most notorious gang of outlaws? Or were they seized off the street somewhere—perhaps at a stoplight—to be slung over the gas tank of a bored-out Harley and carried off into the night, screaming hysterically, while bystanders gaped in horror?

Police strategists, thinking to isolate the Angels, had reserved them a campsite far out of town, on an empty stretch of dunes between Monterey Bay and Fort Ord, an Army basic-training center. The reasoning was sound; the beasts were put off in a place where they could whip themselves into any kind of orgiastic frenzy without becoming dangerous to the citizenry—and if things got out of hand, the recruits across the road could be bugled out of bed and issued bayonets. The police posted a guard on the highway, in case the Angels got restless and tried to get back to town, but there was no way to seal the camp off entirely, nor any provision for handling local innocents who might be drawn to the scene out of curiosity or other, darker reasons not mentioned in police training manuals.

The victims told police they had gone to the beach because they "wanted to look at the cyclists." They were curious—even after several hours at Nick's, which was so crowded that evening that most of the outlaws took to pissing in the parking lot rather than struggle inside to the bathroom.

"Hell, those broads didn't come out there for any singsong," said Terry. "They were loaded and they wanted to get off some leg, but it just got to be too many guys. To start with, it was groovy for em. Then more and more guys came piling over the dunes . . . 'yea, pussy,' you know, that kinda thing . . . and the broads didn't want it. The suede dudes just split; we never saw em again. I don't know for sure how it ended. All I knew then was that they had some mamas out there in the dunes, but me and my old lady went and crashed pretty early. I was so wasted I couldn't even make it with her."

No family newspaper saw fit to quote the Angel version, but six months later, playing pool in a San Francisco bar, Frenchy remembered it this way: "One girl was white and pregnant, the other was colored, and they were with five colored studs. They hung around Nick's about three hours on Saturday night, drinking and talking with our riders, then they came out to the beach with us—them and their five boy friends. Everybody was standing around the fire, drinking wine, and some of the guys were talking to them—hustling em, naturally—and pretty soon somebody asked the two chicks if they wanted to be turned on—you know, did they want to smoke some pot? They said yeah, and then they walked off with some of the guys to the dunes. The spade went with a few guys, and then she wanted to quit, but the pregnant one was really hot to trot; the first four or five guys she was really draggin into her arms, but after that she cooled off too. By this time, though, one of their boy friends had got scared and gone for the cops— and that's all it was."

"The next morning," said Terry, "I rode in with somebody—I forget who—to some drive-in on the highway, where we got some breakfast. When we got back to the beach they had a roadblock set up with those two broads sittin there in the cop car, lookin at everybody. I didn't know what was goin on, but then a cop said, 'You're one,' and they slapped the cuffs on me. Those goddamn girls were gigglin, righteously laughin . . . you know, 'Ha ha, thats one of em.' So off I went to the bucket, for rape.

"When we got to the jail I said, 'Hey, I want to be checked. Let's see a doctor. I ain't had no intercourse in two days.' But they wouldn't go for it. Marvin and Miles and Crazy Cross were already there and we figured we were deep in the shit until they told us bail was only eleven hundred dollars. Then we knew they didn't have much of a case."

Meanwhile, out on Marina Beach, the rest of the Angels were being rounded up and driven north along Highway 156 toward the county line. Laggards were thumped on the shoulders with billy clubs and told to get moving. Side roads were blocked by state troopers while dozens of helmeted deputies—many from neighboring counties—ran the outlaws through the gauntlet. Traffic was disrupted for miles as the ragged horde moved slowly along the road, gunning their engines and raining curses on everything in sight. The noise was deafening and it is hard to imagine what effect the spectacle must have had on the dozens of out-of-state late-summer tourists who pulled over to let the procession come through. Because of the proximity of an Army base, they undoubtedly thought they were making way for a caravan of tanks, or at least something impressive and military—and then to see an army of hoodlums being driven along the road like a herd of diseased sheep—ah, what a nightmare for the California Chamber of Commerce.

At the county line on U.S. 101 a reporter from the *San Francisco Chronicle* talked with Tommy, and with another Angel, named Tiny, a six-foot-six, 240-pound outlaw with a shoulder-length pigtail who later gained nationwide fame for his attack on a Get Out of Vietnam demonstration in Berkeley.

"We're ordinary guys," said Tommy. "Most of us work. About half are married, I guess, and a few own their homes. Just because we like to ride motorcycles, the cops give us trouble everywhere we go. That rape charge is phony and it won't stick. The whole thing was voluntary."

"Shit, our bondsman will have those guys out in two hours," said Tiny. "Why can't people let us alone, anyway? All we want to do is get together now and then and have some fun—just like the Masons, or any other group."

But the presses were already rolling and the eight-column headline said: HELL'S ANGELS GANG RAPE. The Masons haven't had that kind of publicity since the eighteenth century, when Casanova was climbing through windows and giving the brotherhood a bad name. Perhaps the Angels will one day follow the Freemasons into bourgeois senility, but by then some other group will be making outrage headlines: a Hovercraft gang, or maybe some once-bland fraternal group tooling up even now for whatever the future might force on them.

What is the trend in Kiwanis? There are rumors in Oakland of a new militancy in that outfit, a radical ferment that could drastically alter the club's image. In the drift and flux of these times it is easy enough to foresee a Sunday morning, ten or twenty years hence, when a group of middle-aged men wearing dark blazers with Hell's Angels crests on the pockets will be pacing their mortgaged living rooms and muttering sadly at a headline saying: KIWANIS GANG RAPE: FOUR HELD, OTHERS FLEE, RINGLEADERS SOUGHT.

And in some shocked American city a police chief will be saying— as the Monterey chief said in 1964 of the Hell's Angels—"They will not be welcomed back, because of the atmosphere created."

Questions for Discussion

1. Here is a sentence from Hunter Thompson's account of the Monterey run:

   Terry and Scraggs left the house about ten, taking it easy on the two-mile run through downtown Oakland, keeping the engine noise down, aware of the stares from passing motorists and people on street corners, observing stop signs and speed limits, then suddenly accelerating a half block from the house of Tommy, vice-president of the local chapter, where the others were waiting.

This sixty-two-word sentence can be broken up into several shorter sentences, as follows:

Terry and Scraggs left the house about ten. They took it easy on the two-mile run through downtown Oakland. They kept the engine noise down. They were aware of the stares from passing motorists and people on street corners. They observed stop signs and speed limits. Then suddenly they accelerated a half block from the house of Tommy. He was vice-president of the local chapter. The others were waiting there.

Which version is easier to read? Which version sounds more like the writing of a skilled professional? In explaining your answers to these questions, you need not resort to fancy grammatical terminology.

2. What is Hunter Thompson's attitude toward the Hell's Angels? (Is he sympathetic? Hostile? Indifferent?) What is his attitude toward former California Senator George Murphy? To support and explain your answer, refer to the text. Which passages led you to your conclusions?

3. In one sentence, state the main point of Hunter Thompson's account of the Monterey run.

4. What is Hunter Thompson's feeling about the future of American society? Explain how you know. (Pay close attention to the last few paragraphs of the text.)

5. Thompson explains that half of the Hell's Angels are married, some have children, and others work on respectable jobs. Why do you think he does this? How does this relate to his coverage of the rape?

6. Many people think Hunter Thompson's works are often hilariously funny. Point out instances of humor in this selection. (What insight does the humor give you into the nature of the Hell's Angels?)

7. In what ways are the Hell's Angels a good subject for a piece of writing?

MICHAEL HERR

Michael Herr wrote the narration for "Apocalypse Now," the Francis Ford Coppola and John Milius film about the Vietnam War. He spoke from experience, for he had been an Esquire *correspondent in Vietnam in 1967. He has published articles in* Rolling Stone, Esquire, *and* New American Review.

Dispatches, from which this selection was taken, was published in 1977. The book was termed "convulsively brilliant," "nightmarish," and "awesome." Certainly it ranks with the great American novels The Naked and the Dead *and* The Red Badge of Courage *as an account of what war means. It is generally considered the best account of the Vietnam War.*

This selection and "Gear," which follows immediately, can be termed "character sketches," portraits in prose of individual persons who represent whole classes. The character sketch is, in a way, a case study. Through a case study we learn about whole groups of people: their values, their life-styles, and their place in the culture. As you read, think about the kind of person Page symbolizes. At the very least, he is the opposite of the Marine "grunt" who slogged through the jungles and followed orders.

That was also the week that Page came back. . . .

That was also the week that Page came back to Vietnam. *A Scrambler to the Front* by Tim Page, *Tim Page* by Charles Dickens. He came a few days before it started, and people who knew about his luck were making jokes blaming the whole thing on his return. There were more young, politically radical, wigged-out crazies running around Vietnam than anybody ever realized; between all of the grunts turning on and tripping out on the war and the substantial number of correspondents who were doing the same thing, it was an authentic subculture. There were more than enough within the press corps to withstand a little pressure from the upright, and if Flynn was the most sophisticated example of this, Page was the most extravagant. I'd heard about him even before I came to Vietnam ("Look him up. If he's still alive"), and between the time I got there and the time he came back in May, I'd heard so much about him that I might have felt that I knew him if so many people hadn't warned me, "There's just no way to describe him for you. Really, no way."

"Page? That's easy. Page is a child."

"No, man, Page is just crazy."

"Page is a crazy child."

They'd tell all kinds of stories about him, sometimes working up a passing anger over things he'd done years before, times when he'd freaked a little and become violent, but it always got softened, they'd pull back and say his name with great affection. "Page. Fucking Page."

He was an orphan boy from London, married at seventeen and divorced a year later. He worked his way across Europe as a cook in the hotels, drifting east through India, through Laos (where he claims to have dealt with the Spooks, a little teen-age espionage), into Vietnam at the age of twenty. One of the things that everybody said about him was that he had not been much of a photographer then (he'd picked up a camera the way you or I would pick up a ticket), but that he would go places for pictures that very few other photographers were going. People made him sound crazy and ambitious, like the Sixties Kid, a stone-cold freak in a country where the madness raced up the hills and into the jungles, where everything essential to learning Asia, war, drugs, the whole adventure, was close at hand.

The first time he got hit it was shrapnel in the legs and stomach. That was at Chu Lai, in '65. The next time was during the Buddhist riots of the 1966 Struggle Movement in Danang: head, back, arms, more shrapnel. (*A Paris-Match* photograph showed Flynn and a French photographer carrying him on a door, his face half covered by bandages, *"Tim Page blessé à la tête."*) His friends began trying to talk him into leaving Vietnam, saying, "Hey, Page, there's an airstrike looking for you." And there was; it caught him drifting around off course in a Swift boat in the South China Sea, blowing it out of the water under the mistaken impression that it was a Viet Cong vessel. All but three of the crew were killed, Page took over 200 individual wounds, and he floated in the water for hours before he was finally rescued.

They were getting worse each time, and Page gave in to it. He left Vietnam, allegedly for good, and joined Flynn in Paris for a while. He went to the States from there, took some pictures for Time-Life, got busted with the Doors in New Haven, traveled across the country on his own (he still had some money left), doing a picture story which he planned to call "Winter in America." Shortly after the Tet Offensive, Flynn returned to Vietnam, and once Page heard that, it was only a matter of time. When he got back in May, his entrance requirements weren't in order, and the Vietnamese kept him at Tan Son Nhut for a couple of days, where his friends visited him and brought him things. The first time I met him he was giggling and doing an insane imitation of two Vietnamese immigration authorities fighting over the amount of money they were going to hold him up for, "Minh phung, auk nyong bgnyang gluke poo phuc fuck fart, I mean you should have *heard* those beastly people. Where am I going to sleep, who's got a rack for Page? The Dinks have been mucking about with Page, Page is a *very* tired boy."

He was twenty-three when I first met him, and I can remember wishing that I'd known him when he was still young. He was bent, beaten, scarred, he was everything by way of being crazy that everyone had said he was, except that you could tell that he'd never get really nasty again when he flipped. He was broke, so friends got him a place to sleep, gave him piastres, cigarettes, liquor, grass. Then he made a couple of thousand dollars on some fine pictures of the Offensive, and all of those things came back on us, twice over. That was the way the world was for Page; when he was broke you took care of him, when he was not he took care of you. It was above economics. . . .

In April I got a call telling me that Page had been hit again and was not expected to live. He had been up goofing somewhere around Cu Chi, digging the big toys, and a helicopter he was riding in was ordered to land and pick up some wounded. Page and a sergeant ran out to help, the sergeant stepped on a mine which blew his legs off and sent a two-inch piece of shrapnel through Page's forehead above the right eye and deep into the base of his brain. He retained consciousness all the way to the hospital at Long Binh. Flynn and Perry Young were on R&R in Vientiane when they were notified, and they flew immediately to Saigon. For nearly two weeks, friends at Time-Life kept me informed by telephone from their daily cables; Page was transferred to a hospital in Japan and they said that he would probably live. He was moved to Walter Reed Army Hospital (a civilian and a British subject, it took some doing), and they said that he would live but that he'd always be paralyzed on his left side. I called him there, and he sounded all right, telling me that his roommate was this very religious colonel who kept apologizing to Page because he was only in for a check-up, he hadn't been wounded or anything fantastic like that. Page was afraid that he was freaking the colonel out a little bit. Then they moved him to the Institute for Physical Rehabilitation in New York, and while none of them could really explain it medically, it seemed that he was regaining the use of his left arm and leg. The first time I went to see him I walked right past his bed without recognizing him out of the four patients in the room, even though he'd been the first one I'd seen, even though the other three were men in their forties, and fifties. He lay there grinning his deranged, uneven grin, his eyes were wet, and he raised his right hand for a second to jab at me with his finger. His head was shaved and sort of lidded now across the forehead where they'd opened it up ("What did they find in there, Page?" I asked him. "Did they find that quiche lorraine?") and caved in on the right side where they'd removed some bone. He was emaciated and he looked really old, but he was still grinning very proudly as I approached the bed, as if to say, "Well, didn't Page step into it this time?" as though two inches of shrapnel in your brain was the wiggiest goof of them all, that wonderful moment of the Tim Page Story where our boy comes leering, lurching back from death, twin brother to his own ghost.

That was that, he said, *fini Vietnam*, there could be no more odds left, he'd been warned. Sure he was crazy, but he wasn't *that* crazy. He had a bird now, a wonderful English girl named Linda Webb whom he'd met in Saigon. She'd stayed with him in the Long Binh hospital even though the shock and fear of seeing him like that had made her pass out fifteen times on the first evening. "I'd really be the fool, now, to just give that one up, now, wouldn't I?" he said, and we all said, Yes, man, you would be.

On his twenty-fifth birthday there was a big party in the apartment near the hospital that he and Linda had found. Page wanted all of the people to be there who, he said, had bet him years ago in Saigon that he'd never make it past twenty-three. He wore a blue sweat suit with a Mike patch, black skull and bones, on his sleeve. You could have gotten stoned just by walking into the room that day, and Page was so happy to be here and alive and among friends that even the strangers who turned up then were touched by it. "There's Evil afoot," he kept saying, laughing and chasing after people in his wheelchair. "Do no Evil, think ye no Evil, smoke no Evil. . . . Yesh."

A month went by and he made fantastic progress, giving up the chair for a cane and wearing a brace to support his left arm.

"I've a splendid new trick for the doctor," he said one day, flinging his left arm out of the brace and up over his head with great effort, waving his hand a little. Sometimes he'd stand in front of a full-length mirror in the apartment and survey the wreckage, laughing until tears came, shaking his head and saying, "Ohhhhh, fuck! I mean, just *look* at that, will you? Page is a fucking hemi-plegic," raising his cane and stumbling back to his chair, collapsing in laughter again.

He fixed up an altar with all of his Buddhas, arranging prayer candles in a belt of empty .50-caliber cartridges. He put in a stereo, played endlessly at organizing his slides into trays, spoke of setting out Claymores at night to keep "undesirables" away, built model airplanes ("Very good therapy, that"), hung toy choppers from the ceiling, put up posters of Frank Zappa and Cream and some Day-Glo posters which Linda had made of monks and tanks and solid soul brothers smoking joints in the fields of Vietnam. He began talking more and more about the war, often coming close to tears when he remembered how happy he and all of us had been there.

One day a letter came from a British publisher, asking him to do a book whose working title would be "Through with War" and whose purpose would be to once and for all "take the glamour out of war." Page couldn't get over it.

"Take the glamour out of war! I mean, how the bloody hell can you do *that*? Go and take the glamour out of a Huey, go take the glamour out of a Sheridan. . . . Can *you* take the glamour out of a Cobra or getting stoned at China Beach? It's like taking the glamour out of an M-79, taking the glamour out of Flynn." He pointed to a picture he'd taken, Flynn laughing maniacally ("We're winning," he'd said), triumphantly. "Nothing the matter with *that* boy, is there? Would you let your daughter marry that man? Ohhhh, war is *good* for you, you can't take the glamour out of that. It's like trying to take the glamour out of sex, trying to take the glamour out of the Rolling Stones." He was really speechless, working his hands up and down to emphasize the sheer insanity of it.

"I mean, you *know* that, it just *can't be done!*" We both shrugged and laughed, and Page looked very thoughtful for a moment. "The very *idea!*" he said. "Ohhh, what a laugh! Take the bloody *glamour* out of bloody *war!*"

Questions for Discussion

1. Explain the literal meaning of the following sentence: "He was twenty-three when I first met him, and I can remember wishing that I'd known him when he was still young." What would the author have lost if he had stated his idea literally?

2. Explain Page's attitude toward war and why he held that attitude. Does his use of third person in referring to himself have anything to do with his attitude? ("The Dinks have been mucking about with Page. Page is a very tired boy. . . .")

3. What is Michael Herr's attitude toward Page? Explain the reasons for your answer, using passages in the text as evidence.

4. In what ways is Page a casualty of war?

5. What is your reaction to the last two paragraphs of the essay, which ask, "Take the glamour out of war! I mean, how the bloody hell can you do *that*?" Is Page's attitude justified?

6. What are the uses and effects of the *diction* in the following passage?

In April I got a call telling me that Page had been hit again and was not expected to live. He had been up goofing somewhere around Cu Chi, digging the big toys, and a helicopter he was riding in was ordered to land and pick up some wounded.

RICHARD GOLDSTEIN

Born on June 19, 1944, in New York City, Richard Goldstein received his B.A. from Hunter College and then his M.S. from Columbia University in 1966. He has been the editor of US *magazine since 1968, while also contributing articles to the* Village Voice, Vogue, *and* New York *and doing other freelance writing. His books include* One in Seven: Drugs on Campus, *1966;* The Poetry of Rock, *1969;* Goldstein's Greatest Hits: A Book Mostly About Rock 'n' Roll, *1970. In* Contemporary Authors, *Goldstein had the following to say about himself:*

> *He digs sloths and groundhogs. Also late night horror movies and melted popsicles. He became a writer because "my mother used to hit me over the knuckles to improve my penmanship."*

You might ask yourself how the author reveals himself in "Gear."

In this selection, point of view *shifts wildly and thus may be a source of confusion. Perhaps you will want to read "Gear" a second time to straighten out some of the tangles.*

Gear

Too early to get up, especially on Saturday. The sun peeks over his windowsill. Isolated footsteps from the street. Guys who have to work on Saturday. Boy! That's what they'll call you all your life if you don't stay in school. Forty-five definitions, two chapters in *Silas Marner*, and three chem labs. On Sunday night, he will sit in his room with the radio on, bobbing back and forth on his bed, opening the window wide and then closing it, taking a break to eat, to comb his hair, to dance, to hear the Stones—anything. Finally, cursing wildly and making ugly faces at himself in the mirror, he will throw *Silas Marner* under the bed and spend an hour watching his tortoise eat lettuce.

In the bathroom he breaks three screaming pimples. With a tooth-pick he removes four specks of food from his braces, skirting barbed wires and week-old rubber bands. Brooklyn Bridge, railroad tracks, they call him. Metal mouth. They said he smiled like someone was forcing him to. Bent fingers with filthy nails. Caved-in chest with eight dangling hairs. A face that looks like the end of a watermelon, and curly hair—not like the Stones, not at all like Brian Jones—but muddy curls running down his forehead and over his ears. A bump. Smashed by a bat thrown wildly. When he was eight. Hunchback Quasimodo—Igor—Rodan on his head. A bump. Nobody hip has a bump or braces. Or hair like a fucking Frankenstein movie. He licks his braces clean and practices smiling.

Hair straight and heavy. Nose full. Lips bulging like boiling frankfurters. Hung. Bell bottoms and boss black boots. He practices his Brian Jones expressions. Fist held close to the jaw. Ready to spring, ready to spit. Evil. His upper brace catches on a lip.

He walks past his parents' room, where his mother sleeps in a gauzy hairnet, the covers pulled over her chin, her baby feet swathed in yellow calluses. Her hand reaches over to the night table where her eyedrops and glasses lie. He mutters silently at her. The night before there had been a fight—the usual fight, with Mommy shouting "I'll give you money! Sure, you rotten kid! I'll give you clothing so you can throw it all over the floor—that's blood money in those pants of yours!" And him answering the usual "geh-awf-mah-bak" and her: "Don't you yell at me, don't you—did you hear that (to no one). Did you hear how that kid . . . ?" and him slamming the door—the gray barrier—and above the muffled ". . . disrespects his mother . . . He treats me like dirt under his feet! . . . and he wants me to buy him . . . he'll spit on my grave" . . . and finally dad's groaning shuffle and a murmured "Ronnie, you better shut your mouth to your mother," and him whispering silently, the climatic, the utter: "Fucking bitch. Cunt. Cunt."

Now she smiles. So do crocodiles. He loves her. He doesn't know why he cursed, except that she hates it. It was easy to make her cry and though he shivers at the thought of her lying across the bed sobbing into a pillow, her housedress pulled slightly over a varicose thigh, he has to admit doing it was easy.

On the table he sees the pants she bought him yesterday. Her money lining his pocket, he had taken the bus to Fordham Road and in Alexander's he had cased out the Mod rack. Hands shaking, dying for a cigarette, he found the pants—a size small but still a fit. He bought them, carried them home clutched in his armpit, and deposited them before her during prime "Star Trek" TV time.

"Get away. I can't see. Whatsamaddah, your father a glazier or something?" and when he unveiled the pants and asked for the usual cuff-making ritual (when he would stand on the ladder and she, holding a barrage of pins in her mouth, would run the tailor's chalk along his shoe line and make him drag out the old black sewing machine), the fight began—and ended within the hour. The pants, hemmed during "The Merv Griffin Show" as the last labor of the night, now lay exposed and sunlit on the table. $8.95 pants.

They shimmer. The houndstooth design glows against the formica. Brown and green squares are suddenly visible within the gray design. He brushes the fabric carefully so the wool bristles. He tries them on, zipping up the two-inch fly, thinking at first that he has broken the zipper until he realizes that hip-huggers have no fly to speak of. They buckle tightly around his hips, hug his thighs, and flare suddenly at his knees. He races to the mirror and grins.

His hips are suddenly tight and muscular. His waist is sleek and his ass round and bulging. Most important, the pants make him look hung. Like the kids in the park. The odor of stale cigarettes over their clothing, medallions dangling out of their shirts. Their belt buckles ajar. They are hip. They say "Check out that bike." Get bent on Gypsy. Write the numbers of cruising police cars all over the walls. ROT, they call themselves. Reign of Terror. In the park they buzz out on glue, filling paper bags and breathing deeply, then sitting on the grass slopes, watching the cars. Giggling. Grooving. High.

Sometimes they let him keep the models that come with the glue. Or he grubs around their spot until, among the torn bags and oozing tubes, he finds a Messerschmitt or Convair spread across the grass ruins as though it had crashed there.

He unzips his pants and lets them hang on the door where he can watch them from the living room. He takes a box of Oreos from the kitchen, stacking the cookies in loose columns on the rug. He pours a cup of milk and turns on the TV. Farmer Gray runs nervously up and down the screen while a pig squats at ease by his side. His pants are filled with hornets. He runs in a cloud of dust toward a pond which appears and disappears teasingly, leaving Farmer Gray grubbing in the sand. Outasight!

He fills his mouth with three Oreos and wraps his feet around the screen so he can watch Farmer Gray between his legs. Baby habit. Eating cookies on the floor and watching cartoons on Saturday morning. Like thumbsucking. They teased him about it until he threw imaginary furniture into their faces. A soft bulge on his left thumb from years of sucking—cost them a fortune in braces. Always busting his hump.

He kills the TV picture and puts the radio on softly, because he doesn't want to wake Daddy who is asleep on his cot in the middle of the living room, bunched up around the blanket, his face creased in a dream, hands gripping his stomach in mock tension. Daddy snores in soft growls.

He brushes a flock of Oreo crumbs under the TV and rubs a milk stain into the rug. Thrown out of your own bed for snoring. You feel cheap, like Little Bo Peep; beep beep beep beep.

There is nothing to stop him from going downstairs. The guys are out already, slung over cars and around lampposts. The girls are trickling out of the project. It's cloudy, but until it actually rains he knows they will be around the lamppost, spitting out into the street, horsing around, grubbing for hooks, singing. He finishes four more cookies and stuffs half an apple onto his chocolate-lined tongue.

Marie Giovanni put him down bad for his braces. When she laughs her tits shake. Her face is pink; her hair rises in a billowing bouffant. In the hallway, she let Tony get his fingers wet. Yesterday she cut on him; called him metal mouth.

He flicks the radio off, grabs the pants from the hanger, and slides into them. He digs out a brown turtleneck from under a rubble of twisted clothing (they dress him like a ragpicker) and shines his boots with spit. They are chipping and the heels are worn on one side, but they make him look an inch taller, so he wears them whenever he can.

He combs his hair in the mirror. Back on the sides, over the ears, so the curl doesn't show. Over the eyes in the front to cover up his bump. Straight down the back of his neck, so it rests on his collar. He checks his bald spot for progress and counts the hairs that come out in his brush. In two years he knows he will be bald in front and his bump will look like a boulder on his forehead.

He sits on his bed and turns the radio on. From under the phonograph he lifts a worn fan magazine—*Pop* in bright fuchsia lettering—with Zal Yanovsky hunched over one P, Paul McCartney contorted over the other, and Nancy Sinatra touching her toes around the O. He turns to the spread on the Stones and flips the pages until he sees The Picture. Mick Jagger and Marianne Faithfull. Mick scowling, waving his fingers in the air. Marianne watching the camera. Marianne, waiting for the photographer to shoot. Marianne. Marianne, eyes fading brown circles, lips slightly parted in flashbulb surprise, miniskirt spread apart, tits like two perfect cones under her sweater. He had to stop looking at Marianne Faithfull a week ago.

He turns the page and glances at the shots of Brian Jones and then his eyes open wide because a picture in the corner shows Brian in Ronnie's pants. The same check. The same rise and flare. Brian leaning against a wall, his hands on the top of his magic hiphuggers. Wick-ked!

He flips the magazine away and stands in a curved profile against the mirror. He watches the pants move as he does. From a nearby flowerpot he gathers a fingerful of dirt and rubs it over his upper lip. He checks hair, nose, braces, nails, and pants. He likes the pants. They make him look hung. He reaches into his top drawer and pulls out a white handkerchief. He opens his fly and inserts the rolled cloth, patting it in place, and closing the zipper over it. He looks boss. Unfuckinbelievable.

In the elevator Ronnie takes a cigarette from his three-day-old pack and keeps it unlit in his mouth. Marie Giovanni will look at his pants and giggle. Tony will bellow "Check out them pants," and everyone will groove on them. In the afternoon, they will take him down to the park and turn him on, and he will feel the buzz they are always talking about and the cars will speed by like sparks.

Brian Jones thoughts in his head. Tuff thoughts. He will slouch low over the car and smoke with his thumb over the cigarette—the hip way. And when he comes back upstairs they will finally get off his back. Even on Fordham Road, where the Irish kids crack up when he walks by, even in chemistry and gym, they will know who he is and nod a soft "hey" when he comes by. He'll get laid.

Because clothing IS important. Especially if you've got braces and bony fingers and a bump the size of a goddam coconut on your head.

And especially if you're fourteen. Because—ask anyone. Fourteen is shit.

Questions for Discussion

1. One characteristic of Goldstein's style is his use of fragmentary sentences, as in the paragraph on page 141, which contains only two complete sentences:

    Hair straight and heavy. Nose full. Lips bulging like boiling frankfurters. Hung. Bell bottoms and boss black boots. *He practices his Brian Jones expressions.* Fist held close to the jaw. Ready to spring, ready to spit. Evil. *His upper brace catches on a lip.* [italics added]

    In your opinion, is this stylistic device effective or not? What does Goldstein lose or gain by its use?
2. What is the significance of the title "Gear"?
3. This essay is, first of all, a character sketch of a teenager named Ronnie, but it has other purposes, other themes. What are those other themes? What evidence can you cite to support your opinion? (Are Ronnie's character and personality actually Goldstein's central concern, or does he use Ronnie merely as a symbol to deal with broader issues?)
4. What sort of person is Ronnie's mother?
5. How do you feel about Ronnie? Why? What specific details lead you to your attitude toward Ronnie?
6. Does this selection portray a credible fourteen-year-old? Is Ronnie a person with whom you can empathize or sympathize? Why?
7. Do you agree that "clothing IS important"? If so, in what instances do you think it is especially important? If not, explain your own view.
8. List from the text five names or terms with which you're not familiar. Does not recognizing the meaning of "Get bent on Gypsy," or not knowing who Zal Yanovsky is, affect your reaction to "Gear"?
9. How would you describe Ronnie's relation with his mother ("Mommy")?
10. What do you think is the main point of the selection? Is the humorous approach more or less successful in presenting the idea?

11.   In what respect would you regard this selection as fiction? In what respect would you regard it as journalism?

12.   In most writings that you have read, *point of view* (see the explanation in the glossary at the end of this book) is consistent. That is, the readers "see" either through the eyes of the author-narrator or from the standpoint of one of the characters in the piece; but in "Gear," point of view makes abrupt shifts. Point out where those shifts occur and discuss their effects. What does Goldstein lose through these shifts? What does he gain?

ELLEN GOODMAN

Ellen Goodman was born on April 11, 1941, in Newton, Massachusetts, daughter of a lawyer and politician. In 1963, she received her B.A. from Radcliffe College. She and her daughter live in Brookline, Massachusetts.

A feature writer for the Boston Globe, *her column is syndicated in more than two hundred and fifty newspapers. She has also been a commentator on the television shows "Spectrum" and "Today." She was a Nieman Fellow at Harvard in 1973-1974, and in 1980, she received the Pulitzer Prize for distinguished commentary.*

This selection is from Close to Home, *published in 1979.* Turning Points *and* At Large *are her other two books.*

Goodman says, "I tend to go through life like a vacuum cleaner, inhaling all the interesting tidbits in my path, using almost everything I observe, read or report." She also says, "I am more concerned with the struggles between conflicting values than the struggles between conflicting political parties."

Frequently called lighthearted, Goodman can also be completely serious, as here. Note the conflicting values in her essay, and consider how those values have evolved over the last few decades. Note also Goodman's use of repetition to establish her point.

A Description of Rejection

She was brilliant. Everyone involved in the case agreed about that.

She was unattractive. Everyone agreed about that, too.

She was overweight, whiny, argumentative, unkempt—the list goes on—sloppy, hypercritical, unpopular.

The life of Charlotte Horowitz—whose dismissal from a Missouri medical school became a Supreme Court case this week—has become painfully public. A description of rejection.

From all reports, she interacted with the world like a fingernail on a blackboard. She was punished for the crime of being socially unacceptable.

Charlotte Horowitz was older than most of the other students when she was admitted to the University of Missouri–Kansas City Medical School in 1972. She was also brighter, a misfit from New York who won her place despite the admissions officer's report that read, "The candidate's personal appearance is against her. . . ."

By the school's "merit system," she was tops in her medical-school class. As her advisor wrote: "Her past record is the best in the school. Her examination scores are at the very top of the school. She has functioned at a high level and has had no problems with a patient at any time." Yet she was dismissed by the dean on the verge of graduation. The grounds were tardiness, bad grooming and an abrasive personal style.

Of course, the case in front of the Supreme Court won't judge those grounds. It will deal with the issue of due process: whether she was given proper notice and a fair hearing; whether universities and professional schools have to extend certain legal rights to their students.

But the theme of this difficult, emotional story is prejudice. The most deep-rooted way in which we prejudge each other. The sort of discrimination which is universal, almost unrootable. Prejudice toward appearance. Discrimination against what we "see."

The most unattractive children in the classrooms of our youth had their lives and personalities warped by that fact. Their painful experiences of rejection nurtured in them an expectation of rejection. That expectation, like some paranoia, was almost always fulfilled.

It is a mystery why some "unattractive people" wear it in their souls and others don't. Why one becomes Barbra Streisand and another a reject. But often, along the way, some people give up trying to be accepted and become defensively nonconforming. They stop letting themselves care. They become "unkempt, argumentative, abrasive." And the list goes on.

Everyone's self-image is formed in some measure by the way they are seen, the way they see themselves being seen. As their image deteriorates, their personality often shatters along with it. At that point, the rest of us smugly avoid them, stamping them "unacceptable," not because of their "looks" but because of their behavior.

It happens all the time.

There is no law that can protect children from this sort of discrimination. We are all, in that sense, the products as well as the survivors of our childhood. But the cumulative, spiraling effect of appearance on personality is worse for women than for men. If Charlotte Horowitz had been a man, surely her brains would have alleviated her physical unattractiveness. As a woman, her unattractiveness was further handicapped by brains.

As Dr. Estelle Ramey, a professor at Georgetown Medical School and former head of the Association for Women in Science, said: "If the bad fairy ends up the last one at your crib, you'll be cursed as a brilliant unattractive woman."

But this case isn't a question of the curse, the birth penalty, the "life isn't fair" sort of discrimination. It's a story of a university so "blinded" that its officials felt they had the right to throw away a life and a mind because it was housed in a body that was "overweight, sloppy, hypercritical."

"What's been lost in all this," says Dr. Ramey, "is the contribution a brilliant human being might have made in a field which needs all the fine minds we have."

You see, Charlotte Horowitz was brilliant. Everyone involved in the case could, at least, see that.

Questions for Discussion

1. Goodman says the case against Charlotte Horowitz was based on discrimination against her appearance. How does her "whiny" and "abrasive personal style" fit with Goodman's assessment?
2. Should a medical school have the right to dismiss a student on grounds other than academic? If so, on what grounds?
3. How might we prevent unattractive children from having "their lives and personalities warped" by prejudice against appearance?

4. Do you agree with Goodman that physical unattractiveness has a worse effect on a woman's personality than on a man's?

5. A Los Angeles newspaperman said that Goodman's writing "hits people in the gut." What is your personal reaction to the article, its subject and its style?

6. The selection ends with the paragraph, "You see, Charlotte Horowitz was brilliant. Everyone involved in the case could, at least, see that." What things that people couldn't see does Goodman wish to point out?

7. Goodman discusses a court case that was pending when she wrote her essay. What "evidence" does she present in the piece?

8. Do you think the style of the piece is suited to the subject matter? Explain.

9. What further information would you like about the Charlotte Horowitz case? Would Goodman have been able to include that information without changing the format of the piece? If you had to choose another one of the authors of this chapter to supply this additional information, which would you choose? How would the piece change in style and format?

JOHN MCPHEE

Born in 1931 in Princeton, New Jersey, John McPhee attended Princeton and Cambridge universities. His father was a physician, and his wife is a horticulturist. And as you read "Under the Snow," you will be interested in the fact that he has four daughters. He teaches a course, "The Literature of Fact," at Princeton and is a staff writer for The New Yorker.

One of the leading New Journalists, McPhee is able to transform apparently unglamorous subjects into the most engaging prose currently being written. For instance, he has devoted one whole—and fascinating—book to Oranges. Coming into the Country, *his study of Alaska, makes geography, history, and state politics into high drama. In 1986, he did a series of articles for* The New Yorker *on geology, a subject he turned from inanimate stone into human drama.*

One key to McPhee's success as a writer is that he puts everything into human terms. He talks not about just the facts of geology but about how geologists discover those facts, not about canoes but about the drama of one man who builds canoes. As you read this essay, notice how McPhee translates ecological and biological information into dramatic situations.

Under the Snow

When my third daughter was an infant, I could place her against my shoulder and she would stick there like velvet. Only her eyes jumped from place to place. In a breeze, her bright red hair might stir, but she would not. Even then, there was profundity in her repose.

When my fourth daughter was an infant, I wondered if her veins were full of ants. Placing her against a shoulder was a risk both to her and to the shoulder. Impulsively, constantly, everything about her moved. Her head seemed about to revolve as it followed the bestirring world.

These memories became very much alive some months ago when—one after another—I had bear cubs under my vest. Weighing three, four, 5.6 pounds, they were wild bears, and for an hour or so had been taken from their dens in Pennsylvania. They were about two months old, with fine short brown hair. When they were made to stand alone, to be photographed in the mouth of a den, they shivered. Instinctively, a person would be moved to hold them. Picked up by the scruff of the neck, they splayed their paws like kittens and screamed like baby bears. The cry of a baby bear is muted, like a human infant's heard from her crib down the hall. The first cub I placed on my shoulder stayed there like a piece of velvet. The shivering stopped. Her bright-blue eyes looked about, not seeing much of anything. My hand, cupped against her back, all but encompassed her rib cage, which was warm and calm. I covered her to the shoulders with a flap of down vest and zipped up my parka to hold her in place.

I was there by invitation, an indirect result of work I had been doing nearby. Would I be busy on March 14th? If there had been a conflict—if, say, I had been invited to lunch on that day with the Queen of Scotland and the King of Spain—I would have gone to the cubs. The first den was a rock cavity in a lichen-covered sandstone outcrop near the top of a slope, a couple of hundred yards from a road in Hawley. It was on posted property of the Scrub Oak Hunting Club—dry hardwood forest underlain by laurel and patches of snow—in the northern Pocono woods. Up in the sky was Buck Alt. Not long ago, he was a dairy farmer, and now he was working for the Keystone State, with directional antennae on his wing struts angled in the direction of bears. Many bears in Pennsylvania have radios around their necks as a result of the summer trapping work of Alt's son Gary, who is a wildlife biologist. In winter, Buck Alt flies the country listening to the radio, crissing and crossing until the bears come on. They come on stronger the closer to them he flies. The transmitters are not omnidirectional. Suddenly, the sound cuts out. Buck looks down, chooses a landmark, approaches it again, on another vector. Gradually, he works his way in, until he is flying in ever tighter circles above the bear. He marks a map. He is accurate within two acres. The plane he flies is a Super Cub.

The den could have served as a set for a Passion play. It was a small chamber, open on one side, with a rock across its entrance. Between the freestanding rock and the back of the cave was room for one large bear, and she was curled in a corner on a bed of leaves, her broad head plainly visible from the outside, her cubs invisible between the rock and a soft place, chuckling, suckling, in the wintertime tropics of their own mammalian heaven. Invisible they were, yes, but by no means inaudible. What biologists call chuckling sounded like starlings in a tree.

People walking in woods sometimes come close enough to a den to cause the mother to get up and run off, unmindful of her reputation as a fearless defender of cubs. The cubs stop chuckling and begin to cry: possibly three, four cubs—a ward of mewling bears. The people hear the crying. They find the den and see the cubs. Sometimes they pick them up and carry them away, reporting to the state that they have saved the lives of bear cubs abandoned by their mother. Wherever and whenever this occurs, Gary Alt collects the cubs. After ten years of bear trapping and biological study, Alt has equipped so many sows with radios that he has been able to conduct a foster-mother program with an amazingly high rate of success. A mother in hibernation will readily accept a foster cub. If the need to place an orphan arises somewhat later, when mothers and their cubs are out and around, a sow will kill an alien cub as soon as she smells it. Alt has overcome this problem by stuffing sows' noses with Vicks VapoRub. One way or another, he has found new families for forty-seven orphaned cubs. Forty-six have survived. The other, which had become accustomed over three weeks to feedings and caresses by human hands, was not content in a foster den, crawled outside, and died in the snow.

With a hypodermic jab stick, Alt now drugged the mother, putting her to sleep for the duration of the visit. From deeps of shining fur, he fished out cubs. One. Two. A third. A fourth. Five! The fifth was a foster daughter brought earlier in the winter from two hundred miles away. Three of the four others were male—a ratio consistent with the heavy preponderance of males that Alt's studies have shown through the years. To various onlookers he handed the cubs for safekeeping while he and several assistants carried the mother into the open and weighed her with block and tackle. To protect her eyes, Alt had blindfolded her with a red bandanna. They carried her upside down, being extremely careful lest they scrape and damage her nipples. She weighed two hundred and nineteen pounds. Alt had caught her and weighed her some months before. In the den, she had lost ninety pounds. When she was four years old, she had had four cubs; two years later, four more cubs; and now, after two more years, four cubs. He knew all that about her, he had caught her so many times. He referred to her as Daisy. Daisy was as nothing compared with Vanessa, who was sleeping off the winter somewhere else. In ten seasons, Vanessa had given birth to twenty-three cubs and had lost none. The growth and reproductive rates of black bears are greater in Pennsylvania than anywhere else. Black bears in Pennsylvania grow more rapidly than grizzlies in Montana. Eastern black bears are generally much larger than Western ones. A seven-hundred-pound bear is unusual but not rare in Pennsylvania. Alt once caught a big bear like that who had a thirty-seven-inch neck and was a hair under seven feet long.

This bear, nose to tail, measured five feet five. Alt said, "That's a nice long sow." For weighing the cubs, he had a small nylon stuff sack. He stuffed it with bear and hung it on a scale. Two months before, when the cubs were born, each would have weighed approximately half a pound—less than a newborn porcupine. Now the cubs weighed 3.4, 4.1, 4.4, 4.6, 5.6—cute little numbers with soft tan noses and erectile pyramid ears. Bears have sex in June and July, but the mother's system holds the fertilized egg away from the uterus until November, when implantation occurs. Fetal development lasts scarcely six weeks. Therefore, the creatures who live upon the hibernating mother are so small that everyone survives.

The orphan, less winsome than the others, looked like a chocolate-covered possum. I kept her under my vest. She seemed content there and scarcely moved. In time, I exchanged her for 5.6—the big boy in the litter. Lifted by the scruff and held in the air, he bawled, flashed his claws, and curled his lips like a woofing boar. I stuffed him under the vest, where he shut up and nuzzled. His claws were already more than half an inch long. Alt said that the family would come out of the den in a few weeks but that much of the spring would go by before the cubs gained weight. The difference would be that they were no longer malleable and ductile. They would become pugnacious and scratchy, not to say vicious, and would chew up the hand that caressed them. He said, "If you have an enemy, give him a bear cub."

Six men carried the mother back to the den, the red bandanna still tied around her eyes. Alt repacked her into the rock. "We like to return her to the den as close as possible to the way we found her," he said. Someone remarked that one biologist can work a coon, while an army is needed to deal with a bear. An army seemed to be present. Twelve people had followed Alt to the den. Some days, the group around him is four times as large. Alt, who is in his thirties, was wearing a visored khaki cap with a blue-and-gold keystone on the forehead, and a khaki cardigan under a khaki jump suit. A lithe and light-bodied man with tinted glasses and a blond mustache, he looked like a lieutenant in the Ardennes Forest. Included in the retinue were two reporters and a news photographer. Alt encourages media attention, the better to soften the image of the bears. He says, "People fear bears more than they need to, and respect them not enough." Over the next twenty days, he had scheduled four hundred visitors—state senators, representatives, commissioners, television reporters, word processors, biologists, friends—to go along on his rounds of dens. Days before, he and the denned bears had been hosts to the BBC. The Brits wanted snow. God was having none of it. The BBC brought in the snow.

In the course of the day, we made a brief tour of dens that for the time being stood vacant. Most were rock cavities. They had been used before, and in all likelihood would be used again. Bears in winter in the Pocono plateau are like chocolate chips in a cookie. The bears seldom go back to the same den two years running, and they often change dens in the course of a winter. In a forty-five-hundred-acre housing development called Hemlock Farms are twenty-three dens known to be in current use and countless others awaiting new tenants. Alt showed one that was within fifteen feet of the intersection of East Spur Court and Pommel Drive. He said that when a sow with two cubs was in there he had seen deer browsing by the outcrop and ignorant dogs stopping off to lift a leg. Hemlock Farms is expensive, and full of cantilevered cypress and unencumbered glass. Houses perch on high flat rock. Now and again, there are bears in the rock—in, say, a floor-through cavity just under the porch. The owers are from New York. Alt does not always tell them that their property is zoned for bears. Once, when he did so, a "FOR SALE" sign went up within two weeks.

Not far away is Interstate 84. Flying over it one day, Buck Alt heard an oddly intermittent signal. Instead of breaking off once and cleanly, it broke off many times. Crossing back over, he heard it again. Soon he was in a tight turn, now hearing something, now nothing, in a pattern that did not suggest anything he had heard before. It did, however, suggest the interstate. Where a big green sign says, "MILFORD 11, PORT JERVIS 20," Gary hunted around and found the bear. He took us now to see the den. We went down a steep slope at the side of the highway and, crouching, peered into a culvert. It was about fifty yards long. There was a disc of daylight at the opposite end. Thirty inches in diameter, it was a perfect place to stash a body, and that is what the bear thought, too. On Gary's first visit, the disc of daylight had not been visible. The bear had denned under the eastbound lanes. She had given birth to three cubs. Soon after he found her, heavy rains were predicted. He hauled the family out and off to a vacant den. The cubs weighed less than a pound. Two days later, water a foot deep was racing through the culvert.

Under High Knob, in remote undeveloped forest about six hundred metres above sea level, a slope falling away in an easterly direction contained a classic excavated den: a small entrance leading into an intimate ovate cavern, with a depression in the center for a bed—in all about twenty-four cubic feet, the size of a refrigerator-freezer. The den had not been occupied in several seasons, but Rob Buss, a district game protector who works regularly with Gary Alt, had been around to check it three days before and had shined his flashlight into a darkness stuffed with fur. Meanwhile, six inches of fresh snow had fallen on High Knob, and now Alt and his team, making preparations a short distance from the den, scooped up snow in their arms and filled a big sack. They had nets of nylon mesh. There was a fifty-fifty likelihood of yearling bears in the den. Mothers keep cubs until their second spring. When a biologist comes along and provokes the occupants to emerge, there is no way to predict how many will appear. Sometimes they keep coming and coming, like clowns from a compact car. As a bear emerges, it walks into the nylon mesh. A drawstring closes. At the same time, the den entrance is stuffed with a bag of snow. That stops the others. After the first bear has been dealt with, Alt removes the sack of snow. Out comes another bear. A yearling weighs about eighty pounds, and may move so fast that it runs over someone on the biological team and stands on top of him sniffing at his ears. Or her ears. Janice Gruttadauria, a research assistant, is a part of the team. Bear after bear, the procedure is repeated until the bag of snow is pulled away and nothing comes out. That is when Alt asks Rob Buss to go inside and see if anything is there.

Now, moving close to the entrance, Alt spread a tarp on the snow, lay down on it, turned on a five-cell flashlight, and put his head inside the den. The beam played over thick black fur and came to rest on a tiny foot. The sack of snow would not be needed. After drugging the mother with a jab stick, he joined her in the den. The entrance was so narrow he had to shrug his shoulders to get in. He shoved the sleeping mother, head first, out of the darkness and into the light.

While she was away, I shrugged my own shoulders and had a look inside. The den smelled of earth but not of bear. The walls were dripping with roots. The water and protein metabolism of hibernating black bears has been explored by the Mayo Clinic as a research model for, among other things, human endurance on long flights through space and medical situations closer to home, such as the maintenance of anephric human beings who are awaiting kidney transplants.

Outside, each in turn, the cubs were put in the stuff sack—a male and a female. The female weighed four pounds. Greedily, I reached for her when Alt took her out of the bag. I planted her on my shoulder while I wrote down facts about her mother: weight, a hundred and ninety-two pounds; length, fifty-eight inches; some toes missing; severe frostbite from a bygone winter evidenced along the edges of the ears.

Eventually, with all weighing and tagging complete, it was time to go. Alt went into the den. Soon he called out that he was ready for the mother. It would be a tight fit. Feet first, she was shoved in, like a safe-deposit box. Inside, Alt tugged at her in close embrace, and the two of them gradually revolved until she was at the back and their positions had reversed. He shaped her like a doughnut—her accustomed den position. The cubs go in the center. The male was handed in to him. Now he was asking for the female. For a moment, I glanced around as if looking to see who had her. The thought crossed my mind that if I bolted and ran far enough and fast enough I could flag a passing car and keep her. Then I pulled her from under the flap of my vest and handed her away.

Alt and others covered the entrance with laurel boughs, and covered the boughs with snow. They camouflaged the den, but that was not the purpose. Practicing wildlife management to a fare-thee-well, Alt wanted the den to be even darker than it had been before; this would cause the family to stay longer inside and improve the cubs' chances when at last they faced the world.

In the evening, I drove down off the Pocono Plateau and over the folded mountains and across the Great Valley and up the New Jersey Highlands and down into the basin and home. No amount of intervening terrain, though—and no amount of distance—could remove from my mind the picture of the covered entrance in the Pennsylvania hillside, or the thought of what was up there under the snow.

Questions for Discussion

1. In his writing, McPhee always gives readers a great deal of specific data, as he does in "Under the Snow," where we learn the weight of the bear cubs, the length of the sow, the kind of plane Buck Alt flies, and so on. Why is McPhee so specific about details? Does this specificity add to the interest of his writing? Why?

2. On the basis of this essay, what sort of person do you take John McPhee to be? Explain. How does he differ from Hunter Thompson (see pages 122–133) and Tom Wolfe (pages 103–121).

3. What did the cubs mean to McPhee? How do you know?

4. Using "Under the Snow" (and other selections in this chapter) as evidence, support and explain the statement that the new journalism puts the writer-reporter into the forefront of the action.

5. Tom Wolfe wanted to give the reader a sense of a city; Thompson, an idea of what motorcycle club members are like. What does McPhee attempt to convey in this selection? Discuss details or passages from the essay that reinforce this purpose.

─────────── SUGGESTIONS FOR WRITING ───────────

1.   Think about Hunter S. Thompson's essay "Roll 'em boys." Probably you don't belong to an outlaw motorcycle gang like the Hell's Angels, but you are a member of other groups: the friends with whom you normally run around (your "gang"), a fraternity or sorority, a church, a union.

Choose a group of which you are a member and write a report on it.

From Hunter Thompson's piece, you can gain excellent ideas for structuring your own essay. For example, in writing about your organization, you might

> a.   Choose typical characters, just as Hunter Thompson chose Terry the Tramp and Sonny Barger to represent the sort of people one would be likely to find in the Hell's Angels.
> b.   Use a narrative framework. Hunter Thompson embedded his whole essay in the story of the Labor Day run, giving details about the Hell's Angels at appropriate spots. You could choose an event typical of your organization—a church supper, a sorority rush party, the annual Mensa banquet—as the basis for your discussion.

2.   Write a characterization of a place: your residence (whether a college dorm, a white cottage in the suburbs, or an apartment house in the city), your neighborhood, your college—or any other place you know thoroughly. From Tom Wolfe's "Las Vegas (What?) Las Vegas," you can get some ideas for developing your essay. For example, your essay can be a series of sharply drawn scenes, of specific impressions, and these can be set side by side in almost any order. (Ask yourself how Tom Wolfe's essay could be rearranged.) In writing about Las Vegas, Tom Wolfe gives us sounds (the craps dealer's monologue, the cash register sound of the slot machines, Muzak), sights (the titanic, garish neon signs, for example), and characters of two kinds: classes (for example, the old babes at the slot machines) and individuals (for example, Raymond). As you begin to think about your own essay, keep in mind Wolfe's handling of sounds, sights, and characters: his essay might serve as a rough model for your own.

3.   In *Pilgrim at Tinker Creek*, Annie Dillard records experience with the natural world—for example,

> The mockingbird took a single step into the air and dropped. His wings were still folded against his sides as though he were singing from a limb and not falling, accelerating thirty-two feet per second per second [*sic*], through empty air. Just a breath before he would have been dashed to the ground, he unfurled his wings with exact, deliberate care,

revealing the broad bars of white, spread his elegant, white-banded tail, and so floated onto the grass. I had just rounded a corner when his insouciant step caught my eye; there was no one else in sight. The fact of his free fall was like the old philosophical conundrum about the tree that falls in the forest. The answer must be, I think, that beauty and grace are performed whether or not we will or sense them. The least we can do is try to be there.[1]

Of course, we *are* there, in the natural world, if we will but observe.

Report one of your experiences with animals—and remember that cockroaches and camels, rats and rhinoceroses, and alley cats and alligators, not to mention pets and farm animals, are all members of that class.

Before you begin to write or even plan your essay, you might reread "Under the Snow," by John McPhee. From McPhee we learn a great deal about bears in Pennsylvania; his piece is informative. It is also permeated with the author's attitude: his sense of wonder, his love for the cubs.

Yet McPhee never becomes sentimental, thus embarrassing the reader, and one way to avoid sentimentality is to present a vivid account of what happened without commenting on the event. In the following, the one word *greedily* and the brief narration of what McPhee did with the cub convey the emotion that he felt.

> Outside, each in turn, the cubs were put in the stuff sack—a male and a female. The female weighed four pounds. Greedily, I reached for her when Alt took her out of the bag. I planted her on my shoulder while I wrote down facts about her mother.

Make your essay informative in two ways: so the reader will learn something about the animal (or animals) you choose as a subject and also about your attitude toward this animal (or these animals).

4.   Write a character sketch: a "portrait" and account of someone who interests you (for example, a family member, a friend, a teacher or boss). Before you begin to write, read the sketch of "Page" (pages 134–139) and "Gear" (pages 140–146). What techniques do Herr and Goldstein use to bring their characters to life?

5.   Statistics indicate that more money is spent yearly on cosmetics than for charity. In an essay that recalls "Gear" and "A Decription of Rejection," discuss the importance of appearance and other personal and social values.

---

[1]Annie Dillard, *Pilgrim at Tinker Creek* (New York: Bantam, 1975), p. 8.

6. Explain why you would rather go on a Hell's Angels run with Hunter Thompson than bear hunting with John McPhee, or vice versa.

7. Crawford Woods has said, "The whole point of this new picaresque [sort of writing] is that the American style rogue hero must not merely tease or insult the Silent Majority, but abuse it, outrage it, twist it, hurt it, smash it." Discuss two or three characteristics of the people that Tom Wolfe and Hunter Thompson seem to classify as "average Americans," and explain why you find the pictures accurate, unfair, ridiculous, or whatever your assessment is.

8. Rewrite your favorite fairytale in the style of the New Journalism. Choose Hunter Thompson or Tom Wolfe as your model.

9. The following are some reactions to Hunter Thompson's writing:

> "Throughout his career, Thompson's writing has been called self-indulgent, grating and inaccurate." (Leo Litvak)

> "The book [Hell's Angels] should have the widest reader appeal, and should be a must for students of crime, deviance, and social problems . . . and indeed anyone concerned with understanding and controlling genuine outlaws." (Choice)

> "Hunter Thompson evokes the same kind of admiration one would feel for a streaker at Queen Victoria's funeral." (William F. Buckley, Jr.)

> Hunter Thompson "views them [Hell's Angels] as creatures of an irresponsible society, given their image by an irresponsible press embodying the nation's puerile fantasy life." (Elmer Bendinger, Newsweek)

> "Thompson sees the Angels as contemporary folk heroes whose romantic delinquency has a vast appeal in a nation of frightened dullards." (William Hogan)

Using a critical statement of your own or one of those quoted above as your topic sentence, write a critical essay on "Roll 'em boys." Is it a good piece of writing. Why?

If you like, you can choose another selection from this chapter as the subject for your critical essay.

C H A P T E R
4

The Lyric in Prose

Lyric in prose or *prose lyric* is a term invented by the editors of this collection. The usual name for the selections in the present chapter is *personal essay,* a kind of writing that had its beginnings in the nineteenth century. Charles Lamb, William Hazlitt, Thomas De Quincey, and others began to produce highly personal, carefully polished writings that centered on their own concerns and attitudes. One might say that intimacy characterized these extremely popular writings.

But we have decided to call the selections we have chosen "lyrics," and there is good reason for this terminology.

One standard reference source, *A Handbook to Literature*, defines lyric thus: "A brief subjective poem strongly marked by imagination, melody, and emotion, and creating for the reader a single, unified impression." The selections in this chapter are not poems, but otherwise they fit the definition very well. They are relatively brief essays; subjective in that they convey the authors' personal attitudes, values, and emotions; imaginative in their use of images and figures of speech, particularly metaphor; and unified, making a single point.

In *Fables of Identity,* the literary critic Northrop Frye distinguishes between works that tell a story—novels, histories, biographies, and autobiographies—and those that don't. The latter category he calls *thematic*, and the essays in this chapter, the lyrics in prose, are thematic.

Frye tells us, "In thematic literature the author and the reader are the only characters involved. . . ." Annie Dillard and Loren Eiseley—these writers address you directly, in poetic, attitudinal terms, for as the philosopher and critic Kenneth Burke has said, the lyric is "the dancing of an attitude," not primarily the attempt to inform (in the sense of conveying data, facts) or to persuade (as a campaign speech or an ad for breakfast cereal might).

These lyrical essays set out to prove nothing, and although they are not illogical, their power comes from their tone, their nature as personal statements of writers, not from their incontrovertible arguments.

ANNIE DILLARD

Pilgrim at Tinker Creek, *which won the 1974 Pulitzer Prize in nonfiction,
was inspired by the account of a young girl who, after cataract surgery,
saw for the first time. "Seeing for the first time" became the central
metaphor in the book, which is a meditation about seeing the Roanoke
Creek banks and the Blue Ridge mountainsides, and about the author's
seeing herself. It is an account of vision, filled with marvelous
discoveries: a Monarch butterfly, a copperhead, insect pests. "I learn that
ten percent of all the world's species are parasitic insects. . . . Parasitism:
this itch, this gasp in the lung, this coiled worm in the gut, hatching egg
in the sinew, warble-hole in the hide—is a sort of rent, paid by all
creatures who live in the world with us now."*

*Ms. Dillard was born in Pittsburgh in 1948. In 1965, she married
the poet and novelist Richard Henry Wilde Dillard. Her education was at
Hollins College (B.A., 1967; M.A., 1968). Author of a collection of
poems,* Tickets for a Prayer Wheel, *she has been a contributing editor for*
Harper's *magazine and has written for* Atlantic Monthly, Sports
Illustrated, American Scholar, *and other magazines.*

*Dillard's meditations on nature and the human condition are
directly in the American Romantic tradition of Thoreau, whose* Walden *is
the ideal companion piece for* Pilgrim at Tinker Creek.

The Horns of the Altar

I received once as a gift a small, illustrated layman's guide to insect pests. These are insects that for one reason or another are in the way of human culture—or economics. By no means all are parasites. Nevertheless, the book reads like the devil's *summa theologica.* The various insects themselves include cottony-cushion scales, bean beetles, borers, weevils, bulb flies, thrips, cutworms, stink bugs, screw-worms, sawflies, poultry lice, cheese skippers, cheese mites, cluster flies, puss caterpillars, itch mites, and long-tailed mealy bugs. Of cockroaches the book says, "When very abundant, they may also eat human hair, skin, and nails." (The key word, *skin,* is buried.) The full-color pictures show warbled beef and fly-blown gashes, blighted trees and blasted corn, engorged ticks and seething ham, pus-eyed hogs and the wormy nostrils of sheep.

In another book I learn that ten percent of all the world's species are parasitic insects. It is hard to believe. What if you were an inventor, and you made ten percent of your inventions in such a way that they could only work by harassing, disfiguring, or totally destroying the other ninety percent? These things are not well enough known.

There is, for instance, a species of louse for almost every species of everything else. In addition to sucking blood, lice may also eat hair, feathers, the dry scales of moths, and other lice. Birdbanders report that wild birds are universally infested with lice, to each its own. Songbirds often squat in the dust near ant hills and spray themselves with a shower of living ants; it is thought that the formic acid in the ants discourages the presence of lice. "Each species of auk has its own species of louse, found on all individuals examined." The European cuckoo is the sole host to three species of lice, and the glossy ibis to five, each specializing in eating a different part of the host's body. Lice live in the hollow quills of bird's feathers, in wart hog bristles, in Antarctic seals' flippers and pelican pouches.

Fleas are almost as widely distributed as lice, but much more catholic in their choice of hosts. Immature fleas, interestingly, feed almost entirely on the feces of their parents and other adults, while mature fleas live on sucked blood.

Parasitic two-winged insects, such as flies and mosquitos, abound. It is these that cause hippos to live in the mud and frenzied caribou to trample their young. Twenty thousand head of domestic livestock died in Europe from a host of black flies that swarmed from the banks of the Danube in

1923. Some parasitic flies live in the stomachs of horses, zebras, and elephants; others live in the nostrils and eyes of frogs. Some feed on earthworms, snails, and slugs; others attack and successfully pierce mosquitos already engorged on stolen blood. Still others live on such delicate fare as the brains of ants, the blood of nestling songbirds, or the fluid in the wings of lacewings and butterflies.

The lives of insects and their parasites are horribly entwined. The usual story is that the larva of the parasite eats the other insect alive in any of several stages and degrees of consciousness. It is above all parasitic *Hymenoptera*—which for the sake of simplicity I shall call wasps—that specialize in this behavior. Some species of wasps are so "practiced" as parasites that the female will etch a figure-eight design on the egg of another insect in which she has just laid her egg, and other wasps will avoid ovipositing on those marked, already parasitized eggs. There are over one hundred thousand species of parasitic wasps, so that, although many life histories are known, many others are still mysterious. British entomologist R.R. Askew says, "The field is wide open, the prospect inviting." The field may be wide open, but—although most of my favorite entomologists seem to revel in these creatures—the prospect is, to me at least, scarcely inviting.

Consider this story of Edwin Way Teale's. He brought a monarch butterfly caterpillar inside to photograph just as it was about to pupate. The pale green caterpillar had hung itself upside-down from a leaf, as monarch caterpillars have done from time immemorial, in the form of a letter J.

"All that night it remained as it was. The next morning, at eight o'clock, I noticed that the curve in the 'J' had become shallower. Then, suddenly, as though a cord within had been severed, the larva straightened out and hung limp. Its skin was baggy and lumpy. It began to heave as the lumps within pushed and moved. At 9:30 A.M., the first of the six white, fat-bodied grubs appeared through the skin of the caterpillar. Each was about three eighths of an inch in length." This was the work of a parasitic wasp.

There is a parasitic wasp that travels on any adult female praying mantis, feeding on her body wherever she goes. When the mantis lays her eggs, the wasp lays hers, inside the frothy mass of bubbles before it hardens, so that the early-hatching wasp larvae emerge inside the case to eat the developing mantis eggs. Others eat cockroach eggs, ticks, mites, and houseflies. Many seek out and lay eggs on the caterpillars of butterflies and moths; sometimes they store paralyzed, living caterpillars, on which eggs have been laid, in underground burrows where they stay "fresh" for as long as nine months. Askew, who is apparently very alert, says, "The mass of yellowish cocoons of the braconid *Apanteles glomeratus* beneath the shrivelled remains of a large white butterfly caterpillar are a familiar sight."

There are so many parasitic wasps that some parasitic wasps have parasitic wasps. One startled entomologist, examining the gall made by a vegetarian oak gall wasp, found parasitism of the fifth order. This means that he found the remains of an oak gall wasp which had a parasitic wasp which had another which had another which had another which had another, if I count it right.

Other insect orders also include fascinating parasites. Among true bugs are bed-bugs, insects that parasitize dozens of species of bats, and those that parasitize bed-bugs. Parasitic beetles as larvae prey on other insects, and as adults on bees and kangaroos. There is a blind beetle that lives on beavers. The cone-nose bug, or kissing bug, bites the lips of sleeping people, sucking blood and injecting an excruciating toxin.

There is an insect order that consists entirely of parasitic insects called, singly and collectively, stylops, which is interesting because of the grotesquerie of its form and its effects. Stylops parasitize divers other insects such as leaf hoppers, ants, bees, and wasps. The female spends her entire life inside the body of her host, with only the tip of her bean-shaped body protruding. She is a formless lump, having no wings, legs, eyes, or antennae; her vestigial mouth and anus are tiny, degenerate, and nonfunctional. She absorbs food— her host—through the skin of her abdomen, which is "inflated, white, and soft."

The sex life of a stylops is equally degenerate. The female has a wide, primitive orifice called a "brood canal" near her vestigial mouthparts, out in the open air. The male inserts his sperm into the brood canal, whence it flows into her disorganized body and fertilizes the eggs that are floating freely there. The hatched larvae find their way to the brood canal and emerge into the "outside world."

The unfortunate insects on which the stylops feed, although they live normal life spans, frequently undergo inexplicable changes. Their colors brighten. The gonads of males and females are "destroyed," and they not only lose their secondary sexual characteristics, they actually acquire those of the opposite sex. This happens especially to bees, in which the differences between the sexes are pronounced. "A stylopsised insect," says Askew, "may sometimes be described as an intersex."

Finally, completing this whirlwind survey of parasitic insects, there are, I was surprised to learn, certain parasitic moths. One moth caterpillar occurs regularly in the *horns* of African ungulates. One adult, winged moth lives on the skin secretions between the hairs of the fur of the three-fingered sloth. Another adult moth sucks mammal blood in southeast Asia. Last of all, there are the many eye-moths, which feed as winged adults about the open eyes of domestic cattle, sucking blood, pus, and tears.

Let me repeat that these parasitic insects comprise ten percent of all known animal species. How can this be understood? Certainly we give our infants the wrong idea about their fellow creatures in the world. Teddy bears should come with tiny stuffed bear-lice; ten percent of all baby bibs and rattles sold should be adorned with colorful blowflies, maggots, and screwworms. What kind of devil's tithe do we pay? What percentage of the world's species that are *not* insects are parasitic? Could it be, counting bacteria and viruses, that we live in a world in which half the creatures are running from—or limping from—the other half?

The creator is no puritan. A creature need not work for a living; creatures may simply steal and suck and be blessed for all that with a share—an enormous share—of the sunlight and air. There is something that profoundly fails to be exuberant about these crawling, translucent lice and white, fat-bodied grubs, but there is an almost manic exuberance about a creator who turns them out, creature after creature, and sets them buzzing and lurking and flying and swimming about. These parasites are our companions at life, wending their dim, unfathomable ways into the tender tissues of their living hosts, searching as we are simply for food, for energy to grow and breed, to fly or creep on the planet, adding more shapes to the texture of intricacy and more life to the universal dance.

Parasitism: this itch, this gasp in the lung, this coiled worm in the gut, hatching egg in the sinew, warble-hole in the hide—is a sort of rent, paid by all creatures who live in the real world with us now. It is not an extortionary rent: Wouldn't you pay it, don't you, a little blood from the throat and wrists for the taste of the air? Ask the turtle. True, for some creatures it is a slow death; for others, like the stylopsised bee, it is a strange, transfigured life. For most of us Western humans directly it is a pinprick or scabrous itch here and there from a world we learned early could pinch, and no surprise. Or it is the black burgeoning of disease, the dank baptismal lagoon into which we are dipped by blind chance many times over against our wishes, until one way or another we die. Chomp. It is the thorn in the flesh of the world, another sign, if any be needed, that the world is actual and fringed, pierced here and there, and through and through, with the toothed conditions of time and the mysterious, coiled spring of death.

Outright predators, of course, I understand. I am among them. There is no denying that the feats of predators can be just as gruesome as those of the unlovely parasites: the swathing and sipping of trapped hummingbirds by barn spiders, the occasional killing and eating of monkeys by chimpanzees. If I were to eat as the delicate ladybug eats, I would go through in just nine days the entire population of Boys Town. Nevertheless, the most rapacious lurk and charge of any predator is not nearly so sinister as the silent hatching of barely visible, implanted eggs. With predators, at least you have a chance.

One night this summer I had gone looking for muskrats, and was waiting on the long pedestrian bridge over the widest part of the creek. No muskrat came, but a small event occurred in a spider's web strung from the lower rung of the bridge's handrail. As I watched, a tiny pale-green insect flew directly into the spider's web. It jerked violently, bringing the spider charging. But the fragile insect, which was no larger than a fifth of the spider's abdomen, extricated itself from the gluey strands in a flurry, dropped in a deadfall to the hard bridge surface a foot below, stood, shook itself, and flew away. I felt as I felt on the way back from lobar pneumonia, stuffed with penicillin and taking a few steps outside: *vive la chance.*

Recently I have been keeping an informal list of the ones that got away, of living creatures I have seen in various states of disarray. It started with spiders. I used to see a number of daddy-longlegs, or harvestmen, in the summer, and I got in the idle habit of counting their legs. It didn't take me long to notice that hardly ever did an adult of any size cross my path which was still hitting on all eight cylinders. Most had seven legs, some had six. Even in the house I noticed that the larger spiders tended to be missing a leg or two.

Then last September I was walking across a gravel path in full sunlight, when I nearly stepped on a grasshopper. I poked its leg with a twig to see it hop, but no hop came. So I crouched down low on my hands and knees, and sure enough, her swollen ovipositor was sunk into the gravel. She was pulsing faintly—with a movement not nearly so strained as the egg-laying mantis's was—and her right antenna was broken off near the base. She'd been around. I thought of her in the Lucas meadow, too, where so many grasshoppers leaped about me. One of those was very conspicuously lacking one of its big, springlike hind legs—a grasslunger. It seemed to move fairly well from here to there, but then of course I didn't know where it had been aiming.

Nature seems to catch you by the tail. I think of all the butterflies I have seen whose torn hind wings bore the jagged marks of birds' bills. There were four or five tiger swallowtails missing one of their tails, and a fritillary missing two thirds of a hind wing. The birds, too, who make up the bulk of my list, always seem to have been snatched at from behind, except for the killdeer I saw just yesterday, who was missing all of its toes; its slender shank ended in a smooth, gray knob. Once I saw a swallowtailed sparrow, who on second look proved to be a sparrow from whose tail the central wedge of feathers had been torn. I've seen a completely tailless sparrow, a tailless robin, and a tailless grackle. Then my private list ends with one bob-tailed and one tailless squirrel, and a muskrat kit whose tail bore a sizeable nick near the spine.

The testimony of experts bears out the same point: it's rough out there. Gerald Durrell, defending the caging of animals in well-kept zoos, says that the animals he collects from the wild are all either ridden with parasites, recovering from various wounds, or both. Howard Ensign Evans finds the butterflies in his neck of the woods as tattered as I do. A southwest Virginia naturalist noted in his journal for April, 1896, "Mourning-cloaks are plentiful but broken, having lived through the winter." Trappers have a hard time finding unblemished skins. Cetologists photograph the scarred hides of living whales, striated with gashes as long as my body, and hilly with vast colonies of crustaceans called whale lice.

Finally, Paul Siple, the Antarctic explorer and scientist, writes of the Antarctic crab-eater seal, which lives in the pack ice off the continent: "One seldom finds a sleek silvery adult crab-eater that does not bear ugly scars—or two-foot long parallel slashes—on each side of its body, received when it managed somehow to wriggle out of the jaws of a killer whale that had seized it."

I think of those crab-eater seals, and the jaws of the killer whales lined with teeth that are, according to Siple, "as large as bananas." How did they get away? How did not one or two, but most of them get away? Of course any predator that decimates its prey will go hungry, as will any parasite that kills its host species. Predator and prey offenses and defenses (and fecundity is a defense) usually operate in such a way that both populations are fairly balanced, stable in the middle as it were, and frayed and nibbled at the edges, like a bitten apple that still bears its seeds. Healthy caribou can outrun a pack of wolves; the wolves cull the diseased, old, and injured, who stray behind the herd. All this goes without saying. But it is truly startling to realize how on the very slender bridge of chance some of the most "efficient" predators operate. Wolves literally starve to death in valleys teeming with game. How many crab-eater seals can one killer whale *miss* in a lifetime?

Still, it is to the picture of the "sleek silvery" crab-eater seals that I return, seals drawn up by scientists from the Antarctic ice pack, seals bearing again and again the long gash marks of unthinkable teeth. Any way you look at it, from the point of view of the whale or the seal or the crab, from the point of view of the mosquito or copperhead or frog or dragonfly or minnow or rotifer, it is chomp or fast.

Questions for Discussion

1. Dillard says that doing research in the field of parasitic wasps is "scarcely inviting." Yet she does write six pages about parasitic insects. How do you account for the seeming contradiction?

2. "She [the female stylops] is a formless lump, having no wings, legs, eyes, or antennae; her vestigial mouth and anus are tiny, degenerate,

and nonfunctional. . . .The sex life of a stylops is equally degenerate." Explain the meaning of *degenerate* in this context. In what ways does the term not apply?

3. Dillard proposes that "Teddy bears should come with tiny stuffed bear lice; ten percent of all baby bibs and rattles should be adorned with colorful blowflies, maggots, and screw-worms." How do you react to Dillard's suggestion? What was her point in making it?

4. Ten percent of all the world's species are parasitic insects that harass, disfigure, or totally destroy the other ninety percent. How does Dillard distinguish between parasites and predators?

5. What can the selection title mean? What does it suggest? Why do you think Dillard chose this title?

6. Without its specific details, "The Horns of the Altar" would be uninteresting and uninformative. What are some of the effects Dillard achieves with details? Refer to specific passages in the text.

7. Is "The Horns of the Altar" merely about parasitic insects, or does it have a larger purpose, a broader theme? If so, state that theme in a sentence. In other words, write a topic sentence for the essay.

F. GONZALEZ-CRUSSI

F. Gonzalez-Crussi was born in Mexico City and grew up there. He received his M.D. degree from the National University of Mexico, did postdoctoral work in the United States and Canada, and since 1978, has been professor of pathology at Northwestern University and head of the Division of Anatomical Pathology at Children's Memorial Hospital in Chicago. He has written two technical books in his field and more than ninety articles.

He is also, obviously, something of an anthropologist, investigating and thinking about the tribal customs of the modern industrialized world—embalming, for instance.

On Embalming

Ceremony and ritual spring from our heart of hearts: those who govern us know it well, for they would sooner deny us bread than dare alter the observance of tradition. And yet funeral ceremonies can change. The Dayak people of Borneo used to preserve the body of a dead chief in the communal house of the living, a practice they had to abandon under the pressure of Dutch officials who did not take kindly to this form of mixed company. With equally commendable sanitary zeal, authorities in India have been known to oppose the ancient customs of the Parsis of Bombay, Zoroastrian votaries, who place the bodies of their dead atop circular constructions, where, in a matter of hours, vultures dispose neatly of all the fleshy parts. Europeans generally perceived a lurid aura about this ritual and showed little sympathy for what they saw as a "secret cult of death." Yet the Parsi custom dates its origins at least six centuries before the birth of Christ and was inspired by the currently much-vaunted goal of decreasing ecologic contamination: the Zoroastrian believes the dead body so unclean that it would contaminate the "pure elements" of the universe—earth, fire, and water.

In Europe and the United States embalming was practically unknown before the latter part of the eighteenth century. The modern technic of this procedure is generally attributed to the Scottish anatomist William Hunter. Before his day, and in the United States up to the years of the Civil War, cadavers that had to be transported or kept unburied for days were simply packed in ice. There were "cooling boards," concave devices filled with ice in which the body could fit snugly, but, beyond this rudimentary inventiveness, it may be said that corpse technology had not really been put at the service of the common people.

Consider this telling difference between East and West: among the ancient Egyptians, embalming was but one aspect of a life oversaturated with things spiritual and preoccupied with the possible fate of the soul after the body had perished. In the industrial West, there has been an equally universal and all-encompassing preoccupation. It is called desire for profit, and, as will become apparent here, it has done much for the spread of the practice of embalming.

In the West, embalming and greed seem to have been wedded from the beginning. John Hunter, younger brother of the Scottish anatomist, came across an exceptional opportunity to apply his brother's methods. A wealthy woman, Mrs. Martin Van Butchell, under motives obscure and indecipherable, wrote a peculiar will. It was her intention, duly legalized by seals and signatures, that her surviving husband should have control of her fortune only for as long as she would remain above ground. Upon her demise, her husband acted with a determination all the more admirable for being mixed with grief. John Hunter was summoned to the homestead. Mrs. Van Butchell's remains were injected intra-arterially with fluids of recent invention, and the lady ended up, fashionably clad in her best finery, inside a glass-lidded container, before which she received friends and relatives.

After these auspicious beginnings, the career of the embalming practice made impressive gains, but nowhere as sound as in the United States, where the government threw its full weight behind it. Here, embalming became mandatory by law whenever the interval between death and burial exceeds forty-eight hours (twenty-four in some states) or when the body must be transported a certain distance. To say that embalming is big business in America would be, as everyone knows, a great understatement. According to recent statistics, less than 8 percent of the lifeless population of this country is disposed of by cremation, and since alternative methods of disposal, such as cannibalism or Zoroastrian exposure, must be very infrequently practiced in America, it follows that embalming continues to be an economically important activity. This is true from the standpoint of the total economy of the nation as well as from the more restricted viewpoint of individual enterprise.

However spurious or suspect the origins of Western embalming, the pathologist ought to acknowledge his gratitude to the practitioners of this trade. Theirs is an activity that cannot be dismissed as menial, in spite of its frequent unpleasantness. At its most perfected and professional, it is no exaggeration to say that it should be called an art. Without the skillful intervention of dieners, funeral house directors, and morgue attendants, the pathologist's task would be much more onerous and frequently impossible, for it is part of his job to secure bodily parts for conscientious study—in some cases entire mandibles, eyes, femurs, or vertebral columns.

On a rare occasion, the pathologist, at the completion of his task, has looked back on the remains lying on the table and felt a chill upon realizing that professional zeal has caused him to alter the human form in a manner apt to be called a defilement. The dead possess an identity, granted by the living through the agency of intact form; so long as form remains, a cadaver remains "the same one" for associates and relatives, for friend and foe. But without spine or limbs or eyes (which virtually never are removed during an autopsy study), the form is altered and diminished; without ribs, the dead person is a frail manikin; without jaw, the human face is a grotesque mask. For the body to be viewed at this time by the most generous purveyors of identity, his loved ones, could mean disaster.

Such catastrophic events are, happily, almost unheard of. In the exceptional case of removal of a large bodily part, the adroit ministrations of the mortician will avert a sad outcome. In place of absent bones he places rigid rods or sticks; he restores and reconstructs, closes off incisions, and fills up gaps. In the end, like a proud craftsman, he sits back and contemplates his finished production awaiting the final verdict: the "viewing" ceremony. And since the dead are often the worn-out, shattered rejects of life, he can aspire, like a true artist, to improve the work of nature. Cotton pledgets under the eyelids will counteract the effects of dehydration; placed inside the cheeks, they will make the hollowed-out appearance of consumption yield to a more robust semblance of life. The eyes, fixed in a dilated stare of horror, are carefully closed according to the *Manual of the Embalmer* "so that the upper eyelid covers exactly two-thirds of the globe"; then they are smeared with Vaseline to prevent drying. And even the pallor of extreme anemia (the color of shrouds) or advanced jaundice (yellow as gamboge) will disappear under the influence of dyes and bleaching agents mixed in the embalming fluid, distributed under brand names like Blossom and Spring and promoted with catchy slogans in morticians' magazines that read: "As if he were sleeping" or "Bring back the colors of spring." Yes; as long as the somewhat macabre custom of deathwatch endures, the pathologist will need beside him those dexterous assistants whose calling means protection from charges that range between minor fluke and hideous sacrilege.

When younger, I cherished the romantic notion that in the age of the New Kingdom of Egypt secrets of embalming were discovered that surpassed in effectiveness the most advanced technics of our day. The image of priests and mortician-priests uttering magical incantations inside pharaonic tombs and preserving dead bodies from decomposition for two thousand years is sure to fire the romantic fantasy of any youth. It was with some disappointment that I learned that, in terms of sheer technical efficacy, the ancient Egyptians achieved only mediocre results and that their methods are neither mysterious nor unexplainable to us. Apparently, the Egyptians covered the dead with blocks of natre, or natron, a natural salt found in the Nile Valley. Instead of being an esoteric formula, natron turns out to be a mixture of rather commonplace chemicals, namely, sodium carbonate and sodium bicarbonate, with a varying amount of impurities, chiefly sodium sulfate and common salt. Thus the Egyptians merely "salted" their corpses, slowly extracting water, which is indispensable for the enzymatic actions that account for decomposition; at the same time, the salts produced a weak fixation.

The desired effects were more easily achieved by removal of the viscera, which were placed in canopic jars, but the process was slow; a job was not completed in less than a month or two. And at the end of this lengthy preparation, the task was not over for these forebears of the modern embalmer. Followed the laborious swathing with bandages soaked in resins and gum resins and the sprinkling with scents, all of which are now known to possess antibacterial agents. All according to elaborate ritual: the bandage of Nekheb on the well-oiled forehead; the bandage of Hathor on the face; and there was also the gilding of the nails, and the crystal to lighten the face, and carnelian to strengthen the steps of the deceased in the underworld. There followed a strange ceremony that stands in curious opposition to ours. This was called "the opening of the mouth." Mouth and eyes of the recently embalmed cadaver, or its effigy, were pried open by means of specially designed instruments held by a priest, in contrast to our "pious" gesture of closing the same natural orifices in the recently departed. The very concrete ideas of the Egyptians about the voyage awaiting the dead might explain this singular gesture: the deceased had to be in fit condition to pronounce the sacred incantations that were passwords to the beyond. Think of the responsibility of these ancestors of the profession: careless facial bandaging meant considerably more than a pardonable fluke; it meant precluding an immortal soul from gaining salvation, by gagging!

Though divested of their mystery, the ministrations of these predecessors of present-day morticians remain admirable. How many craftsmen, or even renowned artists, today can feel confident that their work will be admired two thousand years hence, as we admire the excellent state of preservation of Seti I? This is not to say that all Egyptian embalmers were equally competent. Archeologists must be uniquely aware that there were bunglers, especially at those times when the suspense attending the undoing of bandages turns to dismay upon discovering, instead of the majestic presence of a ruler come down the ages in gold and lapis lazuli, a heap of crumbling filth swarming with insects. Still, the Egyptian technic was compatible with a respectful and solemn attitude toward the dead. On the authority of a distinguished pathologist, Guido Majno, we know that they neither immersed them in brine, as they did—and we do—with fish, nor roasted them over slow fires, as some South American Indians have been known to do—and as we are wont to do with chickens, producing comparable results. Their procedure was, in the graphic saying of Majno, "mothballing, and with weak mothballs at that."[1]

What is apparent to the modern embalmer, in stark contrast with the ancient calling, is that all these carryings-on are strictly for the benefit of the living. The questions are seriously raised among the practitioners of the trade whether the remains should be "laid out" with glasses on, whether cosmetics should be applied, and whether the placement of dentures is indispensable. Not for a minute is it assumed that the decedent will need to have his vision corrected or his denture fit for biting an apple; nor is he in need of any of the three shades of pink cosmetic distributed by B. and G. Products,

---

[1]Until recently, no author who wrote about embalming for the general public had any firsthand experience with the members of the mètier. This has been corrected with the appearance of an admirable volume, a work demonstrating the highest scholarly achievement and possessing the most engrossing readability, by the distinguished pathologist Guide Majno: *The Healing Hand* (Cambridge: Harvard University Press, 1975).

guaranteed to reproduce "nature's own skin texture . . . the velvety appearance of living tissue." Among the highest spheres of power in the National Funeral Directors Association, the statement that embalming is a procedure designed with the living in mind would not be received without controversy. It is difficult, however, to agree on just how embalming benefits the living. For reasons not hard to guess, officialdom within the NFDA proclaims that an open-coffin ceremony serves laudable purposes, to wit, aiding in the direct expression of grief, providing a suitable atmosphere for mourning, and helping the bereaved to face the finality of death. The problem is one that has been much pondered, without a single answer yet in sight. It is counterargued that the display of the body may be traumatic to certain individuals, especially to children, even when forewarned and instructed on what to expect; that "viewing" is hardly an aid to contemplate death when the "viewee" has been meticulously restored to impart to its external appearance a close semblance of life; that a person's ability to grasp the concept of death is the product of his total life experience, quite independent of "viewing"; and that, in any case, a memorial service is sufficient reminder of the ineluctability of death, thus rendering immaterial the open or closed state of the coffin's lid.

I believe there is at the core of the embalmer's officiousness a desire to remove the harrowing aspects of death, to expunge its painful appearance, and to erase all hurtful experiences for the survivors. I also believe that this is not altogether contemptible. Perhaps this desire to beautify the unavoidable miseries of an essentially finite, hence decaying, existence is a conspicuous feature of the American way of life. At least, such a thesis was proposed and developed by the French philosopher Jacques Maritain, who illustrated it with the following autobiographical anecdote.

Maritain, newly arrived in the United States, was entirely taken by the general civility and democratic warmth which he, like most foreigners, noticed immediately upon arrival. In academic circles, he observed, the students are not treated arrogantly by their professors but consort amicably with them; and the latter, regardless of their rank, see it as their duty to ease the way of learning for the students. This contrasts with the rigid scholastic mores and the unbridgeable chasm that often separates, in other countries, the humble student from the haughty pinnacles of professional arrogance. In public offices, transactions are closed expeditiously and, allowing for the inherently frustrating nature of red tape, with considerably less humiliation than attend dealings with the bureaucracy in other lands. This polite efficiency he found also in his visits to the dentist. Immaculately attired nurses and dental assistants, working in a spotless environment among gleaming equipment, directed him, positioned him, inquired of his needs, and prepared him for the reparative dental work. All was done with the utmost efficiency and with no other interruptions than required by brief, polite questions: "Are you comfortable?" "Is everything all right?"

Suddenly, while sitting in the dentist's chair, the thought came to him that if he were to suffer a fatal heart attack right then, all these professionals, technicians, assistants, and attendants would continue to perform their most attentive, purposeful, and determined services. A cold sweat covered his forehead as he imagined the smiling nurses, professional composure undaunted, laying him out on a bier. Everything would be as orderly, methodical, and efficient as before: his arms would be brought together so that his hands would touch each other in a pious and collected gesture; his body would be smoothly transferred into a well-designed coffin with chromed edges; and all expert finishing touches would be put on his remains by attendants whose unruffled expressions would be the same as when, minutes before, they inquired of him: "Are you comfortable?" and "Is everything all right?" This vision so shockingly conflicted with Maritain's conception of a Catholic passing away to await the Day of Resurrection that he became the first patient ever to change dentists for entirely theological reasons.

Maritain was highly partial to the whitewashing instinct of white Anglo-Saxon America. In this he saw neither insensitivity nor hypocrisy. He believed in an inherent "goodness" of the American people that leads them to attempt to efface all the potentially hurtful aspects of life. Misery and suffering seem, upon but slight reflection, the inescapable lot of life; even more so: part and parcel of life, like breathing. Through a kind of heroic contumaciousness, Americans are impelled to disbelieve this appalling truth. On the positive side, this monumentally wistful attitude forms the basis of their superior technological ingenuity. If life appears to many as a fatal stupefying bondage of sweat and toil, Americans will counter by inventing machines and gadgets to shake the yoke—the same gadgets that, incidentally, will be avidly taken up by those very critics who thunder against the "dehumanizing" perils of American technology. When the funeral customs of Americans are examined by this light, it is not easy to be overly critical of the ceremony of "viewing" an embalmed dead person. Death, like the sun, cannot be viewed directly; it is like an unfathomable void that gives us a sort of metaphysical vertigo if we so much as go near the edge of the cliff. Yet if there is an element of the ridiculous in a custom that substitutes a "restored" corpse, made up to look like a living doll, for the uncontemplable spectacle of death, we must confess that the same is true for most symbolic ritual. And then all harsh criticism recedes in front of the discovery that this is yet another attempt, however naive, of a people bent on removing all unpleasantness from life; a further manifestation of the American's "goodness" that wills universal politeness and whose motto might well be "Cleanliness and contentment for all!"

The ridiculous, however, is the least of dangers in such an attitude. Behind the illusion that life can be a succession of smiling scenes, with neither pain nor passion, lurks the delusion that death without anguish can be bought for money in an over-the-counter transaction. Cash, check, or credit card. And behind this counter hides the ugly mien of philistinism, for which it is impossible to feel much sympathy. In the *Consumers Report on Conventional Funerals and Burial* there is an account of alarming excesses of commercialism that plague these services. In one case, mourners were introduced into a richly furnished antechamber in which each piece of decor represented, one may reasonably suppose, an extra charge on the bill: flowers at so many dollars; background organ music for such a price; and so on.[2] After a while an usher announced that Mrs. X was ready to receive the visitors, and the mourners went, treading on thick carpets between floral arrangements and parting dark draperies, into another room of still more luxurious decor that seemed right out of *faux* Versailles. There, as if she were a duchess, or at least a countess in a second-rate Hollywood motion picture, sat Mrs. X, or rather the remains of Mrs. X, on a canopied bed abundant in lace and ribbons, dressed in a silk robe and propped up by cushions. Mark what private enterprise can do: the death ceremony transformed into a social visit, with a touch of vulgarity proportionate to the size of the payer's pocket! In another case, a Louisiana entrepreneur hit upon the felicitous idea of organizing the "viewing" ceremony around the "drive-in" concept. Mourners could look from the reassuring security of their automobiles into a display room where the decedent was aptly shown in a most collected and well-kept attitude behind a glass window, reposing on a bier whose end was surmounted by a cross framed with blue neon-gas light tubes. While under interrogation by the congressional committee on irregular funeral practices, the businessman defended well his unorthodox services: families could mourn and pay their visit at all hours, without leaving the soothing enclosure of their own automobiles; they did not have to pay any attention to details of their dress or worry about being the targets of gossip, thus being free to express their grief in a wholesome way; and, once their visit was over, they could simply lower the window of their car, sign a thick register book within arm's reach, and "drive on."

Whereas such practices seem to step on the toes of our sense of righteousness, we might do well, before voicing our indignant execration, to probe the public sentiment on the matter. In letters to the syndicated columnist Ann Landers, complaints were expressed on the charging methods of

---

[2]A number of publications have dealt with abuses in the practices of the funeral industry. I acknowledge my heavy debt to the masterfully written study by Jessica Mitford, *The American Way of Death* (New York: Simon and Schuster, 1963), and to the editors of *Consumer Reports* for their highly entertaining and informative book, *Funerals: Consumers' Last Rights* (New York: W. W. Norton, 1977).

funeral directors. In particular, severe reproof went to those who sell expensive garments with which to dress the cadaver. It was thought that luxurious raiment, difficult to justify for the living, is assuredly a wanton waste on the dead. The expensive clothes are often sold because some undertakers prepare photographs (and oil paintings!) of the decedent, which are later sold to the relatives who, grief stricken, are often vulnerable to these swindles. With her proverbial impartiality, the columnist also published letters of persons who took a different view of the subject. Among these, there was a widow who wrote, "I wouldn't take a million dollars for the pictures I made of my husband laid out in his new blue suit. He looked better in that box than he had any time in the last ten years."

As a pathologist who has seen no rise in his life insurance policy premiums despite customary corpse handling, I am naturally skeptical of reports that extoll embalming as a public health blessing. Lack of embalming of cadavers does not seem a cause of devastating epidemics in most countries, and most countries fail to routinely practice this procedure. For the fact that epidemics are uncommon we ought to acknowledge a greater debt to sanitation engineers or public health officials than to embalmers. Bacteria do proliferate in a cadaver, as anyone can confirm who is of sound nose and comes within fifty paces of the autopsy room. Highly pathogenic organisms proliferate too, but elementary precautions of antisepsis, like the wearing of surgical mask and gloves, seem to adequately protect all exposed personnel. Morgue-acquired infections are part of the romance and lore of the autopsy suite, but one hears of the macabre saga mostly secondhand. I have not been impressed by either the frequency or the nefarious quality of infections therein contracted by persons who live there day by day, although the specialized literature mentions individual instances of dire diseases acquired in this environment.

The practice of embalming dead American citizens is so massively successful that, as is well known, a person living in the United States is statistically likelier to live closer to a funeral home than to a police station or a fire department building. This comes from profit consciousness, not from enlightened legislation. The funeral industry is so well organized and so expertly directed that its revenues are unlikely to decrease, even if funeral customs were to change. Should cremation become the most popular form of disposal of remains, private enterprise will prove equal to the challenge and will be ready to diversify, as they say in financial circles, and to control. However, as a pathologist, too, I am not ready to condemn the practice of embalming as a shameless farce or to pass it up as nothing but a sordid hoax played by the greedy on the gullible. Rather, I see in it an impulse, not without nobility, to prevent, or at least decelerate, the ruin of the human body. Commercialism and dishonesty aside, the embalmer obeys that obscure dictate that would have us stave off, or at least retard, the decay of this marvel. It is our primeval vigor, our deepest creative prepotency, our basic fund of antideath energy, that infuses us with the wish, however irrational, to make the corruptible undecaying and the impermanent eternal. The ancients fancied that the soul did not abandon the body on a sudden but even after death it lingered on for forty-two days, departing gradually and as if by stages. Da Vinci reflected on this theme and thought that it was quite fitting that the soul should dally, for the body is so wondrous a habitation that the soul could not find it easy to part with it, and finding it so painful to quit its mortal domicile, it hesitates. Later, that delicately spiritual writer Paul Valéry, on reading the autobiographical passage of Leonardo that contains these reflections, was greatly intrigued. This was for Valéry a metaphysical system of most peculiar originality: that the farewell scene between body and soul should be imagined as capable of "bringing tears to the eyes . . . of the soul"! Leonardo, it is very important to remember, had personally dissected scores of cadavers; his metaphysical construct may strike many as odd, but pathologists and embalmers should find it perfectly natural.

Questions for Discussion

1. "All these carryings on are strictly for the benefit of the living." Do you agree that our funeral rituals are a benefit to the living? Or do you think we have been brainwashed into believing so, to the economic benefit of undertakers and others who benefit from the laws and customs? What is the author's opinion?
2. In what ways would it be accurate to call embalmers parasitic?
3. Along with advances in medical science has come a demand for "used parts," that is, a dead person's organs that can be transplanted into a needy live human. Recently, lawsuits have been filed because of the theft (by undertakers) of organs from deceased loved ones. What are some pros and cons that will emerge in the trials?
4. Do you find the topic of the essay distasteful? Does the author make it more or less repellent? Cite examples or passages from the selection to support your opinion.
5. Other than macabre interest in how other societies have dealt with death, why do you think the author included a history of embalming?
6. Maritain was favorably disposed to the whitewashing tendency in the American people. Why, then, was he horrified by the efficient, clinical ministrations of the dentist's assistants?
7. What arguments does the author make in favor of the practice of embalming? Against?
8. What is the author's overall attitude toward embalming? Cite specific passages to demonstrate your opinion.

9. What is the literal meaning of the two metaphors in the following sentence? "Death, like the sun, cannot be viewed directly; it is like an unfathomable void that gives us a sort of metaphysical vertigo if we so much as go near the edge of the cliff."
10. What is the author's profession? How might that profession influence his attitude toward his subject?

MARY AUSTIN

The book from which the following selection comes was published in 1903. Why such ancient history in a collection that aims to represent modern writing? The answer is simple: Mary Austin is a "modern" writer, very much in the spirit of Annie Dillard.

In his introduction to the 1974 edition of The Land of Little Rain, *T. M. Pearce says,*

> *In many ways, Mary Austin was an "original." As a literary figure, she followed in the footsteps of other naturists, Henry Thoreau, John Burroughs, and John Muir. But she was no solitary like Thoreau, and no woodsman like Muir. Burroughs is closer to her view of the American environment, for he shared her interest in science and the relationship science held to experiencing nature. When Mary Austin did seek solitude, her world was "peopled," not empty. The farm lands near her home in Illinois not only called her attention to the sights and sounds of birds, the patterns of leaves and flowers, and the maze of forest pathways, but they also brought the mystery of forces sustaining all growth as a shelter and sustenance for the human race. The arid regions of the West, too, were not just a panorama of sand, bunchgrass, and wildlife, but an expression of energy to which both people and animals were related.*

Mary Hunter was born in 1868 in Carlinville, Illinois.

She majored in science at Blackburn College. In 1888, the year of her graduation from college, she moved to California to live with her uncles, her father having died a decade earlier. In 1891 she married Stafford Wallace Austin, owner of a vineyard near Bakersfield, California. During her life, she lived in various places in California, including Carmel; from 1925 to her death in 1934, she lived in Santa Fe, New Mexico.

The Land of Little Rain

East away from the Sierras, south from Panamint and Amargosa, east and south many an uncounted mile, is the Country of Lost Borders.

Ute, Paiute, Mojave, and Shoshone inhabit its frontiers, and as far into the heart of it as a man dare go. Not the law, but the land sets the limit. Desert is the name it wears upon the maps, but the Indian's is the better word. Desert is a loose term to indicate land that supports no man; whether the land can be bitted and broken to that purpose is not proven. Void of life it never is, however dry the air and villainous the soil.

This is the nature of that country. There are hills, rounded, blunt, burned, squeezed up out of chaos, chrome and vermilion painted, aspiring to the snowline. Between the hills lie high level-looking plains full of intolerable sun glare, or narrow valleys drowned in a blue haze. The hill surface is streaked with ash drift and black, unweathered lava flows. After rains water accumulates in the hollows of small closed valleys, and, evaporating, leaves hard dry levels of pure desertness that get the local name of dry lakes. Where the mountains are steep and the rains heavy, the pool is never quite dry, but dark and bitter, rimmed about with the efflorescence of alkaline deposits. A thin crust of it lies along the marsh over the vegetating area, which has neither beauty nor freshness. In the broad wastes open to the wind the sand drifts in hummocks about the stubby shrubs, and between them the soil shows saline traces. The sculpture of the hills here is more wind than water work, though the quick storms do sometimes scar them past many a year's redeeming. In all the Western desert edges there are essays in miniature at the famed, terrible Grand Cañon, to which, if you keep on long enough in this country, you will come at last.

Since this is a hill country one expects to find springs, but not to depend upon them; for when found they are often brackish and unwholesome, or maddening, slow dribbles in a thirsty soil. Here you find the hot sink of Death Valley, or high rolling districts where the air has always a tang of frost. Here are the long heavy winds and breathless calms on the tilted mesas where dust devils dance, whirling up into a wide, pale sky. Here you have no rain when all the earth cries for it, or quick downpours called cloud-bursts for violence. A land of lost rivers, with little in it to love; yet a land that once visited must be come back to inevitably. If it were not so there would be little told of it.

This is the country of three seasons. From June on to November it lies hot, still, and unbearable, sick with violent unrelieving storms; then on until April, chill, quiescent, drinking its scant rain and scanter snows; from April to the hot season again, blossoming, radiant, and seductive. These months are only approximate; later or earlier the rain-laden wind may drift up the water gate of the Colorado from the Gulf, and the land sets its seasons by the rain.

The desert floras shame us with their cheerful adaptations to the seasonal limitations. Their whole duty is to flower and fruit, and they do it hardly, or with tropical luxuriance, as the rain admits. It is recorded in the report of the Death Valley expedition that after a year of abundant rains, on the Colorado desert was found a specimen of Amaranthus ten feet high. A year later the same species in the same place matured in the drought at four inches. One hopes the land may breed like qualities in her human offspring, not tritely to "try," but to do. Seldom does the desert herb attain the full stature of the type. Extreme aridity and extreme altitude have the same dwarfing effect, so that we find in the high Sierras and in Death Valley related species in miniature that reach a comely growth in mean temperatures. Very fertile are the desert plants in expedients to prevent evaporation, turning their foliage edgewise toward the sun, growing silky hairs, exuding viscid gum. The wind, which has a long sweep, harries and helps them. It rolls up dunes about the stocky stems, encompassing and protective, and above the dunes, which may be, as with the mesquite, three times as high as a man, the blossoming twigs flourish and bear fruit.

There are many areas in the desert where drinkable water lies within a few feet of the surface, indicated by the mesquite and the bunch grass (*Sporobolus airoides*). It is this nearness of unimagined help that makes the tragedy of desert deaths. It is related that the final breakdown of that hapless party that gave Death Valley its forbidding name occurred in a locality where shallow wells would have saved them. But how were they to know that? Properly equipped it is possible to go safely across that ghastly sink, yet every year it takes its toll of death, and yet men find there sun-dried mummies, of whom no trace or recollection is preserved. To underestimate one's thirst, to pass a given landmark to the right or left, to find a dry spring where one looked for running water—there is no help for any of these things.

Along springs and sunken watercourses one is surprised to find such water-loving plants as grow widely in moist ground, but the true desert breeds its own kind, each in its particular habitat. The angle of the slope, the frontage of a hill, the structure of the soil determines the plant. South-looking hills are nearly bare, and the lower tree-line higher here by a thousand feet. Cañons running east and west will have one wall naked and one clothed. Around dry lakes and marshes the herbage preserves a set and orderly arrangement. Most species have well-defined areas of growth, the best index the voiceless land can give the traveler of his whereabouts.

If you have any doubt about it, know that the desert begins with the creosote. This immortal shrub spreads down into Death Valley and up to the lower timberline, odorous and medicinal as you might guess from the name, wandlike, with shining fretted foliage. Its vivid green is grateful to the eye in a wilderness of gray and greenish white shrubs. In the spring it exudes a resinous gum which the Indians of those parts know how to use with pulverized rock for cementing arrow points to shafts. Trust Indians not to miss any virtues of the plant world!

Nothing the desert produces expresses it better than the unhappy growth of the tree yuccas. Tormented, thin forests of it stalk drearily in the high mesas, particularly in that triangular slip that fans out eastward from the meeting of the Sierras and coastwise hills where the first swings across the southern end of the San Joaquin Valley. The yucca bristles with bayonet-pointed leaves, dull green, growing shaggy with age, tipped with panicles of fetid, greenish bloom. After death, which is slow, the ghostly hollow network of its woody skeleton, with hardly power to rot, makes the moonlight fearful. Before the yucca has come to flower, while yet its bloom is a creamy cone-shaped bud of the size of a small cabbage, full of sugary sap, the Indians twist it deftly out of its fence of daggers and roast it for their own delectation. So it is that in those parts where man inhabits one sees young plants of Yucca *arborensis* infrequently. Other yuccas, cacti, low herbs, a thousand sorts, one finds journeying east from the coastwise hills. There is neither poverty of soil nor species to account for the sparseness of desert growth, but simply that each plant requires more room. So much earth must be preëmpted to extract so much moisture. The real struggle for existence, the real brain of the plant is underground; above there is room for a rounded perfect growth. In Death Valley, reputed the very core of desolation, are nearly two hundred identified species.

Above the lower tree-line, which is also the snowline, mapped out abruptly by the sun, one finds spreading growth of piñon, juniper, branched nearly to the ground, lilac and sage, and scattering white pines.

There is no special preponderance of self-fertilized or wind-fertilized plants, but everywhere the demand for and evidence of insect life. Now where there are seeds and insects there will be birds and small mammals and where these are, will come the slinking, sharp-toothed kind that prey on them. Go as far as you dare in the heart of a lonely land, you cannnot go so far that life and death are not before you. Painted lizards slip in and out of rock crevices, and pant on the white hot sands. Birds, hummingbirds even, nest in the cactus scrub; woodpeckers befriend the demoniac yuccas; out of the stark, treeless waste rings the music of the night-singing mockingbird. If it be summer and the sun well down, there will be a burrowing owl to call. Strange, furry, tricksy things dart across the open places, or sit motionless in the conning towers of the creosote. The poet may have "named all the birds without a gun," but not the fairy-footed, ground-inhabiting, furtive, small folk of the rainless regions. They are too many and too swift; how many you would not believe without seeing the footprint tracings in the sand. They are nearly all night workers, finding the days too hot and white. In mid-desert where there are no cattle, there are no birds of carrion, but if you go far in that direction the chances are that you will find yourself shadowed by their tilted wings. Nothing so large as a man can move unspied upon in that country, and they know well how the land deals with strangers. There are hints to be had here of the way in which a land forces new habits on its dwellers. The quick increase of suns at the end of spring sometimes overtakes birds in their nesting and effects a reversal of the ordinary manner of incubation. It becomes necessary to keep eggs cool rather than warm. One hot, stifling spring in the Little Antelope I had occasion to pass and repass frequently the nest of a pair of meadowlarks, located unhappily in the shelter of a very slender weed. I never caught them sitting except near night, but at midday they stood, or drooped above it, half fainting with pitifully parted bills, between their treasure and the sun. Sometimes both of them together with wings spread and half lifted continued a spot of shade in a temperature that constrained me at last in a fellow feeling to spare them a bit of canvas for permanent shelter. There was a fence in that country shutting in a cattle range, and along its fifteen miles of posts one could be sure of finding a bird or two in every strip of shadow; sometimes the sparrow and the hawk, with wings trailed and beaks parted, drooping in the white truce of noon.

If one is inclined to wonder at first how so many dwellers came to be in the loneliest land that ever came out of God's hands, what they do there and why stay, one does not wonder so much after having lived there. None other than this long brown land lays such a hold on the affections. The rainbow hills, the tender bluish mists, the luminous radiance of the spring, have the lotus charm. They trick the sense of time, so that once inhabiting there you always mean to go away without quite realizing that you have not done it. Men who have lived there, miners and cattle-men, will tell you this, not so fluently, but emphatically, cursing the land and going back to it. For one thing there is the divinest, cleanest air to be breathed anywhere in God's world. Some day the world will understand that, and the little oases on the windy tops of hills will harbor for healing its ailing, house-weary broods. There is promise there of great wealth in ores and earths, which is no wealth by reason of being so far removed from water and workable conditions, but men are bewitched by it and tempted to try the impossible.

You should hear Salty Williams tell how he used to drive eighteen- and twenty-mule teams from the borax marsh to Mojave, ninety miles, with the trail wagon full of water barrels. Hot days the mules would go so mad for drink that the clank of the water bucket set them into an uproar of hideous, maimed noises, and a tangle of harness chains, while Salty would sit on the high seat with the sun glare heavy in his eyes, dealing out curses of pacification in a level, uninterested voice until the clamor fell off from sheer exhaustion. There was a line of shallow graves along that road; they used to count on dropping a man or two of every new gang of coolies brought out in the hot season. But when he lost his swamper, smitten without warning at the noon halt, Salty quit his job; he said it was "too durn hot." The swamper he buried by the way with stones upon him to keep the coyotes from digging him up, and seven years later I read the penciled lines on the pine headboard, still bright and unweathered.

But before that, driving up on the Mojave stage, I met Salty again crossing Indian Wells, his face from the high seat, tanned and ruddy as a harvest moon, looming through the golden dust above his eighteen mules. The land had called him.

The palpable sense of mystery in the desert air breeds fables, chiefly of lost treasure. Somewhere within its stark borders, if one believes report, is a hill strewn with nuggets; one seamed with virgin silver; an old clayey water-bed where Indians scooped up earth to make cooking pots and shaped them reeking with grains of pure gold. Old miners drifting about the desert edges, weathered into the semblance of the tawny hills, will tell you tales like these convincingly. After a little sojourn in that land you will believe them on their own account. It is a question whether it is not better to be bitten by the little horned snake of the desert that goes sidewise and strikes without coiling, than by the tradition of a lost mine.

And yet—and yet—is it not perhaps to satisfy expectation that one falls into the tragic key in writing of desertness? The more you wish of it the more you get, and in the mean time lose much of pleasantness. In that country which begins at the foot of the east slope of the Sierras and spreads out by less and less lofty hill ranges toward the Great Basin, it is possible to live with great zest, to have red blood and delicate joys, to pass and repass about one's daily performance an area that would make an Atlantic seaboard State, and that with no peril, and, according to our way of thought, no particular difficulty. At any rate, it was not people who went into the desert merely to write it up who invented the fabled Hassaympa, of whose waters, if any drink, they can no more see fact as naked fact, but all radiant with the color of romance. I, who must have drunk of it in my twice seven years' wanderings, am assured that it is worth while.

For all the toll the desert takes of a man it gives compensations, deep breaths, deep sleep, and the communion of the stars. It comes upon one with new force in the pauses of the night that the Chaldeans were a desert-bred people. It is hard to escape the sense of mastery as the stars move in the wide clear heavens to risings and settings unobscured. They look large and near and palpitant; as if they moved on some stately service not needful to declare. Wheeling to their stations in the sky, they make the poor world-fret of no account. Of no account you who lie out there watching, nor the lean coyote that stands off in the scrub from you and howls and howls.

Questions for Discussion

1. In the final paragraph of this selection, the author states most bluntly her reason for liking the desert. What is it? What other reasons does she give in the course of her essay?

2. If you were a geographer, you perhaps would define a particular desert by its location, its climatic features (such as rainfall and availability of water), its temperatures, its flora and fauna. Locate the sections in the essay that do just that. In her essay, does the author give an orderly definition of the term desert?

3. Within the text itself are several clues as to the date of composition of "Land of Little Rain." Find them. Does the piece seem dated to you? Why?

4. What is the significance of the reference to the Chaldeans?

5. Is there a discernible thesis in Austin's discussion? If so, what is it?

6. The final paragraph in this essay is, in a way, a summary of the whole text. Explain that summary.

LEWIS THOMAS

Born in 1913, Lewis Thomas completed his M.D. degree at Harvard in 1937. In 1973, after serving with several prestigious institutions and medical schools, he moved to the Sloan-Kettering Institute in New York, one of the world's leading centers for the study and treatment of cancer.

Like Loren Eiseley, an anthropologist, and F. Gonzalez-Crussi, also a physician, Lewis Thomas does not consider himself a professional writer; yet throughout his career, he has taken the time to do superb collections of essays: The Lives of a Cell: Notes of a Biology Watcher *(1974),* The Medusa and the Snail: More Notes of a Biology Watcher *(1979), and* Late-Night Thoughts on Listening to Mahler's Ninth Symphony *(1983). One must ask, "Why does this scientist—who has written 'about two hundred' scientific papers and countless reports and funding proposals—turn again and again to the prose lyric?" The answer must be that in this genre the author is able to say things important to himself in a way that would be impossible in other forms. When he writes for the* American Journal of Pathology, *he is the disinterested scientist-physician; when he turns to his late-night composition of lyrics, he is the passionate, caring human being, no more an expert than you or I but gifted with a brilliant imagination and a dazzling prose style.*

One last question: Are Thomas's "lyrics" finally less important than his scientific papers?

The Unforgettable Fire

The hardest of all tasks for the military people who are occupationally obliged to make plans for wars still to come must be to keep a comprehensive, up-to-date list of guesses as to what the other side might, in one circumstance or another, do. Prudence requires that all sorts of possibilities be kept in mind, including, above all, the "worst-case." In warfare, in this century, the record has already proved that the worst-case will turn out in the end to be the one that happens and, often enough, the one that hadn't been planned for. At the outset of World War I, the British didn't have in mind the outright loss of an entire generation of their best youth, nor did any of the Europeans count on such an unhinging of German society as would lead straight to Hitler. In World War II, when things were being readied, nobody forecast Dresden or Coventry as eventualities to be looked out for and planned against. In Vietnam, defeat at the end was not anywhere on the United States' list of possible outcomes, nor was what happened later in Cambodia and Laos part of the scenario.

We live today in a world densely populated by human beings living in close communication with one another all over the surface of the planet. Viewed from a certain distance it has the look of a single society, a community, the swarming of an intensely social species trying to figure out ways to become successfully interdependent. We obviously need, at this stage, to begin the construction of some sort of world civilization. The final worst-case for all of us has now become the destruction, by ourselves, of our species.

This will not be a novel event for the planet, if it does occur. The fossil record abounds with sad tales of creatures that must have seemed stunning successes in their heyday, wiped out in one catastrophe after another. The trilobites are everywhere, elegant fossil shells, but nowhere alive. The dinosaurs came, conquered, and then all at once went.

Epidemic disease, meteorite collisions, volcanoes, atmospheric shifts in the levels of carbon dioxide, earthquakes, excessive warming or chilling of the earth's surface are all on the worst-case list for parts of the biosphere, one time or another, but it is unlikely that these can ever be lethal threats to a species as intelligent and resourceful as ours. We will not be wiped off the face of the earth by hard times, no matter how hard; we are tough and resilient animals, good at hard times. If we are to be done in, we will do it ourselves by warfare with thermonuclear

From *Late Night Thoughts on Listening to Mahler's Ninth Symphony* by Lewis Thomas. Copyright © 1981 by Lewis Thomas. Reprinted by permission of Viking Penguin Inc.

weaponry, and it will happen because the military planners, and the governments who pay close attention to them, are guessing at the wrong worst-case. At the moment there are really only two groups, the Russians and us, but soon there will be others, already lining up.

Each side is guessing that the other side will, sooner or later, fire first. To guard against this, each side is hell-bent on achieving a weapons technology capable of two objectives: to prevent the other from firing first by having enough missiles to destroy the first-strike salvo before it is launched (which means, of course, its own first strike) and, as a backup, to have for retaliation a powerful enough reserve to inflict what is called "unacceptable damage" on the other side's people. In today's urban world, this means the cities. The policy revision designated as Presidential Directive 59, issued by the Carter White House in August 1980, stipulates that enemy command and control networks and military bases would become the primary targets in a "prolonged, limited" nuclear war. Even so, some cities and towns would inevitably be blown away, then doubtless more, then perhaps all.

The term "unacceptable" carries the implication that there is an acceptable degree of damage from thermonuclear bombs. This suggests that we are moving into an era when the limited use of this kind of weaponry is no longer on the worst-case lists. Strategic weapons are those designed to destroy the whole enemy—armies, navies, cities, and all. Tactical nuclear bombs are something else again, smaller and neater, capable of taking out a fortified point, selectively and delicately removing, say, a tank division. Damage to one's country from strategic weapons may be unacceptable, in these terms, but tactical weapons do not raise this issue.

So it goes. The worst-case is clouds of missiles coming over the horizon, aimed at the cities. And another sort of merely bad-case might be to *neglect* the advantage of small-scale, surgically precise, tactical weapons, needed at crucial moments on conventional battlefields when things are going against one's side. So it seems.

Perhaps it really is the other way round. The worst of all possible scenarios might be the tactical use of a miniaturized thermonuclear bomb, a mere puff alongside the gigantic things stowed on MIRVs.

When we speak of mere puffs, it is useful to give a backward thought to Hiroshima and Nagasaki. We have gotten used to the notion that the two bombs dropped out of our B-29 bombers on August 6 and 9, 1945, were only primitive precursors of what we have at hand today, relatively feeble instruments, even rather quaint technological antiques, like Tiffany lamps. They were indeed nothing but puffs compared to what we now possess. If we and the Russians were to let everything fly at once, we could do, in a matter of minutes, a million times more damage than was done on those two August mornings long ago.

How do you figure a million times? You have to know, to begin with and in some detail, precisely what the Hiroshima and Nagasaki damage was like, and then try to imagine it a millionfold magnified. You don't even have to do that, if your imagination doesn't stretch that far. Any single one of today's best hydrogen bombs will produce at least one thousand times the lethal blast, heat, and radiation that resulted from the Hiroshima or Nagasaki bombs. Nothing would remain alive, no matter how shielded or "hardened," within an area twelve miles in diameter. Taking just one city—Boston, for example—you can begin to guess with some accuracy what just one modern bomb can do, say, tomorrow morning.

One thing for sure, such a bomb would not leave alive anyone to join a committee to prepare a book of sketches and paintings like those published several years ago in *Unforgettable Fire*. The people whose memories are contained in this book were residents of Hiroshima, most of them somewhere within a radius of two miles or so from the hypocenter, the Aioi bridge in the center of town. They survived, and made their drawings thirty years later. With one of today's bombs they would all have been vaporized within a fraction of a second after the explosion. What they recall most vividly, and draw most heartrendingly, are the deaths all around them, the collapsed buildings, and above all the long black strips of skin hanging from the arms and torsos of those still alive. They remember the utter hopelessness, the inability of anyone to help anyone else, the loneliness of the injured alongside the dying. Reading their accounts and wincing at the pictures, one gains the sure sense that no society, no matter how intricately structured, could have coped with that event. No matter how many doctors and hospitals might have been in place and ready to help with medical technology beforehand (as, for instance, in Boston or Baltimore today), at the moment of the fireball all of that help would have vanished in the new sun. As for the radioactivity, a single case of near-lethal radiation can occasionally be saved today by the full resources of a highly specialized, tertiary hospital unit, with endless transfusions and bone-marrow transplants. But what to do about a thousand such cases all at once, or a hundred thousand? Not to mention the more conventionally maimed and burned people, in the millions.

Words like "disaster" and "catastrophe" are too frivolous for the events that would inevitably follow a war with thermonuclear weapons. "Damage" is not the real term; the language has no word for it. Individuals might survive, but "survival" is itself the wrong word. As to the thought processes of the people in high perches of government who believe that they can hide themselves underground somewhere (they probably can) and emerge later on to take over again the running of society (they cannot, in the death of society) or, more ludicrous, the corporate executives who plan to come deranged out of their underground headquarters already installed in the mountains to reorganize the telephone lines or see to the oil business—these people cannot have thought at all.

Hiroshima and Nagasaki: The Physical, Medical and Social Effects of the Atomic Bombings is a 700-page, flatly written description of what happened in August 1945, containing a few photographs and a great many charts and tables to illustrate the abundant details in the text. Here and there, but in only a few paragraphs of the unemotional, factual text, are sentences that reveal the profundity of revulsion and disgust for this weapon and its use by the United States that still remain in the Japanese mind. It is briefly noted that Hiroshima had been spared the extensive fire-bombing to which most other Japanese cities were being subjected in the 1945 summer—there was an eagerly believed rumor that the Americans were sparing the city out of respect because it was known to be a Buddhist religious center—and then later, soon after the A-bombing, it was realized that the city had been preserved free of conventional damage in order to measure with exactitude the effects of the new bomb. It is tersely recalled that the first American journalists to arrive on the scene, a month after the bombing, were interested only in the extent of physical damage and the evidence of the instrument's great power, and it is further noted that no news about the injuries to the people, especially news about radiation sickness, was allowed by the Allied Occupation. *"On 6 September, 1945, the General Headquarters of the Occupational Forces issued a statement that made it clear that people likely to die from A-bomb afflictions should be left to die. The official attitude . . . was that people suffering from radiation injuries were not worth saving."* The Japanese nation is of course now a friendly ally of the United States, peacefully linked to this country, but the people remember. The continuing bitterness of that memory runs far deeper than most Americans might guess. Apart from the 370,000 Hiroshima and Nagasaki survivors still alive, whose lasting evidences of physical and psychological damage are exhaustively documented in *Hiroshima and Nagasaki,* the Japanese people at large are appalled that other nations can still be so blind to the horror.

To get back to cases, worst-cases, what would you guess is the worst of all possibilities today, with the United States and the Soviet Union investing every spare dollar and ruble to build new and more powerful armaments, missiles enough to create artificial suns in every habitable place of both countries, and with France, Britain, India, China, South Africa, maybe Israel, and who knows what other country either stockpiling bombs of their own or preparing to build them? Of all the mistakes to be made, which is the worst?

A very bad one, although maybe not the worst of all, is a technical complication not much talked about in public but hanging over all the military scientists like a great net poised to fall at any moment. It is still a theoretical complication, not yet tested, or, for that matter, even testable, but very terrifying indeed. The notion is this: a good-sized nuclear bomb, say, ten megatons, exploded at a very high altitude, 250 miles or so over a country, or a set of several such bombs over a continent, might elicit such a surge of electromagnetic energy in the underlying atmosphere that all electronic devices on the earth below would be put out of commission—or destroyed outright—all computers, radios, telephones, television, all electric grids, all communications beyond the reach of a human shout. None of the buttons pressed in Moscow or Washington, if either lay beneath the rays, would function. The silos would not open on command, or fire their missiles. During this period the affected country would be, in effect, anaesthetized, and the follow-on missiles from the other side could pick off their targets like fruit from a tree. Only the submarine forces, roaming far at sea, would be able to fire back, and their only signal to fire would have to be the total absence of any signal from home. The fate of the aggressor's own cities would then lie at the fingertips of individual submarine commanders, out of touch with the rest of the world, forced to read the meaning of silence.

If the hypothesis is valid, it introduces a new piece of logic into the game. Metal shielding can be used to protect parts of the military communication lines, and fiber optics lines are already replacing some parts. Nuclear-power plants can be partially shielded, perhaps enough to prevent meltdowns everywhere. But no one can yet be certain of protection against this strange new threat.

Any first strike might have to involve this technical maneuver beforehand, with the risk of counterblows from somewhere in the oceans or from surviving intelligence in land-based missiles, but always with the tempting prospect of an enemy country sitting paralyzed like a rabbit in the headlights of a truck. Guessing wrong either way could be catastrophic, and I imagine the War College faculties on both sides are turning the matter over and over in their minds and on their computers, looking for new doctrine.

But all in all, looking ahead, it seems to me that the greatest danger lies in the easy assumption by each government that the people in charge of military policy in any adversary government are not genuine human beings. We make this assumption about the Russians all the time, and I have no doubt they hold the same belief about us. We know ourselves, of course, and take ourselves on faith: Who among us would think of sending off a cluster of missiles to do a million times more damage to a foreign country than was done at Hiroshima, for any reason? None of us, we would all affirm (some of us I fear with fingers crossed). But there are those people on the other side who do not think as we do, we think.

It may be that the road to the end is already being paved, right now, by those tactical "theater" bombs, the little ones, as small and precise as we can make them. If the other side's tanks are gaining on ours, and we are about to lose an action, let them have one! And when they send one of theirs back in retaliation, slightly larger, let them have another, bigger one. Drive them back, we will say, let them have it. A few such exchanges, and off will go the ICBMs, and down will go, limb by limb, all of mankind.

I hope these two books are widely translated, and then propped under the thoughtful, calculating, and expressionless eyes of all the officials in the highest reaches of all governments. They might then begin to think harder than they now think about the future, their own personal future, and about whether a one-time exchange of bombs between countries would leave any government still governing, or any army officer still in command of anything.

Maybe the military people should sit down together on neutral ground, free of politicians and diplomats, perhaps accompanied by their chief medical officers and hospital administrators, and talk together about the matter. They are, to be sure, a strange and unfamiliar lot, unworldly in a certain sense, but they know one another or could at least learn to know one another. After a few days of discussion, unaffectionately and coldly but still linked in a common and ancient professional brotherhood, they might reach the conclusion that the world is on the wrong track, that human beings cannot fight with such weapons and remain human, and that since organized societies are essential for the survival of the profession of arms it is time to stop. It is the generals themselves who should have sense enough to demand a freeze on the development of nuclear arms, and then a gradual, orderly, meticulously scrutinized reduction of such arms. Otherwise, they might as well begin to learn how spears are made, although their chances of living to use them are very thin, not much better than the odds for the rest of us.

Meanwhile, the preparations go on, the dreamlike rituals are rehearsed, and the whole earth is being set up as an altar for a burnt offering, a monstrous human sacrifice to an imagined god with averted eyes. Carved in the stone of the cenotaph in Hiroshima are the words: REST IN PEACE, FOR THE MISTAKE WILL NOT BE REPEATED. The inscription has a life of its own. Intended first as a local prayer and promise, it has already changed its meaning into a warning, and is now turning into a threat.

Questions for Discussion

1. What, according to Thomas, is the main difference between us and trilobites, dinosaurs, and other species?

2. What are the differences between tactical and strategic weapons? Are these important differences in Thomas's scenario? Explain.

3. If the bombs dropped on Hiroshima and Nagasaki were "relatively feeble instruments, even rather quaint technological antiques, like Tiffany lamps," what comparison to the power of those we have today could you make that would be more meaningful to the reader than the author's "a million times more powerful"? In other words, can you create a metaphor that will convey the author's meaning more forcefully than his direct statement?

4. Does this essay have a topic or thesis sentence? If so, what is it? If not, write one for it.

5. What elements in this text make it a prose lyric, a personal essay, rather than, for instance, an editorial in a newspaper or an article on the nuclear threat in a general interest magazine? Refer specifically to the text itself to back up your answer. (How does "The Unforgettable Fire" differ from *Hiroshima and Nagasaki: The Physical, Medical and Social Effects of Atomic Bombing?*)

6. Who is the "imagined god with averted eyes"?

7. Is Lewis Thomas fair and objective or unfair and prejudiced? Support your opinion by referring to the text.

LOREN EISELEY

During his seventy years from 1907 to 1977, Loren Eiseley became known and admired as an anthropologist, poet, and essayist. After completing his doctorate at the University of Pennsylvania, he taught at the University of Kansas and Oberlin College. In 1947, he moved to the University of Pennsylvania, where he spent the rest of his career. He has contributed to numerous scientific journals and to such magazines as Harper's, Scientific American, Atlantic, *and* Ladies Home Journal. *His best known works among the reading public are two essay collections:* The Immense Journey *(1958) and* The Firmament of Time *(1960).*

Comparing Loren Eiseley with Lewis Thomas and F. Gonzalez-Crussi is inevitable, for all three turned in their writing from the rigors and precision of science to the puzzling, endlessly fascinating questions regarding humanity in a perhaps boundless, little understood universe. As an anthropologist, Eiseley's obsession has been the immense journey of humankind from its beginnings to a conclusion that possibly lies in the not-too-distant future. To express such musings, the prose lyric is the ideal medium.

In the New York Times Book Review, *William Stafford said, "Here is a scientist who is interested in the natural history of the soul. . . ."*

The Hidden Teacher

Sometimes the best teacher teaches only once to a single child or to a grownup past hope.

—ANONYMOUS

The putting of formidable riddles did not arise with today's philosophers. In fact, there is a sense in which the experimental method of science might be said merely to have widened the area of man's homelessness. Over two thousand years ago, a man named Job, crouching in the Judean desert, was moved to challenge what he felt to be the injustice of his God. The voice in the whirlwind, in turn, volleyed pitiless questions upon the supplicant—questions that have, in truth, precisely the ring of modern science. For the Lord asked of Job by whose wisdom the hawk soars, and who had fathered the rain, or entered the storehouses of the snow.

A youth standing by, one Elihu, also played a role in this drama, for he ventured diffidently to his protesting elder that it was not true that God failed to manifest Himself. He may speak in one way or another, though men do not perceive it. In consequence of this remark perhaps it would be well, whatever our individual beliefs, to consider what may be called the hidden teacher, lest we become too much concerned with the formalities of only one aspect of the education by which we learn.

We think we learn from teachers, and we sometimes do. But the teachers are not always to be found in school or in great laboratories. Sometimes what we learn depends upon our own powers of insight. Moreover, our teachers may be hidden, even the greatest teacher. And it was the young man Elihu who observed that if the old are not always wise, neither can the teacher's way be ordered by the young whom he would teach.

For example, I once received an unexpected lesson from a spider.

It happened far away on a rainy morning in the West. I had come up a long gulch looking for fossils, and there, just at eye level, lurked a huge yellow-and-black orb spider, whose web was moored to the tall spears of buffalo grass at the edge of the arroyo. It was her universe, and her senses did not extend beyond the lines and spokes of the great wheel she inhabited. Her extended claws could feel every vibration throughout that delicate structure. She knew the tug of wind, the fall of a raindrop, the flutter of a trapped moth's wing. Down one spoke of the web ran a stout ribbon of gossamer on which she could hurry out to investigate her prey.

Curious, I took a pencil from my pocket and touched a strand of the web. Immediately there was a response. The web, plucked by its menacing occupant, began to vibrate until it was a blur. Anything that had brushed claw or wing against that amazing snare would be thoroughly entrapped. As the vibrations slowed, I could see the owner fingering her guidelines for signs of struggle. A pencil point was an intrusion into this universe for which no precedent existed. Spider was circumscribed by spider ideas; its universe was spider universe. All outside was irrational, extraneous, at best, raw material for spider. As I proceeded on my way along the gully, like a vast impossible shadow, I realized that in the world of spider I did not exist.

Moreover, I considered, as I tramped along, that to the phagocytes, the white blood cells, clambering even now with some kind of elementary intelligence amid the thin pipes and tubing of my body—creatures without whose ministrations I could not exist—the conscious "I" of which I was aware had no significance to these amoeboid beings. I was, instead, a kind of chemical web that brought meaningful messages to them, a natural environment seemingly immortal if they could have thought about it, since generations of them had lived and perished, and would continue to so live and die, in that odd fabric which contained my intelligence—a misty light that was beginning to seem floating and tenuous even to me.

I began to see that among the many universes in which the world of living creatures existed, some were large, some small, but that all, including man's, were in some way limited or finite. We were creatures of many different dimensions passing through each other's lives like ghosts through doors.

In the years since, my mind has many times returned to that far moment of my encounter with the orb spider. A message has arisen only now from the misty shreds of that webbed universe. What was it that had so troubled me about the incident? Was it that spidery indifference to the human triumph?

If so, that triumph was very real and could not be denied. I saw, had many times seen, both mentally and in the seams of exposed strata, the long backward stretch of time whose recovery is one of the great feats of modern science. I saw the drifting cells of the early seas from which all life, including our own, has arisen. The salt of those ancient seas is in our blood, its lime is in our bones. Every time we walk along a beach some ancient urge disturbs us so that we find ourselves shedding shoes and garments, or scavenging among seaweed and whitened timbers like the homesick refugees of a long war.

And war it has been indeed—the long war of life against its inhospitable environment, a war that has lasted for perhaps three billion years. It began with strange chemicals seething under a sky lacking in oxygen; it was waged through long ages until the first green plants learned to harness the light of the nearest star, our sun. The human brain, so frail, so perishable, so full of inexhaustible dreams and hungers, burns by the power of the leaf.

The hurrying blood cells charged with oxygen carry more of that element to the human brain than to any other part of the body. A few moments' loss of vital air and the phenomenon we know as consciousness goes down into the black night of inorganic things. The human body is a magical vessel, but its life is linked with an element it cannot produce. Only the green plant knows the secret of transforming the light that comes to us across the far reaches of space. There is no better illustration of the intricacy of man's relationship with other living things.

The student of fossil life would be forced to tell us that if we take the past into consideration the vast majority of earth's creatures—perhaps over ninety percent—have vanished. Forms that flourished for a far longer time than man has existed upon earth have become either extinct or so transformed that their descendants are scarcely recognizable. The specialized perish with the environment that created them, the tooth of the tiger fails at last, the lances of men strike down the last mammoth.

In three billion years of slow change and groping effort only one living creature has succeeded in escaping the trap of specialization that has led in time to so much death and wasted endeavor. It is man, but the word should be uttered softly, for his story is not yet done.

With the rise of the human brain, with the appearance of a creature whose upright body enabled two limbs to be freed for the exploration and manipulation of his environment, there had at last emerged a creature with a specialization—the brain—that, paradoxically, offered escape from specialization. Many animals driven into the nooks and crannies of nature have achieved momentary survival only at the cost of later extinction.

Was it this that troubled me and brought my mind back to a tiny universe among the grass-blades, a spider's universe concerned with spider thought?

Perhaps.

The mind that once visualized animals on a cave wall is now engaged in a vast ramification of itself through time and space. Man has broken through the boundaries that control all other life. I saw, at last, the reason for my recollection of that great spider on the arroyo's rim, fingering its universe against the sky.

The spider was a symbol of man in miniature. The wheel of the web brought the analogy home clearly. Man, too, lies at the heart of a web, a web extending through the starry reaches of sidereal space, as well as backward into the dark realm of prehistory. His great eye upon Mount Palomar looks into a distance of millions of light-years, his radio ear hears the whisper of even more remote galaxies, he peers through the electron microscope upon the minute particles of his own being. It is a web no creature of earth has ever spun before. Like the orb spider, man lies at the heart of it, listening. Knowledge has given him the memory of earth's history beyond the time of his emergence. Like the spider's claw, a part of him touches a world he will never enter in the flesh. Even now, one can see him reaching forward into time with new machines, computing, analyzing, until elements of the shadowy future will also compose part of the invisible web he fingers.

Yet still my spider lingers in memory against the sunset sky. Spider thoughts in a spider universe—sensitive to raindrop and moth flutter, nothing beyond, nothing allowed for the unexpected, the inserted pencil from the world outside.

Is man at heart any different from the spider, I wonder: man thoughts, as limited as spider thoughts, contemplating now the nearest star with the threat of bringing with him the fungus rot from earth, wars, violence, the burden of a population he refuses to control, cherishing again his dream of the Adamic Eden he had pursued and lost in the green forests of America. Now it beckons again like a mirage from beyond the moon. Let man spin his web, I thought further; it is his nature. But I considered also the work of the phagocytes swarming in the rivers of my body, the unresting cells in their mortal universe. What is it we are a part of that we do not see, as the spider was not gifted to discern my face, or my little probe into her world?

We are too content with our sensory extensions, with the fulfillment of that ice age mind that began its journey amidst the cold of vast tundras and that pauses only briefly before its leap into space. It is no longer enough to see as a man sees—even to the ends of the universe. It is not enough to hold nuclear energy in one's hand like a spear, as a man would hold it, or to see the lightning, or times past, or time to come, as a man would see it. If we continue to do this, the great brain—the human brain—will be only a new version of the old trap, and nature is full of traps for the beast that cannot learn.

It is not sufficient any longer to listen at the end of a wire to the rustlings of galaxies; it is not enough even to examine the great coil of

DNA in which is coded the very alphabet of life. These are our extended perceptions. But beyond lies the great darkness of the ultimate Dreamer, who dreamed the light and the galaxies. Before act was, or substance existed, imagination grew in the dark. Man partakes of that ultimate wonder and creativeness. As we turn from the galaxies to the swarming cells of our own being, which toil for something, some entity beyond their grasp, let us remember man, the self-fabricator who came across an ice age to look into the mirrors and the magic of science. Surely he did not come to see himself or his wild visage only. He came because he is at heart a listener and a searcher for some transcendent realm beyond himself. This he has worshipped by many names, even in the dismal caves of his beginning. Man, the self-fabricator, is so by reason of gifts he had no part in devising—and so he searches as the single living cell in the beginning must have sought the ghostly creature it was to serve.

The young man Elihu, Job's counselor and critic, spoke simply of the "Teacher," and it is of this teacher I speak when I refer to gifts man had no part in devising. Perhaps—though it is purely a matter of emotional reactions to words—it is easier for us today to speak of this teacher as "nature," that omnipresent all which contained both the spider and my invisible intrusion into her carefully planned universe. But nature does not simply represent reality. In the shapes of life, it prepares the future; it offers alternatives. Nature teaches, though what it teaches is often hidden and obscure, just as the voice from the spinning dust cloud belittled Job's thought but gave back no answers to its own formidable interrogation.

A few months ago I encountered an amazing little creature on a windy corner of my local shopping center. It seemed, at first glance, some long-limbed, feathery spider teetering rapidly down the edge of a store front. Then it swung into the air and, as hesitantly as a spider on a thread, blew away into the parking lot. It returned in a moment on a gust of wind and ran toward me once more on its spindly legs with amazing rapidity.

With great difficulty I discovered the creature was actually a filamentous seed, seeking a hiding place and scurrying about with the uncanny surety of a conscious animal. In fact, it *did* escape me before I could secure it. Its flexible limbs were stiffer than milkweed down, and, propelled by the wind, it ran rapidly and evasively over the pavement. It was like a gnome scampering somewhere with a hidden packet—for all that I could tell, a totally new one: one of the jumbled alphabets of life.

A new one? So stable seem the years and all green leaves, a botanist might smile at my imaginings. Yet bear with me a moment. I would like to tell a tale, a genuine tale of childhood. Moreover, I was just old enough to know the average of my kind and to marvel at what I saw. And what I saw was straight from the hidden Teacher, whatever be his name.

It is told in the Orient of the Hindu god Krishna that his mother, wiping his mouth when he was a child, inadvertently peered in and beheld the universe, though the sight was mercifully and immediately veiled from her. In a sense, this is what happened to me. One day there arrived at our school a newcomer, who entered the grade above me. After some days this lad, whose look of sleepy-eyed arrogance is still before me as I write, was led into my mathematics classroom by the principal. Our class was informed severely that we should learn to work harder.

With this preliminary exhortation, great rows of figures were chalked upon the blackboard, such difficult mathematical problems as could be devised by adults. The class watched in helpless wonder. When the preparations had been completed, the young pupil sauntered forward and, with a glance of infinite boredom that swept from us to his fawning teachers, wrote the answers, as instantaneously as a modern computer, in their proper place upon the board. Then he strolled out with a carelessly exaggerated yawn.

Like some heavy-browed child at the wood's edge, clutching the last stone hand ax, I was witnessing the birth of a new type of humanity—one so beyond its teachers that it was being used for mean purposes while the intangible web of the universe in all its shimmering mathematical perfection glistened untaught in the mind of a chance little boy. The boy, by then grown self-centered and contemptuous, was being dragged from room to room to encourage us, the paleanthropes, to duplicate what, in reality, our teachers could not duplicate. He was too precious an object to be released upon the playground among us, and with reason. In a few months his parents took him away.

Long after, looking back from maturity, I realized that I had been exposed on that occasion, not to human teaching, but to the Teacher, toying with some sixteen billion nerve cells interlocked in ways past understanding. Or, if we do not like the anthropomorphism implied in the word *teacher*, then nature, the old voice from the whirlwind fumbling for the light. At all events, I had been the fortunate witness to life's unbounded creativity—a creativity seemingly still as unbalanced and chance-filled as in that far era when a black scaled creature had broken from an egg and the age of the giant reptiles, the creatures of the prime, had tentatively begun.

Because form cannot be long sustained in the living, we collapse inward with age. We die. Our bodies, which were the products of a kind of hidden teaching by an alphabet we are only beginning dimly to discern, are dismissed into their elements. What is carried onward, assuming we have descendants, is the little capsule of instructions such as I encountered hastening by me in the shape of a running seed. We have learned the first biological lesson: that in each generation life passes through the eye of a needle. It exists for a time molecularly and in no recognizable semblance to its adult condition. It *instructs* its way again into man or reptile. As the ages pass, so do variants of the code. Occasionally, a species vanishes on a wind as unreturning as that which took the pterodactyls.

Or the code changes by subtle degrees through the statistical altering of individuals; until I, as the fading Neanderthals must once have done, have looked with still-living eyes upon the creature whose genotype was quite possibly to replace me. The genetic alphabets, like genuine languages, ramify and evolve along unreturning pathways.

If nature's instructions are carried through the eye of a needle, through the molecular darkness of a minute world below the field of human vision and of time's decay, the same, it might be said, is true of those monumental structures known as civilizations. They are transmitted from one generation to another on invisible puffs of air known as words—words that can also be symbolically incised on clay. As the delicate printing on the mud at the water's edge retraces a visit of autumn birds long since departed, so the little scrabbled tablets in perished cities carry the seeds of human thought across the deserts of millennia. In this instance the teacher is the social brain but it, too, must be compressed into minute hieroglyphs, and the minds that wrought the miracle efface themselves amidst the jostling torrent of messages, which, like the genetic code, are shuffled and reshuffled as they hurry through eternity. Like a mutation, an idea may be recorded in the wrong time, to lie latent like a recessive gene and spring once more to life in an auspicious era.

Occasionally, in the moments when an archaeologist lifts the slab over a tomb that houses a great secret, a few men gain a unique glimpse through that dark portal out of which all men living have emerged, and through which messages again must pass. Here the Mexican archaeologist Ruz Lhuillier speaks of his first penetration of the great tomb hidden beneath dripping stalactites at the pyramid of Palenque: "Out of the dark shadows, rose a fairy-tale vision, a weird ethereal spectacle from another world. It was like a magician's cave carved out of ice, with walls glittering and sparkling like snow crystals." After shining his torch over hieroglyphs and sculptured figures, the explorer remarked wonderingly: "We were the first people for more than a thousand years to look at it."

Or again, one may read the tale of an unknown Pharaoh who had secretly arranged that a beloved woman of his household should be buried in the tomb of the god-king—an act of compassion carrying a personal message across the millennia in defiance of all precedent.

Up to this point we have been talking of the single hidden teacher, the taunting voice out of that old Biblical whirlwind which symbolizes nature. We have seen incredible organic remembrance passed through the needle's eye of a microcosmic world hidden completely beneath the observational powers of creatures preoccupied and ensorcelled by dissolution and decay. We have seen the human mind unconsciously seize upon the principles of that very code to pass its own societal memory forward into time. The individual, the momentary living cell of the society, vanishes, but the institutional structures stand, or if they change, do so in an invisible flux not too dissimilar from that persisting in the stream of genetic continuity.

Upon this world, life is still young, not truly old as stars are measured. Therefore it comes about that we minimize the role of the synapsid reptiles, our remote forerunners, and correspondingly exalt our own intellectual achievements. We refuse to consider that in the old eye of the hurricane we may be, and doubtless are, in aggregate, a slightly more diffuse and dangerous dragon of the primal morning that still enfolds us.

Note that I say "in aggregate." For it is just here, among men, that the role of messages, and, therefore, the role of the individual teacher— or, I should say now, the hidden teachers—begin to be more plainly apparent and their instructions become more diverse. The dead Pharaoh, though unintentionally, by a revealing act, had succeeded in conveying an impression of human tenderness that has outlasted the trappings of a vanished religion.

Like most modern educators I have listened to student demands to grade their teachers. I have heard the words repeated until they have become a slogan, that no man over thirty can teach the young of this generation. How would one grade a dead Pharaoh, millennia gone, I wonder, one who did not intend to teach, but who, to a few perceptive minds, succeeded by the simple nobility of an act.

Many years ago, a student who was destined to become an internationally known anthropologist sat in a course of linguistics and heard his instructor, a man of no inconsiderable wisdom, describe some linguistic peculiarities of Hebrew words. At the time, the young student, at the urging of his family, was contemplating a career in theology. As the teacher warmed to his subject, the student, in the back row, ventured excitedly: "I believe I can understand that, sir. It is very similar to what exists in Mohegan."

The linguist paused and adjusted his glasses. "Young man," he said, "Mohegan is a dead language. Nothing has been recorded of it since the eighteenth century. Don't bluff."

"But sir," the young student countered hopefully, "it can't be dead so long as an old woman I know still speaks it. She is Pequot-Mohegan. I learned a bit of vocabulary from her and could speak with her myself. She took care of me when I was a child."

"Young man," said the austere, old-fashioned scholar, "be at my house for dinner at six this evening. You and I are going to look into this matter."

A few months later, under careful guidance, the young student published a paper upon Mohegan linguistics, the first of a long series of studies upon the forgotten languages and ethnology of the Indians of the Northeastern forests. He had changed his vocation and turned to anthropology because of the attraction of a hidden teacher. But just who was the teacher? The young man himself, his instructor, or that solitary speaker of a dying tongue who had so yearned to hear her people's voice that she had softly babbled it to a child?

Later, this man was to become one of my professors. I absorbed much from him, though I hasten to make the reluctant confession that he was considerably beyond thirty. Most of what I learned was gathered over cups of coffee in a dingy campus restaurant. What we talked about were things some centuries older than either of us. Our common interest lay in snakes, scapulimancy, and other forgotten rites of benighted forest hunters.

I have always regarded this man as an extraordinary individual, in fact, a hidden teacher. But alas, it is all now so old-fashioned. We never protested the impracticality of his quaint subjects. We were all too ready to participate in them. He was an excellent canoeman, but he took me to places where I fully expected to drown before securing my degree. To this day, fragments of his unused wisdom remain stuffed in some back attic of my mind. Much of it I have never found the opportunity to employ, yet it has somehow colored my whole adult existence. I belong to that elderly professor in somewhat the same way that he, in turn, had become the wood child of a hidden forest mother.

There are, however, other teachers. For example, among the hunting peoples there were the animal counselors who appeared in prophetic dreams. Or, among the Greeks, the daemonic supernaturals who stood at the headboard while a man lay stark and listened—sometimes to dreadful things. "You are asleep," the messengers proclaimed over and over again, as though the man lay in a spell to hear his doom pronounced. "You, Achilles, you, son of Atreus. You are asleep, asleep," the hidden ones pronounced and vanished.

We of this modern time know other things of dreams, but we know also that they can be interior teachers and healers as well as the anticipators of disaster. It has been said that great art is the night thought of man. It may emerge without warning from the soundless depths of the unconscious, just as supernovae may blaze up suddenly in the farther reaches of void space. The critics, like astronomers, can afterward triangulate such worlds but not account for them.

A writer friend of mine with bitter memories of his youth and estranged from his family, who, in the interim, had died, gave me this account of the matter in his middle years. He had been working, with an unusual degree of reluctance, upon a novel that contained certain autobiographical episodes. One night he dreamed; it was a very vivid and stunning dream in its detailed reality.

He found himself hurrying over creaking snow through the blackness of a winter night. He was ascending a familiar path through a long-vanished orchard. The path led to his childhood home. The house, as he drew near, appeared dark and uninhabited, but, impelled by the power of the dream, he stepped upon the porch and tried to peer through a dark window into his own old room.

"Suddenly," he told me, "I was drawn by a strange mixture of repulsion and desire to press my face against the glass. I knew intuitively they were all there waiting for me within, if I could but see them. My mother and my father. Those I had loved and those I hated. But the window was black to my gaze. I hesitated a moment and struck a match. For an instant in that freezing silence I saw my father's face glimmer wan and remote behind the glass. My mother's face was there, with the hard, distorted lines that marked her later years.

"A surge of fury overcame my cowardice. I cupped the match before me and stepped closer, closer toward that dreadful confrontation. As the match guttered down, my face was pressed almost to the glass. In some quick transformation, such as only a dream can effect, I saw that it was my own face into which I stared, just as it was reflected in the black glass. My father's haunted face was but my own. The hard lines upon my mother's aging countenance were slowly reshaping themselves upon my living face. The light burned out. I awoke sweating from the terrible psychological tension of that nightmare. I was in a far port in a distant land. It was dawn. I could hear the waves breaking on the reef."

"And how do you interpret the dream?" I asked, concealing a sympathetic shudder and sinking deeper into my chair.

"It taught me something," he said slowly, and with equal slowness a kind of beautiful transfiguration passed over his features. All the tired lines I had known so well seemed faintly to be subsiding.

"Did you ever dream it again?" I asked out of a comparable experience of my own.

"No, never," he said, and hesitated. "You see, I had learned it was just I, but more, much more, I had learned that I was they. It makes a difference. And at the last, late, much too late, it was all right. I understood. My line was dying, but I understood. I hope they understood, too." His voice trailed into silence.

"It is a thing to learn," I said. "You were seeking something and it came." He nodded, wordless. "Out of a tomb," he added after a silent moment, "my kind of tomb—the mind."

On the dark street, walking homeward, I considered my friend's experience. Man, I concluded, may have come to the end of that wild being who had mastered the fire and the lightning. He can create the web but not hold it together, not save himself except by transcending his own image. For at the last, before the ultimate mystery, it is himself he shapes. Perhaps it is for this that the listening web lies open: that by knowledge we may grow beyond our past, our follies, and ever closer to what the Dreamer in the dark intended before the dust arose and walked. In the pages of an old book it has been written that we are in the hands of a Teacher, nor does it yet appear what man shall be.

Questions for Discussion

1. A quotation in this essay says that "great art is the night thought of man." What does this mean?
2. Explain the relationship of "The Book of Job" to "The Hidden Teacher."
3. In your own words, explain "the hidden teachers." Why are they hidden? What do we learn from "hidden teachers" that we could not learn from "unhidden teachers"?
4. What lesson did Eiseley learn from the spider? (In this selection he says, "The spider was a symbol of man in miniature.")

5. What is an *allegory*? In what sense is "The Hidden Teacher" allegorical?

6. In "The Hidden Teacher," Eiseley tells the story of a young student who knew about the supposedly dead Mohegan language and who "changed his vocation and turned to anthropology because of the attraction of a hidden teacher." Then Eiseley asks, "But just who was the teacher?" What is your answer to that question?

7. In this selection, we read the account of a dream that a friend of Eiseley had. "And how do you interpret the dream?" asks Eiseley. Answer that question. What is your own interpretation of the dream?

————————   SUGGESTIONS FOR WRITING   ————————

1.   Write a personal essay on the funeral customs in your family or community. What is your attitude toward these customs?

2.   These essays deal with the out-of-the-ordinary, either in subject matter or in the attitude the author takes toward that subject matter. On the one hand, for example, Annie Dillard writes about a commonplace topic, insects, from a unique point of view; on the other, F. Gonzalez-Crussi deals with an unusual topic, embalming.

Do you have an unusual attitude toward a commonplace thing or event? Or do you know a great deal about something that is out of the ordinary? Either would be an excellent topic for an essay, provided you develop your ideas concretely, giving adequate explanations and examples.

3.   Loren Eiseley tells us that dreams "can be interior teachers and healers as well as anticipators of disaster." Has one of your dreams taught you, healed you, or warned you of disaster? Narrate that dream and tell why and how you interpreted it as you did. What was its lasting effect on your life?

4.   Choose any one of the essays you find particularly appealing and do an imitation of it. That is, choose any subject, but write on it as if you were the author of the essay you enjoyed—Annie Dillard, F. Gonzalez-Crussi, Mary Austin, Lewis Thomas, Loren Eiseley.

5.   Tell about your hidden teachers. In writing this essay, you should keep Loren Eiseley's techniques in mind. He relies on examples and stories to convey his points: the spider and its web, the young man who learned Mohegan, the dream of his friend.

If you concretely and specifically tell of one incident in which you learned something, you will have discussed one of your hidden teachers.

6.   In a brief essay, distinguish between *eccentric* and *idiosyncratic* by means of illustrative examples—and perhaps referring to some of the selections in this chapter.

7.   In "The Unforgettable Fire," Lewis Thomas says, "The term 'unacceptable' carries the implication that there is an acceptable degree of damage from thermonuclear bombs."

In an essay, give a tentative answer to this question: Who defines what is acceptable and what is unacceptable in terms of thermonuclear conflict?

According to their opinions, can you divide the definers into camps—hawks and doves, for example? How do the members of a camp differ from one another? What are the details of the positions that members of the various camps take?

In preparing to write this essay, you will certainly want to do a bit of background reading in current periodicals.

Your essay will be a chance for you to sort out ideas and classify them. Indeed, you will probably make comparisons and contrasts.

8. Lewis Thomas unequivocally states that "we obviously need to begin the construction of some sort of world civilization [government]." Should we have a world government, a sort of United Nations that actually controls the member nations, a world confederation such as the United States of America?

Present an in-depth argument on either side of this issue.

9. In "The Hidden Teacher" Loren Eiseley says,

> If nature's instructions are carried through the eye of a needle, through the molecular darkness of a minute world below the field of human vision and of time's decay, the same, it might be said, is true of those monumental structures known as civilizations. They are transmitted from one generation to another on invisible puffs of air known as words—words that can also be symbolically incised on clay.

Eiseley is saying that *writing* transmits civilization.

Investigate the effects of literacy—reading and writing—on societies and individuals and present the results of your research in an essay.

Useful sources of information about the effects of literacy are

Oxenham, John. *Literacy: Writing, Reading and Social Organization.* London: Routledge & Kegan Paul, 1980.

Pattison, Robert. *On Literacy.* New York: Oxford University Press, 1982.

Scribner, Sylvia, and Michael Cole. "The Practice of Literacy." In *The Psychology of Literacy.* Cambridge, Mass.: Harvard University Press, 1981. Pages 234–260.

10. Do a critical review of one of the essays in this chapter—and remember that critical reviews can be either favorable or unfavorable in their judgment of their subjects. (Your review will probably be easier to complete if you choose an essay that you like or dislike a great deal.)

11. Annie Dillard is in many ways the spiritual and artistic heir of Henry David Thoreau, author of the American classic *Walden*.

An ambitious project would be a comparison of two books: *Pilgrim at Tinker Creek*, by Annie Dillard, and *Walden*, by Henry David Thoreau.

Less ambitiously, you could compare "Winter Animals," a chapter from *Walden*, with "The Horns of the Altar."

C H A P T E R

5

History

The first historian in Western culture was the Greek Herodotus, who lived
in the fifth century B.C. His writings center on the wars with Persia but
contain numerous digressions: myths, accounts of customs and of
peoples, and many speculations. Although Herodotus attempted to record
an account of past events, he was not a historian in the modern sense. He
made no attempt to separate fact from myth or to interpret causes and
effects.

Two other fifth-century B.C. Greeks wrote histories that, in spirit and
method, are very much like some modern histories.

Writing the history of the Peloponnesian War, Thucydides attempted
to differentiate fact from fable, a distinction that Herodotus had ignored.
Thucydides kept his focus on events of the war and matters of state,
always pointing out the lessons to be learned from the narrative and
analyzing causes and effects.

The third of the Greek "fathers of history" was Xenophon, whose
major work was the *Anabasis,* an account of the retreat from the battle of
Cunaxa (in 401 B.C.) after the leader of the Greek forces, Cyrus the
Younger, was killed. In his historical writing, Xenophon concentrated on

narrative, on telling the story clearly and interestingly, not primarily on interpretation or drawing lessons from the events.

In the Roman period, Livy was an heir of Xenophon while Tacitus wrote in the mode of Xenophon.

In this chapter, you will find that Daniel J. Boorstin writes very much in the spirit of Thucydides while Barbara Tuchman is the heir of Xenophon's gift for storytelling.

The American historian Hayden White sorts out the problems of historical writing.[1] In brief, White says that writing history is very much like writing a novel; the author sees events as they relate to and influence one another, with a beginning, middle, and conclusion. Of course, the historian uses events that are presumably nonfictional, that have been verified through scrupulous research, and the novelist makes up or imagines events (although the distinction is not at all clear because the historical novel is based on actual events. One might say that the novelist has more freedom than the historian.)

A *chronicle* is a list of events, one after another, as in a journal or the minutes of some organization. The *Anglo-Saxon Chronicle*, begun during the reign of Alfred in the ninth century, is a miscellany, containing entries that sometimes are mere notations and other times are detailed accounts, much in the spirit of Herodotus.

The historian uses the events in the chronicle to create a story. As Hayden White says,

> The arrangement of selected events of the chronicle into a story raises the kinds of questions the historian must anticipate and answer in the course of constructing his narrative. These questions are of the sort: "What happened next?" "How did that happen?" "Why did things happen this way rather than that?" "How did it all come out in the end?"[2]

History being a kind of story, we are left with this frustrating, but fascinating, question: Is there a *real* past, or do we create it according to our own needs and viewpoints?

[1]Hayden White, *Metahistory* (Baltimore and London: Johns Hopkins University Press, 1973), pp. 1–42.
[2]Ibid., p. 7.

DANIEL J. BOORSTIN

The accomplishments and honors of Daniel J. Boorstin are awesome. He was a Rhodes Scholar and took law degrees at both Oxford and Yale; he was admitted to the bar in both the United States and Great Britain; he has been a government official and has taught at Harvard, Swarthmore, and the University of Chicago; he has lectured widely in the United States and abroad; and in 1975, he was appointed Librarian of Congress.

Born in 1914 in Atlanta, the son of a lawyer, Boorstin took his B.A. (summa cum laude) at Harvard in 1934 and thereafter began to produce a distinguished series of books on the law and history: The Mysterious Science of the Law, The Lost World of Thomas Jefferson, The Americans: The Colonial Experience, A Lady's Life in the Rocky Mountains, *and* Democracy and Its Discontents: Reflections on Everyday America, *among others.*

Among the awards conferred on Boorstin are the Francis Parkman Medal of the American Society of Historians and the Pulitzer Prize for The Americans: The Democratic Experience.

In "A Personal Note to the Reader," Boorstin says this about The Discoverers, *the book from which "Charting Heaven and Hell" is taken:*

> My hero is Man the Discoverer. The world we now view from the literate West—the vistas of time, the land and the sea, the heavenly bodies and our own bodies, the plants and animals, history and human societies past and present—had to be opened for us by countless Columbuses. In the deep recesses of the past, they remain anonymous. As we come closer to the present they emerge into the light of history, a cast of characters as varied as human nature. Discoveries become episodes of biography, unpredictable as the new worlds the discoverers opened to us.

In the four major sections of The Discoverers, *Boorstin traces humankind's efforts to comprehend time, the earth and the seas, nature, and society. "Charting Heaven and Hell" is the second chapter in a part of "The Earth and the Seas" entitled, appropriately enough, "The Geography of the Imagination."*

Charting Heaven and Hell

The great obstacle to discovering the shape of the earth, the continents, and the ocean was not ignorance but the illusion of knowledge. Imagination drew in bold strokes, instantly serving hopes and fears, while knowledge advanced by slow increments and contradictory witnesses. Villagers who themselves feared to ascend the mountaintops located their departed ones on the impenetrable heavenly heights.

The heavenly bodies were conspicuous examples of disappearance and rebirth. The sun died every night and was reborn every morning, while the moon was newborn every month. Was this moon the same heavenly body that reappeared at each "rebirth"? Were the stars that were newly lit at each sunset actually the same as those extinguished every dawn? Perhaps, like them, each of us could be extinguished and yet be reborn. It is not surprising that the heavenly bodies, and especially the moon, were widely associated with the resurrection of the dead. We will illustrate these notions from ancient Greece and Rome with some reminders that such notions were not confined to the Mediterranean or the European world.

In earliest Greek antiquity, Hecate, goddess of the moon, was summoner of ghosts, queen of the infernal regions. The cold damp rays of the moon, according to a popular Eastern astrology, corrupted the flesh of the dead and so helped dislodge the soul, which then was freed from its earthly prison to reach the heavens. The ancient Syrians tried to accelerate this process by sacrifices at their tombs on the night when the moonbeams were most potent. In the Eastern Church the dates of the rituals for the dead were fixed to exploit these hopes.

"All who leave the earth go to the moon," declared an Upanishad, an ancient Hindu text, "which is swollen by their breath during the first half of the month." The Manichaean followers of the Persian sage Manes (A.D. 216?–276?) gave the moon a brilliant role in their mystic doctrines, and so compounded the doctrines of Zoroastrianism and of Christianity into an appealing new sect that tempted many early Christians, including Saint Augustine. The moon takes a crescent shape, they explained, when it is being swelled by the luminous souls that it has drawn up from the earth. The moon wanes when it has transferred these souls to the sun. Every month the boat of the moon that sails across the skies takes on a new load of souls, which it regularly passes on to the larger vessel of the sun. The crescent moon, symbol of immortality, adorned funeral monuments of the ancient Babylonians and in Celtic countries, and across Africa. In republican Rome the shoes of senators were decorated with ivory crescents, taken as a symbol of their pure spirits, since noble souls after death were transported to the heavens, where they walked on the moon.

The flight of souls to the moon was no mere metaphor. According to the Stoics, a zone of special physical qualities surrounded the moon. The soul, a burning breath, naturally rose through the air toward the fires of the sky. In the neighborhood of the moon, it found this "Porch" of ether, a substance so like the soul's own essence that the soul stayed floating there in equilibrium. Each soul was a globe of fire endowed with intelligence, and all souls together were a perpetual chorus around the luminous moon. In this case the Elysian Fields would not, as the Pythagoreans had insisted, be on the moon but in the ether surrounding the moon, into which only suitably pure souls could penetrate.

According to popular astronomy, the lowest of the seven planetary spheres was the moon, whose ether was nearest the earth's impure atmosphere. Pythagoreans and Stoics imagined souls returning to earth just after they had crossed the circle of the moon. Therefore "sublunary" (beneath the moon) came to describe everything terrestrial, mundane, or ephemeral.

Perhaps, as European folklore suggested, each person had his own star—bright or dull, according to his station and his destiny—which was illuminated at his birth and disappeared at his death. A shooting star, then, might signifiy some person's death. "Were there then only two stars at the time of Adam and Eve," wondered Bishop Eusebius of Alexandria in the fifth century, "and only eight after the Flood when Noah and seven other persons alone were saved in the Ark?" Everyone was born under either a lucky or an unlucky star. The Latin *astrosus* (ill-starred) meant unlucky, and today we still thank our "lucky stars."

If, as many people have thought, the departing soul becomes a bird fleeing from this earth, would not souls naturally alight on the heavenly bodies? And the multitude of the stars could be explained by the countless generations of the dead. The Milky Way, which some believed was the highway for departed souls, was such a gathering of innumerable departed spirits. Ovid recounts how Venus swooped down invisibly into the Senate and carried Caesar's soul from his bleeding body into the heavens, and how the soul took flame and flew beyond the moon to become a trailing comet. Families consoled themselves with the thought that their members departed from earth had become stars to illuminate the heavens. The Emperor Hadrian, grieving over his favorite Antinous, professed to believe that his friend had become a star which had just appeared. According to Cicero, "nearly the whole heaven is filled with mankind."

Millennia before the discovery of gravitation, the sun, that most potent of heavenly bodies, was said to govern the others, and to be somehow "the heart of the world, source of new-born souls." According to the Pythagoreans (second century B.C.) the sun was Apollo Musagetes, chorus master of the Muses, whose music was the harmony of the spheres.

People who could agree on few other facts about remote regions of the earth somehow agreed on the geography of the afterworld. Even while the shape of most of the earth's surface was still unknown, the Nether World was described in vivid detail. The practice of burying the dead in the earth made it quite natural that people should think that the dead inhabited the Nether World. A subterranean topography seemed to make that afterlife possible and even plausible. Tradition reported that the Romans, at the foundation of their city, followed an old Etruscan custom and dug a pit in the city's center so that ancestors in the Nether World could more easily communciate with the world of the living. Into this pit were thrown gifts—the first fruits of the harvest and a clod of earth from the place whence the city's settlers had come—to ease the lives of the departed and to ensure the continuity of the generations. A vertical shaft ended in a chamber with a roof curved like the heavens, which justified calling this lower-realm a world (*mundus*). The keystone of this vault (the *lapis Manalis*; the stone of the departed spirits) was raised three times a year, on the holidays when the dead could freely return to earth.

In the beginning, life in the Nether World was simply an extension of life above. Which explains why among so many peoples the warrior was buried with his chariot, his horses, his weapons, and his wives, why his tools accompanied the craftsman to the grave, and why the housewife went with her weaving implements and cooking vessels. And so earth-life could go on beneath the earth.

In Greece there arose a sect that named itself after Orpheus, the mythical poet, whose efforts to rescue his beloved wife, Eurydice, from the underworld had made him an expert in the perils of the journey in both directions. About the sixth century B.C. these Orphic Greeks and the Etruscans who followed them developed a mythology of judgment day, an appealing eschatology that we can still see elegantly depicted on their black-figured vases.

The books of many peoples on the Descent into Hades, while varying in the cast of characters, somehow agree on the topography of the infernal regions almost as if they were describing a nearby landscape. The Greeks provided the outlines—an underground realm bounded by the river Styx and governed by Pluto and Proserpina. There were the judges Minos, Aeacus, and Rhadamanthus, the executioners Erinyes (the Furies), and a high-walled prison, Tartarus. Since there was no bridge across the Styx, all the deceased had to be ferried by Charon, a grisly old man in a dark sailor's cloak, who charged an *obolos* for the service, a coin that it became the custom to put in the mouth of the dead to ensure passage. Once across the Styx, all took a common road to the court of judgment. Such judging of the dead was, of course, familiar to the Egyptians and is commonly depicted on the tombs in the Valley of the Kings. In the Greek Nether World the judges, from whom there was no appeal and from whom nothing could be concealed, sent the wicked to the left across a river of fire to the dark tortures of Tartarus and sent the virtuous along the right-hand road toward the Elysian Fields. There were some nice problems of physics here. If, as the Stoics taught, every soul was an upward-tending burning breath, none could descend into the earth. But the Elysian Fields were relocated in the heavens above, and wicked spirits were consigned to the Inferno below.

Was the earth large enough to contain a Tartarus for all those since the beginning of time who had ever deserved its punishments? Perhaps the infernal regions should be found not under the earth but on the lower half of the terrestrial globe, in the southern hemisphere. Virgil followed the traditional geography of the Nether World when he related the descent of Aeneas into Hades. But enlightened Romans like Cicero and Seneca and Plutarch probably had ceased to believe the mythic chart of Hades. The hardheaded Pliny, for example, noted how strange it was that miners who dig deep pits and broad galleries underground had never come upon the infernal regions.

It seems that in ancient Greece and Rome the traditional topography of the Nether World was widely accepted by the populace or, at least, not actively disbelieved. We cannot be sure how many tomb inscriptions were mere metaphor. "I shall not wend mournfully to the floods of Tartarus," read the tomb of a young Roman of the Age of Augustus, announcing that he had become a celestial hero who sent this message from the ether, "I shall not cross the waters of Acheron as a shade, nor shall I propel the dusky boat with my oar; I shall not fear Charon with his face of terror, nor shall old Minos pass sentence on me; I shall not wander in the abode of gloom nor be held prisoner on the bank of the fatal waters." Sarcophagi commonly depicted the mythic characters with their accustomed places on the map of Hades.

Although Platonism and Christianity contradicted each other on countless dogmas, both in different ways confirmed the traditional maps of heaven and of hell. When Neoplatonists in the third century revived Plato's teachings as a sacred text, they defended his vivid description of how souls lived in the bowels of the earth. Porphyry (A.D. 232?–304?), a potent antagonist of Christianity, explained that although each soul was by nature a "fiery breath" tending to rise to the heavens, yet as a soul lowered into the earthly atmosphere it tended to become damp and heavy. During a soul's life on earth, as it became encumbered with the clay of sensual life, it became still denser, until it was naturally dragged into the earthly depths. "It is true," argued

Proclus (410?–485), the last of the great Greek Neoplatonists, and a still vigorous opponent of Christianity, "that the soul by force of its nature aspires to rise to the place which is its natural abode, but when passions have invaded it they weigh it down and the savage instincts which develop in it attract it to the place to which they properly belong, that is, the earth." So it was quite understandable that wicked souls should be consigned to the Nether World. Hell, then, was no mere metaphor, but a vast underground network of rivers and islands, prisons and torture chambers, irrigated by the earth's effluvia and never brightened by the sun.

During the next millennium Christianity gave new credibility and new vividness to the ancient topography of heaven and hell. Few visions were more compelling than those of the strong-willed Saint Hildegard of Bingen (1099–1179), who at the age of eight had been consigned to a nunnery with all the last rites of the dead to signify that she was buried to the world. She wrote eloquent lives of the saints, works on natural history, medicine, and the mysteries of Creation. She saw and described precisely what happened to impenitent sinners:

> I saw a well deep and broad, full of boiling pitch and sulphur, and around it were wasps and scorpions, who scared but did not injure the souls of those therein; which were the souls of those who had slain in order not to be slain.
>
> Near a pond of clear water I saw a great fire. In this some souls were burned and others were girdled with snakes, and others drew in and again exhaled the fire like a breath, while malignant spirits cast lighted stones at them. And all of them beheld their punishment reflected in the water, and thereat were the more afflicted. These were the souls of those who had extinguished the substance of the human form within them, or had slain their infants.
>
> And I saw a great swamp, over which hung a black cloud of smoke, which was issuing from it. And in the swamp there swarmed a mass of little worms. Here were the souls of those who in the world had delighted in foolish merriment.

It was not only in Saint Hildegard's visions but in many others that hell's vivid chambers of horrors became so much more interesting than the bland delights of heaven.

The most persuasive Christian geographer of heaven and hell was, of course, the greatest of Italian poets, Dante Alighieri (1265–1321). His journey to the afterworld was a pilgrimage, a return to anciently familiar scenes. The power of his *Divine Comedy* was multiplied because, unlike most of the polite literature of Europe in its day, it was written not in Latin or another scholar's language, but in Italian, a language "lowly and humble, because it is the vulgar tongue, in which even housewives hold converse." The dominant emotional experience of his life was the death in 1290 of his beloved Beatrice when he was only twenty-five, which induced him to spend most of his active life writing an epic of the afterworld where she had gone.

Dante's great work was a travel epic recounting the author's journey through the realms of the dead. One hundred cantos (14,233 lines) covered "the state of souls after death" in Dante's guided tour through Inferno, Purgatory, and Paradise. He began writing it about 1307 and was still working on it on the day he died. The last thirteen cantos of his completed work would have been lost if after his death Dante had not appeared in a dream to his son Jacopo to explain where they were hidden.

Dante translated medieval learning into a panorama of the afterlife. Virgil, whose scheme of the Nether World Dante accepts, guides him through the Inferno; Beatrice guides him through Paradise, giving way to Saint Bernard only when the presence of God is reached. His geography of the underworld is traditional. Down across the nine chasms of the underworld Virgil guides him, at each level showing the punishments of another category of the damned, until they finally reach Satan himself. Ascending a tunnel to the foot of Mount Purgatory, they climb its seven levels, each level one of the seven deadly sins, on the way to Paradise, where there are nine heavens. The tenth is where God and his angels dwell.

Questions for Discussion

1. Does Boorstin state the gist of his piece? If so, where do you find that statement?

2. Boorstin is writing for nonspecialists—for the educated general reading public, not for professional historians. He is writing, in other words, for persons such as you and me. In what ways does he succeed in his purpose? In what ways does he fail? (How could he make his essay more interesting and meaningful to you? What should be added? Cut out?)

3. Explain the following sentence (p. 219): "The flight of souls to the moon was no mere metaphor." Be sure you consider context before you attempt your explanation. And be sure also that you understand the concept "metaphor," which is discussed in the glossary of this book.

4. Do any present-day beliefs about heaven and hell—and the rituals associated with death—square with the primitive beliefs Boorstin discusses? How so?

5. How did the ancients go about answering "scientific" questions? Think about the discussions in both "Charting Heaven and Hell" and " 'This Is the End of the World': The Black Death" (pp. 225–234).

6. Rewrite the sentences in the third paragraph, changing their word order but preserving all of their ideas. For example, the first sentence can be rewritten in several ways:

—Hecate, goddess of the moon, in earliest Greek antiquity, was summoner of ghosts, queen of the infernal regions.

—In earliest Greek antiquity, Hecate was summoner of ghosts, queen of the infernal regions, goddess of the moon.

After you have rewritten the sentences, evaluate them. Are they clearer or less clear than the originals? Are they more or less forceful? Are they awkward?

BARBARA TUCHMAN

Like the great American historian Francis Parkman—whose Oregon Trail *is a classic—Barbara Tuchman had no special training for her life's work. However, she has a marvelous ability to tell a story (and, after all,* history *is a story) as well as a fine intelligence and scholarly persistence and care. The result has been a series of books, the most popularly successful of which are* The Guns of August, *a Book of the Month Club selection, and* A Distant Mirror.

She was born, in 1912, in New York and has lived in that city all of her life. She took her B.A. at Radcliffe and in 1940 married Lester R. Tuchman, a physician. She has three children: Lucy, Jessica, and Alma.

Tuchman says her goal is to write readable histories: "Historians who put in everything plus countless footnotes aren't thinking of their readers," she says. "There should be a beginning, a middle, and an end, plus an element of suspense to keep a reader turning the pages."

About her lack of professional training as a historian she has this to say: "I never took a Ph.D. It's what saved me, I think. If I had taken a doctoral degree, it would have stifled any writing ability."

"This Is the End of the World": The Black Death

In October 1347, two months after the fall of Calais, Genoese trading ships put into the harbor of Messina in Sicily with dead and dying men at the oars. The ships had come from the Black Sea port of Caffa (now Feodosiya) in the Crimea, where the Genoese maintained a trading post. The diseased sailors showed strange black swellings about the size of an egg or an apple in the armpits and groin. The swellings oozed blood and pus and were followed by spreading boils and black blotches on the skin from internal bleeding. The sick suffered severe pain and died quickly within five days of the first symptoms. As the disease spread, other symptoms of continuous fever and spitting of blood appeared instead of the swellings or buboes. These victims coughed and sweated heavily and died even more quickly, within three days or less, sometimes in 24 hours. In both types everything that issued from the body—breath, sweat, blood from the buboes and lungs, bloody urine, and blood-blackened excrement—smelled foul. Depression and despair accompanied the physical symptoms, and before the end "death is seen seated on the face."

The disease was bubonic plague, present in two forms: one that infected the bloodstream, causing the buboes and internal bleeding, and was spread by contact; and a second, more virulent pneumonic type that infected the lungs and was spread by respiratory infection. The presence of both at once cause the high mortality and speed of contagion. So lethal was the disease that cases were known of persons going to bed well and dying before they woke, of doctors catching the illness at a bedside and dying before the patient. So rapidly did it spread from one to another that to a French physician, Simon de Covino, it seemed as if one sick person "could infect the whole world." The malignity of the pestilence appeared more terrible because its victims knew no prevention and no remedy. . . .

By January 1348 it penetrated France via Marseilles, and North Africa via Tunis. Shipborne along coasts and navigable rivers, it spread westward from Marseille through the ports of Languedoc to Spain and northward up the Rhône to Avignon, where it arrived in March. It reached Narbonne, Montpellier, Carcassonne, and Toulouse between February and May, and at the same time in Italy spread to Rome and Florence and their hinterlands. Between June and August it reached Bordeaux, Lyon, and Paris, spread to Burgundy and Normandy, and crossed the Channel from Normandy into southern England. From Italy during the same summer it crossed the Alps into Switzerland and reached eastward to Hungary.

In a given area the plague accomplished its kill within four to six months and then faded, except in the larger cities, where, rooting into the close-quartered population, it abated during the winter, only to reappear in spring and rage for another six months.

In 1349 it resumed in Paris, spread to Picardy, Flanders, and the Low Countries, and from England to Scotland and Ireland as well as to Norway, where a ghost ship with a cargo of wool and a dead crew drifted offshore until it ran aground near Bergen. From there the plague passed into Sweden, Denmark, Prussia, Iceland, and as far as Greenland. Leaving a strange pocket of immunity in Bohemia, and Russia unattacked until 1351, it had passed from most of Europe by mid-1350. Although the mortality rate was erratic, ranging from one fifth in some places to nine tenths or almost total elimination in others, the overall estimate of modern demographers has settled—for the area extending from India to Iceland—around the same figure expressed in Froissart's casual words: "a third of the world died." His estimate, the common one at the time, was not an inspired guess but a borrowing of St. John's figure for mortality from plague in Revelation, the favorite guide to human affairs of the Middle Ages.

A third of Europe would have meant about 20 million deaths. No one knows in truth how many died. Contemporary reports were an awed impression, not an accurate count. In crowded Avignon, it was said, 400 died daily; 7,000 houses emptied by death were shut up; a single graveyard received 11,000 corpses in six weeks; half the city's inhabitants reportedly died, including 9 cardinals or one third of the total, and 70 lesser prelates. Watching the endlessly passing death carts, chroniclers let normal exaggeration take wings and put the Avignon death toll at 62,000 and even at 120,000, although the city's total population was probably less than 50,000.

When graveyards filled up, bodies at Avignon were thrown into the Rhône until mass burial pits were dug for dumping the corpses. In London in such pits corpses piled up in layers until they overflowed. Everywhere reports speak of the sick dying too fast for the living to bury. Corpses were dragged out of homes and left in front of doorways. Morning light revealed new piles of bodies. In Florence the dead were gathered up by the Compagnia della Misericordia—founded in 1244 to care for the sick—whose members wore red robes and hoods masking the face except for the eyes. When their efforts failed, the dead lay putrid in the streets for days at a time. When no coffins were to be had, the bodies were laid on boards, two or three at once, to be carried to graveyards or common pits. Families dumped their own relatives into the pits, or buried them so hastily and thinly "that dogs dragged them forth and devoured their bodies."

Amid accumulating death and fear of contagion, people died without last rites and were buried without prayers, a prospect that terrified the last hours of the stricken. A bishop in England gave permission to laymen to make confession to each other as was done by the Apostles, "or if no man is present then even to a woman," and if no priest could be found to administer extreme unction, "then faith must suffice." Clement VI found it necessary to grant remissions of sin to all who died of the plague because so many were unattended by priests. "And no bells tolled," wrote a chronicler of Siena, "and nobody wept no matter what his loss because almost everyone expected death. . . . And people said and believed, 'This is the end of the world.' ". . .

Ignorance of the cause augmented the sense of horror. Of the real carriers, rats and fleas, the 14th century had no suspicion, perhaps because they were so familiar. Fleas, though a common household nuisance, are not once mentioned in contemporary plague writings, and rats only incidentally, although folklore commonly associated them with pestilence. The legend of the Pied Piper arose from an outbreak of 1284. The actual plague bacillus, *Pasturella pestis*, remained undiscovered for another 500 years. Living alternatively in the stomach of the flea and the bloodstream of the rat who was the flea's host, the bacillus in its bubonic form was transferred to humans and animals by the bite of either rat or flea. It traveled by virtue of *Rattus rattus*, the small medieval black rat that lived on ships, as well as by the heavier brown or sewer rat. What precipitated the turn of the bacillus from innocuous to virulent form is unknown, but the occurrence is now believed to have taken place not in China but somewhere in central Asia and to have spread along the caravan routes. Chinese origin was a mistaken notion of the 14th century based on real but belated reports of huge death tolls in China from drought, famine, and pestilence which have since been traced to the 1330s, too soon to be responsible for the plague that appeared in India in 1346.

The phantom enemy had no name. Called the Black Death only in later recurrences, it was known during the first epidemic simply as the Pestilence or Great Mortality. Reports from the East, swollen by fearful imaginings, told of strange tempests and "sheets of fire" mingled with huge hailstones that "slew almost all," or a "vast rain of fire" that burned up men, beasts, stones, trees, villages, and cities. In another version, "foul blasts of wind" from the fires carried the infection to Europe, "and now as some suspect it cometh round the seacoast." Accurate observation in this case could not make the mental jump to ships and rats because no idea of animal- or insect-borne contagion existed.

The earthquake was blamed for releasing sulfurous and foul fumes from the earth's interior, or as evidence of a titanic struggle of planets and oceans causing waters to rise and vaporize until fish died in masses and corrupted the air. All these explanations had in common a factor of poisoned air, of miasmas and thick, stinking mists traced to every kind of natural or imagined agency from stagnant lakes to malign conjunction of the planets, from the hand of the Evil One to the wrath of God. Medical thinking, trapped in the theory of astral influences, stressed air as the communicator of disease, ignoring sanitation or visible carriers. The existence of two carriers confused the trail, the more so because the flea could live and travel independently of the rat for as long as a month and, if infected by the particularly virulent septicemic form of the bacillus, could infect humans without reinfecting itself from the rat. The simultaneous presence of the pneumonic form of the disease, which was indeed communicated through the air, blurred the problem further.

The mystery of the contagion was "the most terrible of all the terrors," as an anonymous Flemish cleric in Avignon wrote to a correspondent in Bruges. Plagues had been known before, from the plague of Athens (believed to have been typhus) to the prolonged epidemic of the 6th century A.D., to the recurrence of sporadic outbreaks in the 12th and 13th centuries, but they had left no accumulated store of understanding. That the infection came from contact with the sick or with their houses, clothes, or corpses was quickly observed but not comprehended. Gentile da Foligno, renowned physician of Perugia and doctor of medicine at the universities of Bologna and Padua, came close to respiratory infection when he surmised that poisonous material was "communicated by means of air breathed out and in." Having no idea of microscopic carriers, he had to assume that the air was corrupted by planetary influences. Planets, however, could not explain the ongoing contagion. The agonized search for an answer gave rise to such theories as transference by sight. People fell ill, wrote Guy de Chauliac, not only by remaining with the sick but "even by looking at them." Three hundred years later Joshua Barnes, the 17th century biographer of Edward III, could write that the power of infection had entered into beams of light and "darted death from the eyes."

Doctors struggling with the evidence could not break away from the terms of astrology, to which they believed all human physiology was subject. Medicine was the one aspect of medieval life, perhaps because of its links with the Arabs, not shaped by Christian doctrine. Clerics detested astrology, but could not dislodge its influence. Guy de Chauliac, physician to three popes in succession, practiced in obedience to the zodiac. While his *Cirurgia* was the major treatise on surgery of its time, while he understood the use of anesthesia made from the juice of opium, mandrake, or hemlock, he nevertheless prescribed bleeding and purgatives by the planets and divided chronic from acute diseases on the basis of one being under the rule of the sun and the other of the moon.

In October 1348 Philip VI asked the medical faculty of the University of Paris for a report on the affliction that seemed to threaten human survival. With careful thesis, antithesis, and proofs, the doctors ascribed it to a triple conjunction of Saturn, Jupiter, and Mars in the 40th degree of Aquarius said to have occurred on March 20, 1345. They acknowledged, however, effects "whose cause is hidden from even the most highly trained intellects." The verdict of the masters of Paris became the official version. Borrowed, copied by scribes, carried abroad, translated from Latin into various vernaculars, it was everywhere accepted, even by the Arab physicians of Cordova and Granada, as the scientific if not the popular answer. Because of the terrible interest of the subject, the translations of the plague tracts stimulated use of national languages. In that one respect life came from death.

To the people at large there could be but one explanation—the wrath of God. Planets might satisfy the learned doctors, but God was closer to the average man. A scourge so sweeping and unsparing without any visible cause could only be seen as Divine punishment upon mankind for its sins. It might even be God's terminal disappointment in his creature. Matteo Villani compared the plague to the Flood in ultimate purpose and believed he was recording "the extermination of mankind." Efforts to appease Divine wrath took many forms, as when the city of Rouen ordered that everything that could anger God, such as gambling, cursing, and drinking, must be stopped. More general were the penitent processions authorized at first by the Pope, some lasting as long as three days, some attended by as many as 2,000, which everywhere accompanied the plague and helped to spread it.

Barefoot in sackcloth, sprinkled with ashes, weeping, praying, tearing their hair, carrying candles and relics, sometimes with ropes around their necks or beating themselves with whips, the penitents wound through the streets, imploring the mercy of the Virgin and saints at their shrines. In a valid illustration for the *Très Riches Heures* of the Duc de Berry, the Pope is shown in a penitent procession attended by four cardinals in scarlet from hat to hem. He raises both arms in supplication to the angel on top of the Castel Sant'Angelo, while white-robed priests bearing banners and relics in golden cases turn to look as one of their number, stricken by the plague, falls to the ground, his face contorted with anxiety. In the rear, a gray-clad monk falls beside another victim already on the ground as the townspeople gaze in horror. (Nominally the illustration represents a 6th century plague in the time of Pope Gregory the Great, but as medieval artists made no distinction between past and present, the scene is shown as the artist would have seen it in the 14th century.) When it became evident that these processions were sources of infection, Clement VI had to prohibit them.

In Messina, where the plague first appeared, the people begged the Archbishop of neighboring Catania to lend them the relics of St. Agatha. When the Catanians refused to let the relics go, the Archbishop dipped them in holy water and took the water himself to Messina, where he carried it in a procession with prayers and litanies through the streets. The demonic, which shared the medieval cosmos with God, appeared as "demons in the shape of dogs" to terrify the people. "A black dog with a drawn sword in his paws appeared among them, gnashing his teeth and rushing upon them and breaking all the silver vessels and lamps and candlesticks on the altars and casting them hither and thither. . . . So the people of Messina, terrified by this prodigious vision, were all strangely overcome by fear."

The apparent absence of earthly cause gave the plague a supernatural and sinister quality. Scandinavians believed that a Pest Maiden emerged from the mouth of the dead in the form of a blue flame and flew through the air to infect the next house. In Lithuania the Maiden was said to wave a red scarf through the door or window to let in the pest. One brave man, according to legend, deliberately waited at his open window with drawn sword and, at the fluttering of the scarf, chopped off the hand. He died of his deed, but his village was spared and the scarf long preserved as a relic in the local church.

Beyond demons and superstition the final hand was God's. The Pope acknowledged it in a Bull of September 1348, speaking of the "pestilence with which God is afflicting the Christian people." To the Emperor John Cantacuzene it was manifest that a malady of such horrors, stenches, and agonies, and especially one bringing the dismal despair that settled upon its victims before they died, was not a plague "natural" to mankind but "a chastisement from Heaven." To Piers Plowman "these pestilences were for pure sin."

The general acceptance of this view created an expanded sense of guilt, for if the plague were punishment there had to be terrible sin to have occasioned it. What sins were on the 14th century conscience? Primarily greed, the sin of avarice, followed by usury, worldliness, adultery, blasphemy, falsehood, luxury, irreligion. Giovanni Villani, attempting to account for the cascade of calamity that had fallen upon Florence, concluded that it was retribution for the sins of avarice and usury that oppressed the poor. Pity and anger about the condition of the poor, especially victimization of the peasantry in war, was often expressed by writers of the time and was certainly on the conscience of the century. Beneath it all was the daily condition of medieval life, in which hardly an act or thought, sexual, mercantile, or military, did not contravene the dictates of the Church. Mere failure to fast or attend mass was sin. The result was an underground lake of guilt in the soul that the plague now tapped.

That the mortality was accepted as God's punishment may explain in part the vacuum of comment that followed the Black Death. An investigator has noticed that in the archives of Périgord references to the war are innumerable, to the plague few. Froissart mentions the great death but once, Chaucer gives it barely a glance. Divine anger so great that it contemplated the extermination of man did not bear close examination. . . .

St. Roch, credited with special healing powers, who had died in 1327, was the particular saint associated with the plague. Inheriting wealth as a young man, as had St. Francis, he had distributed it to the poor and to hospitals, and while returning from a pilgrimage to Rome had encountered an epidemic and stayed to help the sick. Catching the malady himself, he retreated to die alone in the woods, where a dog brought him bread each day. "In these sad times," says his legend, "when reality was so somber and men so hard, people ascribed pity to animals." St. Roch recovered and, on appearing in rags as a beggar, was thought to be a spy and thrown into jail, where he died, filling the cell with a strange light. As his story spread and sainthood was conferred, it was believed that God would cure of the plague anyone who invoked his name. When this failed to occur, it enhanced the belief that, men having grown too wicked, God indeed intended their end. As Langland wrote,

> God is deaf now-a-days and deigneth not hear us,
> And prayers have no power the Plague to stay.

In a terrible reversal, St. Roch and other saints now came to be considered a source of the plague, as instruments of God's wrath. "In the time of that great mortality in the year of our Lord 1348," wrote a professor of law named Bartolus of Sassoferrato, "the hostility of God was stronger than the hostility of man." But he was wrong.

The hostility of man proved itself against the Jews. On charges that they were poisoning the wells, with intent "to kill and destroy the whole of Christendom and have lordship over all the world," the lynchings began in the spring of 1348 on the heels of the first plague deaths. The first attacks occurred in Narbonne and Carcassonne, where Jews were dragged from their houses and thrown into bonfires. While Divine punishment was accepted as the plague's source, people in their misery still looked for a human agent upon whom to vent the hostility that could not be vented on God. The Jew, as the eternal stranger, was the most obvious target. He was the outsider who had separated himself by choice from the Christian world, whom Christians for centuries had been taught to hate, who was regarded as imbued with unsleeping malevolence against all Christians. Living in a distinct group of his own kind in a particular street or quarter, he was also the most feasible target, with property to loot as a further inducement.

The accusation of well-poisoning was as old as the plague of Athens, when it had been applied to the Spartans, and as recent as the epidemics of 1320–21, when it had been applied to the lepers. At that time the lepers were believed to have acted at the instigation of the Jews and the Moslem King of Granada, in a great conspiracy of outcasts to destroy Christians. Hundreds were rounded up and burned throughout France in 1322 and the

Jews heavily punished by an official fine and unofficial attacks. When the plague came, the charge was instantly revived against the Jews:

> . . . rivers and fountains
> That were clear and clean
> They poisoned in many places . . .

wrote the French court poet Guillaume de Machaut.

The antagonism had ancient roots. The Jew had become the object of popular animosity because the early Church, as an offshoot of Judaism striving to replace the parent, had to make him so. His rejection of Christ as Saviour and his dogged refusal to accept the new law of the Gospel in place of the Mosaic law made the Jew a perpetual insult to the newly established Church, a danger who must be kept distinct and apart from the Christian community. This was the purpose of the edicts depriving Jews of their civil rights issued by the early Church Councils in the 4th century as soon as Christianity became the state religion. Separation was a two-way street, since, to the Jews, Christianity was at first a dissident sect, then an apostasy with which they wanted no contact.

The theory, emotions, and justifications of anti-Semitism were laid at that time—in the canon law codified by the Councils; in the tirades of St. John Chrysostom, Patriarch of Antioch, who denounced the Jews as Christ-killers; in the judgment of St. Augustine, who declared the Jews to be "outcasts" for failing to accept redemption by Christ. The Jews' dispersion was regarded as their punishment for unbelief.

The period of active assault began with the age of the crusades, when all Europe's intramural antagonisms were gathered into one bolt aimed at the infidel. On the theory that the "infidel at home" should likewise be exterminated, massacres of Jewish communities marked the crusaders' march to Palestine. The capture of the Holy Sepulcher by the Moslems was blamed on "the wickedness of the Jews," and the cry "HEP! HEP!" for *Hierosolyma est Perdita* (Jerusalem is lost) became the call for murder. What man victimizes he fears; thus, the Jews were pictured as fiends filled with hatred of the human race, which they secretly intended to destroy. . . .

Survivors of the plague, finding themselves neither destroyed nor improved, could discover no Divine purpose in the pain they had suffered. God's purposes were usually mysterious, but this scourge had been too terrible to be accepted without questioning. If a disaster of such magnitude, the most lethal ever known, was a mere wanton act of God or perhaps not God's work at all, then the absolutes of a fixed order were loosed from their moorings. Minds that opened to admit these questions could never again be shut. Once people envisioned the possibility of change in a fixed order, the end of an age of submission came in sight; the turn to individual conscience lay ahead. To that extent the Black Death may have been the unrecognized beginning of modern man.

Questions for Discussion

1. Structurally, this selection has clearcut parts; the essay would be easy to outline. Find the major sections of the essay and apply a summarizing title to each. For example, the first section can be said to run from the beginning through the eighth paragraph on p. 228, concluding with "This is the end of the world." It might be titled "The Spread of the Plague." What, in your analysis, are the boundaries of the other sections, and what would you title them?

2. Tuchman gives many details, including statistics, about the plague. What is the effect of these details? Does the author tell the reader more than he or she wants to know? Are there instances in which you wanted more information?

3. On page 229, Tuchman tells us, "Clerics detested astrology, but could not dislodge its influence." And astrology is alive and well today. Why? What do you think about astrology?

4. Explain what Tuchman means by the following sentence: "Divine anger so great that it contemplated the extermination of man did not bear close examination" (p. 231).

5. Explain why Tuchman says that "the Black Death may have been the unrecognized beginning of modern man" (p. 234). Can one say that the phrase states the gist of the selection? Explain.

6. Compare and contrast the fourteenth-century reaction to the plague with public reaction to a modern "plague," such as AIDS. In what respects do the reactions differ, and in what ways are they similar?

7. Argue that all plagues, ancient and modern, either are or are not finally the work of God.

8. In what ways were fourteenth-century explanations of the plague like early explanations of heaven and hell? (See "Charting Heaven and Hell" earlier in this chapter.)

9. People in the fourteenth century held numerous beliefs about the causes of the plague. What were these beliefs, and what do they tell you about making generalizations concerning an era?

STEPHEN BIRMINGHAM

After starting his career as a novelist, Stephen Birmingham found his ideal subject matter in the histories of the very rich, as in "Our Crowd": The Great Jewish Families of New York *(1967),* Real Lace: America's Irish Rich *(1973), and* Certain People: America's Black Elite *(1977). In the* Atlantic, *Phoebe Adams characterized Birmingham as "a persistent explorer of ethnic byways provided they are paved with gold."*

Birmingham, the son of a lawyer, was born in 1932. He took his bachelor's degree, Phi Beta Kappa, from Williams College. He worked in advertising from 1955 to 1967 after two years of service in the army. He is married and has three children. His home is in Mt. Adams, Ohio.

The Gangsters

Thus, the caste lines remained firmly drawn. The Russians did indeed seem enterprising; the Germans would admit that. But they also seemed brash, aggressive, pushy, loud, argumentative. They had not acquired the fine sheen of social polish that the Germans had striven so hard, and for so long, to possess. At a Jewish fund-raising gathering at Felix Warburg's Fifth Avenue house, a black-tie affair, two men were spotted who were not wearing dinner jackets. "They must be Russians," one of Mr. Warburg's sons whispered. The Russians, in other words, might have become successful, but they had not yet, in the Germans' eyes, become ladies and gentlemen.

Even more perplexing, perhaps, was the fact that Russian Jews were not going into endeavors that were considered solid and respectable, such as stockbrokerage and investment banking and insurance. They were going into chancier fields. Since many Russian men and women had arrived with some experience as tailors and seamstresses, they had gone into tailoring and dressmaking, and were now taking over the entire garment industry, and in the process turning it into what would become the largest single industry in New York City. Previously, nearly all the cloak manufacturers had been Germans, and prior to 1900, the average American woman had been very poorly dressed. Rich women shopped for fashions in Europe, or had dressmakers to copy the European designs that appeared in American fashion magazines. But poorer women dressed in what amounted to sacks, with neither fit nor style. But once the Russians entered the business, all that began to change. The Germans had been merely merchants, but the Russians were artists and artisans. In addition to the concept of sizing, they brought with them a knowledge and appreciation of the colors and textures and weights of fabrics. Having worked as tailors in Russia, they know how a pleat should fall, how a hem should hang, where a gusset or a gore or a dart should be placed. Russian furriers understood the qualities of furs by the feel and by the smell of untreated pelts, and they knew how sections of kid could be pieced together to conform to the shapes of women's hands. Once they had mastered the mechanics of the garment industry—the machines that had been unavailable in the old country—they were able to introduce to it literally thousands of innovations, to perfect and revolutionize the industry. With the new techniques of mass production, they were able to offer women stylish, well-fitting clothes off the racks at low prices, and by 1920 fashion was available to even the lowliest waitress or shopgirl. They had invented American fashion.

Still, to the Germans, it seemed an unbusinesslike enterprise, for what could be chancier, more unpredictable, than fashion, which was subject to shifting tastes, whims, and sudden fads? Fashion, furs, diamonds, jewelry—all wildly fluctuating commodities, all even riskier than show business. But the Russian Jews seemed to thrive on risks.

Crime, meanwhile, could hardly be considered a business at all. What could be a more win-or-lose, go-for-broke career than a life outside the law? That the East Side had produced a number of criminals was well known, and the attitude toward these people among the Russian-Jewish community was somewhat ambivalent. On the one hand, Jewish parents did not point out these men to their children as examples of American success. And yet, at the same time, there was a certain grudging admiration for men who could buck the system and get away with it. The Jewish criminal wore snappy clothes, drove an expensive car, was good to his wife, and could afford to send his sons to Harvard instead of the City College of New York. There was a certain glamour about him, rather like a Hollywood movie star. Crime, after all, was another way out of the ghetto, and nobody could be faulted for wanting to get out. And, for some, it was proving a very *rapid* way out of the ghetto—as whirlwind a way as Rose Pastor's engagement and marriage. Also, for otherwise perfectly legitimate Jewish businessmen, it was often useful to have a friend with "connections" who could get things done expeditiously, without going through a lot of legal red tape. Union problems, for example, could often be handled with a little muscle from certain quarters. And so the Jewish criminal was not regarded, among Jews, as an enemy of society, but more as a part of the general American landscape. By 1920, Meyer Lansky had become part of this panorama.

There are at least two versions of how Meyer Lansky first became friendly with another tough young East Sider named Salvatore Lucania, later to become known as Charles "Lucky" Luciano. Lansky liked to recall that they had first encountered each other at what had threatened to become a Lower East Side street battle between the Italians and the Jews, and how Luciano had been attracted by the tiny—fully grown, he was only a few inches over five feet tall—Lansky's spunk and nerve. Luciano had called off the fight and later taken Lansky under his protection, gratis. Luciano would recall the initial meeting somewhat differently. Luciano had been earning extra pin money collecting pennies from Jewish youths for protection, but when he approached Lansky with the usual proposition, Lansky had replied, "Fuck you!" Impressed, Luciano had offered to supply Lansky with free protection, to which Lansky had replied, "Shove your protection up your ass!" Realizing that they were kindred spirits, the two became lifelong friends and business associates. This friendship, too, marked the beginning of a Jewish-Italian alliance against a common East Side enemy, the Irish.

Soon, into the Lansky-Luciano group came another, somewhat older Jewish youth named Benjamin Siegel. Siegel was a well-built, good-looking fellow who had quite a way with the ladies, and whose ambition in those days was to become a movie star. It was not such a farfetched notion, since one of his best friends was a young actor named George Raft. Raft had been a street fighter and gambler out of Hell's Kitchen, and had boxed his way up from a number of small-time clubs all the way to Madison Square Garden, where he realized that he hadn't the fighting ability to reach top boxing circles. He had turned to dancing in nightclubs and revues, and became famous overnight for teaching the young Prince of Wales to do the Charleston. From there, it was on to Broadway and Hollywood. His friend Benny Siegel, though, had kind of a wild streak in him. Most Jewish and Italian street toughs eschewed knives and guns, but Siegel was always armed with one weapon or another, and would brandish these at the slightest provocation. For this behavior, and other bizarre habits—it was said that Siegel invented the game called Russian roulette—he was labeled "crazy as a bedbug," which earned him the nickname "Bugsy," though this was an appellation his friends were careful never to use to his face. Bugsy Siegel, as we shall see, eventually did get to Hollywood, though not in the manner he had originally planned.

Into this loosely organized but very effective fraternity came other Lower East Side Jews: Abe "Kid Twist" Reles, whose nickname derived from the fact that even as a kid he was adept at the "twist" of extortion; Arnold "the Brain" Rothstein, much admired for his ability to conceive and carry out grand schemes, and who came up with the notion of fixing the 1919 [baseball] World Series between the Chicago White Sox and the Cincinnati Reds. Then there was Jacob "Greasy Thumb" Guzik, whose thumb, it was said, was stained green from collecting bribes and blackmail; and Abner "Longie" Zwillman, whose nickname referred to the uncommon length of a certain anatomical endowment; and Louis "Lepke" Buchalter, whose doting mother called him "Lepkele," or "little Louis," and whose early career had involved picking pockets and robbing pushcarts. But from the very beginning of the organization, there was only one man who was its acknowledged leader—the little Caesar

who planned the battles, deployed the troops, settled internal arguments, and, with his mathematical genius, kept the books—and that
was Meyer Lansky. If much of the brawn of the group was supplied by
others, it was Lansky who supplied the brains.

Lansky never liked to think of his chosen means of livelihood as
anything other than a business. It might not be a legitimate business,
but it was still a business, and Lansky tried to keep it on as businesslike
a level—no tampering with the books—as possible. It was a business, as
he saw it, that was designed to cater to certain basic human needs—a
service business. Human beings liked to gamble, and would gamble
whether gambling was legal or not, and so Lansky and his associates
would put themselves at the service of gamblers. At the same time,
Lansky had his own strict moral code. He would not, for example,
involve himself in prostitution. Prostitution could also be rationalized
as fulfilling a human need, but Lansky would have none of it. Some of
his partners called him a prude for this, and in a way he was. But he
was also something of a snob. He considered prostitution dehumanizing, but it also got one mixed up with all the wrong sort of people. As a
boy, he had seen a beautiful Jewish prostitute named Rachel, to whom
he had taken a fancy, beaten to death in a back alley by her Jewish
pimp. The grisly, sordid scene remained etched in his mind.

He felt the same way about trafficking in narcotics. Again, the
people who were in the drug trade struck him as lowlifes whom he
wouldn't want to be seen with, and the addicts they served were the
dregs of humanity. Lansky had his standards. In many ways, if you
overlooked his source of income, Meyer Lansky was a young gentleman
of the old school. As he began to prosper from his gambling operations,
he remained a conservative fellow. His friend Bugsy Siegel might favor
loud neckties and flashy sport coats, but Lansky always dressed quietly
in well-cut three-button suits—which, with his slight figure, he usually
bought in the boy's department of Macy's. He did not look like a "gangster," nor did he act like one. In manner, he was genial, soft-spoken—
except, of course, when crossed. He was also a devoutly pious Jew and
faithfully kept the Sabbath.

Still, Lansky and Company's business might have remained a relatively small one had it not been for an event that, for an organization
dedicated to serving human needs, amounted to nothing less than a
windfall. On January 16, 1919, the Eighteenth Amendment to the Constitution of the United States was ratified, to become law one year later.
The amendment banned the manufacture, sale, and transportation of
liquor, wine, beer, or other intoxicating substances. Nine months later,
over President Wilson's veto, the Volstead Act was passed by Congress,

toughening the Prohibition laws and setting up the machinery for their enforcement. The Women's Christian Temperance Union had been triumphant; the "noble experiment" had begun.

Perhaps never in the history of government folly had an experiment so doomed to failure been undertaken, and certainly never had a scheme so outwardly drenched in piety and righteousness been embarked upon with so much cynicism. America had been a drinking nation since pre-Colonial times, and there was nothing to indicate that Prohibition could change this. Instead, Prohibition was an open invitation to break the law, and to break it in the most daring, glamorous, and exciting ways. Drinking in America had always been associated with parties and good times, and now Prohibition offered Americans a chance to go on a prolonged, illegal binge. Even as Prohibition was being enacted into law, the very legislators who had voted for it were planning ways of obtaining their own personal supplies of liquor. The "year of grace" allowed wealthy hoarders plenty of time to stock their cellars for years to come. Furthermore, it gave legitimate bars and restaurants time to convert to illicit speakeasies, so that by the early 1920s, there were thousands in the city of New York alone. It also allowed men like Meyer Lansky and his friends the time to develop an elaborate game plan for buying and marketing alcoholic beverages, so that when the Volstead Act finally went into effect, they had a virtually foolproof strategy for working around the law. On the very eve of Prohibition, nightclub comics joked about the various ways of obtaining liquor that would become available the following day. Had it not been for Prohibition, men like Lansky, Luciano, and Siegel might have continued as operators of small-time gambling parlors, living in a series of cold-water tenement flats. But Prohibition offered a golden door to riches—for Lansky, what would become one of the larger personal fortunes in America—all for helping Americans defy an unpopular law. The profits, as Lanksy saw them, would be far greater than those from gambling operations; the penalties were far less; and the chance of those penalties being enforced was infinitesimal. Once again, he was in a service business. And he was not yet twenty.

There were two kinds of bootleggers, from the beginning. One dealt in cheap, watered-down liquor and in homemade brews from basement stills. The other dealt in the real thing. Lansky counseled his associates to join the latter group. Partly, it was his snobbish nature. But also, he reasoned, dealing in cut, ersatz liquor—in which a bottle labeled "Scotch" might actually be only colored water, raw alcohol, and a splash of real Scotch for flavor—meant that one's clientele would consist mostly of skid-row bums and the sleaziest bars; there would be little repeat business. If, on the other hand, one could offer good, uncut, imported Scotches and gins that had not been tampered with, one would be dealing with the well-heeled—along with the most expensive bars and clubs—who would pay anything for top quality and who, once they had learned to trust their bootlegger, would come back for more of the same. Lansky had also read a book called *Making Profits*, written a few years earlier by a Harvard professor of economics named William Taussig. In it, Professor Taussig had outlined the law of supply and demand. What it meant, Lansky explained to his less literate associates, was, "If you have a lot of what people want and can't get, then you can supply the demand and shovel in the dough." Among his friends, this quickly became known as "Lansky's Law," and it would become the basic precept by which organized crime would live from that point onward, just as legitimate capitalist society lived by it, and had been living by it, all along.

But there was more to it than that. As Prohibition began to lift the underworld from what had been a loosely organized group of friends, relatives, and acquaintances into the stratosphere of Big Business, the many ramifications of the Volstead Act became quickly clear. For the average consumer, Prohibition meant essentially one thing: the cost of liquor went up, to cover the costs of the risks involved. But times were prosperous, and the average consumer understood the situation, and cheerfully paid the price. There was money to be made in all directions. Foreign distillers could raise their prices for the illicit American market. The speakeasies that instantly sprang up across the countryside became instantly prosperous, since they could charge their "member" customers more for drinks by the glass than had previously been charged in legal bars. Soon it was estimated that there were at least twenty-two thousand speakeasies on the island of Manhattan alone—far more than there had ever been legitimate bars. (One popular speakeasy on West Fifty-second Street, Jack and Charlie's 21 Club, operated by two brothers named Kriendler, was the forerunner of today's posh and elegant "21" Restaurant as well as the prestigious "21"-brand liquors.) The makers of fruit juices, mixers, and sweeteners also made money, since the flavors of inferior liquors could be disguised by colas and syrups. (The mixed "cocktail" was a Prohibition invention of necessity.) Bootleggers in the smallest towns could make money. Even poor Italians on the Lower East Side, who had been brewing their own wines and spirits in their homes for years, found themselves proprietors of profitable neighborhood liquor stores. Into all these sources of money Meyer Lansky plunged. As his network of connections in other American cities grew, where local gamblers knew as well as he that their patrons spent more at the gaming tables when their inhibitions had been loosened by alcohol, it was natural that his group should extend its operations into the illegal import of liquor.

Some of the earliest attempts to smuggle liquor into the United States were clumsy and naive. The term "bootlegging," for example, derived from stuffing bottles of liquor into the tops of oversized boots to foil customs inspectors at American borders. Some carried in liquor strapped to their persons under bulky coats.*

For American bootleggers, the handiest source of liquor was Canada, with its long and relatively unguarded border, much of which was wilderness, and as bootlegging grew more profitable, its methods became more sophisticated. Before crossing the border, for example, a truck driver with a load of contraband would select a dirt road, and then attach heavy chains to his rear bumper. He would then charge across the border, refusing to stop for the customs inspector, while his dragging chains kicked up so much dust that he was impossible to follow.

Liquor made its way into Canada from England, Ireland, Scotland, and Europe by way of two tiny French islands (actually a *département* of France) off the Newfoundland coast that most people had never heard of, Saint Pierre and Miquelon. Here the shipments were uncrated for redistribution to the American bootleg market, and most of the wooden houses on the principal, virtually treeless island of Saint Pierre were built with lumber obtained from cast-off liquor crates. From Canada, a particularly popular route of shipment was by boat across Lake Erie, where long stretches of shoreline on both the American and Canadian sides were unpopulated, but where old logging roads led inland from the shore to connect with main arteries. One of Meyer Lansky's first assignments to his underlings was to have maps drawn of these uncharted roads. In his youth, he had worked briefly as an automobile mechanic, and had learned quite a lot about cars. A side operation was organized to service, repair, and camouflage stolen trucks and other vehicles that were used to transport liquor to the marketplace.

Meanwhile, bootlegging had suddenly become a glamorous occupation, and the bootlegger a glamorous figure. Bootleggers in the early 1920s were like cowboy heroes out of the Old West who took the law into their own hands, and women chattered about their favorite bootleggers as they might about their favorite hairdressers ("We've found the most wonderful new bootlegger . . ."). In small towns, the bootlegger gained almost the same respect and social status as the local doctor,

*This author's own mother, returning from Europe, made her way safely, if clinking slightly and looking somewhat overweight, with bottles plunged into her girdle and a bottle in each cup of her brassiere.

lawyer, or undertaker. In the cities, bootleggers were invited to all the best parties, and had their pick of the most desirable women. The term "gangster" was used almost reverentially, and Hollywood gangster movies achieved great popularity. A number of silent film stars of the era—Pola Negri, Gloria Swanson, Renée Adorée—were said to have taken gangster lovers. In the best hotels and restaurants, men reputed to be gangsters were given the best tables. When gangsters were recognized, children asked for their autographs.

There were dangers involved in bootlegging, of course, but they were relatively slight. Despite the desperate efforts of American lawmen to police the Canadian border, it was estimated that only five percent of the smuggled booty was ever successfully stopped or confiscated—and any legitimate salesman who succeeded in getting ninety-five percent of his merchandise sold would have considered himself more than fortunate. Occasionally, there were unsettling incidents. In 1927, a convoy of trucks carrying liquor from Ireland was ambushed outside of Boston. The Irish guards who were in charge of the shipment opened fire on the ambushers, and before the shooting was over eleven men lay dead.

The ambushers, who were working for the Lansky organization, were able to make off with the whiskey, but Lansky himself was furious. Whiskey, he roared, was replaceable, but human lives were not. Besides, eleven bodies strewn along the roadside meant that there would be police and federal investigations—the last things he wanted. His men had been instructed that, whenever any actual shooting started, they should run for their lives, and no doubt the Lansky employee who returned the Irish fire would have been disciplined, were it not for the fact that he was already dead.

Later, Lansky learned that the "importer" of the Irish whiskey whom he had robbed was the son of a Boston bartender, Joseph P. Kennedy. For the rest of his life, Lansky would claim that Joseph Kennedy had passed on his vendetta to his sons, Bobby and John, and that Bobby Kennedy's efforts, as United States attorney general, to root out organized crime were in fact a personal attempt to "get even" with Lansky for that long-ago hijacking.

Questions for Discussion

1. "History is merely gossip," said Oscar Wilde. What instances in this chapter fit Oscar Wilde's assessment? What value is there in

such gossip? What justification is there for passing such information on to succeeding generations?

2. Compare the Prohibition era with today's drug culture. Does "Lansky's Law" still apply?

3. Why do you think people found the bootleggers glamorous?

4. How can we account for the legislators' hypocrisy in passing the Volstead Act while hoarding away personal stores of liquor?

5. In the introduction to this chapter, you found characterizations of the histories of Herodotus, Thucydides, and Xenophon. Which of the three is Birmingham's work more nearly like? Why?

6. If Birmingham were a Thucydides, he would probably derive a moral lesson from his narrative. What would that lesson be? State the lesson in one stylistically polished sentence.

7. Explain the characteristics that make the Birmingham selection a history rather than a chronicle.

WILLIAM L. SHIRER

William L. Shirer was in the right place at the right time. After graduating from Coe College in 1925, he set off for Europe and soon found a job writing for the Paris edition of the Chicago Tribune, *attempting to establish himself as a poet and short story writer, and then turned his attention to the European political scene. Reporting from various European capitals, Shirer witnessed firsthand many of the major developments leading to World War II.*

He returned to the United States in 1940 and continued as a reporter for both radio and newspaper until he was blacklisted during the McCarthy era. His forced retirement gave him time in which to research and write his masterpiece, The Rise and Fall of the Third Reich. *Completed after ten years of work, this epic book draws on Shirer's own recollections, captured German documents, and historical records to chart the twenty-year history of Nazism.*

The Rise and Fall of the Third Reich *won the National Book Award in 1961.*

The Mission of Count von Stauffenberg

This was a man of astonishing gifts for a professional Army officer. Born in 1907, he came from an old and distinguished South German family. Through his mother, Countess von Uxkull-Gyllenbrand, he was a great-grandson of Gneisenau, one of the military heroes of the war of liberation against Napoleon and the cofounder, with Scharnhorst, of the Prussian General Staff, and through her also a descendant of Yorck von Wartenburg, another celebrated general of the Bonaparte era. Klaus's father had been Privy Chamberlain to the last King of Wuerttemberg. The family was congenial, devoutly Roman Catholic and highly cultivated.

With this background and in this atmosphere Klaus von Stauffenberg grew up. Possessed of a fine physique and, according to all who knew him, of a striking handsomeness, he developed a brilliant, inquisitive, splendidly balanced mind. He had a passion for horses and sports but also for the arts and literature, in which he read widely, and as a youth came under the influence of Stefan George and that poetic genius's romantic mysticism. For a time the young man thought of taking up music as a profession, and later architecture, but in 1926, at the age of nineteen, he entered the Army as an officer cadet in the 17th Bamberg Cavalry Regiment—the famed *Bamberger Reiter*.

In 1936 he was posted to the War Academy in Berlin, where his all-round brilliance attracted the attention of both his teachers and the High Command. He emerged two years later as a young officer of the General Staff. Though, like most of his class, a monarchist at heart, he was not up to this time an opponent of National Socialism. Apparently it was the anti-Jewish pogroms of 1938 which first cast doubts in his mind about Hitler, and these increased when in the summer of 1939 he saw that the Fuehrer was leading Germany into a war which might be long, frightfully costly in human lives, and, in the end, lost.

Nevertheless, when the war came he threw himself into it with characteristic energy, making a name for himself as a staff officer of General Hoepner's 6th Panzer Division in the campaigns in Poland and France. It was in Russia that Stauffenberg seems to have become completely disillusioned with the Third Reich. He had been transferred to the Army High Command (OKH) early in June 1940, just before the assault on Dunkirk, and for the first eighteen months of the Russian campaign spent most of his time in Soviet territory, where, among other things, he helped organize the Russian "volunteer" units from among the prisoners of war. By this time, according to his friends, Stauffenberg believed that while the Germans were getting rid of Hitler's tyranny these Russian troops could be used to overthrow Stalin's. Perhaps this was an instance of the influence of Stefan George's wooly ideas.

The brutality of the S.S. in Russia, not to mention Hitler's order to shoot the Bolshevik commissars, opened Stauffenberg's eyes as to the master he was serving. As chance had it, he met in Russia two of the chief conspirators who had decided to make an end to that master: General von Tresckow and Schlabrendorff. The latter says it took only a few subsequent meetings to convince them that Stauffenberg was their man. He became an active conspirator. . . .

Shortly after 6 o'clock on the warm, sunny summer morning of July 20, 1944, Colonel Stauffenberg, accompanied by his adjutant, Lieutenant Werner von Haeften, drove out past the bombed-out buildings of Berlin to the airport at Rangsdorf. In his bulging briefcase were papers concerning the new *Volksgrenadier* divisions on which at 1 P.M. he was to report to Hitler at the "Wolf's Lair" at Rastenburg in East Prussia. In between the papers, wrapped in a shirt, was a time bomb.

It was identical to the one which Tresckow and Schlabrendorff had planted in the Fuehrer's airplane the year before and which had failed to explode. Of English make, as we have seen, it was set off by breaking a glass capsule, whose acid then ate away a small wire, which released the firing pin against the percussion cap. The thickness of the wire governed the time required to set off the explosion. On this morning the bomb was fitted with the thinnest possible wire. It would dissolve in a bare ten minutes.

At the airport Stauffenberg met General Stieff, who had produced the bomb the night before. There they found a plane waiting, the personal craft of General Eduard Wagner, the First Quartermaster General of the Army and a ringleader in the plot, who had arranged to put it at their disposal for this all-important flight. By 7 o'clock the plane was off, landing at Rastenburg shortly after 10 A.M. Haeften instructed the pilot to be ready to take off for the return trip at any time after twelve noon.

From the airfield a staff car drove the party to the Wolfsschanze headquarters, set in a gloomy, damp, heavily wooded area of East Prussia. It was not an easy place to get into or, as Stauffenberg undoubtedly noted, out of. It was built in three rings, each protected by mine fields, pillboxes and an electrified barbed-wire fence, and was patrolled day and night by fanatical S.S. troops. To get into the heavily guarded inner compound, where Hitler lived and worked, even the highest general had to have a special pass, good for one visit, and pass the personal inspection of S.S. Oberfuehrer Rattenhuber, Himmler's chief of security and commander of the S.S. guard, or of one of his deputies. However, since Hitler himself had ordered Stauffenberg to report, he and Haeften, though they were stopped and their passes examined, had little trouble in getting through the three check points. After breakfast with Captain von Moellendorff, adjutant to the camp commander, Stauffenberg sought out General Fritz Fellgiebel, Chief of Signals at OKW.

Fellgiebel was one of the key men in the plot. Stauffenberg made sure that the General was ready to flash the news of the bombing to the conspirators in Berlin so that action there could begin immediately. Fellgiebel was then to isolate the Fuehrer headquarters by shutting off all telephone, telegraph and radio communications. No one was in such a perfect position to do this as the head of the OKW communications network, and the plotters counted themselves lucky to have won him over. He was indispensable to the success of the entire conspiracy.

After calling on General Buhle, the Army's representative at OKW, to discuss the affairs of the Replacement Army, Stauffenberg walked over to Keitel's quarters, hung up his cap and belt in the anteroom and entered the office of the Chief of OKW. There he learned that he would have to act with more dispatch than he had planned. It was now a little after 12 noon, and Keitel informed him that because Mussolini would be arriving by train at 2:30 P.M. the Fuehrer's first daily conference had been put forward from 1 P.M. to 12:30. The colonel, Keitel advised, must make his report brief. Hitler wanted the meeting over early.

Before the bomb could go off Stauffenberg must have wondered if once again, and on what was perhaps his last try, fate was robbing him of success. Apparently he had hoped too that this time the conference with Hitler would be held in the Fuehrer's underground bunker, where the blast from the bomb would be several times more effective than in one of the surface buildings. But Keitel told him the meeting would be in the *Lagebaracke*—the conference barracks. This was far from being the flimsy wooden hut so often described. During the previous winter Hitler had had the original wooden structure reinforced with concrete walls eighteen inches thick to give protection against incendiary and splinter aerial bombs that might fall nearby. These heavy walls would add force to Stauffenberg's bomb.

He must soon set it to working. He had briefed Keitel on what he proposed to report to Hitler and toward the end had noticed the OKW Chief glancing impatiently at his watch. A few minutes before 12:30 Keitel said they must leave for the conference immediately or they would be late. They emerged from his quarters, but before they had taken more than a few steps Stauffenberg remarked that he had left his cap and belt in the anteroom and quickly turned to go back for them before Keitel could suggest that his adjutant, a Lieutenant von John, who was walking alongside, should retrieve them for him.

In the anteroom Stauffenberg swiftly opened his briefcase, seized the tongs with the only three fingers he had, and broke the capsule. In just ten minutes, unless there was another mechanical failure, the bomb would explode.

Keitel, as much a bully with his subordinates as he was a toady with his superiors, was aggravated at the delay and turned back to the building to shout to Stauffenberg to get a move on. They were late, he yelled. Stauffenberg apologized for the delay. Keitel no doubt realized that it took a man as maimed as the colonel a little extra time to put on his belt. As they walked over to Hitler's hut Stauffenberg seemed to be in a genial mood and Keitel's petty annoyance—he had no trace of suspicion as yet—was dissipated.

Nevertheless, as Keitel had feared, they were late. The conference had already begun. As Keitel and Stauffenberg entered the building the latter paused for a moment in the entrance hall to tell the sergeant major in charge of the telephone board that he expected an urgent call from his office in Berlin, that it would contain information he needed to bring his report up to the minute (this was for Keitel's ear), and that he was to be summoned immediately when the call came. This too, though it must have seemed most unusual—even a field marshal would scarcely dare to leave the Nazi warlord's presence until he had been dismissed or until the conference was over and the Supreme Commander had left *first*—did not arouse Keitel's suspicions.

The two men entered the conference room. About four minutes had ticked by since Stauffenberg reached into his briefcase with his tongs and broke the capsule. Six minutes to go. The room was relatively small, some thirty by fifteen feet, and it had ten windows, all of which were wide open to catch the breezes on this hot, sultry day. So many open windows would certainly reduce the effect of any bomb blast. In the middle of the room was an oblong table, eighteen by five feet, made of thick oak planks. It was a peculiarly constructed table in that it stood not on legs but on two large heavy supports, or socles, placed near the ends and extending to nearly the width of the table. This interesting construction was not without its effect on subsequent history.

When Stauffenberg entered the room, Hitler was seated at the center of the long side of the table, his back to the door. On his immediate right were General Heusinger, Chief of Operations and Deputy Chief of Staff of the Army, General Korten, Air Force Chief of Staff, and Colonel Heinz Brandt, Heusinger's chief of staff. Keitel took his place immediately to the left of the Fuehrer and next to him was General

Jodl. There were eighteen other officers of the three services and the S.S. standing around the table, but Goering and Himmler were not among them. Only Hitler, playing with his magnifying glass—which he now needed to read the fine print on the maps spread before him—and two stenographers were seated.

Heusinger was in the midst of a lugubrious report on the latest breakthrough on the central Russian front and on the perilous position, as a consequence, of the German armies not only there but on the northern and southern fronts as well. Keitel broke in to announce the presence of Colonel von Stauffenberg and its purpose. Hitler glanced up at the one-armed colonel with a patch over one eye, greeted him curtly, and announced that before hearing his report he wanted to have done with Heusinger's.

Stauffenberg thereupon took his place at the table between Korten and Brandt, a few feet to the right of Hitler. He put his briefcase on the floor, shoving it under the table so that it leaned against the *inside* of the stout oaken support. It was about six feet distant from the Fuehrer's legs. The time was now 12:37. Five minutes to go. Heusinger continued to talk, pointing constantly to the situation map spread on the table. Hitler and the officers kept bending over to study it.

No one seems to have noticed Stauffenberg stealing away. Except perhaps Colonel Brandt. This officer became so absorbed in what his General was saying that he leaned over the table the better to see the map, discovered that Stauffenberg's bulging briefcase was in his way, tried to shove it aside with his foot and finally reached down with one hand and lifted it to the *far side* of the heavy table support, which now stood between the bomb and Hitler. This seemingly insignificant gesture probably saved the Fuehrer's life; it cost Brandt his. There was an inexplicable fate involved here. Colonel Brandt, it will be remembered, was the innocent officer whom Tresckow had induced to carry a couple of "bottles of brandy" back on Hitler's plane from Smolensk to Rastenburg on the evening of March 13, 1943, and he had done so without the faintest suspicion that they were in reality a bomb—the very make of bomb which he had now unostentatiously moved farther away under the table from the warlord. Its chemical had by this time almost completed the eating away of the wire that held back the firing pin.

Keitel, who was responsible for the summoning of Stauffenberg, glanced down the table to where the colonel was supposed to be standing. Heusinger was coming to the end of his gloomy report and the OKW Chief wanted to indicate to Stauffenberg that he should make ready to report next. Perhaps he would need some aid in getting his papers out of his briefcase. But the young colonel, he saw to his extreme annoyance, was not there. Recalling what Stauffenberg had told the telephone operator on coming in, Keitel slipped out of the room to retrieve this curiously behaving young officer.

Stauffenberg was not at the telephone. The sergeant at the board said he had hurriedly left the building. Nonplused, Keitel turned back to the conference room. Heusinger was concluding, at last, his report on the day's catastrophic situation. *"The Russian,"* he was saying, *"is driving with strong forces west of the Duna toward the north. His spearheads are already southwest of Dunaburg. If our army group around Lake Peipus is not immediately withdrawn, a catastrophe . . ."*

It was a sentence that was never finished.

At that precise moment, 12:42 P.M., the bomb went off.

Stauffenberg saw what followed. He was standing with General Fellgiebel before the latter's office in Bunker 88 a couple of hundred yards away, glancing anxiously first at his wrist watch as the seconds ticked off and then at the conference barracks. He saw it go up with a roar in smoke and flame, as if, he said later, it had been hit directly by a 155-mm. shell. Bodies came hurtling out of the windows, debris flew into the air. There was not the slightest doubt in Stauffenberg's excited mind that every single person in the conference room was dead or dying. He bade a hasty farewell to Fellgiebel, who was now to telephone the conspirators in Berlin that the attempt had succeeded and then cut off communications until the plotters in the capital had taken over the city and proclaimed the new government.

Stauffenberg's next task was to get out of the Rastenburg headquarters camp alive and quickly. The guards at the check points had seen or heard the explosion at the Fuehrer's conference hall and immediately closed all exits. At the first barrier, a few yards from Fellgiebel's bunker, Stauffenberg's car was halted. He leaped out and demanded to speak with the duty officer in the guardroom. In the latter's presence he telephoned someone—whom is not known—spoke briefly, hung up and turned to the officer, saying, "Herr Leutnant, I'm allowed to pass."

This was pure bluff, but it worked, and apparently, after the lieutenant had dutifully noted in his log: *"12:44. Col. Stauffenberg passed through,"* word was sent along to the next check point to let the car through. At the third and final barrier, it was more difficult. Here an alarm had already been received, the rail had been lowered and the guard doubled, and no one was to be permitted to enter or leave. Stauffenberg and his aide, Lieutenant Haeften, found their car blocked by a very stubborn sergeant major named Kolbe. Again Stauffenberg demanded the use of the telephone and rang up Captain von Moellendorff, adjutant to the camp commander. He complained that "because of the explosion," the guard would not let him through. "I'm in a hurry. General Fromm is waiting for me at the airfield." This also was bluff. Fromm was in Berlin, as Stauffenberg well knew.

Hanging up, the colonel turned to the sergeant. "You heard, Sergeant, I'm allowed through." But the sergeant was not to be bluffed. He himself rang through to Moellendorff for confirmation. The captain gave it.

The car then raced to the airport while Lieutenant Haeften hurriedly dismantled a second bomb that he had brought along in his briefcase, tossing out the parts on the side of the road, where they were later found by the Gestapo. The airfield commandant had not yet received any alarm. The pilot had his engines warming up when the two men drove onto the field. Within a minute or two the plane took off.

It was now shortly after 1 P.M. The next three hours must have seemed the longest in Stauffenberg's life. There was nothing he could do as the slow Heinkel plane headed west over the sandy, flat German plain but to hope that Fellgiebel had been able to get through to Berlin with the all-important signal, that his fellow plotters in the capital had swung immediately into action in taking over the city and sending out the prepared messages to the military commanders in Germany and in the West, and that his plane would not be forced down by alerted Luftwaffe fighters or by prowling Russian craft, which were increasingly active over East Prussia. His own plane had no long-distance radio which might have enabled him to tune in on Berlin and hear the first thrilling broadcasts which he expected the conspirators would be making before he landed. Nor, for this lack, could he himself communicate with his confederates in the capital and give the signal that General Fellgiebel might not have been able to flash.

His plane droned on through the early summer afternoon. It landed at Rangsdorf at 3:45 P.M. and Stauffenberg, in high spirits, raced to the nearest telephone at the airfield to put through a call to General Olbricht to learn exactly what had been accomplished in the fateful three hours on which all depended. To his utter consternation he found that nothing had been accomplished. Word about the explosion had come through by telephone from Fellgiebel shortly after 1 o'clock but the connection was bad and it was not quite clear to the conspirators whether Hitler had been killed or not. Therefore nothing had been done. The Valkyrie orders had been taken from Olbricht's safe but not sent out. Everyone in the Bendlerstrasse had been standing idly by waiting for Stauffenberg's return. General Beck and Field Marshal von Witzleben, who as the new head of state and Commander in Chief of the Wehrmacht, respectively, were supposed to have started issuing immediately the already-prepared proclamations and commands and to have gone on the air at once to broadcast the dawn of a new day in Germany, had not yet showed up.

Questions for Discussion

1. Briefly summarize "The Mission of Count von Stauffenberg." What is the gist of the narrative?
2. Did you find Shirer's account of the plot to kill Hitler an interesting story? Explain.
3. In your opinion, was Stauffenberg justified in trying to kill Hitler? What justification does Shirer give?
4. What techniques does Shirer use to create our attitudes toward his characters?
5. Which author is the better storyteller, Shirer or Birmingham? Explain your judgment.
6. Discuss the qualities of this episode that would make good material for a film.

_____ SUGGESTIONS FOR WRITING _____

1.   Below are two passages about the brutal exploitation of Africans in the nineteenth century. One is from a history, Alan Moorehead's splendid study *The White Nile*, and the other is from Joseph Conrad's classic novella *Heart of Darkness*.

Using these two passages as your evidence, write a brief essay in which you begin to explain the nature of history by contrasting it with fiction.

Some features you might consider are the following:

    1.   The narrator. How involved in the action is the narrator? Is he an observer-reporter, merely telling what went on, or is he a participant in the events? How much does the narrator know about the thoughts and emotions of his subjects?

    2.   The content. How does the content, or subject matter, of the history differ from that of the fiction?

    3.   The style. Are there differences in the kind of language used in the two selections? What are these differences? What kind of imagery—details of sense experience (touch, smell, sight, sound)—do the authors use?

    4.   The purpose. What seems to be the purpose of each passage? In your opinion, how does each author want his work to affect readers?

Don't stop with these four suggestions. See what else you can discover by closely comparing the two passages.

    1.   With a tradition of at least two thousand years of slaving behind them none of the east coast Arab dealers had as yet dreamed of giving up the trade. Slaving was in the Arab blood: no Arab regarded the trade as any more evil or abnormal than, presumably, a horse-dealer regards as evil or abnormal the buying and selling of horses today.

And so the caravans were still raiding into the interior; the dhows, with their cargoes close-packed beneath the decks, were still successfully running the blockade of warships; and Zanzibar market was as crowded as ever. Prices varied a good deal according to the season of the year and the supply, but in 1856 a dealer could still count on obtaining £4 or £5 for an adult slave in Zanzibar and somewhat more for a female. Between twenty and forty thousand slaves were still imported into the island every year, about one-third of these being reserved for work on the plantations (which was still legal), and the remainder being destined, illegally, for export to Arabia, Persia, Egypt, Turkey and even further afield. There was a tremendous wastage even among those slaves who had survived the journey from their villages inland to the coast: some thirty per cent of the males died of disease and malnutrition every year in Zanzibar and had to be replaced. Moreover the attempt to control the export trade had increased the hardships of the slaves. Prices were going up, and consequently it paid the dealer to cram more and more of his victims into the dhows: if just one vessel in four got through it was enough to make a profit. The ships were now built, [Sir Richard Francis] Burton says, "with 18 inches between the decks, one pint of water a head was served out per diem and five wretches were stowed away instead of two."

—Alan Moorehead, *The White Nile* (New York: Vintage Books, 1983), p. 21.

2. My purpose was to stroll into the shade for a moment; but no sooner within than it seemed to me I had stepped into the gloomy circle of some Inferno. The rapids were near, and an uninterrupted, uniform, headlong, rushing noise filled the mournful stillness of the grove, where not a breath stirred, not a leaf moved, with a mysterious sound—as though the tearing pace of the launched earth had suddenly become audible.

Black shapes crouched, lay, sat between the trees, leaning against the trunks, clinging to the earth, half coming out, half effaced within the dim light, in all the attitudes of pain, abandonment, and despair. Another mine on the cliff went off, followed by a slight shudder of the soil under my feet. The work was going on. The work! And this was the place where some of the helpers had withdrawn to die.

They were dying slowly—it was very clear. They were not enemies, they were not criminals, they were nothing earthly now—nothing but black shadows of disease and starvation, lying confusedly in the greenish gloom. Brought from all the recesses of the coast in all the legality of time contracts, lost in uncongenial surroundings, fed on unfamiliar food, they sickened, became inefficient, and were then allowed to crawl away and rest. These moribund shapes were free as air—and nearly as thin. I began to distinguish the gleam of the eyes under the trees. Then, glancing down, I saw a face near my hand. The black bones reclined at full length with one shoulder against the tree, and slowly the eyelids rose and the sunken eyes looked up at me, enormous and vacant, a kind of blind, white flicker in the depths of the orbs, which died out slowly. The man seemed young—almost a boy—but you know with them it's hard to tell. I found nothing else to do but to offer him one of my good Swede's ship's biscuits I had in my pocket. The fingers closed slowly on it and held—there was no other movement and no other glance. He had tied a bit of white worsted around his neck—Why? Where did he get it? Was it a badge—an ornament—a charm—a propitiatory act? Was there any idea at all connected with it? It looked startling round his black neck, this bit of white thread from beyond the seas.

—Joseph Conrad, *Heart of Darkness*

2. Keeping in mind the distinction between chronicle and history that was discussed in the introduction to this chapter, write the history of a recent event you are familiar with. For example, has a noteworthy event happened on your campus within the last few months? How about watershed moments in an organization to which you belong, or in local government?

Think carefully about your sources of information: written records (such as newspapers), participants in the event (whom you can interview), "experts" who will give you their interpretations, locations you can visit to get a concrete sense of scene.

3.   In his *History of England*, Lord Macaulay said, "Those who compare the age in which their lot has fallen with a golden age which exists only in imagination, may talk of degeneracy and decay; but no man who is correctly informed as to the past, will be disposed to take a morose or desponding view of the present."

Compare the present time with one or two of the eras dealt with in this chapter and argue that Macaulay is or is not correct in his view that the present is no worse than the past.

4.   Pick a time, past or future, in which you would like to live at least briefly. Write an essay describing in detail the time and place, the people and their activities, and your role there. Make it clear why you would like to be transplanted. (In preparing to write this essay, you might want to learn more about the time you have chosen. Encyclopedias are good sources of historical knowledge, and there are many excellent discussions of given periods. For instance, *The Greek Way* and *The Roman Way*, by Edith Hamilton, would give you a vivid sense of life in classical times; Moulton's *Medieval Panorama* is longer and more difficult than Hamilton's book, but well worth reading. You might also enjoy Frederick Lewis Allen's *Only Yesterday*, which characterizes the 1920s in America. The point is this: many resources are at your disposal.)

5.   Meyer Lansky "had his own strict moral code," which did not coincide with laws and with the prevailing social code. Write an essay about someone you know who has similarly developed a private, personal code of conduct. What is this code, and how does it justify flouting society's rules? What are your own views about private codes of ethics that contradict societal standards?

6.   Think of a turning point in past or recent history, some event that changed the course of human destiny. (For example, America's entry into the Vietnam War was momentous for this country; the decision in 1986 to go ahead with the blast-off of the space shuttle *Challenger* resulted in the death of the whole crew and a slowdown in and reappraisal of America's space effort; the Supreme Court's decision, in July 1986, to allow exclusion of death penalty opponents from juries immediately changed the nature of criminal justice.) Assume the stance of an armchair quarterback in regard to the event. Explain what actually happened and how you would have arranged matters differently to bring about more satisfactory results.

7.   In an essay, answer the following questions:

a.   Of what use is a knowledge of history?

b. How have you gained your own knowledge of history? (Think not only of classes in school and books but also of firsthand experience, such as visits to the Smithsonian Institution, travel through historical areas, and the stories you have heard from family members and friends. What have you learned from television and motion pictures?)

c. If a knowledge of history is important, how could history be taught more effectively?

8. Choose a historical character who interests you: for example, Abraham Lincoln, Eleanor Roosevelt, Richard Nixon, Ingrid Bergman. Find diverse viewpoints about this person and his or her effects on history: commentators who idealize their subject almost to the point of sainthood; others who attempt, in your opinion, to present a balanced view; and others who debunk their subjects iconoclastically, shattering the myth.

Which viewpoint is more convincing? Why?

After you have seen three versions of the same historical character, use them, plus your own knowledge of and opinions about the character, to write the "definitive" version.

9. Imagine you are an amnesiac returning home but with no one to greet you. Write a two-page history of your life based entirely on the artifacts you find in your place of residence. In other words, you are an archeologist, reconstructing your past only from what you can "dig up" in the place where you lived before the amnesia set in.

Now review your sketch and think about what seems to be missing. Write one further page describing either what the evidence does not show or what you yourself overlooked.

C H A P T E R
6

The Social Sciences

With their beginnings in the eighteenth century, the social sciences are relative latecomers as fields of knowledge. In the 1700s, the passion of many thinkers for economics, the first of the social sciences to develop, resulted in such classic studies as Adam Smith's *An Inquiry into the Nature and Causes of the Wealth of Nations*, in which Smith set forth his theory of the division of labor and argued that value arises from the labor expended in the production process.

The nineteenth century—in which anthropology, political science, psychology, and sociology defined themselves—might be called "the age of theories" in the social sciences, for such thinkers as Comte, Marx, and Spenser propounded sweeping theories to account for social phenomena.

In his *Cours de philosophie positive* (The Course of Positive Philosophy), Auguste Comte (1798–1857) argued that a sociology using the methods of positivism—observation and experimentation, that is, the scientific method—could create a virtually perfect society. Karl Marx (1818–1883), who had been influenced by Adam Smith, proposed that inevitable laws of history would bring about the ascendancy of the working class; the socialist state was, in Marx's view, as certain as the return of Halley's comet. Herbert Spencer (1820–1903), in effect, banned metaphysical speculation; he argued that we can know only phenomena and not the ultimate sources of those phenomena. Furthermore, Spencer did much to promulgate Darwin's theory of evolution, which explained the genesis of humankind in terms of phenomena, not of miracles.

Herbert Spencer in a sense prepared the way for the social sciences of the twentieth century, with their emphasis on empirical methods rather than broad-scale theorizing.

In our century, one of the greatest issues in the social sciences has been the debate over *behaviorism*, the psychological theory introduced by J. B. Watson in 1913. Behaviorist doctrine holds that observable, outward responses to stimuli can explain both animal and human behavior; the behaviorist says to the cognitivist (who takes "mind" as a given), "Suppose there is such an entity as mind. How do you gain access to it? You can observe only the results of thinking, that is, behavior, not the thinking itself." The selection from B. F. Skinner in this chapter represents the behaviorist view of thought and mind.

As you will learn from the essay by Howard Gardner, behaviorism has been largely abandoned as an explanatory model for human psychology and society, but, especially in the work of B. F. Skinner, during much of this century it powerfully influenced all of the social sciences and consequently had a major impact on fields as diverse as psychotherapy and educational theory and practice, serving, in fact, as a counterstatement to Freudianism.

At present, social scientists—the sociologist Clifford Geertz, for example—are saying that interpreting social phenomena is very much like interpreting texts: the Bible or *Hamlet*. The exact meaning you ascribe to the text—or to the social phenomenon—will depend to a large extent on your point of view (your own beliefs, your social background, your reasons for interpreting, and so on). Thus, it can be said that we are in an age of skepticism or pluralism, questioning the old belief that in every text and situation there was one—and only one—meaning, which could be discovered with enough hard and careful work.

The selections that follow are interesting in and of themselves, and they provide an overview of writing and thinking in the social sciences. Both Howard Gardner and B. F. Skinner are prominent psychologists, representing opposed views of such concepts as "mind." In an anthropological study of culture, Margaret Mead writes about family life in New Guinea. John Kenneth Galbraith is an economist and one of America's foremost social and political gadflies.

JOHN KENNETH GALBRAITH

John Kenneth Galbraith, probably the best known economist in America, describes himself as a writer, and it is indeed his lively writing that has helped make him such a widely read author.

Born in Iona Station, Ontario, Canada, Galbraith received his bachelor's degree from the University of Toronto and his master's and Ph.D. from the University of California. His career has since swung back and forth from serving in the United States government to academic posts. From 1939 to 1942, Galbraith was in charge of the price division of the Office of Price Administration, which set the price-control levels for the nation. Ultimately, he became the administrator of the department. He has been a professor of economics at Harvard since 1949, but has also served, during leaves of absence, as the American ambassador extraordinary and plenipotentiary in India for John Kennedy and as presidential advisor to Kennedy and Lyndon Johnson. Professor Galbraith is the author of numerous books, the most famous of which are The Affluent Society, The New Industrial State, *and* The Great Crash, 1929.

Of Paper

A number of circumstances explain the pioneering role of the American colonies in the use of paper money. War, as always, forced financial innovation. Also paper money, like the Bank of England loans, was a substitute for taxation, and, where taxes were concerned, the colonists were exceptionally obdurate; they were opposed to taxation without representation, as greatly remarked, and they were also, a less celebrated quality, opposed to taxation with representation. "That a great reluctance to pay taxes existed in all the colonies, there can be no doubt. It was one of the marked characteristics of the American people long after their separation from England."[1] Paper money was also seen during colonial times, and not wrongly, as an antidote for economic discontent. Also the colonies were generally prevented by the mother country from sponsoring banks—thus bank notes, the obvious alternative to government notes, were excluded. And something must be credited to an instinct for monetary experiment—perhaps to the belief that, along with all of the other wonders of the New World, there existed also the possibility, original and unique in history, of creating money to make men rich.

The instinct for monetary experiment dates from the earliest days of settlement. The colonists, as every history tells, were endemically short of money. Almost all explanations attribute this shortage to the absence of any local source of gold and silver and to the commercial policy of the mother country which, reflecting the mercantilist belief that all significant wealth consisted of gold and silver, insouciantly sucked these metals away from the settlers. Both explanations are improbable. Many countries or communities had gold and silver in comparative abundance without mines. Venice, Genoa, Bruges had no Mother Lode. (Nor today does Hong Kong or Singapore.) While the colonists were required to pay in hard coin for what they bought from Britain, they also had products—tobacco, pelts, ships, shipping services—for which British merchants would have been willing, and were quite free, to expend gold and silver. Much more plausibly, the shortage of hard money in the colonies was another manifestation of Gresham. From the very beginning the colonists experimented with substitutes for metal. The substitutes, being less well regarded than gold or silver, were passed on to others and thus were kept in circulation. The good gold or silver was kept by those receiving it or

[1]G. S. Callender, *Selections from the Economic History of the United States, 1765–1860* (Boston: Ginn and Co., 1909), p. 123.

used for those purchases, including those in the mother country, for which the substitutes were unacceptable.

The first substitute was taken over from the Indians. From New England to Virginia in the first years of settlement, the wampum or shells used by the Indians became the accepted small coinage. In Massachusetts in 1641, it was made legal tender, subject to some limits as to the size of the transaction, at the rate of six shells to the penny. However, within a generation or two it began to lose favor. The shells came in two denominations, black and white, the first being double the value of the second. It required but small skill and a smaller amount of dye to convert the lower-denomination currency into the higher. Also the acceptability of wampum depended on its being redeemed by the Indians in pelts. The Indians, in effect, were the central bankers for the wampum monetary system, and beaver pelts were the reserve currency into which wampum could be converted. This convertibility sustained the purchasing power of the shells. As the seventeenth century passed and settlement expanded, the beavers receded to the ever more distant forests and streams. Pelts ceased to be available, wampum ceased, accordingly, to be convertible and thus, in line with expectation, it lost in purchasing power. Soon it disappeared from circulation except as small change.

Tobacco, although regionally more restricted, was far more important than wampum. It came into use as money in Virginia a dozen years after the first permanent settlement in Jamestown in 1607. Twenty-three years later, in 1642, it was made legal tender by the General Assembly of the colony by the interestingly inverse device of outlawing contracts that called for payment in gold or silver. The use of tobacco as money survived in Virginia for nearly two centuries and in Maryland for a century and a half—in both cases until the Constitution made money the concern solely of the Federal government. The gold standard, by the common calculation, lasted from 1879 until the cancellation of the final attenuated version by Richard Nixon in 1971. Viewing the whole span of American history, tobacco, though more confined as to region, had nearly twice as long a run as gold.

Initially the tobacco passed from hand to hand in the manner of paper and coins. Apart from being somewhat friable, it had two other characteristics of considerable importance. As a medium of exchange that was grown instead of mined, minted or printed, its supply was uniquely a matter not of luck, organization or state authority but of individual will. And it lent itself with exceptional readiness to depreciation in quality. Both characteristics of tobacco were energetically exploited. From the earliest days of the Virginia and Maryland settlements, colonial governments were concerned with arrangements for limiting the production of tobacco and thus sustaining its purchasing power. In 1666, a treaty was negotiated among Virginia, Maryland

and Carolina (as it then was), agreeing to a one-year suspension of all tobacco production. In 1683, the failure of a similar effort sent bands roaming the countryside destroying tobacco plants and leading the Virginia Assembly to decree that, if such operations were conducted by eight or more marauders, the participants should be adjudged guilty of treason and suffer death.

Although high production brought a sharp inflation of prices as denoted in pounds of tobacco, tobacco as money had a marked charm for producers. The overproduction of farm products, their often inelastic demand and the resulting disastrous prices have regularly made it hard for farmers to meet interest or payments on mortgages or other debts. At low prices an excessive quantity of wheat, cotton or livestock was required. So long as tobacco was money, the same quantity serviced the given debt, for the debt was written in pounds of leaf. The law of 1642 forbidding contracts that called for gold and silver was a thoughtful concession by tobacco planters to themselves. Being troubled by creditors who, not wanting to be paid off in cheap tobacco, were contracting to receive something more substantial, notably gold or silver, the planters took the logical step of outlawing such a menace.

The price of tobacco in British currency was, *pari passu*, the rate of exchange between the money of Virginia and Maryland and sterling. When the price of tobacco was tenpence a pound, that was the rate of exchange; i.e., the Virginia or Maryland tobacco pound was worth tenpence sterling. When the price of tobacco dropped to fivepence, the rate of exchange was fivepence for one tobacco pound. As between price level and exchange rate there was thus an effortless and automatic accommodation with no lag. It was an early and exceptionally elegant manifestation of what is now called a floating exchange rate and by the *cognoscenti*, a float.

A pound of poor tobacco still being a pound of tobacco, there was obvious advantage in favoring that of lowest quality if it could be produced at lower cost. And this led Gresham's Law to operate with exceptional power on the resulting product. No one passed on good tobacco if scraps, stems or leaf of suffocating tendency were available instead. On the north shore of Lake Erie in Ontario, tobacco is an important crop. In my youth there a neighbor named Norman Griswold, whose farm was to the south of ours, sustained his nicotine addiction by odds and ends of leaf which were passed on to him from neighboring farmers and which he cured himself. Norman's approach, in a south wind, would be known a full fifteen minutes before he materialized. All authorities agree that such was the tobacco that the Virginia and Maryland planters put in circulation first.

It was, in fact, the counterpart of the clipped and sweated coins that the Amsterdam merchants had found so troublesome. And the eventual remedy was the same. Public warehouses, the counterpart of the Bank of Amsterdam, were established. There the tobacco was weighed and graded, and certificates representing a defined quality and quantity were then issued. These passed into circulation. In 1727, tobacco certificates or notes became full legal tender in Virginia and continued to serve until nearly the end of the century. So close was the association between tobacco and money that the paper currency of New Jersey, not a tobacco-growing state, carried on its face a tobacco leaf as well as the exigent warning: "To counterfeit is *Death*."

In South Carolina during the later colonial years rice, for a time, served as money in much the same fashion as tobacco in Virginia and Maryland. Elsewhere there were numerous lesser experiments with grain, cattle, whiskey and brandy, all of which at one time or another were declared legal tender for debts. The use of whiskey and brandy as money makes exceptionally poignant the injunctions, common through American history, against drinking up one's fortune. None of these substitutes was important as compared with paper money.

Questions for Discussion

1. Many people think economics is a dry, arcane subject, yet Galbraith's writings are popular with general readers, and *Money* is a lively book. What does Galbraith do as a writer to make his discussion interesting and enjoyable? You can start to answer this question by thinking about the title of the book, *Money: Whence It Came, Where It Went*. What is the effect of this title?

2. Explain (a) why the first paragraph of the essay can be viewed as the whole essay in miniature and (b) the advantages and disadvantages of beginning a piece of writing in such a way.

3. Was wampum or tobacco closer to paper money as a medium of exchange? Explain your answer.

4. Does Galbraith use words with which you were not familiar before you read this selection? Argue that this use of unfamiliar words is or is not justified.

5. At one point, Galbraith stresses a point by using the same structure for two adjacent sentences:

   When the price of tobacco was tenpence a pound, that was the rate of exchange; i.e., the Virginia or Maryland tobacco pound was worth tenpence sterling.
   When the price of tobacco dropped to fivepence, the rate of exchange was fivepence for one tobacco pound.

Point out other instances in which Galbraith relies on the *form* of his language to emphasize his meaning.

6. Do you understand Galbraith's explanation of "a floating exchange rate"? If so, explain the concept in your own words.

7. What are the disadvantages of paper money?

MARGARET MEAD

Margaret Mead's career as an anthropologist began in 1925 when she studied the adolescent girls in Samoa. The results of her research, published as the well-known book Coming of Age in Samoa, *conclude that adolescence is not necessarily a troubled time in the maturation process, a thesis that ran contrary to the general belief of the day, and even now her book is the subject of debate as to what constitutes proper anthropological methodology.*

Mead received her bachelor's degree from Barnard College in 1923, her master's from Columbia in 1924, and her Ph.D. from Columbia in 1929. She continued to study in the Pacific region, visiting the Admiralty Islands of New Guinea three times over the course of thirty-seven years and Bali twice in a period of twenty-seven years as she pursued her study of the problems of primitive societies coping with modernization. Margaret Mead was employed by the American Museum of Natural History in New York from 1926 until her death in 1978. She is the author or editor of over thirty books.

The Family Life

A Manus child's family is very different from the picture of American family life. True, it consists of the same people: father, mother, one or two brothers or sisters, sometimes a grandmother, less frequently a grandfather. At night the doorways are barricaded carefully and the parents insist that the children be all home at sundown except on moonlight nights. After the evening meal the children are laid on mats for sleep, or allowed to fall asleep in the elders' arms, then gently laid down. The bundles of cocoanut leaves light the dark corners of the house fitfully. At first glimpse this looks like the happy intimate family of our own preference, where strangers are excluded and the few people who love each other best are closeted together around the fire.

But a closer knowledge of Manus homes reveals many differences. Young men do not have houses of their own, but live in the backs of the houses of their older brothers or young uncles. When two such families live together the wife of the younger man must avoid the older man. She never enters his end of the house, partitioned off by hanging mats, when he is at home. The children, however, can run about freely between the two families, but the continual avoidance, the avoidance of all personal names, and the fact that the younger man is dependent upon the older, tends to strain relationships between the two little households. The Manus are prevailingly paternal, a man usually inherits from his father or brother, a wife almost always goes to live in her husband's place.

But although the family group is small, and the tie between children and parents close, the relationship between husband and wife is usually strained and cold. Father and mother seem to the child to be two disparate people both playing for him against each other. The blood ties of his parents are stronger than their relationship to each other, and there are more factors to pull them apart than there are to draw them together. A glance into some of these Peri families will illustrate the fundamental feeling tone which exists between husbands and wives.

Let us take for instance the family of Ndrosal. Ndrosal is a curly-haired, handsome waster, quick to boast and slow to perform. His first wife bore him two boys and died. His sister's husband adopted the elder; the younger stayed with him to be cared for by his new wife, a tall, straight-limbed woman from a faraway village. The new wife straightway bore him a girl which refused to thrive. Month after month the baby fretted and wailed in the little hanging cradle its father fashioned for it. While the baby was so ill it might not be taken from the house on any pretext nor might the mother leave it for more than a few minutes. Month after month she stayed in the house swinging the cradle, growing pale and wan herself. Food was not too plentiful. Ndrosal was very devoted to his elder sister, a woman of definite and unmistakable character. She was middle-aged, a woman of affairs, always busy and always needing her brother's help. When the baby became ill, she took the other child, so both of Ndrosal's little boys were in his sister's house. He loved to carry them about on his back, to lie prone and let them play over his body; or take them fishing. So he spent most of his time in his sister's house next door, and when he made a good haul of fish, most of it went into his sister's pot. His wife had no close relatives in the village, but one day a younger sister of her husband brought her some crabs. Crabbing is woman's work, so there had been no shell fish in the house for months. She cooked them eagerly, careless of the fact that one of the varieties was forbidden to all members of her husband's family. Her husband came home late, empty handed, and demanded his supper. His wife served him crabs, and in answer to his questions professed to be pretty sure that the tabu variety was not among them. Cooked, it was impossible to distinguish them. He began to eat his supper, grumbling over her short answer and lack of concern with his tabus. Almost immediately the baby started to cry. His younger sister and her husband were temporarily lodged in the back of the house. His sister went to the cradle but the baby still wailed. Ndrosal turned sternly to his wife, "Give that child thy breast." "She's nursed enough to-day. She's not hungry, only sick," the wife answered. "Nurse her, dost thou hear me, thou useless woman! Thou woman belonging to worthlessness. Thou root of lying and lack of thought, who carest neither for thy husband's tabus nor for his child." Rising, he poured out the stream of expletive upon her. Still she lingered over her supper, tearful, sullen, convinced that the child wasn't hungry, until the enraged husband seized his lime gourd and flung a pint of powdered lime into her eyes. The scalding tears slaked the lime and burned her eyes horribly as she stumbled blindly from the house, wailing. One of the women who gathered at the sound of trouble took her home with her, and the little baby with her. Ndrosal went to his sister's house to sleep, and when the younger boy sleepily cuddled his father and asked why his adopted mother was crying, he was told gruffly that his mother was a bad woman who refused to feed his little sister. . . .

. . . She is a stranger among strange spirits, spirits who nevertheless exercise a rigid espionage over her behaviour.

All this is galling enough to the young girl and she grows more and more sulky day by day as she sits among her relatives-in-law, cooking for feasts, or goes with them to the bush to work sago. If she does not conceive promptly, she is very likely to run away. Sometimes her relatives persuade her to return and she vacillates back and forth for several years before a child is born. When she does conceive, she is drawn closer, not to the father of her child, but to her own kin. She may not tell her husband that she is pregnant. Such intimacy would shame them both. Instead, she tells her mother and her father, her sisters and her brothers, her aunts and her cross cousins. Her relatives set to work to prepare the necessary food for the pregnancy feasts. Still nothing is said to the husband. His wife repulses his advances more coldly than ever and his dislike and resentment of her increases. Then some chance word reaches his ears, some rumour of the economic preparations his brothers-in-law are making. A child is to be born to him, so the neighbours say. Still he cannot mention the point to his wife, but he waits for the first feast when canoes laden with sago come to his door. The months wear on, marked by periodic feasts for which he must make repayment. His relatives help him but he is expected to do most of it himself. . . .

. . . The rift between the two widens.

A few days before the birth of the child the brother or cousin or uncle of the expectant mother divines for the place of birth. If he does not have the power to handle the divining bones himself, a relative will do it for him. The divination declares whether the child shall be born in the house of its father or of its maternal uncle. If the former is the verdict, the husband must leave his house and go to his sister's. This is usually only done when the couple have a house of their own, a very rare occurrence in the case of a man's first child. His brother-in-law and his wife and children move into his house. Or else his wife is taken away, sometimes to another village. From the moment her labour begins he may not see her. The nearest approach he can make to the house is to bring fish to the landing platform. For a whole month he wanders aimlessly about, sleeping now at one sister's, now at another's. Only after his brother-in-law has worked or collected enough sago, one or two tons at least, to make the return feast, can his wife return to him, can he see his child.

Meanwhile the mother is very much occupied with her new baby. For a month she must stay inside the house, hidden by a mat curtain, her food must be cooked on a special fire in special dishes. Only after dark may she slip out and bathe hastily in the sea. Life is more pleasant for her than it has been since before her marriage. All of her female relatives stop in to chat with her, those with milk suckle her child for her during their call. Her brothers' wives cook for her, bring her betel nut and pepper leaf, humour her as an invalid. Her husband, whom she has not learned to love, is not missed. She hugs her baby to her breast, runs her pursed lips along its little arms, and is happy. . . .

. . . This festival of return to her husband gives her no pleasure. Very often on the plea that she is ill or that her child is crying for her she leaves the procession and goes home. The feast goes on merrily. Her absence is not missed. She is only a pawn, an occasion for financial transactions.

Finally, after dark, the time has come to make "the journey of the breasts": to return her to her husband. This is a profitable business for the women who accompany her so there is much wrangling among the women of the house as to which kindred shall punt the canoe. . . . The practised women punt the laden canoe to the house of her husband's sister, where her husband has lived since their separation. The wife climbs upon the platform and sits there quietly. Her husband may be within the house but it is not necessary that he be there. He gives no sign. After a little she climbs back into the canoe and returns to her baby, to the crowded house and the new wrangling over the sago payments involved in the journey. Only after the last reckoning is settled will the guests disperse. Her brother's wife is the last to go, gathering up her belongings and muttering because her own children have fallen ill among the spirits of strangers. The young wife goes to sleep, wearily, and late that night the husband returns.

Now begins a new life. The father takes a violent proprietary interest in the new baby. It is his child, belongs to his kin, is under the protection of his spirits. He watches his wife with jealous attention, scolds her if she stirs from the house, berates her if the baby cries. He can be rougher with her now. The chances are that she will not run away, but will stay where her child will be well cared for. For a year mother and baby are shut up together in the house. For that year the child still belongs to its mother. The father only holds it occasionally, is afraid to take it from the house. But as soon as the child's legs are strong enough to stand upon and its small arms adept at clutching, the father begins to take the child from the mother. Now that the child is in no need of such frequent suckling, he expects his wife to get to work, to go to the mangrove swamp to work sago, to make long trips to the reef for shell fish. She has been idle long enough for, say the men, "a woman with a new baby is no use to her husband, she cannot work." The plea that her child needs her would not avail. The father is delighted to play with the child, to toss it in the air, tickle it beneath its armpits, softly blow on its bare, smooth skin. He has risen at three in the morning to fish, he has fished all through the cold dawn, punted the weary way to the market, sold some of his fish for good bargains in taro, in betel nut, in taro leaves. Now he is free for the better part of the day, drowsy, just in the mood to play with the baby.

From her brother too come demands upon the woman. He worked well for her during her pregnancy. Now he must meet his obligations to his wife's people. His sister must help him. From every side she is bidden to leave the baby to its doting father and go about her affairs. Children learn very young to take advantage of this situation. Father is obviously the most important person in the home; he orders mother about, and hits her if she doesn't "hear his talk." Father is even more indulgent than mother. It is a frequent picture to see a little minx of three leave her father's arms, quench her thirst at her mother's breast, and then swagger back to her father's arms, grinning over-bearingly at her mother. The mother sees the child drawn further and further away from her. At night the child sleeps with the father, by day she rides on his back. He takes her to the shady island which serves as a sort of men's club house where all the canoes are built and large fish traps made. Her mother can't come on this island except to feed the pigs when no men are there. Her mother is ashamed to come there but she can rollick gaily among the half-completed canoes. When there is a big feast, her mother must hide in the back of the house behind a hanging mat. But she can run away to father in the front of the house when the soup and betel nut are being given out. Father is always at the centre of interest, he is never too busy to play. Mother is often busy. She must stay in the smoky interior of the house. She is forbidden the canoe islands. It is small wonder that the father always wins the competition: the dice are loaded from the start.

And then the mother becomes pregnant again, another baby which will be her own for a year is on its way. She withdraws more from the struggle and begins to wean the present baby. The weaning is slow. The child is spoiled, long accustomed to eating other foods, it is used to being given its mother's breast whenever it cries for it. The women tie bundles of hair to their nipples to repel the children. The weaning is said to last well into pregnancy. The child is offended by its mother's withdrawal and clings still closer to its father. So on the eve of the birth of a new baby, the child's transfer of dependence to its father is almost complete. The social patterning of childbirth reaffirms that dependence. While the mother is occupied with her new baby, the older child stays with its father. He feeds it, bathes it, plays with it all day. He has little work or responsibility during this period and so more time to strengthen his position. This repeats itself for the birth of each new child. The mother welcomes birth; again she will have a baby which is her own, if only for a few months. And at the end of the early months the father again takes over the younger child. Occasionally he may keep a pre-dominant interest in the older child, especially if the older is a boy, the younger a girl, but usually there is room in his canoe for two or three little ones. And the elder ones of five and six are not pushed out of the canoe, they leave it in the tiny canoes which father has hewn for them. At the first upset, the first rebuff, they can come swimming back into the sympathetic circle of the father's indulgent love for his children.

As the father's relation to his child is continually emphasised, so the mother is always being reminded of her slighter claims. If her father is ill in another village, and she wishes to go, her husband cannot keep her, but he keeps her two-year-old son. Some woman of his kin will suckle the child if he cries and the father will care for him tenderly. The woman goes off for her uncertain voyage, torn between her blood kin and her child. This is in cases of perfectly ordinary relations between husband and wife. In case of a quarrel she will take her young children with her if she runs away from her husband. But even here five- and six-year-olds make their own choices and often elect to stay with their father.

Questions for Discussion

1. Why does Mead use the past tense in talking about Ndrosal and his wife and the present tense in discussing the marriage?

2. What are some similarities between the New Guinea society and present-day American upwardly mobile families?

3. Marriage in the Manus society serves the useful function of providing an orderly means of propagation. In what ways do the marriage ceremony and the sago feast for the reunion of the new parents provide an economic function?

4. Mead opens the selection with a portrait of a peaceful family life at the end of the day but then goes on to offer evidence that belies this vision of harmony among the Manus. Do you think Mead might have unconsciously or purposefully left out examples of family life that do not support her thesis?

5. In her study of the Manus society, Mead focuses on the major rites. Suppose an anthropologist were studying your family group. What would be missed if the focus were on such major events as christenings, weddings, bar mitzvahs, birthdays, graduation ceremonies, and funerals?

6. In your opinion, why did the Manus accept Mead when the women held the lowest position in this intensely antifeminist society?

B. F. SKINNER

Howard Gardner, whose essay appears later in this chapter, represents cognitive *psychology. Burrhus Frederic Skinner represents the opposite camp,* behaviorism. *As the introduction to this section of the book points out, behaviorists claim that it makes no sense to talk about "mind," for all we can observe is behavior—hence, the term* behavioral psychology. *Associated with behaviorism are, of course, the terms* stimulus *and* response.

Skinner was born in 1904 in Susquehanna, Pennsylvania, and took his doctoral degree at Harvard in 1931. After serving on the faculties of the University of Minnesota and Indiana University, he returned to Harvard in 1948 and ultimately became Edgar Pierce Professor of Psychology in 1958.

In addition to his scholarly works, Skinner has written a Utopian novel, Walden Two *(1961). In the following selection, he explains why he believes it is futile to speculate about mind, one of the most important and controversial ideas of the twentieth century.*

What Is Man?

Perhaps the last stronghold of autonomous man is that complex "cognitive" activity called thinking. Because it is complex, it has yielded only slowly to explanation in terms of contingencies of reinforcement. When we say that a person *discriminates* between red and orange, we imply that discrimination is a kind of mental act. The person himself does not seem to be doing anything; he responds in different ways to red and orange stimuli, but this is the result of discrimination rather than the act. Similarly, we say that a person *generalizes*—say, from his own limited experience to the world at large—but all we see is that he responds to the world at large as he has learned to respond to his own small world. We say that a person *forms a concept or an abstraction*, but all we see is that certain kinds of contingencies of reinforcement have brought a response under the control of a single property of a stimulus. We say that a person *recalls* or *remembers* what he has seen or heard, but all we see is that the present occasion evokes a response, possibly in weakened or altered form, acquired on another occasion. We say that a person *associates* one word with another, but all we observe is that one verbal stimulus evokes the response previously made to another. Rather than suppose that it is therefore autonomous man who discriminates, generalizes, forms concepts or abstractions, recalls or remembers, and associates, we can put matters in good order simply by noting that these terms do not refer to forms of behavior.

A person may take explicit action, however, when he solves a problem. In putting a jigsaw puzzle together he may move the pieces around to improve his chances of finding a fit. In solving an equation he may transpose, clear fractions, and extract roots to improve his chances of finding a form of the equation he has already learned how to solve. The creative artist may manipulate a medium until something of interest turns up. Much of this can be done covertly, and it is then likely to be assigned to a different dimensional system, but it can always be done overtly, perhaps more slowly but also often more effectively, and with rare exceptions it must have been learned in overt form. The culture promotes thinking by constructing special contingencies. It teaches a person to make fine discriminations by making differential reinforcement more precise. It teaches techniques to be used in solving problems. It provides rules which make it unnecessary to be exposed to the contingences from which the rules are derived, and it provides rules for finding rules.

Self-control, or self-management, is a special kind of problem solving which, like self-knowledge, raises all the issues associated with privacy. We have discussed some techniques in connection with aversive control in Chapter 4. It is always the environment which builds the behavior with which problems are solved, even when the problems are to be found in the private world inside the skin. None of this has been investigated in a very productive way, but the inadequacy of our analysis is no reason to fall back on a miracle-working mind. If our understanding of contingencies of reinforcement is not yet sufficient to explain all kinds of thinking, we must remember that the appeal to mind explains nothing at all.

In shifting control from autonomous man to the observable environment we do not leave an empty organism. A great deal goes on inside the skin, and physiology will eventually tell us more about it. It will explain why behavior is indeed related to the antecedent events of which it can be shown to be a function. The assignment is not always correctly understood. Many physiologists regard themselves as looking for the "physiological correlates" of mental events. Physiological research is regarded as simply a more scientific version of introspection. But physiological techniques are not, of course, designed to detect or measure personalities, ideas, attitudes, feelings, impulses, thoughts, or purposes. (If they were, we should have to answer a third question in addition to those raised in Chapter 1: How can a personality, idea, feeling, or purpose affect the instruments of the physiologist?) At the moment neither introspection nor physiology supplies very adequate information about what is going on inside a man as he behaves, and since they are both directed inward, they have the same effect of diverting attention from the external environment.

Much of the misunderstanding about an inner man comes from the metaphor of storage. Evolutionary and environmental histories change an organism, but they are not stored within it. Thus, we observe that babies suck their mothers' breasts, and we can easily imagine that a strong tendency to do so has survival value, but much more is implied by a "sucking instinct" regarded as something a baby possesses which enables it to suck. The concept of "human nature" or "genetic endowment" is dangerous when taken in that sense. We are closer to human nature in a baby than in an adult, or in a primitive culture than in an advanced, in the sense that environmental contingencies are less likely to have obscured the genetic endowment, and it is tempting to dramatize that endowment by implying that earlier stages have survived in concealed form: man is a naked ape, and "the paleolithic bull which survives in man's inner self still paws the earth whenever a threatening gesture is made on the social scene." But anatomists and physiologists will not find an ape, or a bull, or for that matter instincts. They will find anatomical and physiological features which are the product of an evolutionary history.

The personal history of the individual is also often said to be stored within him. For "instinct" read "habit." The cigarette habit is presumably something more than the behavior said to show that a person possesses it; but the only other information we have concerns the reinforcers and the schedules of reinforcement which make a person smoke a great deal. The contingencies are not stored; they have simply left a changed person.

The environment is often said to be stored in the form of memories: to recall something we search for a copy of it, which can then be seen as the original thing was seen. As far as we know, however, there are no copies of the environment in the individual *at any time*, even when a thing is present and being observed. The products of more complex contingencies are also said to be stored; the repertoire acquired as a person learns to speak French is called a "knowledge of French."

Traits of character, whether derived from contingencies of survival or contingencies of reinforcement, are also said to be stored. A curious example occurs in Follett's *Modern American Usage:* "We say *He faced these adversities bravely*, aware without thought that the bravery is a property of the man, not of the facing; a brave act is poetic shorthand for the act of a person who shows bravery by performing it." But we call a man brave because of his acts, and he behaves bravely when environmental circumstances induce him to do so. The circumstances have changed his behavior; they have not implanted a trait or virtue.

Philosophies are also spoken of as things possessed. A man is said to speak or act in certain ways because he has a particular philosophy— such as idealism, dialectical materialism, or Calvinism. Terms of this kind summarize the effect of environmental conditions which it would now be hard to trace, but the conditions must have existed and should not be ignored. A person who possesses a "philosophy of freedom" is one who has been changed in certain ways by the literature of freedom.

The issue has had a curious place in theology. Does man sin because he is sinful, or is he sinful because he sins? Neither question points to anything very useful. To say that a man is sinful because he sins is to give an operational definition of sin. To say that he sins because he is sinful is to trace his behavior to a supposed inner trait. But whether or not a person engages in the kind of behavior called sinful depends upon circumstances which are not mentioned in either question. The sin assigned as an inner possession (the sin a person "knows") is to be found in a history of reinforcement. (The expression "God-fearing" suggests such a history, but piety, virtue, the immanence of God, a moral sense, or morality does not. As we have seen, man is not a moral animal in the sense of possessing a special trait or virtue; he has built a kind of social environment which induces him to behave in moral ways.)

These distinctions have practical implications. A recent survey of white Americans is said to have shown that "more than half blamed the inferior educational and economic status of blacks on 'something about Negroes themselves.' " The "something" we further identified as "lack of motivation," which was to be distinguished from *both* genetic and environmental factors. Significantly, motivation was said to be associated with "free will." To neglect the role of the environment in this way is to discourage any inquiry into the defective contingencies responsible for a "lack of motivation."

Questions for Discussion

1. A blurb on the jacket of *Beyond Freedom and Dignity* states that B. F. Skinner proposes "a systematic and scientific program to alter the nature of man." How should people be altered? Do you think one person could or should decide this matter?

2. Explain what Skinner seems to mean by "the nature of man."

3. Do you agree with Skinner that "It is always the environment which builds the behavior with which problems are solved, even when the problems are to be found in the private world inside the skin"?

4. Skinner says the questions of whether people sin because they are sinful or are sinful because they sin are not very useful because "man is not a moral animal." Explain why you agree or disagree.

5. The last paragraph in the selection discusses motivation. What might be some "defective contingencies responsible for a 'lack of motivation' "?

6. Do you see an analogy between the proponents of artificial intelligence and Skinner's idea of the contingencies of response in their use of a systems approach and insistence that thinking can only be described by the results? Explain.

7. One tradition in psychology has assumed that humans were inner-directed by their needs and desires. Skinner probably would not argue with the notion that these drive people in their actions but would disagree about the origins of the needs and desires. Explain.

8. In your own words, explain the argument Skinner advances in the last paragraph of his essay. Is that argument valid? Explain why or why not.

HOWARD GARDNER

Howard Gardner, a developmental psychologist, has studied the human ability to use symbols—and the difficulties that go along with that use. He received his bachelor's degree from Harvard in 1965 and a Ph.D. from that institution in 1971. He is associated with Harvard, Boston University School of Medicine, and Boston Veterans Administration Medical Center. He has won the National Psychology Award for Excellence in the Media and the prestigious MacArthur Prize Fellowship for creative work. He is the author of Art, Mind, and Brain *(1982) and* Frames of Mind: The Theory of Multiple Intelligences *(1983).*

In the following selection, he clearly explains the theoretical bases of cognitive science. This piece of writing is a superb example of how a complex and arcane subject can be conveyed to readers outside the field of the author's expertise.

Key Theoretical Inputs to Cognitive Science

Mathematics and Computation

The years around the turn of the century were of exceptional importance in mathematics and logic. For nearly two thousand years, the logic of syllogistic reasoning developed in classical times by Aristotle had held sway; but thanks to the work of the German logician Gottlob Frege, a new form of logic, which involved the manipulation of abstract symbols, began to evolve toward the end of the nineteenth century. Then, in the early twentieth century, as I shall elaborate in chapter 4, the British mathematical logicians Bertrand Russell and Alfred North Whitehead sought, with considerable success, to reduce the basic laws of arithmetic to propositions of elementary logic. The Whitehead-Russell work influenced a whole generation of mathematically oriented thinkers, including both Norbert Wiener and John von Neumann, two of the most important contributors to the founding of cognitive science.

In the 1930s, the logical-mathematical work that ultimately had the greatest import for cognitive science was being carried out by a then relatively unknown British mathematician, Alan Turing. In 1936, he developed the notion of a simple machine (subsequently dubbed a "Turing machine") which could in principle carry out any possible conceivable calculation. The notions underlying this "theoretical" machine were simple. All one needed was an infinitely long tape which could pass through the machine and a scanner to read what was on the tape. The tape itself was divided into identical squares, each of which contained upon it either a blank or some kind of slash. The machine could carry out four moves with the tape: move to the right, move to the left, erase the slash, or print the slash. With just these simple operations, the machine could execute any kind of program or plan that could be expressed in a binary code (for example, a code of blanks and slashes). More generally, so long as one could express clearly the steps needed to carry out a task, it could be programmed and carried out by the Turing machine, which would simply scan the tape (no matter what its length) and carry out the instructions.

Turing's demonstration—and the theorem he proved—was of profound importance for those researchers interested in computing devices. It suggested that a binary code (composed simply of zeros and ones) would make possible the devising and execution of an indefinite number of programs, and that machines operating on this principle could be constructed. As Turing himself pondered computing devices, he became increasingly enthusiastic about their possibilities. In fact, in 1950 (shortly before his untimely death by suicide in his early forties) he suggested that one could so program a machine that it would be impossible to discriminate *its* answers to an interlocutor from those contrived by a living human being—a notion immortalized as the "Turing machine test." This test is used to refute anyone who doubts that a computer can really think: if an observer cannot distinguish the responses of a programmed machine from those of a human being, the machine is said to have passed the Turing test.

The implications of these ideas were quickly seized upon by scientists interested in human thought, who realized that if they could describe with precision the behavior or thought processes of an organism, they might be able to design a computing machine that operated in identical fashion. It thus might be possible to test on a computer the plausibility of notions about how a human being actually functions, and perhaps even to construct machines about which one could confidently assert that they think just like human beings.

In building upon Turing's ideas, John von Neumann pursued the notion of devising a program to instruct the Turing machine to reproduce itself. Here was the powerful idea of a *stored program*: that is, the computer could be controlled through a program that itself was stored within the computer's internal memory, so that the machine would not have to be laboriously reprogrammed for each new task. For the first time, it became conceivable that a computer might prepare and execute its own programs.

The Neuronal Model

A second line of thinking important for those involved in founding cognitive science was put forth during the early 1940s by Warren McCulloch, the second speaker at the Hixon Symposium, and Walter Pitts, a young logician. Again, the core idea was disarmingly simple, though the actual mathematical analysis was anything but trivial. McCulloch and Pitts showed that the operations of a nerve cell and its connections with other nerve cells (a so-called neural network) could be modeled in terms of logic. Nerves could be thought of as logical statements, and the all-or-none property of nerves firing (or not firing) could be compared to the operation of the propositional calculus (where a statement is either true or false). This model allowed one to think of a neuron as being activated and then firing another neuron, in the same way that an element or a proposition in a logical sequence can imply some other proposition: thus, whether one is dealing with logic or neurons, entity A plus entity B can imply entity C. Moreover, the analogy between neurons and logic could be thought of in electrical terms—as signals that either pass, or fail to pass, through a circuit. The end result of the McCulloch-Pitts demonstration: "Anything that can be exhaustively and unambiguously described . . . is . . . realizable by a suitable finite neural network."

The designers of the new computational devices were intrigued by the ideas put forth by McCulloch and Pitts. Thanks to their demonstration, the notion of a Turing machine now looked in two directions— toward a nervous system, composed of innumerable all-or-none neurons; and toward a computer that could realize any process that can be unambiguously described. Turing had demonstrated the possibility in principle of computing machines of great power, while McCulloch and Pitts had demonstrated that at least one redoubtable machine—the human brain—could be thought of as operating via the principles of logic and, thus, as a powerful computer.

Ultimately, McCulloch may have carried his own chain of reasoning too far. He was convinced that fundamental problems of epistemology could be stated and solved only in light of the knowledge of the central nervous system, and he tied his claims about thinking very closely to what was known during his own time about the nervous system. Some commentators even feel that the search by McCulloch and his associates for a direct mapping between logic machines and the nervous system was a regressive element in the development of cognitive science: rather than trying to build machines that mimic the brain at a physiological level, analogies should have been propounded and pursued on a much higher level—for example, between the *thinking* that goes on in human problem solving and the *strategies* embodied in a computer program. On the other hand, it was due in part to McCulloch's own analysis that some of the most important aspects of the nervous system came to be better understood: for he sponsored research on the highly specific properties of individual nerve cells. Moreover, very recently computer scientists have once again been drawing directly on ideas about the nature of and connections among nerve cells. . . . On balance, his polymathic spirit seems to have been a benign catalyst for the growth of cognitive science.

The Cybernetic Synthesis

Even as John von Neumann, working at Princeton, was trying to piece together evidence from mathematics, logic, and the nervous system, mathematician Norbert Wiener was engaged in parallel pursuits at the Massachusetts Institute of Technology. Even more than von Neumann, Wiener had been a mathematical prodigy and, like his counterpart, had made fundamental discoveries in mathematics while still in his early twenties (Wiener had worked on Brownian motion; von Neumann, on quantum theory). Clearly, in these early choices, both men exhibited a practical bent in their mathematics: further, they aspired to influence the growth of science and technology within their society.

During the 1930s and 1940s, Norbert Wiener, by then ensconced at M.I.T., became involved in a variety of worldly projects. In working on servomechanisms—devices that kept anti-aircraft artillery, guided missiles, and airplanes on course—he had come to think about the nature of feedback and of self-correcting and self-regulating systems, be they mechanical or human. He collaborated closely with Vannevar Bush, who had pioneered in the development of analog computers. Wiener was also struck by the importance of the work of his sometimes colleagues McCulloch and Pitts, particularly by the suggestive analogies between a system of logical connections and the human nervous system.

Wiener went beyond all of his contemporaries in his missionary conviction that these various scientific and technological developments cohered. Indeed, in his mind they constituted a new science—one founded on the issues of control and communication, which he deemed to be central in the middle of the twentieth century. He first publicly formulated this point of view in a 1943 paper, "Behavior, Purpose, and Teleology," in which he and his fellow authors put forth the notion that problems of control engineering and communication engineering are inseparable; moreover, they center not on the techniques of electrical engineering, but rather on the much more fundamental notion of the message—"whether this should be transmitted by electrical, mechanical, or nervous means." The authors introduced a then-radical notion: that it is legitimate to speak of machines that exhibit feedback as "striving toward goals," as calculating the difference between their goals and their actual performance, and as then working to reduce those differences. Machines were purposeful. The authors also developed a novel notion of the central nervous system. As Wiener later put it:

> The central nervous system no longer appears as a self-contained organ, receiving inputs from the senses and discharging into the muscles. On the contrary, some of its most characteristic activities are explicable only as circular processes, emerging from the nervous system into the muscles, and re-entering the nervous system through the sense organs, whether they be proprioceptors or organs of the special senses. This seemed to us to mark a new step in the study of that part of

neurophysiology which concerns not solely the elementary processes of nerves and synapses but the performance of the nervous system as an integrated whole.

The parallels to Lashley's ideas about neural organization—and the challenge to behaviorist reflexology—are striking indeed.

Before long, Wiener had contrived a synthesis of the various interlocking ideas and presented it in the landmark volume *Cybernetics* (first published in 1948, the same year as the Hixon Symposium). He introduced his neologistic science as follows: "We have decided to call the entire field of control and communication theory, whether in the machine or in the animal, by the name Cybernetics." In the following pages, he set down an integrated vision—a linkage of developments in understanding the human nervous system, the electronic computer, and the operation of other machines. And he underscored his belief— echoing von Neumann and McCulloch and Pitts—that the functioning of the living organism and the operation of the new communication machines exhibited crucial parallels. Though Wiener's synthesis was not ultimately the one embraced by cognitive science (it came closer to achieving that exalted status in the Soviet Union), it stands as a pioneering example of the viability of such an interdisciplinary undertaking.

Information Theory

Another key progenitor of cognitive science was Claude Shannon, an electrical engineer at M.I.T. who is usually credited with devising information theory. Already as a graduate student at M.I.T. in the late 1930s, Shannon had arrived at a seminal insight. He saw that the principles of logic (in terms of true and false propositions) can be used to describe the two states (on and off) of electromechanical relay switches. In his master's thesis, Shannon provided an early suggestion that electrical circuits (of the kind in a computer) could embody fundamental operations of thought. . . .

During the next ten years, working in part with Warren Weaver, Shannon went on to develop the key notion of information theory: that information can be thought of in a way entirely divorced from specific content or subject matter as simply a single decision between two equally plausible alternatives. The basic unit of information is the *bit* (short for "binary digit"): that is, the amount of information required to select one message from two equally probable alternatives. Thus, the choice of a message from among eight equally probable alternatives required three bits of information: the first bit narrowed the choice from one of eight to one of four; the second, from one of four to one of two; the third selects one of the remaining alternatives. Wiener explained the importance of this way of conceptualization: "Information is information, not matter or energy. No materialism which does not admit this can survive at the present day."

Thanks to Wiener's insights, it became possible to think of information apart from a particular transmission device: one could focus instead on the efficacy of *any* communication of messages via *any* mechanism, and one could consider cognitive processes apart from any particular embodiment—an opportunity upon which psychologists would soon seize as they sought to describe the mechanisms underlying the processing of any kind of information. Only very recently have cognitive scientists begun to wonder whether they can, in fact, afford to treat all information equivalently and to ignore issues of content.

Neuropsychological Syndromes

A comparable contribution to an incipient cognitive science came from a remote and unexpected scientific corner—the profiles of cognitive incapacities following damage to the human brain. Paradoxically, this area of science relies heavily on the travesties of war. As in the era of the First World War, much was learned during the Second World War about aphasia (language deficit), agnosia (difficulty in recognition), and other forms of mental pathology consequent upon injury to the brain. Laboratories in New York, Oxford, Paris, Berlin, and Moscow were all busily engaged in working with victims of brain damage. When the neuropsychological researchers began to communicate their findings to one another, considerable convergence was noted even across cultural and linguistic boundaries. For instance, aphasia assumed similar forms despite wide differences across languages. There was, it seemed, much more regularity in the organization of cognitive capacities in the nervous system than was allowed for by wholly environmental accounts of mental processes. Furthermore, the patterns of breakdown could not be readily explained in terms of simple stimulus-response disruption. Rather, in many cases, the hierarchy of behavioral responses was altered. For example, in certain forms of aphasia, the general sentence frame was preserved, but subjects could not correctly slot individual words into the frame. In other aphasias, the sentence frame broke down, but individual content words carried meaning. Thus was struck yet another blow against reflex-arc models of thought. At the same time, the particular profiles of abilities and disabilities that emerge in the wake of brain damage provided many pregnant suggestions about how the human mind might be organized in normal individuals.

By the late 1940s, in areas as diverse as communication engineering and neuropsychology, certain themes were emerging principally in the United States, Great Britain, and the Soviet Union. Though I have stressed the American version of this story, comparable accounts could be presented from other national perspectives as well. Scholars in these fields were not only writing but were eagerly meeting with one another to discuss the many exciting new perspectives. Herbert Simon, ultimately one of the founders of cognitive science but then a graduate student at the University of Chicago, recalls a kind of "invisible college" in the 1940s. He knew McCulloch at Chicago; he knew of Shannon's master's thesis at M.I.T.; he knew that Wiener and von Neumann were working on issues in symbolic logic which had grown out of the philosophical writings of Whitehead, Russell, and Frege. Simon himself was studying at Chicago with Rudolf Carnap, who was then putting forth key notions about the syntax of logic. Such leading biologists (and Hixon symposiasts) as Ralph Gerard, Heinrich Klüver, Roger Sperry, and Paul Weiss were working in nearby laboratories on issues of the nervous system. Many of the same influences were rubbing off during this period on Jerome Bruner, Noam Chomsky, John McCarthy, George Miller, Allen Newell, and other founders of cognitive science.

Questions for Discussion

1. In your own words, summarize the selection.
2. Was the selection relatively easy or relatively difficult to understand? Explain your answer.
3. Why is cognitive science considered a social science rather than a physical science? Explain how you would classify it and why.
4. Rewrite the paragraph beginning with "During the next ten years" so a person with no scientific background could understand it.
5. To what sort of society might the theories and findings discussed by Gardner lead?
6. For many years, scientists—like journalists—were expected to be objective. In what ways is this selection objective? In what ways are the author's biases apparent?
7. Be prepared to discuss this important question: How is it possible to differentiate statements of fact from dogmatic assertions?
8. How can we prevent further bifurcation of our society into what the British scientist and man of letters C. P. Snow calls "the two cultures," one made up of scientists and the other of humanists, neither really understanding the other?

9. Explain why cybernetics is fundamentally opposed to behaviorism. (For brief explanations of behaviorism, see the introduction to this section and the introduction to the selection by B. F. Skinner. Also, read or reread the Skinner selection.)

10. Explain the differences between Skinner's concept of the contingency of reinforcement and Gardner's presentation of the hierarchy of response.

11. On pages 280–281, Gardner explains the Turing test. Do you think that Skinner would consider this test valid? Explain.

———————— SUGGESTIONS FOR WRITING ————————

1. In regard to the selection by Margaret Mead, imagine the effects of Women's Liberation on this New Guinea tribe. How would someone like Ndrosal react when his wife refused to obey him? In an essay, develop a complete documentary that might be titled "Coming of Women's Liberation in New Guinea."

2. The main dispute about sociology, similar to the disputes about many other social sciences and physical sciences, is whether its purpose is to understand behavior or to work to cause social change. (Some people refer to the argument as "pure science versus applied science.") Argue for or against the proposition that social scientists should be involved with the social and political processes necessary to bring about change.

3. Are values universal, or are they culture-specific? Think of some values common in the USA: thrift, the work ethic, education, literacy, monogamy, the tabu against eating human flesh. And think of values in other cultures: polygamy, the practice of cannibalism, ritual wastefulness, human sacrifice. Develop an argument that certain values are, or should be, universal, or an argument that all values are, and should be, relative to the culture under consideration.

4. In the United States, various ethnic groups—Chicanos, Blacks, Vietnamese, Chinese, Samoans, Amerindians, and many others—want to retain their own cultures and, in some cases, their own languages. On the other hand, America, "the melting pot," has a long tradition of integration: by the second generation, immigrant families have assimilated and in their life-styles are no different from the families who trace back to the Mayflower. In an essay, give your reasoned opinion about one of the following issues:

    a. Ethnic groups should be encouraged to integrate as rapidly as possible. If this is your position, explain what might be done to encourage and facilitate that integration.

    b. Ethnic groups should maintain their identities. If you take this position, explain your reasoning and outline the problems of a multicultural society.

    c. Ethnic groups should maintain their identities, but should be full participants in American life: economic, social, and political. What are the advantages of this position? How might the ideal be carried out?

5. The people Margaret Mead studied in New Guinea developed a life-style and family system very different in most ways from that in the United States. Although you are not an anthropologist, you probably do have ideas about how customs and social practices

develop. In a speculative essay, give hypothetical explanations for the development of the Manus culture that Mead talks about.

6.   Write a history of your own use of money as it has changed through the years. Start with whatever allowance you received as a child, and explain how the means of exchange have broadened (include checks, credit cards, credit, and whatever else is appropriate). Your approach can be lighthearted or serious, but relate your discussion to the uses of money in society at large.

7.   Think of the fairy-tale characters you have encountered in your reading and viewing. In an essay, categorize these characters, and explain the bases for your categories.

8.   Howard Gardner's essay details the various scientific developments that have influenced cognitive psychology. Using Gardner's selection as a model, write a brief essay in which you explain the influences that have gone into the development of your favorite musical group (e.g., a rock band, string quartet, or an orchestra).

9.   B. F. Skinner has written a "novel" about the perfect society, *Walden Two*. Read this book and then write the summary of a movie script that George Lucas (of *Star Wars* fame) might use as the basis for a film.

10.   Many people use Skinnerian principles to motivate people or to deter them from certain actions. For example, the aversive therapy used in smoking clinics is basically Skinnerian, and many parents pay their children money for receiving good grades. The ultimate threat of aversive stimulus is the death penalty. Is capital punishment effective? If so, why? If not, why not? In your essay, take account of B. F. Skinner's argument.

11.   The selection from B. F. Skinner's *Beyond Freedom and Dignity* provides an extended definition of the term *thinking*. Write an extended definition of a term that interests you—for example: *playing, working, cheating, learning, competing.*

C H A P T E R
7

The Sciences

In what sense are the sciences exact?

Many people see the difference between the sociologist and the physicist as the difference between a scientist who can never be sure and one who can prove with certitude. Such is not the case, however. The physicist also deals with principles of uncertainty. Witness the history of science as represented by three men, Isaac Newton, Albert Einstein, and Niels Bohr. Isaac Newton proposed a model of the universe that would be valid in all cases. Albert Einstein showed Newton's laws to be true only in special cases and then formulated his own theory of relativity. Some of Albert Einstein's own ideas were disproved when Niels Bohr showed that God indeed did play dice with the universe, in that a principle of randomness is constantly at work in the cosmos.

Science is fascinating in and of itself, but without application to our own lives, it often seems to be an elaborate construction existing outside of the everyday world like an elaborate game of "Dungeons and Dragons." Writing for the layperson, the science writer often takes great pains to show the practical side of science, the application of theory to practice. But as the following selections demonstrate, science, philosophy, and metaphysics are simply different approaches to the same goal, the accurate description of the world and the pursuit of "ultimate reality."

Writing is such a commonplace activity that normally we give very little thought to it. We write letters to friends, endorse checks, and compose essays for class assignments without consciously realizing that we are manipulating symbols in order to communicate with others and, in many cases, to formulate our own thoughts. The fact that language is a set of symbols is made evident, however, when the layperson or student begins working within the sciences. The physicist uses the language of mathematics to describe the relationship of forces whereas the chemist uses schematics to describe the relationship of elements to one another within compounds. In either case, however, the scientist is constructing a model of what is believed to be the true world "out there." But models are never the "real thing," only an approximation and therefore subject to revision, whether in minor details or in revolutionary ways.

Scientific writing for laypeople is difficult because the language of science is not intelligible to nonscientists. Therefore, the writer must often use analogies and similes. In essence, the writer is using a model of a model. If a model, by definition, must be inaccurate in some way or another, then the model of the model is subject to an even greater degree of imprecision. In reading through the following selections, note how the authors describe a scientific theory. What analogies do they use to bring the theory alive, and what limitations to their descriptions do they themselves make apparent?

DIAN FOSSEY (1932–1985)

Before her untimely death in 1985, Dian Fossey was regarded as the world's foremost expert on the mountain gorillas of Africa, which are the subject of the following selection. Fossey received her bachelor's degree in 1954 from San Jose State College and entered the occupational therapy field the following year. It was another eleven years before she began her study of the gorillas under the sponsorship of the noted anthropologist Louis Leakey. Through her observations, Fossey found that each of these animals has an individual personality and traits that resemble those of humans; she discovered, furthermore, that these great apes are notably more gentle than was commonly believed. Her life, however, was not simply that of the passive observer/naturalist. Six months after arriving in Africa, a civil war developed in the Republic of the Congo. Fossey was placed under arrest but managed to escape to Rwanda with an old Land Rover and a revolver hidden in a Kleenex box. In later years, she became alarmed at the drastic reduction in the gorilla population due to poaching and land cultivation. Fossey battled the Rwandan government, arguing for conservation of the land, and organized the first patrols designed to prevent illegal hunting and capturing of the animal. In 1985, Fossey was found hacked to death at the Karisoke Research Center, which she founded in 1967. At the time of this writing, her murder remains unsolved.

This selection is a perfect example of a scientific account based on a journal or log, the raw material from which anthropologists, ethnologists, and other natural scientists draw their theories and conclusions. As you read, notice how Fossey has interspersed her own attitudes and reflections with the objective observation of her subjects.

The Natural Demise of Two Gorilla Families: Groups 8 and 9

During the first two months of study at Karisoke, my daily contacts with the gorillas were fairly evenly distributed between Group 4—which ranged on the southwestern and western Visoke slopes under the leadership of a silverback I had named Whinny—and Group 5—led by Beethoven on the southeastern mountain slopes. The composition of the two groups totaled 29 animals, but half of them had not been fully identified, and I could only speculate about the degrees of relatedness between the older individuals. My speculations were based on the frequencies of close affiliative associations between group members compared with aggressive, antagonistic reactions. Physical similarities such as noseprints, hair coloring, and evidence of syndactyly or strabismus were also extremely important in determining kinship ties within any group. The cohesive nature of gorilla groups fortunately provides one with a high degree of reliability regarding each offspring's sire. The early days of the research were spent trying to clarify the composition of the two main groups and seeking clues that would reveal the genetic connections between the individuals of the study groups available to me.

In this period, a third group entered the study area for the first time since my arrival and was subsequently named Group 8. (Group 6 was a fringe group; "Group 7" was a mistake—a failure to recognize Group 5 members on an occasion when they were feeding apart from one another.) I first saw Group 8 through binoculars from some five hundred feet up on Visoke's slopes. Even at that distance it was possible to distinguish an extensively silvered old male, a young silverback, a handsome blackback in his prime, two young males, and, bringing up the rear, a doddering old female. Unaware of my presence, they slowly ambled and fed throughout the nettle zone adjacent to Visoke's slopes before crossing a wide cattle trail that led into the forest. While watching the group I could not help being impressed by the manner in which all of the animals periodically paused in their feeding to allow the elderly female to catch up with them.

The following day I tracked Group 8 into the saddle area west of Visoke and contacted them from a distance of about sixty feet. They gave me the calmest reception I had ever received from an unhabituated group. The first individual to acknowledge my presence was the young silverback, who strutted onto a rock and stared with compressed lips before going off to feed. I named him Pugnacious, Pug for short. He was followed by the extremely attractive blackback, who nipped off a leaf to hold between his lips for a few seconds before spitting it out, a common displacement activity known as symbolic feeding and indicative of mild unease. After whacking at some

From *Gorillas in the Mist* by Dian Fossey. Reprinted by permission of Houghton Mifflin Company.

vegetation, the magnificent male swaggered out of sight into dense foliage seemingly quite pleased with himself. I named him Samson. Next, the two young adults scampered into view and impishly flipped over on to their backs to stare at me from upside-down positions, giving the impression they were wearing lopsided grins. In time they were named Geezer and Peanuts. When the elderly female came into view, she gazed briefly at me in a totally uninterested manner before sitting down next to Peanuts and maneuvering her patchy rump almost into his face for grooming. I named her Coco because of her somewhat light chocolate-colored hair, and it was in her memory that the first Karisoke reclaimed captive was named sixteen months later.

Lastly, the old silverback came forward. In all my years of research I never met a silverback so dignified and commanding of respect. His silvering extended from the sides of his cheekbones, along neck and shoulders, enveloped his back and barrel, and continued down the sides of both thighs. Having little to go by in comparison, except for zoo gorillas, I estimated his age at approximately fifty years, possibly more. The nobility of his character compelled me to seek a name for him immediately. In Swahili, *rafiki* means "friend." Because friendship implies mutual respect and trust, the regal silverback became known as Rafiki.

Geezer and Pug closely resembled one another in having slightly pig-snouted profiles unlike the facial characteristics of the other three males or Coco. Physical traits, coupled with the affinity of the two males, suggested common parents. I thought it likely that their mother, who would have had to be an elderly Group 8 female because of their ages, had died before my arrival into the study area. For the same reasons of striking physical resemblances and rapport, Coco was thought to be the mother of Samson and Peanuts, both males sired beyond any doubt by Rafiki.

Coco and Rafiki often shared the same nest, resembling a gracefully aging old married couple who needed no words to strengthen their respect of one another. Coco's serene presence among the males of Group 8 frequently prompted mutual grooming, a social and functional activity involving meticulous hair parting done either orally with the lips or manually with the fingers in search of ectoparasites, dry-skin flakes, and vegetation debris such as burrs. Usually, after Coco's initiation, most of the other Group 8 members would follow suit and, within minutes, there might be a chain of intently grooming gorillas.

Response behavior—actions prompted by the presence of a human being—were only occasionally given by Group 8 members and seemed to convey elements of braggadocio, daring, and curiosity rather than aggression or fear. This unusual group with no young to protect seemed to accept or trust my presence from the start and to "enjoy" the break in their daily routine that I offered. Samson, in particular, reacted more than others but seemingly with a sense of self-enjoyment. Peanuts often tried to mimic Samson's actions. The two resembled a chorus line when standing upright for almost simultaneous chestbeats closely followed by several kicks of their right legs. When finished with their repertoire, they stood and stared at me as if gauging the effect of their performance. Samson also relished the noise made when he broke branches, and his massive weight guaranteed him many satisfying crashes. Once he climbed a tall dead sapling directly over my head. Like a logger, he deliberately preplanned the direction in which the tree would be felled. After several energetic bounces and swings, he managed to bring the tree down right by the side of my body before running off with a smug grin.

*   *   *

Often I am asked about the most rewarding experience I have ever had with gorillas. The question is extremely difficult to answer because each hour with the gorillas provides its own return and satisfaction. The first occasion when I felt I might have crossed an intangible barrier between human and ape occurred about ten months after beginning the research at Karisoke. Peanuts, Group 8's youngest male, was feeding about fifteen feet away when he suddenly stopped and turned to stare directly at me. The expression in his eyes was unfathomable. Spellbound, I returned his gaze—a gaze that seemed to combine elements of inquiry and of acceptance. Peanuts ended this unforgettable moment by sighing deeply, and slowly resumed feeding. Jubilant, I returned to camp and cabled Dr. Leakey I'VE FINALLY BEEN ACCEPTED BY A GORILLA.*

Two years after our exchange of glances, Peanuts became the first gorilla ever to touch me. The day had started out as an ordinary one, if any day working from Karisoke might be considered ordinary. I felt unusually compelled to make this particular day outstanding because the following morning I had to leave for England for a seven-month period to work on my doctorate. Bob Campbell and I had gone out to contact Group 8 on the western-facing Visoke slopes. We found them feeding in the middle of a shallow ravine of densely growing herbaceous vegetation. Along the ridge leading into the ravine grew large *Hagenia* trees that had always served as good lookout spots for scanning the surrounding terrain. Bob and I had just settled down on a comfortable moss-cushioned *Hagenia* tree trunk when Peanuts, wearing his "I want to be entertained" expression, left his feeding

---

*Nine years after Dr. Leakey's death in 1972 I learned that he had carried the cable in his pocket for months, even taking it on a lecture tour to America. I was told that he read it proudly, much as he once spoke to me of Jane Goodall's outstanding success with chimpanzees.

group to meander inquisitively toward us. Slowly I left the tree and pretended to munch on vegetation to reassure Peanuts that I meant him no harm.

Peanuts' bright eyes peered at me through a latticework of vegetation as he began his strutting, swaggering approach. Suddenly he was at my side and sat down to watch my "feeding" techniques as if it were my turn to entertain him. When Peanuts seemed bored with the "feeding" routine, I scratched my head, and almost immediately, he began scratching his own. Since he appeared totally relaxed, I lay back in the foliage, slowly extended my hand, palm upward, then rested it on the leaves. After looking intently at my hand, Peanuts stood up and extended his hand to touch his fingers against my own for a brief instant. Thrilled at his own daring, he gave vent to his excitement by a quick chestbeat before going off to rejoin his group. Since that day, the spot has been called *Fasi Ya Mkoni*, "the Place of the Hands." The contact was among the most memorable of my life among the gorillas.

Habituation of Group 8 progressed far more rapidly than with other groups because of the consistency of Rafiki's tolerant nature and the important fact that the group had no infants to protect; thus they did not need to resort to highly defensive behavior. Their "youngster" was old Coco, who received solicitous attention from the others. Coco seemed to be even older than Rafiki and had a deeply wrinkled face, balding head and rump, graying muzzle, and flabby, hairless upper arms. She was also missing a number of teeth, causing her to gum her food rather than chew it. She often sat hunched over with one arm crossed over her chest while the other hand rapidly patted the top of her head in a seemingly involuntary motion. Sitting in this manner, with mucus draining from her eyes, her lower lip hanging down, Coco presented a pathetic picture. I suspected that her senses of hearing and seeing were considerably dulled by age.

The remarkable displays of affection between Coco, Rafiki, Samson, and Peanuts could be described as poignant, though this was not surprising when one considered the number of years the family had probably shared together. One day I was able to hide myself from the group feeding on a wide open slope 130 feet away from me. They were widely spread out with Rafiki at the top, moving uphill, and Coco far at the bottom, wandering erratically on a feeding course that led away from the rest of the group. Rafiki suddenly stopped eating, paused as if listening for something, and gave a sharp questioning type of vocalization. Coco obviously heard it, for she paused in her wanderings and turned in the general direction of the sound. Rafiki, out of sight from her, sat and gazed downhill. The other group members followed his example as though they were waiting for her to catch up. Coco began climbing slowly, stopping occasionally to determine their whereabouts before again meandering in the general direction of the patient males. Once within sight of Rafiki, the elderly female moved directly to him, exchanged a greeting series of soft belch vocalizations until reaching his side. They looked directly into each other's face and embraced. She placed her arm over his back and he did likewise over hers. Both walked uphill in this fashion, murmuring together like contented conspirators. The three young males followed the couple, feeding along the way, while the young silverback, Pugnacious, watched them intently from a farther, more discreet distance. He too then disappeared out of sight over the top of the hill. I did not let Group 8 know of my presence that day since I felt that to intrude upon them for an open contact would have been improper.

Working on Visoke's western slopes usually gave me the opportunity to contact Groups 4 and 8 on the same day within an area of nearly two square miles. Alternating contacts with Groups 4 and 8 provided almost daily knowledge of their respective range routes and locations. Thus, in December 1967, I was puzzled to hear a series of screams, *wraaghs*, and chestbeats coming from an unknown group located about halfway out in the five-mile-wide saddle area between Mts. Visoke and Mikeno, a region that only Group 8 had been known to frequent.

The search was started for the "ghost group," which, when finally found, was named Group 9. The dominant silverback, one in his prime, perhaps twenty-five to thirty years old, was named Geronimo. He was a most distinctive male, with a triangular red blaze of hair in the middle of his massive brow ridge and luxuriant blue-black body hair that framed bulging pectoral muscles resembling steel cables. Geronimo's supportive male, about eleven years old, was a blackback named Gabriel, because he was usually the first to spot my presence and inform the group with chestbeats or vocalizations. The degree of physical resemblance between the two adult males suggested they probably had a common sire. One young adult female was all too easy to identify because of a recent trap injury which had rendered her right hand useless. The hand, with its swollen pink fingers, hung limply from the wrist and was frequently cradled by the young female. Within two weeks the young female became adept at preparing food by using her right arm or foot to stabilize vegetation stalks and her mouth or left hand for the more intricate tasks, such as peeling or discarding unwanted parts of a plant. She was able to climb or descend trees by hooking her right arm around branches and tree trunks instead of using her injured hand. Within two months after first being observed, she was no longer seen with the group and was assumed dead. The dominant female among Geronimo's harem of four was named Maidenform because of her long pendulous breasts. Each of Group 9's four adult females had at least one dependent offspring, which indicated Geronimo's degree of reproductive success.

The addition of Group 9 to the study area provided a total of 48 individuals in four distinct groups, a population with both an adult male-to-female ratio and an adult-to-immature ratio of 1:1.1 at the start of 1968.

By this time Coco, the aged female of Group 8, could no longer be considered capable of reproduction. Peanuts, estimated as nearly six years of age, had probably been her last offspring. Group 8, therefore, had no breeding females, and Rafiki, the old but still potent silverback leader of the group, sought physical interactions with Group 4, which contained four females who were either approaching or had recently reached sexual maturity.

Encounters between distinct social units increase in frequency when range areas overlap, or if there is a disproportionate ratio of males to females, as was the case on Visoke's western slopes during the early years of the study. It was not long before Groups 4 and 8 met for a physical interaction instigated by Rafiki after following Group 4 for several days.

The two groups first met in a section of ridges separated by deep ravines at the edge of Group 8's range on the southwestern-facing slopes of Visoke. Climbing toward the loudly vocalizing animals, I looked ahead and saw what appeared to be an aerial act of five flying silverbacks: three from Group 4 and Rafiki and Pug of Group 8 leapt from tree to tree, charged parallel to one another, chestbeat, and broke branches along the ridge with crashing, splintering sounds. Their powerful muscular bodies varied in shades from white to tones of dull gray, and formed a vivid contrast to the green forest background. So engrossed were the displaying silverbacks that they seemed unconscious of my presence.

Hoping to remain unnoticed, I crept to a nearby *Hagenia* tree and found old Coco resignedly huddled against the tree trunk—one hand tapping the top of her head and the other arm crossed against her chest. She glanced at me calmly and heaved a big sigh as if expressing patient tolerance of the commotion going on around her. Occasionally Peanuts rushed down to her side to reassure himself that she was there. After brief embraces he would rejoin Group 8's second young adult male, Geezer, with chestbeats directed toward the three silverbacks of Group 4.

Excitement, rather than aggression, dominated this first observed physical interaction between Groups 4 and 8. While watching the discretion of the parallel displays between the two dominant silverbacks—Rafiki of Group 8 and Whinny of Group 4—I received the impression that both were equally experienced and were thus capable of avoiding overt combat because of mutual respect based on numerous previous interactions. Late that afternoon the two groups separated, though they continued to exchange hootseries and chestbeats for several hours, communications that seemed to become more taunting as the distance between the two familial units increased.

Two months later, in February 1968, Rafiki had ceased trying to interact with either Group 4 or Group 9, which were then also ranging on Visoke's western slopes. Old Coco had weakened, and because of her difficulty in keeping up with the group, Rafiki adjusted their travel and feeding pace to meet hers. On February 23 I found no sign of either Coco or Rafiki after contacting Group 8. Only the four males—Pug, Geezer, Samson, and Peanuts—were to be seen wrestling playfully together as carefree as boys at a summer camp. Backtracking the group's trail, I found that Coco and Rafiki had night-nested together in connecting nests for the past two nights, but I completely lost all trail sign after that. Two days later Rafiki returned to Group 8 alone. Coco's body was never found.

The old female's disappearance and assumed death resulted in a lack of cohesion among the five males. Their intragroup squabbles became more frequent and they resumed interactions with Groups 4 and 9, whose ranges overlapped their own.

Group 8's first encounter with Group 9 was held only days after Coco's disappearance and several ridges away from where she last had been seen. The tracker and I came upon Group 9 at unexpectedly close range, giving my assistant just time enough to dive under a large *Hagenia* tree before the gorillas became aware of us. Because of tall vegetation, I climbed into the same tree to gain a better view of Group 9. Within moments loud brush-breaking sounds were heard coming from below. Hiding myself in the tree's heavy vine growth, I was surprised to see Rafiki leading his bachelor band directly toward Group 9 without the chestbeats or hootseries that usually precede an intergroup encounter. The only obvious evidence of excitement at the initiation of the contact was the overpowering silverback odor, most of which was coming from Rafiki. Almost immediately Samson and Peanuts began mingling with three young adults of Group 9. Rafiki calmly made a day nest directly below me in the hollow bole of the *Hagenia*, unaware of the presence of myself or the tracker. Previously I had considered a gorilla's sense of smell superior to that of a human, but this observation did not support the supposition.

After nearly thirty minutes of quiet, my accidental breaking of a tree branch sounded like a pistol shot in the stillness of the resting period. Rafiki jumped from his nest and glared upward through the heavily vined skirts of the tree. Then the majestic silverback strutted deliberately around the trunk before posing stiffly some four feet below me. In an accusing manner he stared into my face nervously chewing his lips, one indication of his stress. Trying to act as innocent as possible and with anxiety only for the cramps in my legs, I gazed at the sky, yawned, and scratched myself while the old male indignantly displayed around the base of the tree unaware of the tracker huddled out of sight only several feet away from him.

Although curious about Rafiki's tolerance of a human's presence, the members of Group 9 eventually moved off to feed after contributing their own chestbeats and alarm vocalizations to this unexpected encounter. Rafiki instantly followed them, though I couldn't help but feel he had enjoyed being the intermediary between a gorilla-habituated human and a nonhuman-habituated group of gorillas.

*   *   *

The northwestern slopes of Visoke offered several ridges of *Pygeum afri-canum* trees shared by both Groups 8 and 9. The fruits of this tree are highly favored by gorillas, though such site-specific food prompts competition and increases opportunities for interactions between distinct social units. Groups 8 and 9 often met along the ridges for prolonged interactions because of their interest in obtaining the fruits.

Rafiki, more dominant and experienced than Geronimo, usually established Group 8's claim to the most prolifically fruiting trees higher on the slopes and Geronimo's Group 9 raided the lower-ridge trees. It was an amazing sight to watch the 350-pound silverbacks climbing onto thin tree limbs about 60 feet above the ground and harvesting with mouth and hands as many fruits as they could collect before climbing down to sit close to the tree trunks to gorge on their yield.

On one occasion Peanuts and Geezer, bored with the long feeding period, playfully galloped downhill toward several of Group 9's immature youngsters. The two Group 8 males failed to see Geronimo bringing up the rear of his group. Giving harsh pig-grunts, Geronimo immediately charged uphill. This caused the two young males to brake to a stop and momentarily stand bipedally, their arms around one another, their expressions panic-stricken. Then both rapidly turned and ran back toward their group, all the while screaming fearfully. Geronimo pursued them to the top of the ridge, where he encountered Rafiki, who was running down to the defense of Peanuts and Geezer. Discretion prevailed when Geronimo turned heel and herded his group away from the bachelors.

The absence of Coco, coupled by frequent interactions with other groups, increased the unrest among the all-male Group 8. Pug and Geezer finally left their natal group to travel together on Visoke's northern slopes in a range area not too far removed from that of Group 8. Their departure left Rafiki only with his and Coco's presumed progeny, Samson and Peanuts. For nearly a year, however, squabbles continued between Rafiki and his oldest son. The friction occurred most often when the three males interacted with other groups and Samson's excitement grew beyond Rafiki's toleration. The old male had little difficulty in subduing Samson by either running or strutting directly toward his sexually maturing son, who would immediately assume a typical submissive posture by bowing down on his forearms, his gaze averted from his father and his rump upward. Rafiki needed only to maintain his stilted pose for a few seconds, his head hair erect, his gaze directed toward Samson, before temporary harmony was restored within the group.

Three and a half years after Coco's death Rafiki acquired two females, Macho and Maisie, from Group 4 during a violent physical interaction in

June 1971. During the encounter Peanuts' right eye was permanently injured from a bite wound inflicted by Uncle Bert, the young silverback who had inherited the leadership of Group 4 three years previously following the death of his father, Whinny.

With the acquisition of the two new females Rafiki seemed invigorated. He staunchly defended his harem against Samson, thereby causing more friction between father and son. It was obvious that Samson was wasting breeding years by remaining in his natal group. He was prompted to leave just as Pugnacious and Geezer had done nearly a year before. Samson became a peripheral silverback, one who travels three hundred to six hundred feet from his natal group before setting out to establish his own range area and gain experience from interactions with other gorilla groups in order to acquire and retain his own females. Both peripheral and lone travel are usually necessary stages for any maturing male unless breeding opportunities are available within his natal group. Samson's departure left Rafiki with Maisie and Macho, the two young females taken from Group 4, and with young Peanuts.

Unexpectedly, Samson returned from his distant ranging area and managed to take Maisie away from Rafiki in September 1971. Fourteen months later Maisie and Samson were observed with a newly born infant. In June 1973 Rafiki proved his own virility when his only female, Macho, gave birth to a female infant named Thor.

Group 8 remained an oddly composed group, consisting of Rafiki, his young mate Macho, his eleven-year-old son Peanuts, and his newborn daughter Thor. Seemingly content with his little family, Rafiki no longer sought other groups. When Thor was about six months old Rafiki was observed in one last interaction with Group 4. I noticed that the regal old silverback's chestbeats and hootseries lacked resonance and strength, though his physical appearance seemed as impressive as ever. Possibly he had been avoiding other groups because he realized his physical limitations brought on by age.

*   *   *

In November 1971, five months after Rafiki had taken Macho from Group 4, the trackers and I began an intensive search for Group 9, whom we had not seen for seven months. They were finally found in the saddle area between Visoke and Mikeno, in almost exactly the same spot where they first had been contacted four years earlier. Instead of the thirteen robust individuals I had expected to find, only five remained in Group 9. The once powerful body of Geronimo had become gaunt, his muscular chest concave, his blue-black body hair dull and patchy. His right hand was deformed and contracted, perhaps as the result of a trap injury, and more wounds were visible along back and thighs. I might never have recognized Geronimo had it not been for the faded vestige of red hair in the center of his forehead and the presence of Maidenform, one of the four females he previously had in Group 9. I tried to conceal myself from their view, but after an hour the ailing male knew that a human being was nearby. Wearing a troubled facial expression, Geronimo, with tremendous physical effort, kept trying to stand bipedally to scout the surrounding area. His fear odor was strong, alarming his two females and their young, who clustered near him ready to flee. I had to reveal my presence but was satisfied when Geronimo seemed to recognize me and his group slowly resumed feeding farther west in the saddle area toward Mt. Mikeno.

I never saw Geronimo again, though Maidenform and several other females of Group 9 were later observed in two different groups ranging on Visoke's northwestern slopes and the saddle area west of Visoke. Whether poachers or natural causes were responsible for Geronimo's ultimate disappearance, I shall never know, but I feel that he died of natural causes. For several years his dung had become increasingly mucoid, often crawling with *Anoplocephala cestoda*, and he certainly had not appeared well when last seen. His death, of course, meant the end of Group 9 as a distinct social unit, because no gorilla family group can endure without a silverback leader.

With Group 9 no longer using the northwestern slopes of Visoke, chances for interactions between Groups 4 and 8 decreased markedly as additional range area reduced the amount of overlap between the two groups. Rafiki, however, remained content to pass the days slowly with his oddly assorted small Group 8, although Peanuts sometimes wandered alone as far as eight tenths of a mile away as if in quest of other groups for social interactions.

The social environment of little Thor, now eleven months old, was in definite contrast to that of Group 5's gregarious young with their numerous peer affiliations. The absence of playmates deprived Thor of rich learning opportunities. Her motor skills lagged about three months behind most eleven-month-old gorilla infants raised with the stimulus of interacting with others of their own age. Thor had to rely upon her mother, Macho, for tactile play and surrounding vegetation for solo play. Thor weighed about seven pounds less than the average eleven-month-old and was seldom seen more than ten feet from Macho at an age when other infants often played out of sight of their mothers. In addition to the lack of social incentives, Thor might have been less venturesome because she was Macho's firstborn and her mother therefore lacked previous experience in handling offspring.

My beloved Rafiki, a friend for seven years, was never able to witness the development of his last offspring beyond her eleventh month. In April 1974 the regal monarch of the mountain died of pneumonia and pleurisy, leaving Macho, Thor, and Peanuts as the sole remnants of Group 8. For about six days before his death Rafiki moved and fed very little, but during this period Macho and Peanuts circled around the weakening old silverback within distances of one hundred to two hundred feet for feeding purposes.

I received the news of Rafiki's death in Kigali, Rwanda, upon return from Cambridge, England. A student, on his way back to England, knocked at my hotel door carrying a large plastic bag that seeped liquid and an odor of putrefaction. Without preamble the student stated, "This is Rafiki's skin and I want to take it home with me." The ghoulish statement hit me with shattering force. This gruesome violation of the majesty, strength, and dignity of Rafiki seemed an intolerable sacrilege. I promptly confiscated the trophy, revolted by the request.

Rafiki's young silverback son Peanuts, about twelve years old at this time, was found traveling with Macho and Thor. Four weeks later, the inevitable happened. With the regal old leader dead and only the inexperienced Peanuts in "command" of Macho—an adult female without strong group affiliations—Uncle Bert led Group 4 into what had been Group 8's range. Peanuts was certainly no match for Uncle Bert. Twenty-seven days after Rafiki's death, eleven-month-old Thor was killed during a violent physical interaction between the two groups. Uncle Bert bit the infant fatally in the skull and groin, both typical infanticide wounds causing almost instant death. Macho carried Thor's body the remainder of the day before leaving it about thirty feet from her night nest. Eleven days following the infanticide, Macho was observed copulating with the sexually immature Peanuts. Five months later Uncle Bert took Macho away from the young male in yet another violent physical confrontation.

There followed a nineteen-month trial-and-error period for Peanuts, as he sought unsuccessfully to obtain females from other groups. Like all young silverbacks without breeding opportunities in their natal groups, he needed this travel period alone in order to gain experience in interactions for the acquisition of other individuals to begin his own group and to develop the necessary leadership skills required to hold his new group together against intrusion by other, more adept silverbacks. I found it distressing to encounter Peanuts wandering through the forest alone since I could easily recall him as a frolicking youngster living within his small family group.

Finally, in November 1975, Peanuts was found traveling with a younger animal I named Beetsme because of uncertainty as to the new gorilla's sex or background. Beetsme showed an unusual tolerance of observers and, since it had been acquired from the northwestern slopes where Group 9 had previously ranged, I felt that the animal was possibly one of Geronimo's offspring who had now matured to an estimated age of about ten years. For two months Beetsme and Peanuts wandered together until Uncle Bert again intervened and took Beetsme into Group 4.

Possibly to avoid further encounters with Uncle Bert, Peanuts shifted his range to the northern slopes of Visoke and out of Karisoke's study area. An entire year passed with only an occasional sighting or trail sign to confirm that Peanuts was still traveling alone. Then, in March 1977, Peanuts was found with five other adults, three of whom strongly resembled Geronimo's females. About fifteen years old now, Peanuts was considered sexually mature, but his vitality had dwindled considerably. The young male had never fully recovered from the bite wound received during the interaction in June 1971 when his father, Rafiki, had succeeded in acquiring Macho and Maisie from Group 4. The right side of Peanuts' face remained swollen, and his right eye was draining profusely. I thought it unlikely that Peanuts would be able to hold the females he had gained and that, indeed, Group 8 had ended with the death of noble Rafiki just as Group 9 had come to a close with Geronimo's disappearance and assumed death.

Questions for Discussion

1. According to Fossey, one of her most rewarding experiences with the gorillas was the first time the animals accepted her presence, when she "crossed an intangible barrier between human and ape." Was this event scientifically important or merely a personal triumph for the author? Explain.

2. How did Fossey limit the scope of her study? Cite a situation in which these limits barred her from obtaining interesting information on a group's life history? Why do you think she imposed the limits?

3. Explain some of the difficulties in studying the life history of a gorilla group.

4. Fossey anthropomorphizes the gorillas. Explain how this kind of figurative language helps make the selection clearer to the reader. Cite examples.

5. Fossey uses the technical terms *syndactyly* and *strabismus*. What do they mean? Is the author justified in using them, or should she have used nontechnical terms for the concepts? In general, when is technical jargon justified?

6. Fossey arrives at many of her conclusions through educated guesses rather than from firsthand observation. Locate several examples in the text. How does Fossey justify her conclusions? Is such educated guesswork valid in scientific writing?

7. Do you feel that you now have a fairly good idea of how gorilla bands organize themselves? Select passages that clarify matters for you. If you do not understand the principles by which gorillas organize their bands, what might the author have supplied to help you understand her point?

8. Good characterization makes writing come alive. Pick one gorilla and explain how Fossey describes the animal to differentiate it from the others. Note how both physical appearance and personality are detailed.

STEPHEN JAY GOULD (1941–)

Son of a court reporter father and an artist mother, Gould was born in New York City. He took his A.B. at Antioch College in 1963 and his Ph.D. at Columbia in 1967. He is now a professor of geology at Harvard.

Gould is a highly respected scientist who can speak to laypeople without degrading either his subject or his audience. His writings include Ever Since Darwin: Reflections in Natural History *(1977);* The Panda's Thumb: More Reflections in Natural History *(1980), from which the following selection was taken; and* Hen's Teeth and Horse's Toes: Further Reflections in Natural History *(1983).*

The following selection is relaxed and informal in tone even though its argument is complex. The essay is an outstanding example of how a skilled writer can make technical subjects accessible to the general public.

Gould makes his subject matter both understandable and interesting by presenting his scientific argument in terms of a human drama, the main characters of which are Darwin and Wallace.

"Natural Selection and the Human Brain: Darwin vs. Wallace"

In the south transept of Chartres cathedral, the most stunning of all medieval windows depicts the four evangelists as dwarfs sitting upon the shoulders of four Old Testament prophets—Isaiah, Jeremiah, Ezekiel, and Daniel. When I first saw this window as a cocky undergraduate in 1961, I immediately thought of Newton's famous aphorism—"if I have seen farther, it is by standing on the shoulders of giants"—and imagined that I had made a major discovery in unearthing his lack of originality. Years later, and properly humbled for many reasons, I learned that Robert K. Merton, the celebrated sociologist of science from Columbia University, had devoted an entire book to pre-Newtonian usages of the metaphor. It is titled, appropriately, *On the Shoulders of Giants*. In fact, Merton traces the bon mot back to Bernard of Chartres in 1126 and cites several scholars who believe that the windows of the great south transept, installed after Bernard's death, represent an explicit attempt to capture his metaphor in glass.

Although Merton wisely constructs his book as a delightful romp through the intellectual life of medieval and Renaissance Europe, he does have a serious point to make. For Merton has devoted much of his work to the study of multiple discoveries in science. He has shown that almost all major ideas arise more than once, independently and often virtually at the same time—and thus, that great scientists are embedded in their cultures, not divorced from them. Most great ideas are "in the air," and several scholars simultaneously wave their nets.

One of the most famous of Merton's "multiples" resides in my own field of evolutionary biology. Darwin, to recount the famous tale briefly, developed his theory of natural selection in 1838 and set it forth in two unpublished sketches of 1842 and 1844. Then, never doubting his theory for a moment, but afraid to expose its revolutionary implications, he proceeded to stew, dither, wait, ponder, and collect data for another fifteen years. Finally, at the virtual insistence of his closest friends, he began to work over his notes, intending to publish a massive tome that would have been four times as long as the *Origin of Species*. But, in 1858, Darwin received a letter and manuscript from a young naturalist, Alfred Russel Wallace, who had independently constructed the theory of natural selection while lying ill with malaria on an island in the Malay Archipelago. Darwin was stunned by the detailed similarity. Wallace even claimed inspiration from the same nonbiological source—Malthus' *Essay on Population*. Darwin, in great anxiety, made the expected gesture of magnanimity, but devoutly hoped that some way might be found to preserve his legitimate priority. He wrote to Lyell: "I would far rather burn my whole book, than that he or any other man should think that I have behaved in a paltry spirit." But he added a suggestion: "If I could honorably publish, I would state that I was induced now to publish a sketch . . . from Wallace having sent me an outline of my general conclusions." Lyell and Hooker took the bait and came to Darwin's rescue. While Darwin stayed home, mourning the death of his young child from scarlet fever, they presented a joint paper to the Linnaean Society containing an excerpt from Darwin's 1844 essay together with Wallace's manuscript. A year later, Darwin published his feverishly compiled "abstract" of the longer work—the *Origin of Species*. Wallace had been eclipsed.

Wallace has come down through history as Darwin's shadow. In public and private, Darwin was infallibly decent and generous to his younger colleague. He wrote to Wallace in 1870: "I hope it is a satisfaction to you to reflect—and very few things in my life have been more satisfactory to me— that we have never felt any jealousy towards each other, though in one sense rivals." Wallace, in return, was consistently deferential. In 1864, he wrote to Darwin: "As to the theory of Natural Selection itself, I shall always maintain it to be actually yours and yours only. You had worked it out in details I had never thought of, years before I had a ray of light on the subject, and my paper would never have convinced anybody or been noticed as more than an ingenious speculation, whereas your book has revolutionized the study of Natural History, and carried away captive the best men of the present age."

This genuine affection and mutual support masked a serious disagreement on what may be the fundamental question in evolutionary theory— both then and today. How exclusive is natural selection as an agent of evolutionary change? Must all features of organisms be viewed as adaptations? Yet Wallace's role as Darwin's subordinate alter ego is so firmly fixed in popular accounts that few students of evolution are even aware that they ever differed on theoretical questions. Moreover, in the one specific area where their public disagreement is a matter of record—the origin of human intellect—many writers have told the story backwards because they failed to locate this debate in the context of a more general disagreement on the power of natural selection.

All subtle ideas can be trivialized, even vulgarized, by portrayal in uncompromising and absolute terms. Marx felt compelled to deny that he was a marxist, while Einstein contended with the serious misstatement that he meant to say "all is relative." Darwin lived to see his name appropriated for an extreme view that he never held—for "Darwinism" has often been defined, both in his day and in our own, as the belief that virtually all evolutionary change is the product of natural selection. In fact Darwin often complained, with uncharacteristic bitterness, about this misappropriation of his name. He wrote in the last edition of the *Origin* (1872): "As my conclusions have lately been much misrepresented, and it has been stated that I attribute the modification of species exclusively to natural selection, I may be permitted to remark that in the first edition of this work, and subsequently, I placed in a most conspicuous position—namely, at the close of the Introduction—the following words: 'I am convinced that natural selection has been the main but not the exclusive means of modification.' This has been of no avail. Great is the power of steady misrepresentation."

However, England did house a small group of strict selectionists—"Darwinians" in the misappropriated sense—and Alfred Russel Wallace was their leader. These biologists did attribute all evolutionary change to natural selection. They viewed each bit of morphology, each function of an organ, each behavior as an adaptation, a product of selection leading to a "better" organism. They held a deep belief in nature's "rightness," in the exquisite fit of all creatures to their environments. In a curious sense, they almost reintroduced the creationist notion of natural harmony by substituting an omnipotent force of natural selection for a benevolent deity. Darwin, on the other hand, was a consistent pluralist gazing upon a messier universe. He saw much fit and harmony, for he believed that natural selection holds pride of place among evolutionary forces. But other processes work as well, and organisms display an array of features that are not adaptations and do not promote survival directly. Darwin emphasized two principles leading to nonadaptive change: (1) organisms are integrated systems and adaptive change in one part can lead to nonadaptive modifications of other features ("correlations of growth" in Darwin's phrase); (2) an organ built under the influence of selection for a specific role may be able, as a consequence of its structure, to perform many other, unselected functions as well.

Wallace stated the hard hyper-selectionist line—"pure Darwinism" in his terms—in an early article of 1867, calling it "a necessary deduction from the theory of natural selection."

> None of the definite facts of organic selection, no special organ, no characteristic form or marking, no peculiarities of instinct or of habit, no relations between species or between groups of species, can exist but which must now be, or once have been, useful to the individuals or races which possess them.

Indeed, he argued later, any apparent nonutility must only reflect our faulty knowledge—a remarkable argument since it renders the principle of utility impervious to disproof a priori: "The assertion of 'inutility' in the case of any organ . . . is not, and can never be, the statement of a fact, but merely an expression of our ignorance of its purpose or origin."

All the public and private arguments that Darwin pursued with Wallace centered upon their differing assessments of the power of natural selection. They first crossed swords on the issue of "sexual selection," the subsidiary process that Darwin had proposed in order to explain the origin of features that appeared to be irrelevant or even harmful in the usual "struggle for existence" (expressed primarily in feeding and defense), but that could be interpreted as devices for increasing success in mating—elaborate antlers of deer, or tail feathers of the peacock, for example. Darwin proposed two kinds of sexual selection—competition among males for access to females, and choice exercised by females themselves. He attributed much of the racial differentiation among modern humans to sexual selection, based upon different criteria of beauty that arose among various peoples. (His book on human evolution—The *Descent of Man* (1871)—is really an amalgam of two works: a long treatise on sexual selection throughout the animal kingdom, and a shorter speculative account of human origins, relying heavily upon sexual selection.)

The notion of sexual selection is not really contrary to natural selection, for it is just another route to the Darwinian imperative of differential reproductive success. But Wallace disliked sexual selection for three reasons: it compromised the generality of that peculiarly nineteenth-century view of natural selection as a battle for life itself, not merely for copulation; it placed altogether too much emphasis upon the "volition" of animals, particularly in the concept of female choice; and, most importantly, it permitted the development of numerous, important features that are irrelevant, if not actually harmful, to the operation of an organism as a well-designed machine. Thus, Wallace viewed sexual selection as a threat to his vision of animals as works of exquisite craftsmanship, wrought by the purely material force of natural selection. (Indeed, Darwin had developed the concept largely to explain why so many differences among human groups are irrelevant to survival based upon good design, but merely reflect the variety of capricious criteria for beauty that arose for no adaptive reason among various races. Wallace did accept sexual selection based upon male combat as close enough to the metaphor of battle that controlled his concept of natural selection. But he rejected the notion of female choice, and greatly distressed Darwin with his speculative attempts to attribute all features arising from it to the adaptive action of natural selection.)

In 1870, as he prepared the *Descent of Man*, Darwin wrote to Wallace: "I grieve to differ from you, and it actually terrifies me and makes me constantly distrust myself. I fear we shall never quite understand each other." He struggled to understand Wallace's reluctance and even to accept his friend's faith in unalloyed natural selection: "You will be pleased to hear," he wrote to Wallace, "that I am undergoing severe distress about protection and sexual selection; this morning I oscillated with joy towards you; this evening I have swung back to [my] old position, out of which I fear I shall never get."

But the debate on sexual selection was merely a prelude to a much more serious and famous disagreement on that most emotional and contentious subject of all —human origins. In short, Wallace, the hyper-selectionist, the man who had twitted Darwin for his unwillingness to see the action of natural selection in every nuance of organic form, halted abruptly before the human brain. Our intellect and morality, Wallace argued, could not be the product of natural selection; therefore, since natural selection is evolution's only way, some higher power—God, to put it directly—must have intervened to construct this latest and greatest of organic innovations.

If Darwin had been distressed by his failure to impress Wallace with sexual selection, he was now positively aghast at Wallace's abrupt about-face at the finish line itself. He wrote to Wallace in 1869: "I hope you have not murdered too completely your own and my child." A month later, he remonstrated: "If you had not told me, I should have thought that [your remarks on Man] had been added by some one else. As you expected, I differ grievously from you, and I am very sorry for it." Wallace, sensitive to the rebuke, thereafter referred to his theory of human intellect as "my special heresy."

The conventional account of Wallace's apostasy at the brink of complete consistency cites a failure of courage to take the last step and admit man fully into the natural system—a step that Darwin took with commendable fortitude in two books, the *Descent of Man* (1871) and the *Expression of the Emotions* (1872). Thus, Wallace emerges from most historical accounts as a lesser man than Darwin for one (or more) of three reasons, all related to his position on the origins of human intellect: for simple cowardice; for inability to transcend the constraints of culture and traditional views of human uniqueness; and for inconsistency in advocating natural selection so strongly (in the debate on sexual selection), yet abandoning it at the most crucial moment of all.

I cannot analyze Wallace's psyche, and will not comment on his deeper motives for holding fast to the unbridgeable gap between human intellect and the behavior of mere animals. But I can assess the logic of his argument, and recognize that the traditional account of it is not only incorrect, but precisely backwards. Wallace did not abandon natural selection at the human threshold. Rather, it was his peculiarly rigid view of natural selection that led him, quite consistently, to reject it for the human mind. His position never varied—natural selection is the only cause of major evolutionary change. His two debates with Darwin—sexual selection and the origin of human intellect—represent the same argument, not an inconsistent Wallace championing selection in one case and running from it in the other. Wallace's error on human intellect arose from the inadequacy of his rigid selectionism, not from a failure to apply it. And his argument repays our study today, since its flaw persists as the weak link in many of the most "modern" evolutionary speculations of our current literature. For Wallace's rigid selectionism is much closer than Darwin's pluralism to the attitude embodied in our favored theory today, which, ironically in this context, goes by the name of "Neo-Darwinism."

Wallace advanced several arguments for the uniqueness of human intellect, but his central claim begins with an extremely uncommon position for his time, one that commands our highest praise in retrospect. Wallace was one of the few nonracists of the nineteenth century. He really believed that all human groups had innately equal capacities of intellect. Wallace defended his decidedly unconventional egalitarianism with two arguments, anatomical and cultural. He claimed, first of all, that the brains of "savages" are neither much smaller nor more poorly organized than our own: "In the brain of the lowest savages, and, as far as we know, of the prehistoric races, we have an organ . . . little inferior in size and complexity to that of the highest type." Moreover, since cultural conditioning can integrate the rudest savage into our most courtly life, the rudeness itself must arise from a failure to use existing capacities, not from their absence: "It is latent in the lower races, since under European training native military bands have been formed in many parts of the world, which have been able to perform creditably the best modern music."

Of course, in calling Wallace a nonracist, I do not mean to imply that he regarded the cultural practices of all peoples as equal in intrinsic worth. Wallace, like most of his contemporaries, was a cultural chauvinist who did not doubt the evident superiority of European ways. He may have been bullish on the capability of "savages," but he certainly had a low opinion of their life, as he mistook it: "Our law, our government, and our science continually require us to reason through a variety of complicated phenomena to the expected result. Even our games, such as chess, compel us to exercise all these faculties in a remarkable degree. Compare this with the savage languages, which contain no words for abstract conceptions; the utter want of foresight of the savage man beyond his simplest necessities; his inability to combine, or to compare, or to reason on any general subject that does not immediately appeal to his senses."

Hence, Wallace's dilemma: all "savages," from our actual ancestors to modern survivors, had brains fully capable of developing and appreciating all the finest subtleties of European art, morality and philosophy; yet they used, in the state of nature, only the tiniest fraction of that capacity in constructing their rudimentary cultures, with impoverished languages and repugnant morality.

But natural selection can only fashion a feature for immediate use. The brain is vastly overdesigned for what it accomplished in primitive society; thus, natural selection could not have built it:

A brain one-half larger than that of the gorilla would . . . fully have sufficed for the limited mental development of the savage; and we must therefore admit that the large brain he actually possesses could never have been solely developed by any of those laws of evolution, whose essence is, that they lead to a degree of organization exactly proportionate to the wants of each species, never beyond those wants. . . . Natural selection could only have endowed savage man with a brain a few degrees superior to that of an ape, whereas he actually possesses one very little inferior to that of a philosopher.

Wallace did not confine this general argument to abstract intellect, but extended it to all aspects of European "refinement," to language and music in particular. Consider his views on "the wonderful power, range, flexibility, and sweetness of the musical sounds producible by the human larynx, especially in the female sex."

The habits of savages give no indication of how this faculty could have been developed by natural selection, because it is never required or used by them. The singing of savages is a more or less monotonous howling, and the females seldom sing at all. Savages certainly never choose their wives for fine voices, but for rude health, and strength, and physical beauty. Sexual selection could not therefore have developed this wonderful power, which only comes into play among civilized people. It seems as if the organ had been prepared in anticipation of the future progress in man, since it contains latest capacities which are useless to him in his earlier condition.

Finally, if our higher capacities arose before we used or needed them, then they cannot be the product of natural selection. And, if they originated in anticipation of a higher intelligence: "The inference I would draw from this class of phenomena is, that a superior intelligence has guided the development of man in a definite direction, and for a special purpose." Wallace had rejoined the camp of natural theology and Darwin remonstrated, failed to budge his partner, and finally lamented.

The fallacy of Wallace's argument is not a simple unwillingness to extend evolution to humans, but rather the hyper-selectionism that permeated all his evolutionary thought. For if hyper-selectionism is valid—if every part of every creature is fashioned for and only for its immediate use—then Wallace cannot be gainsaid. The earliest Cro-Magnon people, with brains bigger than our own, produced stunning paintings in their caves, but did not write symphonies or build computers. All that we have accomplished since then is the product of cultural evolution based on a brain of unvarying capacity. In Wallace's view, that brain could not be the product of natural selection, since it always possessed capacities so far in excess of its original function.

But hyper-selectionism is not valid. It is a caricature of Darwin's subtler view, and it both ignores and misunderstands the nature of organic form and function. Natural selection may build an organ "for" a specific function or group of functions. But this "purpose" need not fully specify the capacity of that organ. Objects designed for definite purposes can, as a result of their structural complexity, perform many other tasks as well. A factory may install a computer only to issue the monthly pay checks, but such a machine can also analyze the election returns or whip anyone's ass (or at least perpetually tie them) in tic-tack-toe. Our large brains may have originated "for" some set of necessary skills in gathering food, socializing, or whatever; but these skills do not exhaust the limits of what such a complex machine can do. Fortunately for us, those limits include, among other things, an ability to write, from shopping lists for all of us to grand opera for a few. And our larynx may have arisen "for" a limited range of articulated sound needed to coordinate social life. But its physical design permits us to do more with it, from singing in the shower for all to the occasional diva.

Hyper-selectionism has been with us for a long time in various guises; for it represents the late nineteenth century's scientific version of the myth of natural harmony—all is for the best in the best of all possible worlds (all structures well designed for a definite purpose in this case). It is, indeed, the vision of foolish Dr. Pangloss, so vividly satirized by Voltaire in *Candide*—the world is not necessarily good, but it is the best we could possibly have. As the good doctor said in a famous passage that predated Wallace by a century, but captures the essence of what is so deeply wrong with his argument: "Things cannot be other than they are. . . . Everything is made for the best purpose. Our noses were made to carry spectacles, so we have spectacles. Legs were clearly intended for breeches, and we wear them." Nor is Panglossianism dead today—not when so many books in the pop literature on human behavior state that we evolved our big brain "for" hunting and then trace all our current ills to limits of thought and emotion supposedly imposed by such a mode of life.

Ironically then, Wallace's hyper-selectionism led right back to the basic belief of the creationism that it meant to replace—a faith in the "rightness" of things, a definite place for each object in an integrated whole. As Wallace wrote, quite unfairly, of Darwin:

> He whose teachings were at first stigmatized as degrading or even atheistical, by devoting to the varied phenomena of living things the loving, patient, and reverent study of one who really had faith in the beauty and harmony and perfection of creation, was enabled to bring to light innumerable adaptations, and to prove that the most insignificant parts of the meanest living things had a use and a purpose.

I do not deny that nature has its harmonies. But structure also has its latent capacities. Built for one thing, it can do others—and in this flexibility lies both the messiness and the hope of our lives.

Questions for Discussion

1. Gould's first two paragraphs seem to be a fairly chatty introduction to the rest of the essay. Explain why this introduction is or is not effective. Can you suggest a better introduction?

2. Contrast the first two paragraphs and the concluding paragraph. Why do you think that the final paragraph is so short? Do you feel that the concluding paragraph raises unresolved issues? Explain.

3. In the paragraph (p. 310) beginning "However, England did house a small group of strict selectionists," Gould characterizes Wallace's view of the universe as one believing in "nature's 'rightness,' in the exquisite fit of all creatures to their environments," and Darwin's as "gazing upon a messier universe." Explain why some individuals or groups today could be characterized as Wallace-ites in their beliefs about the universe and why others might be characterized as Darwinian.

4. Gould claims that scientific discoveries are, in part, a result of the current culture. Do you agree? Explain. Can you give examples of discoveries that are clearly a result of culture?

5. Explain the fallacy of "hyper-selectionism." What were its consequences in Wallace's reasoning? (On page 309, Gould says, "All subtle ideas can be trivialized, even vulgarized, by portrayal in uncompromising and absolute terms. Marx felt compelled to deny that he was a marxist, while Einstein contended with the serious misstatement that he meant to say 'all is relative.' " What can a person who writes about science learn from Gould's analysis of hyper-selectionism?

6. In your own words, explain "what may be the fundamental question in evolutionary theory. . . . How exclusive is natural selection as an agent of evolutionary change?"

7. Explain why Wallace's "logic" led him to conclude that human intellect could not be the result of the process of natural selection.

8. Explain "Panglossianism."

9. What does the following sentence tell you about Charles Darwin's personality? "Then, never doubting his theory for a moment, but afraid to expose its revolutionary implications, he proceeded to stew, dither, wait, ponder, and collect data for another fifteen years."

GARY ZUKAV

The Dancing Wu Li Masters, *from which "General Nonsense" was taken, is a book about physics and consciousness, conceived at an Esalen Institute conference on that subject in 1976.*

The following selection is an extended definition, *an explanatory device that is essential when a writer is attempting to introduce readers to complex and unfamiliar subject matter. You can view this definition as a "preface" to the selection that follows, Nigel Calder's account of the search for black holes.*

General Nonsense

In 1958, David Finkelstein published a paper in which he theorized, on the basis of Einstein's general theory of relativity, a phenomenon that he called a "one-way membrane." Finkelstein showed that under certain conditions involving an extremely dense gravitational field, an invisible threshold can occur into which light and physical objects can enter, but from which they never again can escape.*

The following year, a young graduate student at the University of London heard Finkelstein, who was speaking there as a guest lecturer, explain his one-way membrane. The idea caught his attention and then his imagination. The young student was Roger Penrose. Expanding on Finkelstein's discovery, he developed it into the modern theory of the "Black Hole."†

A black hole is an area of space which appears absolutely black because the gravitation there is so intense that not even light can escape into the surrounding areas.‡ Gravitation is negligible on the laboratory level, but quite important when bodies of large mass are concerned. Therefore, the exploration of black holes naturally became a joint venture of physicists and astronomers.

Astronomers speculated that a black hole may be one of several possible products of stellar evolution. Stars do not burn indefinitely. They evolve through a life cycle which begins with hydrogen gas and sometimes ends with a very dense, burned-out, rotating mass. The exact end product of this process depends upon the size of the star undergoing it. According to one theory, stars which are about three times the size of our sun or larger end up as black holes. The remains of such stars are unimaginably dense. They may be only a few miles in diameter and yet contain the entire mass of a star three times larger than the sun. Such a dense mass produces a gravitational field strong enough to pull everything in its vicinity into it, while at the same time allowing nothing, not even light, to escape from it.

Excerpt from *The Dancing Wu Li Masters* by Gary Zukav. Copyright © 1979 by Gary Zukav by permission of William Morrow & Company.

*This phenomenon was theorized by Pierre-Simon La Place in 1795 using Newtonian physics. Finkelstein was the first physicist to formulate it from the modern point of view, i.e., relativity theory. This modern formulation triggered the current theories on the black hole.

†The very first modern paper on black holes was done by J. R. Oppenheimer and S. Snyder in 1939. The current theories of the black hole, i.e., black hole singularities which are beyond space-time, were developed independently by R. Penrose and S. W. Hawking.

‡To a first approximation. Physicists currently theorize that black holes actually shine due to photons and other particles quantum-tunneling out of the one-way membranes.

Surrounding this remainder of a star is an "event horizon." An event horizon is created by the enormous gravitational field of the burned-out star. It functions precisely like Finkelstein's one-way membrane. Anything within the gravitational field of this mass quickly is pulled toward it, and once past the event horizon, never can return. It is the event horizon which constitutes the essential feature of the black hole. What happens to an object that passes through an event horizon is even more fantastic than the wildest (currently) science fiction.

If the black hole is not rotating, the object will be pulled directly to the center of the black hole to a point called the singularity. There it literally will be squeezed out of existence, or as physicists say, to zero volume. At the black hole singularity all of the laws of physics break down completely, and even space and time disappear. It is speculated that everything which is sucked into a black hole is spilled out again on "the other side"—the "other side" being another universe!

If the black hole is rotating, an object that is sucked into the event horizon could miss the black hole singularity (which is shaped like a "ring" in a rotating black hole) and emerge into another time and another place in this universe (through "wormholes"), or into another universe (through "Einstein-Rosen bridges"). In this way, rotating black holes may be the ultimate time machines.

Although black holes are almost invisible, we can search for observable phenomena that may be characteristic of them. The first of these is a large amount of electromagnetic radiation. A black hole continuously attracts hydrogen atoms, cosmic particles, and everything else to it. As these particles and objects are drawn to the black hole, they steadily accelerate through its gravitational field until they approach the velocity of light itself. This causes tremendous amounts of electromagnetic radiation. (Any accelerating charged particle creates electromagnetic radiation.)

The second observable characteristic of an invisible black hole is its effect on a nearby visible star. If a visible star can be found which moves as though it were revolving around an invisible star (i.e., as though it were half of a binary star system), we might speculate that it actually *is* revolving around an invisible star, and that its invisible partner is a black hole.

NIGEL CALDER (1931–   )

Nigel Calder was born in London and studied at Cambridge
University, where he received both a bachelor's and a master's
degree. He began his career as a staff writer for the New Scientist,
which he eventually edited from 1962 to 1966. Mr. Calder is the
author and editor of more than twenty books dealing with the
sciences, written often in conjunction with television documentaries
that he has produced with either the British Broadcasting
Corporation or the Public Broadcasting System. Einstein's Universe,
from which the following selection is taken, is one such work.
Although his scientific interests are diverse, Calder shows a penchant
for speculative writing based on the most current scientific thought,
having written, for example, about colonization of outer space,
nuclear war, and global weather shifts. He won UNESCO's Kalinga
Prize for the Popularization of Science in 1972.

In recounting the history of how black holes were discovered,
Calder explains and illustrates the scientific method: formulating a
problem, collecting data through observation and experimentation,
and forming and testing hypotheses. The essay is, then, another
example of how narrative can serve as the basis for presenting
concepts as well as stories.

As you read "Cosmic Whirlwind," think about the issues raised
by critic Eliot Fremont-Smith, who says about Calder's explanation
of Einstein's theory of relativity,

> The trouble is that at crucial points it isn't simple at all; it's
> horrendously complex, convoluted, and contradictory. This makes one
> fret—not so much over the difficulties of relativity as over the
> accumulating evidence that, as a layman, one isn't measuring up.

Cosmic Whirlwind

A recent and spectacular example of Einstein's ideas in action is the explanation they offer for a stupendous whirlwind of stars discovered in the galaxy M87. 'M' stands for Charles Messier who hunted comets from a tower in Paris 200 years ago. To avoid wasting time on fuzzy objects in the sky that were *not* comets, he decided to map them, to be rid of them as it were. In 1784 Messier published a catalogue of about a hundred of these annoying smudges. They are now known to include the most fascinating objects in the sky. Quite unaware that he would be remembered for his catalogue more than for his comets, Messier resumed his main work as an industrious inhabitant of Isaac Newton's universe, in which comets were the most amazing phenomena.

At Kitt Peak in Arizona in the late 1970s a group of astronomers used the 150-inch telescope to peer into the heart of M87, one of Messier's discarded objects lying in the constellation of Virgo. From London, Alec Boksenberg and Keith Shortridge had brought special electronic equipment capable of counting individual particles of light gathered from the depths of space. Another Englishman, Wallace Sargent, had joined them from the California Institute of Technology. Roger Lynds, an American astronomer based at Kitt Peak, and David Hartwick from Canada completed the observing team. They were all inhabitants of Albert Einstein's universe, wherein the prodigies were not comets but black holes.

When Einstein promulgated his law of gravity in 1915, the possibility of nature creating black holes—dark pitfalls in space from which nothing could ever escape—was implicit in the equations. And in April 1978 the Kitt Peak team announced evidence for the existence of a giant black hole in the heart of M87. It was a shocking thing, billions of times more massive than the Sun and capable of gobbling entire stars or clusters of stars, with ease.

As a galaxy, M87 is a vast agglomeration of stars like the Milky Way, the discus-like galaxy of which the Sun is a modest member among hundreds of billions of other stars. But M87 is even bigger, and more ball-like. It is a conspicuous member of a collection of galaxies known as the Virgo Cluster, which sprawls across a large area of the sky comparatively close to us. By present estimates M87 is about 50 million light-years away—that is to say, the light entering a telescope tonight, travelling at 186,000 miles a second, had to set off on its journey from M87 more than 50 million years ago, when our ancestors were primitive tree-dwelling primates. The astronomers' use of the travel-time of light to judge distances was ready-made for the marriage of space and time at which Einstein officiated. And his cosmic equations of 1917 implied that the whole universe could be expanding, with galaxies moving apart at high speed. That turned out to be the case and M87 is travelling away from us at a speed of about 700 miles per second.

In a minority of galaxies, astronomers discern great upheavals. M87 is one of the closest of these special objects. When radio astronomy began in earnest after the second World War, M87 was one of the first objects detected as a strong source of radio waves. Looking more intently, optical astronomers made out a faint luminous jet protruding from the galaxy like a lollipop stick a billion billion miles long, and blue in colour. Two decades later, when rockets and satellites going above the Earth's atmosphere detected X-rays coming from various directions in the sky, many of the X-ray sources were inside the Milky Way Galaxy; but M87 was one of the most conspicuous X-ray sources beyond it.

Altogether, M87 was very energetic. Yet it was a comparatively mild-mannered member of those special classes of galaxies which plainly radiated far more energy than they ought to—more energy, that is to say, than could be accounted for by the ordinary burning of all the stars of which they were composed. These exploding galaxies seemed to be related to the quasars which were discovered in the early 1960s: very small, distant objects, also giving off intense energy. What could be powering such violent eruptions far away in space? The theorists canvassed all sorts of ideas, from catastrophic collisions between large numbers of stars to the action of 'anti-matter', which is capable of annihilating ordinary matter. Einstein's theory of gravity came to the rescue and in the 1970s the opinion of many astronomers hardened in favour of black holes as the energy-source of exploding galaxies and quasars.

The idea was that a great star-swallower lay in the heart of a galaxy. When stars or gas came close to it they swirled in, faster and faster, like water approaching a plug-hole. The falling matter would radiate ever-more-intense energy, up to the moment of oblivion. This process could also hurl out jets of matter from the whirlpool. The small-looking quasars were interpreted as very distant exploding galaxies, in which the central turmoil was intense enough to be plain even when the outlying stars were far too faint to be seen.

The team at Kitt Peak wanted to know how fast the stars in M87 were moving. The stars of any galaxy orbit around its centre, in much the same way as the Earth travels around the Sun; the Sun and we with it are orbiting around the centre of the Milky Way at 170 miles per second. If there is a massive collection of matter at the core of a galaxy, stars near to the core will move faster in their orbits. Discover the speed of the innermost stars of the galaxy and you can, in effect, 'weigh' the core.

That required a precision impossible before Boksenberg developed his electronic light-detector in 1973. It is called the image photon counting system; it registers individual particles of light, or photons, when they dislodge electrons from a sensitive surface exposed to the light. Einstein's interpretation of this 'photo-electric effect' established the modern view of the nature of light and the energy it carries; he was the discoverer of the photons that Boksenberg counted.

In M87 the astronomers looked for a smearing or de-tuning of the frequencies of particular kinds of light. Break up starlight into a spectrum, like a rainbow, red at one side and blue at the other; you will then see dark or bright lines at particular positions along the spectrum. They are like stations on a radio tuning dial and these lines correspond to light of precise frequencies absorbed or emitted by particular kinds of atoms in the stars. But for stars in rapid motion, like those swirling around the centre of M87, the frequency of the light changes. Peter Young at the California Institute of Technology used the results from Kitt Peak to build up a picture of the galaxy. The stars near the core of M87 were orbiting at about 250 miles per second. The mass of the core, necessary to sustain such motions, was 5000 million times heavier than the Sun. If there was an enormous number of stars at the core, corresponding to that mass, the heart of the galaxy would be very bright indeed. If, perhaps, dust were obscuring the view, you would expect the light to be reddened, like the Sun at sunset. But in the core of M87 the astronomers saw neither a dazzling mass of stars, nor a dusty red effulgence, but a lacklustre glow with a bluish tinge. In short, the appearance of the core contradicted the calculation of its mass unless it contained a black hole.

The Kitt Peak observations of M87 indicated that the central mass was confined within a region with a diameter of 700 light-years at the most—already a tight enough squeeze for the putative billions of stars. But if the black-hole theory is right the entire mass must in reality lie inside a sphere only about one light-day in diameter. Before the end of 1978, Boksenberg took his electronic detector to the 200-inch telescope on Palomar mountain in California, for an even closer look at M87, while Sargent also turned to a worldwide combination of radio telescopes, in Spain and California, to try to narrow down the region of the central mass. Thus did Einstein's theories continue to inspire and instruct the most modern research.

If you are puzzling out the origin of the energy in M87, or in any other violent object in the universe, you have a cosmic rule of thumb. The equivalence of mass and energy, as specified by Einstein, prescribes the maximum energy extractable from any aggregation of matter whatsoever. His formula $E = mc^2$, still amazing and frightening more than seventy years after he wrote it down, will be the subject of the next chapter.

Questions for Discussion

1. The cover of *Einstein's Universe*, from which the selection by Calder was taken, claims that it presents "relativity made plain." Can a skilled writer make any subject understandable to generally educated readers? If your answer is yes, explain why you think that such a "translation" is possible. If your answer is no, explain what you think is lost in the "translation."

2. Point out at least five instances of metaphorical language Calder uses to present a scientific concept, as in the first sentence: "stupendous whirlwind of stars." How do these metaphors help you understand the concepts the author discusses?

3. In your own words, explain the metaphor "the marriage of space and time at which Einstein officiated."

4. Explain why Zukav's explanation of "event horizon" (pages 318–319) does or does not satisfy you. Would it be satisfactory for an expert in the field of astrophysics?

DOUGLAS RICHARD HOFSTADTER (1945–   )

Hofstadter, the son of a professor, was born in New York City. He received his B.S. (with distinction) from Stanford in 1965 and took his M.S. (1972) and Ph.D. (1975) at the University of Oregon. He is currently on the faculty of Indiana University, where he teaches computer science. Hofstadter is an accomplished pianist and a polyglot fluent in French and able to speak German, Italian, Spanish, and Swedish.

Goedel, Escher, and Bach: An Eternal Golden Braid, from which the following selection is taken, won the Pulitzer Prize for nonfiction and the American Book Award, both in 1980. In the book, Hofstadter argues that if we truly understand any process that demands thought—that is, intellect—we can write a computer program that will be a model of that process. For instance, if we truly understood the nature of human language, we could construct a computer that would use language in a way identical with human language use—a HAL, like the computer in "2001."

In this selection, a masterly "translation" of scientific thought, you will find a mathematical argument explained in natural language, succinctly and clearly. Hofstadter subtly raises philosophical questions regarding knowledge: How much must be assumed as self-evident, and how much can be proved?

The Basic Laws of Arithmetic

Suppose that you lay down a few sticks:

$$/ \ // \ //// \ / \ /$$

Now you count them. At the same time, somebody else counts them, but starting from the other end. Is it clear that the two of you will get the same answer? The result of a counting process is independent of the way in which it is done. This is really an assumption about what counting is. It would be senseless to try to prove it, because it is so basic; either you see it or you don't—but in the latter case, a proof won't help you a bit.

From this kind of assumption, one can get to the commutativity and associativity of addition (i.e., first that $b+c=c+b$ always, and second that $b+(c+d)=(b+c)+d$ always). The same assumption can also lead you to the commutativity and associativity of multiplication; just think of many cubes assembled to form a large rectangular solid. Multiplicative commutativity and associativity are just the assumptions that when you rotate the solid in various ways, the number of cubes will not change. Now these assumptions are not verifiable in all possible cases, because the number of such cases is infinite. We take them for granted; we believe them (if we ever think about them) as deeply as we could believe anything. The amount of money in our pocket will not change as we walk down the street, jostling it up and down; the number of books we have will not change if we pack them up in a box, load them into our car, drive one hundred miles, unload the box, unpack it, and place the books in a new shelf. All of this is part of what we mean by *number*.

There are certain types of people who, as soon as some undeniable fact is written down, find it amusing to show why that "fact" is false after all. I am such a person, and as soon as I had written down the examples above involving sticks, money, and books, I invented situations in which they were wrong. You may have done the same. It goes to show that numbers as abstractions are really quite different from the everyday numbers which we use.

People enjoy inventing slogans which violate basic arithmetic but which illustrate "deeper" truths, such as "1 and 1 make 1" (for lovers), or "1 plus 1 plus 1 equals 1" (the Trinity). You can easily pick holes in those slogans, showing why, for instance, using the plus-sign is inappropriate in both cases. But such cases proliferate. Two raindrops running down a windowpane merge; does one plus one make one? A cloud breaks up into two clouds—more evidence for the same? It is not at all easy to draw a sharp line between cases where what is happening could be called "addition," and where some other word is wanted. If you think about the question, you will probably come up with some criterion involving separation of the objects in space, and making sure each one is clearly distinguishable from all the others. But then how could one count ideas? Or the number of gases comprising the atmosphere? Somewhere, if you try to look it up, you can probably find a statement such as, "There are 17 languages in India, and 462 dialects." There is something strange about precise statements like that, when the concepts "language" and "dialect" are themselves fuzzy.

Ideal Numbers

Numbers as realities misbehave. However, there is an ancient and innate sense in people that numbers ought not to misbehave. There is something clean and pure in the abstract notion of number, removed from counting beads, dialects, or clouds; and there ought to be a way of talking about numbers without always having the silliness of reality come in and intrude. The hard-edged rules that govern "ideal" numbers constitute arithmetic, and their more advanced consequences constitute number theory. There is only one relevant question to be asked, in making the transition from numbers as practical things to numbers as formal things. Once you have decided to try to capsulize all of number theory in an ideal system, is it really possible to do the job completely? Are numbers so clean and crystalline and regular that their nature can be completely captured in the rules of a formal system?

When I speak of the properties of natural numbers, I don't just mean properties such as the sum of a particular pair of integers. That can be found out by counting, and anybody who has grown up in this century cannot doubt the mechanizability of such processes as counting, adding, multiplying, and so on. I mean the kinds of properties which mathematicians are interested in exploring, questions for which no counting-process is sufficient to provide the answer—not even theoretically sufficient. Let us take a classic example of such a property of natural numbers. The statement is: "There are infinitely many prime numbers." First of all, there is no counting process which will ever be able to confirm, or refute, this assertion. The best we could do would be to count primes for a while and concede that there are "a lot." But no amount of counting alone would ever resolve the question of whether the number of primes is finite or infinite. There could always be more. The statement—and it is called "Euclid's Theorem" (notice the capital "T")—is quite unobvious. It may seem reasonable, or appealing, but it is not obvious. However, mathematicians since Euclid have always called it true. What is the reason?

Euclid's Proof

The reason is that *reasoning* tells them it is so. Let us follow the reasoning involved. We will look at a variant of Euclid's proof. This proof works by showing that whatever number you pick, there is a prime larger than it. Pick a number—N. Multiply all the positive integers starting with 1 and ending with N; in other words, form the factorial of N, written "$N!$". What you get is divisible by every number up to N. When you add 1 to $N!$, the result

> can't be a multiple of 2 (because it leaves 1 over, when you divide by 2);
>
> can't be a multiple of 3 (because it leaves 1 over, when you divide by 3);
>
> can't be a multiple of 4 (because it leaves 1 over, when you divide by 4);
>
> can't be a multiple of N (because it leaves 1 over when you divide by N);

In other words, $N! + 1$, if it is divisible at all (other than by 1 and itself), only is divisible by numbers greater than N. So either it is itself prime, or its prime divisors are greater than N. But in either case we've shown there must exist a prime above N. The process holds no matter what number N is. Whatever N is, there is a prime greater than N. And thus ends the demonstration of the infinitude of the primes.

This last step, incidentally, is called *generalization*, and we will meet it again later in a more formal context. It is where we phrase an argument in terms of a single number (N), and then point out that N was unspecified and therefore the argument is a general one.

Euclid's proof is typical of what constitutes "real mathematics." It is simple, compelling, and beautiful. It illustrates that by taking several rather short steps one can get a long way from one's starting point. In our case, the starting points are basic ideas about multiplication and division and so forth. The short steps are the steps of reasoning. And though every individual step of the reasoning seems obvious, the end result is not obvious. We can never check directly whether the statement is true or not; yet we believe it, because we believe in reasoning. If you accept reasoning, there seems to be no escape route; once you agree to hear Euclid out, you'll have to agree with his conclusion. That's most fortunate—because it means that mathematicians will always agree on what statements to label "true," and what statements to label "false."

This proof exemplifies an orderly thought process. Each statement is related to previous ones in an irresistible way. This is why it is called a "proof" rather than just "good evidence." In mathematics the goal is always to give an ironclad proof for some unobvious statement. The very fact of the steps being linked together in an ironclad way suggests that there may be a *patterned structure* binding these statements together. This structure can best be exposed by finding a new vocabulary—a stylized vocabulary, consisting of symbols—suitable only for expressing statements about numbers. Then we can look at the proof as it exists in its translated version. It will be a set of statements which are related, line by line, in some detectable way. But the statements, since they're represented by means of a small and stylized set of symbols, take on the aspect of *patterns*. In other words, though when read aloud, they seem to be statements about numbers and their properties, still when looked at on paper, they seem to be abstract patterns—and the line-by-line structure of the proof may start to look like a slow transformation of patterns according to some few typographical rules.

Getting Around Infinity

Although Euclid's proof is a proof that *all* numbers have a certain property, it avoids treating each of the infinitely many cases separately. It gets around it by using phrases like "whatever N is," or "no matter what number N is." We could also phrase the proof over again, so that it uses the phrase "all N." By knowing the appropriate context and correct ways of using such phrases, we never have to deal with infinitely many statements. We deal with just two or three concepts, such as the word "all"—which, though themselves finite, embody an infinitude; and by using them, we sidestep the apparent problem that there are an infinite number of facts we want to prove.

We use the word "all" in a few ways which are defined by the thought processes of reasoning. That is, there are *rules* which our usage of "all" obeys. We may be unconscious of them, and tend to claim we operate on the basis of the *meaning* of the word; but that, after all, is only a circumlocution for saying that we are guided by rules which we never make explicit. We have used words all our lives in certain patterns, and instead of calling the patterns "rules," we attribute the courses of our thought processes to the "meanings" of words. That discovery was a crucial recognition in the long path towards the formalization of number theory.

If we were to delve into Euclid's proof more and more carefully, we would see that it is composed of many, many small—almost infinitesimal—steps. If all those steps were written out line after line, the proof would appear incredibly complicated. To our minds it is clearest when several steps are telescoped together, to form one single sentence. If we tried to look at the proof in slow motion, we would begin to discern individual frames. In other words, the dissection can go only so far, and then we hit the "atomic" nature of reasoning processes. A proof can be broken down into a series of tiny but discontinuous jumps which seem to flow smoothly when perceived from a higher vantage point. In Chapter VIII, I will show one way of breaking the proof into atomic units, and you will see how incredibly many steps are involved. Perhaps it should not surprise you, though. The operations in Euclid's brain when he invented the proof must have involved millions of neurons (nerve cells), many of which fired several hundred times in a single second. The mere utterance of a sentence involves hundreds of thousands of neurons. If Euclid's thoughts were that complicated, it makes sense for his proof to contain a huge number of steps! (There may be little direct connection between the neural actions in his brain, and a proof in our formal system, but the complexities of the two are comparable. It is as if nature wants the complexity of the proof of the infinitude of primes to be conserved, even when the systems involved are very different from each other.)

In Chapters to come, we will lay out a formal system that (1) includes a stylized vocabulary in which all statements about natural numbers can be expressed, and (2) has rules corresponding to all the types of reasoning which seem necessary. A very important question will be whether the rules for symbol manipulation which we have then formulated are really of equal power (as far as number theory is concerned) to our usual mental reasoning abilities—or, more generally, whether it is theoretically possible to attain the level of our thinking abilities, by using some formal system.

Questions for Discussion

1. Hofstadter's discussion is not aimed at mathematicians; rather, he is writing for laypersons who do not understand such basic principles as "natural numbers." Explain the techniques he uses to con-

vey his concepts. In your opinion, how successful is Hofstadter in carrying out his purpose?

2. Hofstadter states that Euclid's proof has many steps. However, a mathematician's formal proof would be only a few lines. Your mathematics teacher might ask you to flesh out the proof with several intermediate steps involving obvious properties of numbers. Finally, however, you still would have fewer steps than the "many, many" small steps Hofstadter says make up the basic proof. In using more steps for your proof, what meaning systems other than numbers would you call on? Explain. (For example, what semantic problems would you encounter? How would formal logic apply? Does common sense have anything to do with mathematical proof?)

3. Traditionally, logical processes are classed as either inductive or deductive. Point out Hofstadter's use of both induction and deduction in this selection. (A desk dictionary will probably give you an adequate definition of the two terms, or you can go to a general encyclopedia for a more extended discussion.)

4. Throughout the selection, Hofstadter is interested in pattern recognition (e.g., mathematical symbols and proofs, and so forth). What do patterns tell us about the nature of the universe?

5. Why might a mathematician who already understands the concepts Hofstadter explains nonetheless enjoy this selection?

6. Why, according to Hofstadter, is the following statement strange? "There are 17 languages in India, and 462 dialects." Would Hofstadter find the following statistical statement equally strange? "In Plain City, 2.35 persons live in each single-family dwelling." Explain.

―――――――――   SUGGESTIONS FOR WRITING   ―――――――――

1.   Explain how some implement or instrument works. For example, you might explain a reflecting telescope, a hydrometer, an automobile's internal combustion engine, a blender, a vacuum cleaner—any household device, common machine, or gadget. Use analogies to make your explanation clear to nonexperts.

2.   Discuss the impact of some machine, device, or instrument on society.

3.   Evolutionism versus creationism is very much an issue currently. Attempting to be unbiased and objective, explain the arguments of each side. (Your best source for these arguments is current periodicals.)

4.   Develop an argument either in favor of or against evolutionism or creationism.

5.   If you are a science major, perhaps you would like to write about a great accomplishment in your field—for example, Newton and gravity, Mendeleev and the periodic table, or Mendel and the laws of genetics; assume the role of a scientist writing for the lay public, as do the authors in this chapter of *The Literature of Fact*.

Explain how the development came about. What sort of person was the scientist who made the breakthrough? What resistance did he or she encounter? What prepared the way for the discovery or invention?

With a bit of research in the library, you can gather biographical and historical information that will enable you to give a scientific explanation in terms of a human drama, a biographical sketch. (For models of biographical writing, see the biography chapter earlier in this book.)

6.   Use the information in the selections by Nigel Calder and Gary Zukav as the basis for a science fiction story.

7.   A naturalist is basically an observer, carefully watching nature and recording his or her observations. Choose an animal or group of animals to observe and do a naturalist's report, using Dian Fossey's chapter as a general model.

As your subject or subjects, you might choose your own pet, birds that frequent your backyard, a cat that prowls your neighborhood, the ground squirrels in the park. The main point is to gather specific data by careful observation and to organize your observations so they do not appear to be mere chaos to your reader.

8.   Write a report on any of the pseudosciences that have come and gone throughout history: alchemy, phrenology, astrology, and many others. For example, if you happen to be a chemistry major,

you will probably be interested in alchemy, and a psychology or physiology major will find phrenology to be an example of how masses of people can believe utterly false "scientific" claims.

As an alternative, a report on quack medical cures—either in the past or at present—would interest you as you researched your subject and would also interest your readers.

Your contribution to the essay will be the viewpoint, critical intelligence, and perhaps humor that you bring to your subject.

9.   A subject that is likely to be under debate for the next several years—and one that is very much in the news at this writing—is the Strategic Defense Initiative (SDI), the so-called "Star Wars." Explain the arguments in favor of and against SDI. (Probably scientists on your campus have opinions on the subject or are even involved in SDI research. You can interview these people.) What is your reasoned judgment? Should the United States proceed with SDI or not?

10.   Explain your reaction to panglossianism, which, as Stephen Jay Gould explains, is the belief that "things cannot be other than they are. . . . Everything is made for the best purpose."

C H A P T E R
8

The Arts

What are the uses of art? Some, perhaps, view it as mere diversion, a way to kill time when one has nothing better to do. And indeed, some works are so shallow as to be nothing other than diversions—for example, many television shows, much decorative art in public places, and perhaps the majority of popular novels. We experience these once, enjoy them mildly, and then forget them. But there are other kinds of art, works in which we become absorbed, that trouble or elate us, and to which we return again and again.

Because of their power, great works of art provide a special kind of knowledge. They engage the whole person, intellectually and emotionally. An economic theory might explain poverty, but only a story can convey the experience of being poor. A physiologist can measure the changes in glandular, circulatory, and respiratory function brought about by love, but only a poem can explain what it means to be in love.

Works of art are always in a "frame," set apart from the everyday. Whether we are contemplating the "Mona Lisa," reading *Moby Dick*, or listening to Leonard Bernstein's *Mass*, this "framing" allows us to pay a special kind of attention. We know that it is part of the world but that its value does not come from its practical usefulness.

In *Studies in Classic American Literature*, D. H. Lawrence put it this way: "Art has two great functions. First, it provides an emotional experience. And then, if we have the courage of our own feelings, it becomes a mine of practical truth."

As M. H. Abrams points out in his important book *The Mirror and the Lamp*, critics can ask questions about *the message* of the work of art (or what we can learn from it), about *the artist* and his or her purpose, about *the effect of the work on its audience*, and about *the structure and style of the work*. The essays in this chapter ask these questions about photography as an art form; Elvis Presley, one of America's most influential popular artists; Charlie Chaplin, the legendary clown and movie maker; and Mark Twain, America's quintessential storyteller.

SHELLEY FISHER FISHKIN

Shelley Fisher Fishkin is the Director of the Poynter Fellowship in Journalism at Yale University, where she has also taught American Literature. She received her Ph.D. degree in American Studies.

In her book From Fact to Fiction, *she uses materials from biography, literary criticism, literary theory, and social history to trace the development of literary tradition since the 1830s, with her main emphasis showing how the study of the role of journalism in that shaping has been neglected. She contends that one can learn more about* Huckleberry Finn *from the files of the Keokuk* Post *and other Twain journalism than from "a shelf-ful of Spanish picaresque novels."*

Mark Twain

In 1867 Twain left for a trip around the world as a traveling correspondent for the *San Francisco Alta California*. His letters from abroad would be printed by Horace Greeley's *New York Tribune* and James Gordon Bennett's *New York Herald* as well, and would win him unprecedented fame. They would also provide him with the chance to experiment in print with the kind of ironic deflation and juxtaposition that would later play such a key role in *Adventures of Huckleberry Finn*. Most important, perhaps, they provided him with the opportunity to explore the project of creating a narrative comprised of a montage of multiple styles and modes—a project which would be central, as well, to his later novel. Twain's work as a traveling correspondent in 1867 acclimated him to the very form which he would choose, consciously or not, for *Huckleberry Finn*, a novel which is, at its core, an extended travel letter from a correspondent who has much in common with the correspondent who set sail on the *Quaker City*.

One of Twain's central projects in these letters (and in the volume in which they would be eventually collected with some revisions, *The Innocents Abroad*) is to help extricate the reader from the false, hackneyed, empty, or misleading images, attitudes, and perspectives that church legends, travel guidebooks, and certain stylized genres of fiction tended to export and promote. A healthy and established tradition of dissent from the romantic treatment of Europe had been in existence for some time before Twain set sail on the *Quaker City*, as Bernard DeVoto has observed. The stance was not new; but the superiority with which Twain carried it off was. Not every text Twain unmasks is necessarily pernicious; rather, his repeated pattern of challenging images, symbols, and auras to jibe with the realities they purport to represent is designed to get the reader into the habit of being suspicious of *all* texts, both harmless and harmful ones.

By highlighting the deception entailed by the narrow focus of guidebooks, romantic novels, and church legends, Twain helps his reader avoid being victimized by these misleading texts. "I can almost tell, in set phrase what [my shipmates] will say when they see Tabor, Nazareth, Jericho and Jerusalem—*because I have seen the books they will smouch their ideas from*. These authors write pictures and frame rhapsodies, and lesser men follow and see with the author's eyes instead of their own . . ." Like Whitman, Twain was disturbed by people's willingness, as Whitman had put it, to "take things at second or third hand," to "look through the eyes of the dead . . . [and] feed on the spectres in books." In his chapter on Galilee he takes

From *From Fact to Fiction* by Shelley Fisher Fishkin. Copyright © 1985. The Johns Hopkins University Press, Baltimore/London, pp. 66–68, 79–84.

his readers (much as Whitman had) through an object lesson in how they might go about seeing with "their own" eyes.

First he quotes the lush, overblown, sentimental, and romantic descriptions of Galilee one finds in various travel books and juxtaposes them to a stark view of the scene as it actually is—"an unobtrusive basin of water, some mountainous desolation, and one tree." Then night falls and Twain takes a different tack: "when the day is done, even the most unimpressible must yield to the dreamy influences of this tranquil starlight. The old traditions of the place steal upon his memory . . ." Twain then shares with the reader his own shimmering poetic reverie inspired by Galilee "in the starlight." His point is not that one must forswear the subtle shadows and sublime lights that the imagination can impart to a scene which, from a purely objective standpoint, is physically bare and unimpressive. It is that one cannot see the scene itself *or* the marvelous shadows and lights one's imagination can impart to it if one simply parrots uncritically the views others have recorded.

While not totally immune from the flaws it attributes to other texts, Twain's own narrative successfully challenges the authority of those texts as guides for the world they purport to describe. By focusing solely on the elegant palace or cathedral, for example, the guidebook implicitly denies the reality of the slum down the road or the beggar at the gate. The opulence, grace, and beauty represented by the palace or cathedral, Twain points out again and again, through artful enlargement of context, are often bought by denying the basic human needs of the masses that live in its shadow. Twain's own text deflates the false pretenses of a culture which, on the one hand, aspires to be respected as the height of civilization but which at the same time systematically degrades the lives of its own citizens. Thus the opulence of Versailles is dimmed by the close proximity (geographically and within the text) of the degradation of the slum at Faubourg St. Antoine. The king's magnificent palace at Naples is put in perspective by the miserable vagabond on the curb in front. The Italy so often described by the guidebooks as "one vast museum" is characterized by Twain as "one vast museum of magnificence and misery."

Twain deflates the language in which the culture is described in conventional texts not only by enlarging the context of the scene painted, but also by presenting it through the eyes of a narrator who seems oblivious to the import of the contradictory details he strings together. This narrator, who seems to accept unquestioningly the "accepted" view of things, seems always unaware of the ways in which the facts he relates to the reader cancel out that view. Thus he tells us, straight-faced, that "among the most precious relics" at the cathedral at Milan "were a stone from the Holy Sepulchre, a part of the crown of thorns (they have a whole one at Notre Dame), a fragment of the purple robe worn by the Saviour, a nail from the Cross and

a picture of the Virgin and Child painted by the veritable hand of St. Luke."
All this is excellent preparation for the writer who will artfully undercut, in
1884, the level of civilization achieved in a household like the Grangerfords',
where people are as ready to hang up another sentimental verse about death
as they are ready to take another life, or where people pack rifles when they
go to church to hear sermons on brotherly love. . . .

Many of the "fictions" deflated in *Huckleberry Finn* are familiar ones
for Twain: romantic novels—stories of pirates and robbers, military exploits,
and amorous adventure (in particular tales of writers such as Sir Walter Scott,
Thomas Moore, Alexandre Dumas, and William Harrison Ainsworth), sentimental verse, political bombast, and Sunday-school primers, to name a few.
Throughout the book the dangers (as well as the absurdities) of letting texts
serve as guides for action are thoroughly explored.

The literary fabrications of writers such as Alexandre Dumas (as interpreted by Tom Sawyer) defraud Jim of his dignity and transform a genuinely
heroic life into a hodgepodge gothic romance. Sunday-school conventions of
right and wrong nearly lead Huck to deprive Jim of his hard-earned freedom
after their long journey in quest of it. In *Huckleberry Finn* characters continually accept without question the authority of texts which estrange them
from the world around them and each other.

The Grangerfords are particularly estranged from themselves and their
world, and texts of various sorts contribute a good deal to their self-delusion.
The books, the poetry, the verse, and the storybook good manners they have
help them feel cultivated and refined; they blind them to the barbarism and
brutality underlying their way of life.

Twain had described a household like that of the Grangerfords in *Life
on the Mississippi*. There he had deflated the pretensions directly, calling the
home "a pathetic sham." In the novel he takes a more circuitous route, and
one which forces the reader to see for himself the gaps between the artificial
trappings of civilization and civilized behavior.

"Books, piled and disposed, with cast-iron exactness, according to an
inherited and unchangeable plan" in the journalism become, in the fiction,
simply books "piled up perfectly exact, on each corner of the table." In
Huckleberry Finn Twain establishes the dangers of acting "according to an
inherited and unchangeable plan" not by direct statement, but by subtly
reiterating and intertwining, in almost fugal style, the multiple fictions
which conspire to kill Buck Grangerford and his family. The "perfectly
exact" piles of books introduce the theme of the unexamined rigidity and
preordained order which characterize the families' attempts to make the
scoreboard of death equally balanced and exact. The sermon on brotherly
love in a church lined with guns introduces the theme of hypocrisy, of things
masquerading as that which they are not. The charade of chivalry straight

out of Walter Scott—seen in the context of the accompanying butchery, cowardice, and general barbarism—echoes this theme. The sentimental verse that so cheapens death in the Grangerford household implicitly reinforces the feud that so cheapens life.

The fictions—the veneer of culture, civilization, refinement, and morality that both families accept as embodiments of their way of life—blind them to the violence at the core of the way they live. The innocent narrator of the novel is much more effective at revealing those contradictions than the wordly narrator of the journalism had been. Twain's editorializing comments on the house in the journalism are deleted in the fiction, replaced by Huck's naïve enthusiasm. The reader is made to see the real nature of the hypocrisy for himself as he takes in both the scene itself and Huck's innocent response to it. Described in *Life on the Mississippi* as "a pathetic sham," the Grangerford home is simply admired by Huck for having "so much style."

If Huck is impressed by "style," the reader is not. Indeed, throughout the book, "style" is associated with artificiality, fabrication, and lies. The absence of "style" is the absence of words. Indeed, when Huck is most in touch with his environment—as he is in the famous daybreak passage on the raft—he is silent. "Not a sound, anywheres," the passage begins, "perfectly still." When confronted by a bloody feud that a romantic novelist might have spun into a lengthy chivalric tome, Huck prefers to use as few words as possible; "style" is incompatible with the fact that people he cares about have just been needlessly killed. "I don't want to talk much about the next day," Huck says, "I reckon I'll cut it pretty short."

While the reader of *Huckleberry Finn* is taught to be suspicious of "style," he is also taught to be suspicious of structures made with "style." Twain throws into question the authority of *any* text by crafting a book composed of multiple fictions, each an ironic commentary on another. *Adventures of Huckleberry Finn* contains scores of tales supposedly invented by the characters—tales which exist as ironic challenges to each other, and as ironic commentaries on Huck's primary text. By making his book a chaotic mélange of fictive forms, Twain prevents any one form from exercising authority or manifesting autonomy and makes his reader conscious of the ultimately fictive and arbitrary nature of all texts, including the one at hand.

Huck invents more than half a dozen fictional life histories for himself, improvised according to expediency. Huck's fictions begin, appropriately, with his staging of his own death. As far as society is concerned, Huck Finn no longer exists after his "murder" in the cabin; any identities Huck now assumes are those he creates for himself. The fictions Huck creates, filled with either sick relations or poor orphans, are themselves artful compressions of the plots and themes of popular sentimental fiction. He becomes, in quick succession, Sarah Williams, whose mother is sick; "runaway 'prentice' " George Peters fleeing a "mean old farmer" in his daughter's clothes; worried kin of "pap, and mam, and sis, and Miss Hooker," who are trapped on the wreck of the "Walter Scott"; frustrated seeker of help for "Pap, Mam and Mary Ann," plagued with smallpox on the raft; Arkansas orphan George Jackson who fell off the steamboat; a Pike County orphan with nothing to his name but his "nigger Jim"; "Adolphus," loyal servant of the brothers Wilks; and "Tom Sawyer."

All of the fictional tales Huck crafts exist as ironic counterparts to the primary text of his allegedly real autobiography, which retains, somehow, a convincing authenticity despite the competing "autobiographies" which exist alongside it. But even the primary text of the book self-consciously acknowledges its own fictive nature. Huck admits in the first paragraph that he owes his existence, as far as the reader is concerned, to a book that was made by Mr. Mark Twain.

Stories invented, repeated, or reported by other characters in the book often serve as ironic commentaries on each other. In two adjacent chapters, for example, Jim relates the story of how he discovered that his daughter was "deef and dumb," and the Duke and King improvise the script for the "deef and dumb" act with which they will try to defraud the daughters of Peter Wilks. Jim's confession of shame and guilt and the two charlatans' shameless plotting thus exist in ironic juxtaposition to one another, highlighting the authentically moving quality of the one, and the outrageously heartless quality of the other.

Another good example of ironic juxtaposition is the relationship between the tale Tom Sawyer tells in chapter 3 and the story Jim relates in chapter 8.

In chapter 3, Tom tells Huck a version of a tale from *Arabian Nights*, explaining where genies come from and what they do. Huck asks, "Who makes them tear around so?" and Tom answers,

> "Why, whoever rubs the lamp or ring. They belong to whoever rubs the lamp or ring, and they've got to do whatever he says. If he tells them to build a palace forty miles long, out of di'monds, and fill it full of chewing gum, or whatever you want, and fetch an emperor's daughter from China for you to marry, they've got to do it. And more—they've got to waltz that palace around over the country wherever you want it, you understand."
>
> "Well," say I, "I think they are a pack of flatheads for not keeping the palace themselves 'stead of fooling them away like that. And what's more—if I was one of them I would see a man in Jericho before I would drop my business and come to him for the rubbing of an old tin lamp."
>
> "How you talk, Huck Finn. Why, you'd *have* to come when he rubbed it, whether you wanted to or not."
>
> "What, and I as high as a tree and as big as a church? All right, then: I *would* come; but I lay I'd make that man climb the highest tree there was in the country."

"Shucks, it ain't no use to talk to you, Huck Finn. You don't seem to know anything, somehow—perfect sap-head."

Huck does, in fact, go out in the woods and rub a lamp until he sweats "like an Injun, calculating to build a palace and sell it" before concluding for certain that "all that stuff was only just one of Tom Sawyer's lies."

Not inculcated, as Tom Sawyer is, with genie lore from *Arabian Nights*, Huck takes a fresh view of Tom's tale and finds it patently absurd; he sees no basis for the arbitrary authority the lamp-rubber exercises over a being many times his size and strength.

In chapter 8, Jim tells Huck the story of why he "run off":

Ole missus—dat's Miss Watson—she pecks on me all de time, en treats me pooty rough, but she awluz said she woudn' sell me down to Orleans. But I noticed dey wuz a nigger trader roun' de place considable lately, en I begin to git oneasy. Well, one night I creeps to de do' pooty late, en de do' warn't quite shet, en I hear old missus tell de widder she gwine to sell me down to Orleans, but she didn' want to, but she could git eight hund'd dollars for me, en it 'uz sich a big stack o' money she couldn' resis'. De widder she try to git her to say she wouldn' do it, but I never waited to hear de res'. I lit out mighty quick, I tell you.

While Huck is quick to see the arbitrariness and absurdity inherent in the lamp-rubber's control over the genie, he fails to see that Miss Watson's control over Jim is equally arbitrary. Jim is as bound (by the legal documents that let a slaveholder "own" her slaves) to follow Miss Watson's bidding to go to New Orleans as the genie is bound (by the conventions of genie lore) to go wherever the lamp-rubber bids *him* to go. Huck himself, of course, fails to make this leap of insight. Indeed, throughout *Huckleberry Finn*, Huck fails to understand that slavery creates lines of authority and power as arbitrary as any in *Arabian Nights*.

From the first time Huck hears the reason Jim ran off ("people would call me a low down Ablitionist, and despise me for keeping mum—but that don't make no difference"), to the last time he wrestles with the problem of giving Jim up ("All right then, I'll *go* to hell"), Huck fails to recognize as arbitrary and illegitimate the system that keeps Jim in bondage. The brilliantly crafted dramatic irony that results from the reader's awareness of the limitations of Huck's world view thus challenges the authority and trustworthiness of the primary text, as the other ironic juxtapositions in the book challenge the authority of any given interpolated tale. Instead of presenting a vision of the world, Twain presents multiple competing visions, many of which cancel each other out. By crafting a work of art that points up its own limitations, he thrusts his reader back into the world of fact.

In his travel letters from Europe and the Holy Land, and in the volume in which he collected them, *The Innocents Abroad,* Twain had not yet figured out how to prevent his text from becoming as illegitimate an authority as all the guidebooks that went before it. His goal was to help his reader see "with his own eyes," but Twain's anti-guidebook guidebook had too many features of the texts it parodied to be wholly successful in this goal. In *Huckleberry Finn,* however, Twain crafted a text that recedes from view just as it seems to be most solidly present. Critics were amply forewarned: "NOTICE," begins the book, the page before chapter 1, "Persons attempting to find a motive in this narrative will be prosecuted; persons attempting to find a moral in it will be banished; persons attempting to find a plot in it will be shot. BY ORDER OF THE AUTHOR."* While no readers seeking these elements have been "prosecuted," "banished," or "shot" as Twain warned, they have been sorely tried and coyly evaded. On one level Twain's book seems to be a lesson in the difficulty of reading a book. As he succeeds in crafting an object lesson in how to question the authority of texts, Twain here succeeds, where he earlier failed, in teaching his reader to see "with his own eyes instead of the eyes of those who travelled . . . before him."

Questions for Discussion

1. Does the author provide enough background information with which to place *Adventures of Huckleberry Finn* in context with other writings of the time? Why is it necessary to provide such context?
2. How does this selection relate to the issue that *Adventures of Huckleberry Finn* should be banned because it presents racist viewpoints and uses racist language?

* Critics disappointed with the ending of *Huckleberry Finn* have focused on Twain's failure to resolve the deep moral and political questions he raised in the first part of the book.

Twain may have been more successful grappling with these problems on a personal level. During the years when he was struggling to complete this troublesome manuscript, he was also attempting to combat the destructive legacy of slavery by supporting the undergraduate and professional education of several promising black students.

In a newly discovered letter that Twain wrote the year *Huckleberry Finn* was published in this country, he explained to the dean of the Yale Law School the reason he wanted to pay the expenses of a black student named Warner T. McGuinn, whom he had met briefly, on one occasion: "I do not believe I would very cheerfully help a white student who would ask a benevolence of a stranger, but I do not feel so about the other color. We have ground the manhood out of them, & the shame is ours, not theirs; & we should pay for it." (SLC to Francis Wayland, December 24, 1885, in the private collection of Nancy and Richard Stiner.) McGuinn went on to become a respected newspaper editor and a renowned Baltimore attorney, community leader, and civil rights activist.

3. In what ways pointed out by the author is Huckleberry Finn a complex character for the reader?

4. Mark Twain forces the reader to question the authority of the text in *Adventures of Huckleberry Finn*. How does this stylistic ploy relate to the main point of the story?

5. The book from which this chapter was taken is titled *From Fact to Fiction*. How does fact, as for example, in newspaper reports and history books, differ from fiction, as in novels and short stories? Clearly, the following is a nonanswer to this question: "Fact is true and fiction is not true."

6. What would Mark Twain say about the advantages of writing about experiences yourself rather than reading what others have written?

7. In your own words explain Fishkin's point in the paragraph on page 339 that begins "First he quotes the lush, overblown, sentimental, and romantic descriptions of Galilee one finds in various travel books . . ." and ends with this: "It is that one cannot see the scene itself *or* the marvelous shadows and lights one's imagination can impart to it if one simply parrots uncritically the views others have recorded."

RICHARD SCHICKEL

Richard Schickel is known best as Time *magazine's principal film critic, but he is also the author of more than fifteen books that, for the most part, deal with the movies but also cover such other topics as Carnegie Hall, tennis, and the Spanish artist Francisco Goya. He has been associated with periodicals since graduating from the University of Wisconsin in 1956 with a bachelor's degree, at which time he became a reporter for* Sports Illustrated. *He also worked for* Look, Show, *and* Life *magazines before arriving at* Time. *Mr. Schickel has written, produced, and/or directed popular television documentaries dealing with the movies, such as* The Men Who Made the Movies *and* Life Goes to the Movies. *Schickel is an easy critic to read, employing very little jargon to make his point, and yet in the following essay on Charlie Chaplin he makes a complicated argument about ego getting in art's way. While you read the selection, notice how the point threads its way around the biographical details provided.*

A Chaplin Overview

Praise, at this point, seems superfluous. Chaplin has received it, in fullest measure from his peers ("the greatest artist that was ever on the screen"—Stan Laurel, "the greatest comedian who ever lived"—Buster Keaton, "the greatest artist that ever lived"—Mack Sennett, "the best ballet dancer that ever lived, and if I get a chance I'll kill him with my bare hands"—W. C. Fields); from the critics ("It seems unlikely that any dancer or actor can ever have excelled him in eloquence, variety and poignancy of motion"—James Agee, "one of the few great comic geniuses who have appeared so far in history"—Robert Warshow, "Chaplin's career is a cinematic biography on the highest level of artistic expression"—Andrew Sarris); and from the highest levels of the literary world ("the only genius developed in motion pictures"—George Bernard Shaw, "among his age's first artists"—Edmund Wilson).

One could fill an essay with such quotations and still have plenty left over. Moreover, one would, in the end, have a sentence or two from nearly every critic and every artist one respects. So it is disturbing not to join, full-voiced, in a chorus where only Fields, that lovely man, manages to sound an unawed, human note. It is especially difficult to maintain a degree of critical reserve after Chaplin, following a quarter century of self-imposed exile, came among us again—two weeks short of his eighty-third birthday, so obviously on a sentimental, farewell journey to a land that is to him, as Sarris wisely put it, "a fantasy and a delusion, marvelous world that he may . . . revisit, but will never reconquer," at least in the way he once did when he graciously accepted our unconditional surrender to his art. One is so anxious not to appear insensitive before a creator whose chief stock in trade was a preternatural sensitivity, so anxious not to be mistaken for the kind of right-wing crazy who hounded him about his really quite innocent politics and morals, coloring his essential loneliness with the terrible bitterness that seems only now to be fading to bearable levels.

It is, I think, a measure not merely of Chaplin's art, but of his really incredible ego, that one simply cannot find an article that presumes to criticize him—or even to view his life and work with decent objectivity—which does not begin as this one has: apologetically. He has made us feel that any flaws we detect in his work must be flaws in ourselves. He has involved us, as no performing artist ever has, in the drama of his life, the longest-running soap opera on record, and he has forced us for the most part, to discuss it in the terms he has dictated. To put the matter simply, no entertainer in history has so imposed himself on the consciousness of his times for so long a time—almost a half century now.

Nearly everyone who has cared about Chaplin's art has been convinced that in the Tramp or the Little Fellow, to use the terms invariably employed in discussing Chaplin's great creation, we had a very direct expression of the artist's personality—"so simple and unaffected," despite the onslaught of previously unimagined celebrity. Certainly Chaplin has wanted us to believe that. And up to a point, one does. Surely what is best and wisest in him can be found in the Tramp.

But are we really to think that's all that is significant about the man? If we were talking about the great primitives in his line—Buster Keaton, for example, or Stan Laurel—the matter could rest there. Between what we knew of them as men and what we saw of them on screen there was no important discontinuity. That is simply not true of Chaplin. The feeling of anyone born after, say, 1930 for the Little Fellow is bound to be rather abstract; we simply did not experience the excitement of discovery, that sense of possessing (and being possessed by) the Little Fellow that earlier generations felt. We knew who he was, of course, and our elders endlessly guaranteed his greatness to us. But he remained something of an abstraction: a figure to be appreciated, but impossible to love in the way he was loved by those who had been present at the creation.

What we were involved in was the larger drama of Chaplin's life—a drama, as it turned out, in one of the classic twentieth-century molds, that of the artist-visionary in conflict with his age. It was, and is, infinitely more fascinating than any of the Little Fellow's adventures—with its author even now engaged in creating for us an aesthetically satisfying conclusion.

This drama is divided, as all classic, epic works should be, into five acts, which might be subtitled "Self-Discovery," "Success," "Struggle," "Tragedy," and—when the audience at the Academy Award presentations rose to give him an ovation, and everybody forgave everybody—the last act, "Triumph."

Like his greatest routines, the Chaplin drama has a simplicity, an inevitability (and a self-consciousness) that is awesome. Of course fate helped him out a little bit, especially with his opening scenes, for he was born into poverty, the son of a drunken father and a mother who went mad. It was a Dickensian childhood, but one which turned out to have its uses as the source of his art, which he began to perfect at an early age, becoming the leading comedian in one of the Fred Karno comedy troupes where he learned the classic English music-hall style. As everyone knows, it was with a Karno company that Chaplin came to the United States—a leading comedian at age twenty-one—and it was while working with it that he was discovered by Mack Sennett in 1914.

The English comic style was not Sennett's; Chaplin's relationship with his new, roughneck colleagues was edgy. A lot of his best bits were cut out of his early Keystones, Chaplin claims. As the world would soon know, however, Chaplin has always had what any unique artist must have to survive: utter confidence in the correctness of his own judgment. He fought out the stylistic issue with the Keystone crowd, finally finding a way to demonstrate what he had been trying to tell them. It happened one day when Sennett was observed glumly studying a hotel-lobby set, chewing on his cigar. "We need some gags here," he muttered, then turned to Chaplin and told him, "Put on a comedy make-up. Anything will do."

At which point, if life were as well-managed as a movie, the clouds should have broken and beams of sunlight should have lit Chaplin's way to the wardrobe. For his time had come. "I thought I would dress in baggy pants, big shoes, a cane, and a derby hat. I wanted everything a contradiction: the pants baggy, the coat tight, the hat small, and the shoes large." The mustache was added, he says, because Sennett had expected him to be much older and Chaplin thought it would age him without hiding his expression.

He continues: "I had no idea of the character. But the moment I was dressed, the clothes and make-up made me feel the person he was. I began to know him, and by the time I walked onto the stage he was fully born." He claims—and one is a trifle dubious about this—that he was able instantly to describe his creation to Sennett in rather poetic terms *before* a foot of film had been shot: "You know this fellow is many-sided, a tramp, a gentleman, a poet, a dreamer, a lonely fellow, always hopeful of romance and adventure. He would have you believe he is a scientist, a musician, a duke, a polo player. However, he is not above picking up cigarette butts or robbing a baby of its candy. And, of course, if the occasion warrants it, he will kick a lady in the rear—but only in extreme anger."

Perhaps he really was that articulate that quickly. Perhaps not. No doubt, however, he was inspired, sensed there was something more here than just another role, something through which he could express more of his feelings and visions than he ever had before. Most critics, however, believe it required most of the rest of his year with Sennett, plus a good bit of the following year (with the Essanay production company), before the Tramp began to demonstrate all the dimensions Chaplin ascribes to him on, as it were, their first meeting. In particular, the undercurrent of pathos, which in time was to become a veritable torrent, was not visible for another year.

Still, the public almost immediately observed that something wonderful had been wrought. The demand for films featuring the Little Fellow was immediate and huge. The 1915 Essanay contract called for $1200 a week and a $10,000 bonus on signing. A year later he was to receive $675,000 for a year's work with Mutual, and a little more than a year after that, in 1917, Chaplin signed his famous million-dollar contract with First National. Close with his money, and determined never to suffer again the kind of poverty he had so recently escaped, Chaplin began accumulating one of the great show-business fortunes.

He was entitled to it. For in an age when forty or fifty prints of a movie comedy could satisfy the demand for other actors' work, distributors had to make up close to two hundred prints of Chaplin's films—for which they could charge well above the going rates. It was a golden time. It required only a simple poster of the Tramp bearing the legend I AM HERE TODAY to bring the people in. And the two-reel length of these early comedies was perfectly suited to his gifts. Agee wrote: "Before Chaplin came to pictures people were content with a couple of gags per comedy; he got some kind of laugh every second," mainly "through his genius for what might be called *inflection*—the perfect, changeful shading of his physical and emotional attitudes toward the gag." Every writer has his favorite moments in these two-reelers. Agee, for example, loved Chaplin's drunken bout with a malevolent Murphy bed in *One A.M.*; Gilbert Seldes cites *The Pawnshop*, where Chaplin includes business with a feather duster, then a sequence in which he tries to dry dishes by passing them through a clothes wringer, and then some nonsense with a clock where a simple inspection leads to disaster, as all the clockworks litter the screen. Both men mention, as the quintessential Chaplin moment, a sequence in *A Night Out* where Ben Turpin, himself far gone in booze, is dragging a stiffened Chaplin through the streets after the bars have closed. Chaplin awakens, sees how splendidly his friend is serving him, and reaches out to pluck and delicately sniff a flower.

There are lots of ways to put it: he found poetry in the ordinary, he transcended reality, he extended the range of pantomime to previously unimagined dimensions. Yet none of them quite explain his phenomenal appeal. Chaplin has never been generous in acknowledging influences, but some critics have noticed a correlation between his work and that of Max Linder, who had earlier brought something of the European comic tradition to the screen through his Pathé shorts. Edmund Wilson has emphasized how much Chaplin owed to the classic turns of the English music halls. And despite his protests, it is clear that Chaplin learned a great deal from Sennett, especially about pacing and the use of the chase as a climax.

In short, he summarized much that had gone before, linking the art of screen comedy to a much older tradition. This was very significant to those intellectuals who began to take the movies seriously in the teens and twenties of this century. For, if nothing else, it gave them a classy frame of reference in which to place Chaplin. In turn, their writing has been extremely valuable to Chaplin, insuring his reputation as an artist against both direct assault and the more insidious danger of neglect during the long periods when he was absent from the screen. In effect, they committed us to him irrevocably. Through all the long years when most of them were exercising their contempt for movies in general, Chaplin was always cited as the medium's one unquestioned, unquestionable artist, the individualist amid the corporate herd, a man clinging to his peculiar vision while everyone else went hooting off in pursuit of momentary fads. Or submitted to degrading manipulation by the studios. Or simply faded away as his great contemporaries (and sometime United Artists partners) did—Griffith, Fairbanks, Pickford.

Yet this fact remains: Chaplin never again achieved the perfection of those first years. The little films of the Little Fellow were, in effect, solo ballets. As such, they had no more need of plot, of subsidiary characterizations, of great themes than one of Nijinsky's variations did. Despite the reams of appreciative analysis written about the early films, the pleasure we derived from them was essentially kinesthetic and therefore non- (and even perhaps anti-) intellectual. One could go on watching them for a lifetime. Indeed, one has.

But popular arts like the movies are cruel in their demand for novelty. And so are the intellectuals who have taken such arts for their province. No matter what they *thought* they thought, there was in their endless nattering over Chaplin an implicit demand for "development," for big ideas and statements. No doubt Chaplin made the same demands on himself. Beginning with *The Kid* in 1920 he began to inject larger and larger doses of pure sentiment into his work. No less than Griffith's, his was essentially a Victorian sensibility and he turned naturally to a rather cloying sweetness when he was forced, by the public demand for feature-length films, to extend his works.

There were other problems as well. As Edmund Wilson accurately noticed in 1925, "His gift is primarily the actor's, not the director's or the artist's. All the photographic, the plastic development of the movies, which is at present making such remarkable advances, seems not to interest Chaplin. His pictures are still in this respect nearly as raw as *Tillie's Punctured Romance* or any other primitive comedy." He added, presciently, that Chaplin "is jealous of his independence . . . he is very unlikely to allow himself to be written for, directed, or even advised."

The issues were more complex than Wilson could possibly have known at the time. In retrospect it seems significant that Chaplin did not appear in an important role in *A Woman of Paris*—a 1923 picture which was, after all, his first production for United Artists, the company he had helped establish. It betokened, perhaps, a certain restiveness with the Tramp character. Or was it the beginning of a lack of confidence in the Little Fellow as a means of expressing all that Chaplin was beginning to feel about modern life? At any rate—despite the notable exception of *The Gold Rush*—Chaplin's art and his production pace grew hesitant. From the time *A Woman of Paris* was completed to 1940, when *The Great Dictator* appeared, Chaplin made just five films, the last of which, of course, contained his final appearance as the Tramp—and in a role that was quite overwhelmed by Chaplin's impersonation of Hynkel, the dictator.

The coming of sound, naturally, was a threatening problem, solved in *City Lights* and *Modern Times* by the simple expedient of ignoring the microphone and filling the track with music, sound effects, and an occasional burst of gibberish. But dramatic as Chaplin's confrontation was with a technological advance he disliked, and exciting as his triumph over it was (no other screen artist dared so radical a strategy), I do not think it was fear of movies that talked which stayed Chaplin's hand.

Andrew Sarris has pointed out that "for Chaplin, his other self on the screen has always been the supreme object of contemplation," adding that his much-disapproved late work, *Limelight*, about a clown who lost his hold on the audience, was "an imaging [of] his own death, a conception of sublime egoism unparalleled in the world cinema," since "to imagine one's own death, one must imagine the death of the world."

Here, I think, we approach the center of the Chaplin enigma, the reason why he has discomfited so many observers for so many years. It is that every stylistic and technical change which has come to the movies since the end of World War I has implicitly interfered with his (and our) contemplation of his screen self. Length, of course, implies the necessity for subplots and the presence of other actors in significant roles. Very distracting. The growth in movie "plasticity" that Wilson spoke of was similarly likely to disrupt our concentration on the nuances of his art. And talk was perceived to be fatally interruptive.

He was in a double bind. He was an artist universally beloved because he had created a universal symbol of the common man's virtues, flaws, and aspirations, a man whose presence had helped to create a great audience for a new medium at the same time that he had given the medium respectability as an art form. Yet as the century wore on, the common man increasingly showed himself to be capable of the most terrible crimes and indifferences; to be the dupe of such evil mass movements as fascism.

At the same time, the movies, Chaplin's medium, underwent radical change, became more and more resistant to his particular gifts. Otis Ferguson, the first great populist critic of movies since Vachel Lindsay, said of *Modern Times* that it was "about the last thing they should have called the Chaplin picture. . . . Its times were modern when the movies were younger and screen motion was a little faster and more jerky than life, and sequences came in forty-foot spurts." Ferguson called it "a feature picture made up of several one- or two-reel shorts" and proposed titles like *The Shop, The Jailbird, The Watchman, The Singing Waiter*. Like everyone else, he could see the momentary beauties of these sequences, but they did not, he thought, make Chaplin "a first-class picturemaker. He may personally surmount his period, but as director-producer he can't carry his whole show with him, and I'll take bets that if he keeps on refusing to learn any more

than he learned when the movies themselves were just learning, each succes-
sive picture he makes will seem, on release, to fall short of what went
before."

This is a sadly accurate prediction. There is not a subsequent Chaplin
film that does not contain its sublime moments: the dance with the balloon
globe and the scenes with Jack Oakie in *The Great Dictator*, the sequence
where he tries to bump off Martha Raye in *Monsieur Verdoux*, the wonderful
concert with Buster Keaton in *Limelight*. Still, the Tramp was dead, done in,
as Robert Warshow observed, because the essentially innocent relationship
between him and his society could no longer be sustained. "The satiric point
of the relationship lay precisely in [the] element of fortuitousness . . . it
happened that the Tramp and the society were in constant collision, but
neither side was impelled to draw any conclusions from this. The absurdity
in the Tramp's behavior consisted in its irrelevance to the preoccupations of
the society; the viciousness of the society consisted in its failure to make
any provision for the Tramp, its complete indifference to his fate."

In truly modern times, this kind of relationship was impossible. "Now
the two were compelled to become conscious of each other, openly and
continuously, and the quality of innocence . . . could no longer be preserved
between them." As Warshow observes, the factory in *Modern Times* is "a
living, malevolent organism," as is the state in *The Great Dictator*. There is
no longer even a thin margin where the Tramp could survive. And so he was
put to rest.

Now Chaplin began to act out in life the drama that Warshow saw
going on close to the surface of his art. There was the desperate preachment
of love-as-panacea at the end of *Dictator*, embarrassing because the speech is
not truly felt, remains merely an empty oration—though one imagines
Chaplin thought he meant it at the time. In *Verdoux* the climactic speech is
bitter: How is Verdoux, the murderer of a handful of lonely women—and for
the justifiable end of supporting his dear family—worse than all the muni-
tions manufacturers, etc., etc.?

In these pictures the stale ideologies of the age fill the gap between the
world's reality and an artistic vision now inadequate to that reality. Finally
there is the self-pity of *Limelight*, the reported savagery of *A King in New
York*, the sheer emptiness and lack of energy of *A Countess from Hong
Kong*. Yes, age had taken its toll and our expectations about great men are
excessive, unsatisfiable. But there is something more disturbing than that in
the late films. For what we see surfacing in them is something that we may
well have been aware of right from the start, yet dismissed as unworthy of
us.

That, of course, is the increasingly shrill egoism of the artist, a quality
transcending mere self-consciousness, and preventing those of us who were

not part of the first, uncomplicated love affair between Chaplin and the public from surrendering to his insistent demand for a continuance of that affair in the old simple terms.

Of course, one despised Chaplin's enemies and their inquiries into his politics and his morals; and yet one responded automatically, not with the warmth and spirit with which one might try to defend a public figure with whom our relationship was less complex. There was a sense, which we could not articulate at the time, that Chaplin had, no doubt unconsciously, conspired in the creation of that comfortable exile which he wanted us to understand as tragedy. One could see that he was increasingly bewildered by the world, increasingly unable to encompass his feelings about it (and pre-scriptions for it) in the metaphors he employed in lieu of the Little Fellow in his films. One was aware, too, of his loss of touch with his roots—and ours.

He was seen abroad only occasionally and then largely in the company of those few world-class celebrities who were his peers. When he addressed the rest of us he was distant, abstract, patronizing. He preached love of mankind in general, but appeared incapable of affectionate gestures toward anyone outside his family circle, that ever-expanding extension of himself. And the art was not what it had been—not even so brilliant a rationale as Warshow's could save *Verdoux* for us. Or *Limelight*. The world had changed and he had changed.

Awed by accomplishments we had to rediscover, trying to re-create the innocent times in which they had seemed so astonishing, one found one's direct suspicions confirmed by *My Autobiography* in 1964. The first third of it is wonderful, one of the great portraits of turn-of-the-century life, rich in color, anecdote, feeling. But the last two-thirds? They are cold, simplistic, a dreary listing of the great man's encounters with other great men, none of whom are as interesting as he is. And he is too interesting, too complex to be discussed. Now all the doubts, all the hesitation that the good critics had noted in their appreciations rose hauntingly before us. And one sensed that the most important reservations one had harbored were not based on the accidents of age, of political nonsense, of the tragedy of history. One saw that his art was based not on holding a mirror up to life, but up to himself, that our presence, necessary as it was to satisfy his drive for power (which Samuel Goldwyn, who knew something about the subject, called the most developed he had ever encountered) was essentially an intrusion on what was, really, a perfect love, that of the artist for his creation—which was, alas, himself.

The guilt that wells up as one writes those words is palpable. Even now one imagines the failure to be one's own, not his. And anyway, one does not wish to spoil, even in a small way, the conclusion of the Chaplin drama, the necessary, inevitable reconciliation between him and his public. The art *was* there. Every man who loves the movies is in his debt. And as long as that love persists we will take our children to see his first works, that they may know the beauty and innocence of film's beginnings, before the corruption began, before the distortions of power, of celebrity, of the alienation of men from their idols and from their very selves, were incorporated, enhanced by this terrible, wonderful machinery.

The ironies of this life, this career are endless. Let us stop. Let us, at last, honor him as simply as we can. As he seems to want us to, the King—and not only in New York.

Questions for Discussion

1. The author divides Chaplin's life into five "acts": self-discovery, success, struggle, tragedy, and triumph. According to Schickel, what part did Chaplin have in "writing" each of them himself? Does the author give the reader enough information to make a judgment in each case?

2. In what ways was Chaplin's egoism an asset, and in what ways was it a detriment?

3. It is Schickel's contention that Chaplin's ego was much greater than that of other artists. Do you think Schickel made his point convincingly? Why? Is the case supported throughout the text or in only one or two places?

4. What difficulties are there in learning about Chaplin's artistry years after his life's work has been completed? How might one go about overcoming these difficulties?

5. In talking about the first time Chaplin was asked to put on a costume for a Mack Sennett comedy, Schickel writes that "if life were as well-managed as a movie, the clouds should have broken and beams of sunlight should have lit Chaplin's way to the wardrobe." What tone does this sentence convey, coming as it does just before Chaplin's own statement that "by the time I walked onto the stage he [the famous tramp character] was fully born"?

6. What reasons does Schickel give for believing that Chaplin's feature-length films were not as artistically successful as his silent shorts? How do those reasons relate to the central theme?

7. Do you read movie reviews to decide which movies to see or to learn more about the movies you have just seen? Is Richard Schickel a critic you would be interested in reading? Explain.

8. Everyone is familiar with the little tramp character, but perhaps there are readers who have never seen an actual Chaplin movie. If you have not, did this selection still make sense? Why? What changes in the article would have helped you?

GREIL MARCUS

Born in 1945, Greil Marcus received both a bachelor's and a master's degree in American political thought from the University of California at Berkeley. His career in journalism began with a music column written for the San Francisco Express-Times, *an influential underground newspaper of the late 1960s. He is a contributing editor for* Rolling Stone *and has written for* Creem, Newsday, Take One, *and the* Village Voice. *Citing D. H. Lawrence's* Studies in Classic American Literature, *Leslie Fiedler's* Love and Death in the American Novel, *and Alexis de Toqueville's* Democracy in America, *among others, as sources of inspiration, Marcus is interested in American rock and roll music as a source of social insight and applies an academic approach to the subject matter. While reading the following selection on Elvis Presley, think about how Marcus's writing differs from the "Oh, wow!" coverage of popular music offered by, for example, your daily newspaper.*

Elvis Presliad

Fanfare

Elvis Presley is a supreme figure in American life, one whose presence, no matter how banal or predictable, brooks no real comparisons. He is honored equally by long-haired rock critics, middle-aged women, the City of Memphis (they finally found something to name after him: a highway), and even a president.* Beside Elvis, the other heroes of this book seem a little small-time. If they define different versions of America, Presley's career almost has the scope to take America in. The cultural range of his music has expanded to the point where it includes not only the hits of the day, but also patriotic recitals, pure country gospel, and really dirty blues; reviews of his concerts, by usually credible writers, sometimes resemble biblical accounts of heavenly miracles. Elvis has emerged as a great *artist*, a great *rocker*, a great *purveyor of schlock*, a great *heart throb*, a great *bore*, a great *symbol of potency*, a great *ham*, a great *nice person*, and, yes, a great American.

Twenty years ago Elvis made his first records with Sam Phillips, on the little Sun label in Memphis, Tennessee; then a pact was signed with Col. Tom Parker, shrewd country hustler. Elvis took off for RCA Victor, New York, and Hollywood. America has not been the same since. Elvis disappeared into an oblivion of respectability and security in the sixties, lost in interchangeable movies and dull music; he staged a remarkable comeback as that decade ended, and now performs as the transcendental Sun King that Ralph Waldo Emerson only dreamed about—and as a giant contradiction. His audience expands every year, but Elvis transcends his talent to the point of dispensing with it altogether. Performing a kind of enormous victory rather than winning it, Elvis strides the boards with such glamour, such magnetism, that he allows his audience to transcend their desire for his talent.

From *Mystery Train: Images of America in Rock 'N' Roll Music* by Greil Marcus. Copyright © 1975 by Greil Marcus. Reprinted by permission of the publisher, E. P. Dutton, a division of NAL Penguin Inc.

*Richard Nixon had Elvis over to the White House once, and made him an honorary narcotics agent. Nixon got his picture taken with the King. An old story, though, from rock critic Stu Werbin: "It seems that the good German who arranges the White House concerts for the President and his guests managed to travel the many channels that lead only in rare instances to Col. Tom Parker's phone line. Once connected, he delivered what he considered the most privileged invitation. The President requests Mr. Presley to perform. The Colonel did a little quick figuring and then told the man that Elvis would consider it an honor. For the President, Elvis's fee, beyond traveling expenses and accommodations for his back-up group, would be $25,000. The good German gasped.

'Col. Parker, nobody gets paid for playing for the President!'

'Well, I don't know about that, son,' the Colonel responded abruptly, 'but there's one thing I do know. Nobody asks Elvis Presley to play for nothing.' " (*Creem*, March, 1972).

Action is irrelevant when one can simply delight in the presence of a man who has made history, and who has triumphed over it.

Mark now, the supreme Elvis gesture. He takes the stage with a retinue of bodyguards, servants, singers, a band, an orchestra; he applies himself vaguely to the hits of his past, prostrates himself before songs of awesome ickiness; he acknowledges the applause and the gasps that greet his every movement (applause that comes thundering with such force you might think the audience merely suffers the music as an excuse for its ovations); he closes with an act of show-biz love that still warms the heart; but above all, he throws away the entire performance.

How could he take it seriously? How could anyone create when all one has to do is appear? "He *looks* like Elvis Presley!" cried a friend, when the Big E stormed forth in an explosion of flashbulbs and cheers, "What a burden to live up to!" It is as if there is nothing Elvis could do to overshadow a performance of his myth. And so he performs from a distance, laughing at his myth, throwing it away only to see it roar back and trap him once again.

He will sing, as if suffering to his very soul, a song called "This Time, You [God, that is] Gave Me a Mountain," which sums up his divorce and his separation from his little girl. Having confessed his sins, he will stand aside, head bowed, as the Special Elvis Presley Gospel Group sings "Sweet, Sweet Feeling (In This Place)." Apparently cleansed of his sins, he will rock straight into the rhythm and blues of "Lawdy, Miss Clawdy" and celebrate his new-found freedom with a lazy grin. But this little melodrama of casual triumph will itself be a throwaway. As with the well-planned sets, the first-class musicians, the brilliant costumes, there will be little life behind the orchestration; the whole performance will be flaccid, the timing careless, all emotions finally shallow, the distance from his myth necessitating an even greater distance from the musical power on which that myth is based.

Elvis gives us a massive road-show musical of opulent American mastery; his version of the winner-take-all fantasies that have kept the world lined up outside the theaters that show American movies ever since the movies began. And of course we respond: a self-made man is rather boring, but a self-made king is something else. Dressed in blue, red, white, ultimately gold, with a superman cape and covered with jewels no one can be sure are fake, Elvis might epitomize the worst of our culture—he is bragging, selfish, narcissistic, condescending, materialistic to the point of insanity. But there is no need to take that seriously, no need to take anything seriously. "Aw, shucks," says the country boy; it is all a joke to him; his distance is in his humor, and he can exit from this America unmarked, unimpressed, and uninteresting.

"From the moment he comes out of the wings," writes Nik Cohn, "all the pop that has followed him is made to seem as nothing, to be blown away like chaff." That is *exactly* what that first moment feels like, but from that point on, Elvis will go with the rest of it, singing as if there are no dangers or delights in the world grand enough to challenge him. There is great satisfaction in his performance, and great emptiness.

It is an ending. It is a sure sign that a culture has reached a dead end when it is no longer intrigued by its myths (when they lose their power to excite, amuse, and renew all who are a part of those myths—when those myths just bore the hell out of everyone); but Elvis has dissolved into a presentation of his myth, and so has his music. The emotion of the best music is open, liberating in its commitment and intangibility; Elvis's presentation is fixed. The glorious oppression of that presentation parallels the all-but-complete assimilation of a revolutionary musical style into the mainstream of American culture, where no one is challenged and no one is threatened.

History without myth is surely a wasteland; but myths are compelling only when they are at odds with history. When they replace the need to make history, they too are a dead end, and merely smug. Elvis's performance of his myth is so satisfying to his audience that he is left with no musical identity whatsoever, and thus he has no way to define himself, or his audience—except to expand himself, and his audience. Elvis is a man whose task it is to dramatize the fact of his existence; he does not have to create something new (or try, and fail), and thus test the worth of his existence, or the worth of his audience.

Complete assimilation really means complete acceptance. The immigrant who is completely assimilated into America has lost the faculty of adding whatever is special about himself to his country; for any artist, complete assimilation means the adoption of an aesthetic where no lines are drawn and no choices are made. That quality of selection, which is what is at stake when an artist comes across with his version of anything, is missing. When an artist gives an all-encompassing Yes to his audience (and Elvis's Yes implicitly includes everyone, not just those who say Yes to *him*), there is nothing more he can tell his audience, nothing he can really do for them, except maybe throw them a kiss.

Only the man who says No is free, Melville once wrote. We don't expect such a stance in popular culture, and anyone who does might best be advised to take his trade somewhere else. But the refusal that lurks on the margins of the affirmation of American popular culture—the margins where Sly Stone and Randy Newman have done their best work—is what gives the Yes of our culture its vitality and its kick. Elvis's Yes is the grandest of all, his presentation of mastery the grandest fantasy of freedom, but it is finally a counterfeit of freedom: it takes place in a world that for all its openness (Everybody Welcome!) is aesthetically closed, where nothing is left to be mastered, where there is only more to accept. For all its irresistible excitement and enthusiasm, this freedom is complacent, and so the music that it produces is empty of real emotion—there is nothing this freedom could be for, nothing to be won or lost.

At best, when the fans gather around—old men and women who might see their own struggles and failures ennobled in the splendor of one who came from the bottom; middle-aged couples attending to the most glamorous nightclub act there is; those in their twenties and thirties who have grown with Elvis ever since he and they created each other years ago (and who might have a feeling he and they will make their trip through history together, reading their history in each other)—at best, Elvis will confirm all who are there *as* an audience. Such an event, repeated over and over all across the land, implies an America that is as nearly complete as any can be. But what is it worth?

When Elvis sings "American Trilogy" (a combination of "Dixie," "The Battle Hymn of the Republic," and "All My Trials," a slave song), he signifies that his persona, and the culture he has made out of blues, Las Vegas, gospel music, Hollywood, schmaltz, Mississippi, and rock 'n' roll, can contain any America you might want to conjure up. It is rather Lincolnesque; Elvis recognizes that the Civil War has never ended, and so he will perform The Union.

Well, for a moment, staring at that man on the stage, you can almost believe it. For if Elvis were to bring it off—and it is easy to think that only he could—one would leave the hall with a new feeling for the country; whatever that feeling might be, one's sense of place would be broadened, and enriched.

But it is an illusion. A man or woman equal to the song's pretension would have to present each part of the song as if it were the whole story, setting one against each other, proving that one American really could make the South live, the Union hold, and slavery real. But on the surface and beneath it, Elvis transcends any real America by evading it. There is no John Brown in his "Battle Hymn," no romance in his "Dixie," no blood in his slave song. He sings with such a complete absence of musical personality that none of the old songs matter at all, because he has not committed himself to them; it could be anyone singing, or no one. It is in this sense, finally, that an audience is confirmed, that an America comes into being; lacking any real fear or joy, it is a throwaway America where nothing is at stake. The divisions America shares are simply smoothed away.

But there is no chance anyone who wants to join will be excluded. Elvis's fantasy of freedom, the audience's fantasy, takes on such reality that there is nothing left in the real world that can inspire the fantasy, or threaten it. What *is* left is for the fantasy to replace the world; and that, night after night, is what Elvis and his audience make happen. The version of the American dream that is Elvis's performance is blown up again and again, to contain more history, more people, more music, more hopes; the air gets thin but the bubble does not burst, nor will it ever. This is America when it has outstripped itself, in all of its extravagance, and its emptiness is Elvis's ultimate throwaway.

Questions for Discussion

1. Greil Marcus starts with the assumption that Elvis is the king of rock and roll. What passages in the selection tell you this? What changes would be necessary in the selection if the writer were trying to convince skeptics of Elvis's supremacy?

2. The author assumes that the reader knows a great deal about Elvis Presley. What changes would be necessary if the selection were aimed at readers who know little or nothing about Elvis?

3. The subtitle to the book is *Images of America in Rock 'N' Roll Music*. What part of America does Elvis represent, according to the author?

4. Marcus writes, "It is a sure sign that a culture has reached a dead end when it is no longer intrigued by its myths. . . ." Furthermore, "It is a sure sign that an artist has reached a dead end when he or she becomes a myth." In what ways does the author support this contention?

5. What is Marcus's point about Elvis performing the *American Triology*? In formulating an answer, consider the following questions:

   a. Do the songs ("Dixie," "Battle Hymn of the Republic," and "All My Trials") contradict one another? (Think about the groups of people for whom each each song was written.)

   b. How does the example of the *American Trilogy* relate to Marcus's theory that the artist is at odds with society or at least on the fringes?

   c. Find another example in the text in which the author finds a theme that transcends the literal meaning of the songs? Do you think that Marcus is correct in his interpretation?

6. Both Schickel and Marcus include quotes from other critics in their overviews. In what way(s) are the quotes in each of the articles used in the same manner? In what way(s) do they differ in use? In answering this question consider the following:

   a. Why do the quotes in each article occur in the opening paragraph?

   b. Do the quotes seem excessive in their praise?

   c. Does each article agree or disagree with the quotes?

   d. Is each article in part an elaboration on the quotes?

SUSAN SONTAG

One of America's most prominent thinkers and critics, Susan Sontag was born in New York City in 1933; she received her bachelor's degree from the University of Chicago in 1951 and a master's from Harvard in both English (1954) and philosophy (1955). Ms. Sontag has been an instructor at Columbia, Rutgers, and the City University of New York. She has written novels, short stories, essays, and criticism and has also directed motion pictures. Among her best-known works are Against Interpretation (1966) and a novel and screenplay, Duet for Cannibals (1968).

In an interview she said, "I don't think there is one way of rendering experience which is correct. I believe in a plurality of experience. . . . There are different kinds of sensibility, different kinds of demands made on art, different self-conceptions of what the artist is. . . . Writing is a mysterious activity."

She reports having had the experience of being obsessed by photographs; her interest in them is due to her belief that photography gives us "an immense amount of knowledge that normally is not our experience."

No matter how many times the following selection is read, new points, ideas, nuances become apparent with each reading. The density and depth of the ideas are counterbalanced by the relative simplicity of diction and method: a point is asserted, then verified by detailed explanations or use of clarifying examples.

On Photography

Humankind lingers unregenerately in Plato's cave, still reveling, its age-old habit, in mere images of the truth. But being educated by photographs is not like being educated by older, more artisanal images. For one thing, there are a great many more images around, claiming our attention. The inventory started in 1839 and since then just about every-thing has been photographed, or so it seems. This very insatiability of the photographing eye changes the terms of confinement in the cave, our world. In teaching us a new visual code, photographs alter and enlarge our notions of what is worth looking at and what we have a right to observe. They are a grammar and, even more importantly, an ethics of seeing. Finally, the most grandiose result of the photographic enterprise is to give us the sense that we can hold the whole world in our heads—as an anthology of images.

To collect photographs is to collect the world. Movies and television programs light up walls, flicker, and go out; but with still photographs the image is also an object, lightweight, cheap to produce, easy to carry about, accumulate, store. In Godard's *Les Carabiniers* (1963), two sluggish lumpen-peasants are lured into joining the King's Army by the promise that they will be able to loot, rape, kill, or do whatever else they please to the enemy, and get rich. But the suitcase of booty that Michel-Ange and Ulysse triumphantly bring home, years later, to their wives turns out to contain only picture postcards, hundreds of them, of Monuments, Department Stores, Mammals, Wonders of Nature, Methods of Transport, Works of Art, and other classified treasures from around the globe. Godard's gag vividly parodies the equivocal magic of the photographic image. Photographs are perhaps the most mysterious of all the objects that make up, and thicken, the environment we recognize as modern. Photographs really are experience captured, and the camera is the ideal arm of consciousness in its acquisitive mood.

To photograph is to appropriate the thing photographed. It means putting oneself into a certain relation to the world that feels like knowledge—and, therefore, like power. A now notorious first fall into alienation, habituating people to abstract the world into printed words, is supposed to have engendered that surplus of Faustian energy and psychic damage needed to build modern, inorganic societies. But print seems a less treacherous form of leaching out the world, of turning it into a mental object, than photographic images, which now provide most of the knowledge people have about the look of the past and the reach of the present. What is written about a person or an event is frankly an interpretation, as are handmade visual statements, like paintings and drawings. Photographed images do not seem to be statements about the world so much as pieces of it, miniatures of reality that anyone can make or acquire.

Photographs, which fiddle with the scale of the world, themselves get reduced, blown up, cropped, retouched, doctored, tricked out. They age, plagued by the usual ills of paper objects; they disappear; they become valuable, and get bought and sold; they are reproduced. Photographs, which package the world, seem to invite packaging. They are stuck in albums, framed and set on tables, tacked on walls, projected as slides. Newspapers and magazines feature them; cops alphabetize them; museums exhibit them; publishers compile them.

For many decades the book has been the most influential way of arranging (and usually miniaturizing) photographs, thereby guaranteeing them longevity, if not immortality—photographs are fragile objects, easily torn or mislaid—and a wider public. The photograph in a book is, obviously, the image of an image. But since it is, to begin with, a printed, smooth object, a photograph loses much less of its essential quality when reproduced in a book than a painting does. Still, the book is not a wholly satisfactory scheme for putting groups of photographs into general circulation. The sequence in which the photographs are to be looked at is proposed by the order of pages, but nothing holds readers to the recommended order or indicates the amount of time to be spent on each photograph. Chris Marker's film, *Si j'avais quatre dromadaires* (1966), a brilliantly orchestrated meditation on photographs of all sorts and themes, suggests a subtler and more rigorous way of packaging (and enlarging) still photographs. Both the order and the exact time for looking at each photograph are imposed; and there is a gain in visual legibility and emotional impact. But photographs transcribed in a film cease to be collectable objects, as they still are when served up in books. . . .

Recently, photography has become almost as widely practiced an amusement as sex and dancing—which means that, like every mass art form, photography is not practiced by most people as an art. It is mainly a social rite, a defense against anxiety, and a tool of power.

Memorializing the achievements of individuals considered as members of families (as well as of other groups) is the earliest popular use of photography. For at least a century, the wedding photograph has been as much a part of the ceremony as the prescribed verbal formulas. Cameras go with family life. According to a sociological study done in France, most households have a camera, but a household with children is twice as likely to have at least one camera as a household in which there are no children. Not to take pictures of one's children, particularly when they are small, is a sign of parental indifference, just as not turning up for one's graduation picture is a gesture of adolescent rebellion.

Through photographs, each family constructs a portrait-chronicle of itself—a portable kit of images that bears witness to its connectedness. It hardly matters what activities are photographed so long as photographs get taken and are cherished. Photography becomes a rite of family life just when, in the industrializing countries of Europe and America, the very institution of the family starts undergoing radical surgery. As that claustrophobic unit, the nuclear family, was being carved out of a much larger family aggregate, photography came along to memorialize, to restate symbolically, the imperiled continuity and vanishing extendedness of family life. Those ghostly traces, photographs, supply the token presence of the dispersed relatives. A family's photograph album is generally about the extended family—and, often, is all that remains of it.

As photographs give people an imaginary possession of a past that is unreal, they also help people to take possession of space in which they are insecure. Thus, photography develops in tandem with one of the most characteristic of modern activities: tourism. For the first time in history, large numbers of people regularly travel out of their habitual environments for short periods of time. It seems positively unnatural to travel for pleasure without taking a camera along. Photographs will offer indisputable evidence that the trip was made, that the program was carried out, that fun was had. Photographs document sequences of consumption carried on outside the view of family, friends, neighbors. But dependence on the camera, as the device that makes real what one is experiencing, doesn't fade when people travel more. Taking photographs fills the same need for the cosmopolitans accumulating photograph-trophies of their boat trip up the Albert Nile or their fourteen days in China as it does for lower-middle-class vacationers taking snapshots of the Eiffel Tower or Niagara Falls.

A way of certifying experience, taking photographs is also a way of refusing it—by limiting experience to a search for the photogenic, by converting experience into an image, a souvenir. Travel becomes a strategy for accumulating photographs. The very activity of taking pictures is soothing, and assuages general feelings of disorientation that are likely to be exacerbated by travel. Most tourists feel compelled to put the camera between themselves and whatever is remarkable that they encounter. Unsure of other responses, they take a picture. This gives shape to experience: stop, take a photograph, and move on. The method especially appeals to people handicapped by a ruthless work ethic—

Germans, Japanese, and Americans. Using a camera appeases the anxiety which the work-driven feel about not working when they are on vacation and supposed to be having fun. They have something to do that is like a friendly imitation of work: they can take pictures.

People robbed of their past seem to make the most fervent picture takers, at home and abroad. Everyone who lives in an industrialized society is obliged gradually to give up the past, but in certain countries, such as the United States and Japan, the break with the past has been particularly traumatic. In the early 1970s, the fable of the brash American tourist of the 1950s and 1960s, rich with dollars and Babbittry, was replaced by the mystery of the group-minded Japanese tourist, newly released from his island prison by the miracle of overvalued yen, who is generally armed with two cameras, one on each hip.

Photography has become one of the principal devices for experiencing something, for giving an appearance of participation. One full-page ad shows a small group of people standing pressed together, peering out of the photograph, all but one looking stunned, excited, upset. The one who wears a different expression holds a camera to his eye; he seems self-possessed, is almost smiling. While the others are passive, clearly alarmed spectators, having a camera has transformed one person into something active, a voyeur: only he has mastered the situation. What do these people see? We don't know. And it doesn't matter. It is an Event: something worth seeing—and therefore worth photographing. The ad copy, white letters across the dark lower third of the photograph like news coming over a teletype machine, consists of just six words: ". . . Prague . . . Woodstock . . . Vietnam . . . Sapporo . . . Londonderry . . . LEICA." Crushed hopes, youth antics, colonial wars, and winter sports are alike—are equalized by the camera. Taking photographs has set up a chronic voyeuristic relation to the world which levels the meaning of all events.

A photograph is not just the result of an encounter between an event and a photographer; picture-taking is an event in itself, and one with ever more peremptory rights—to interfere with, to invade, or to ignore whatever is going on. Our very sense of situation is now articulated by the camera's interventions. The omnipresence of cameras persuasively suggests that time consists of interesting events, events worth photographing. This, in turn, makes it easy to feel that any event, once underway, and whatever its moral character, should be allowed to complete itself—so that something else can be brought into the world, the photograph. After the event has ended, the picture will still exist, conferring on the event a kind of immortality (and importance) it would never otherwise have enjoyed. While real people are out there killing themselves or other real people, the photographer stays behind his or her camera, creating a tiny element of another world: the image-world that bids to outlast us all.

Photographing is essentially an act of non-intervention. Part of the horror of such memorable coups of contemporary photojournalism as the pictures of a Vietnamese bonze reaching for the gasoline can, of a Bengali guerrilla in the act of bayoneting a trussed-up collaborator, comes from the awareness of how plausible it has become, in situations where the photographer has the choice between a photograph and a life, to choose the photograph. The person who intervenes cannot record; the person who is recording cannot intervene. Dziga Vertov's great film, *Man with a Movie Camera* (1929), gives the ideal image of the photographer as someone in perpetual movement, someone moving through a panorama of disparate events with such agility and speed that any intervention is out of the question. Hitchcock's *Rear Window* (1954) gives the complementary image: the photographer played by James Stewart has an intensified relation to one event, through his camera, precisely because he has a broken leg and is confined to a wheelchair; being temporarily immobilized prevents him from acting on what he sees, and makes it even more important to take pictures. Even if incompatible with intervention in a physical sense, using a camera is still a form of participation. Although the camera is an observation station, the act of photographing is more than passive observing. Like sexual voyeurism, it is a way of at least tacitly, often explicitly, encouraging whatever is going on to keep on happening. To take a picture is to have an interest in things as they are, in the status quo remaining unchanged (at least for as long as it takes to get a "good" picture), to be in complicity with whatever makes a subject interesting, worth photographing—including, when that is the interest, another person's pain or misfortune.

Questions for Discussion

1. Explain Sontag's attitude toward photography as both art and commodity.
2. In what ways does the photographer influence the look of the photograph?
3. The opening sentence alludes to Plato's myth of cave. In what ways does this myth relate to Sontag's ideas about photography?
4. Does the author have a central thesis? If so, explain it.
5. Do you find the selection to be free-flowing or highly ordered? In answering this question, you might consider the following paragraph. In what ways is it, in miniature, like the essay as a whole?

A new sense of the notion of information has been constructed around the photographic image. The photograph is a thin slice of space as well as time. In a world ruled by photographic images, all borders ("framing") seem arbitrary. Anything can be separated, can be made discontinuous, from anything else: all that is necessary is to frame the subject differently. (Conversely, anything can be made adjacent to anything else.) Photography reinforces a nominalist view of social reality as consisting of small units of apparently infinite number—as the number of photographs that could be taken of anything is unlimited. Through photographs, the world becomes a series of unrelated, freestanding particles; and history, past and present, a set of anecdotes and *faits divers*. The camera makes reality atomic, manageable, and opaque. It is a view of the world which denies interconnectedness, continuity, but which confers on each moment the character of a mystery. Any photography has multiple meanings; indeed, to see something in the form of a photograph is to encounter a potential object of fascination. The ultimate wisdom of the photographic image is to say: "There is the surface. Now think—or rather feel, intuit—what is beyond it, what the reality must be like if it looks this way." Photographs, which cannot themselves explain anything, are inexhaustible invitations to deduction, speculation, and fantasy.

How does the structure relate to Sontag's purpose?

6. One commentator on Sontag's work says, "It is easy to read, but hard to understand." Explain why you think that this statement is or is not valid in relation to "On Photography"?

7. Explain what Sontag means when she says, "Only that which narrates can make us understand." (You might think about Gould's explanation in "Natural Selection and the Human Brain" or Calder's "Cosmic Whirlwind.")

———————————— SUGGESTIONS FOR WRITING ————————————

1.   You have read about photography, Elvis Presley, Charlie Chaplin, and Mark Twain. If you had a free Saturday (on a dreary February day, too damp and dismal for outdoor exercise), would you prefer to visit a photographic exhibit, listen to recordings of Elvis Presley's music, watch Charlie Chaplin films, or read Mark Twain? In an essay, explain and argue in favor of your choice. (From your point of view, is one art form—graphic arts, music, film, literature—superior?)

2.   Write a brief critical overview of an artist (musician, writer, painter, or the like) that you either admire or think is overrated. Be sure to discuss major periods of the person's artistic career and relate them to your central thesis. You might want to refer to "A Chaplin Overview" before you start.

3.   Two old adages have it that life influences art, and art influences life. One might say that Shelley Fishkin deals with the influence of life on art and Susan Sontag deals with the influence of art on life. Does Marcus, in writing about Elvis Presley, deal with the influence of life on art or vice versa? And what about Schickel on Chaplin? In any case, the four selections in this chapter are evidence that the questions about life and art are very much alive.

Choose a figure whom you admire and enjoy, from any artistic realm (music, film, painting, dance, literature) and from any period in history (including contemporary), and write about one of the following:

   a.   the influence of that person's life on his or her art

   b.   the influence of that person's art on your life (or our lives) today

3.   In her essay, Susan Sontag is essentially answering this question: "What does photography mean?" Write an essay in answer to the following question: "What does _____ mean?" You can fill the blank with a sport (football, hockey), an art form (ballet, folk singing), or a social custom (Thanksgiving dinner, Friday night bash).

4.   Using Sontag's arguments, respond in a well-developed essay to the cliché "one picture is worth a thousand words." You might want to include your own arguments about the value of pictures versus words.

5.   Who is your favorite musician, artist, or author? Explain why he or she is your favorite. In developing this essay, think about your own values and history. How do the works of the artist satisfy your needs, meet your interests, and coincide with the culture to which you belong?

6.   The "nonfiction novel" is an extremely popular genre: Truman Capote's *In Cold Blood*, Norman Mailer's *Executioner's Song*, Joseph Wambaugh's *Onion Field*, Irving Stone's *Agony and the Ecstasy*, and many others. Choose a nonfiction novel you will enjoy reading, and then, in an essay, discuss the line between fiction and fact as you find it in the novel. What does the author do to turn the raw ore of fact into fiction? Fishkin's discussion of Mark Twain will give you some starting places.

7.   In her essay, Shelley Fishkin says, "The absence of 'style' is the absence of words." In other words, every writer has a style.

In an essay, compare the styles of Sontag, Marcus, Schickel, and Fishkin.

Here are some questions that will help you with your analysis:

a.   What sort of vocabulary does the author use? Common words? Slang? Specialized words? "Snobbish" words?

b.   What kinds of sentences do the authors produce? Long and complex? Short and simple?

c.   What about figures of speech? Metaphor? Irony? Similes?

d.   Is the essay well organized? How could organization be improved?

In your essay, be sure to give examples of the data you find through your analysis.

8.   Many people claim that cinema, televison, rock 'n' roll, and photography are not "Art." In an essay argue for or against that position for one of these media.

9.   In another chapter of this book, Michael Herr writes about the Vietnam War, raising the issue of the artist as a recorder who does not intervene and does not judge. In fact, Susan Sontag says that one problem with photography is its apparent aloofness. "The person who intervenes cannot record; the person who is recording cannot intervene."

What is art's responsibility toward life? Should the writer also be a propagandist for causes in which he or she believes? Should photographers attempt to sway political opinion with their choices of subjects? Even in the case of musicians, should they compose that which will further doctrines and causes?

10.   In his "Defense of Poetry," Percy Bysshe Shelley said, "Poets are the unacknowledged legislators of the world." If you substitute "artists" for "poets," is Shelley's statement defensible? In

what ways do artists legislate for the world? Indeed, one might ask whether art has an influence—for good or for ill—in our society. (Sontag says, "They [photographs] are a grammar and, even more importantly, an ethics of seeing.")

Glossary

allegory. A narrative in which the characters, actions, and scenes are
symbols of abstractions, such as faith or honesty. In *The Pilgrim's
Progress*, the seventeenth-century book by John Bunyan, the journey
represents the progress of the Christian soul, and the chief character
is named Christian. In one episode, Christian struggles through the
Slough of Despond and in another meets the Giant Despair. In some
allegories, the symbols are not as obvious as they are in Bunyan's
work.

analogy. Comparing an unknown or imperfectly known thing or concept
to something that is known. For example, the following analogy can
explain the *Reader's Guide to Periodical Literature* to someone who
has not used it, but who does understand how to use a card
catalogue in a library. "The *Reader's Guide* is an index of articles
published in generally nontechnical magazines, such as *Time* or the
Atlantic. It is like the card catalogue of a library, listing books by (1)
their authors or editors, (2) their titles, and (3) their subjects."

argument. 1. A reason given as proof. 2. A summary or an abstract of a
work. 3. The main point or **thesis** of a work.

chronicle. A list of events in their chronological order. Unlike a history, a chronicle does not interpret the events.

cliché. A stale, overused expression ("loomed on the horizon," "[someone is] all heart," "It takes a heap o' livin' to make a house a home," "[a dog] is man's best friend," "Only God can make a tree").

coherence. See form.

comparison and **contrast.** Comparison indicates the similarities of items, and contrast points out the differences in items, whether abstractions (communism and socialism) or concrete items (Cadillacs and Lincolns).

complex sentence. A sentence containing a principal (independent) clause and one or more dependent clauses: Sherlock Holmes smiled [independent] because he had discovered the person [dependent] who stole the necklace [dependent].

connotation. The suggested shades of meaning of words. *Mentally ill, insane,* and *bonkers* all refer to an abnormal state of mind; but *mentally ill* is less harsh than *insane,* and *bonkers* is a slang term that would be inappropriate in a serious discussion of the condition.

context. The parts of a text that surround a word, phrase, or passage and that shed light on its meaning. To determine the meaning of a word, phrase, or passage, the reader must normally take the context into consideration.

denotation. The specific dictionary definition of a word, as opposed to *connotation.*

diction. One's choice of words. If one uses slang, one's diction is slangy. In the following pairs, the first items represent formal diction and the second items are informal: journey/trip, profession/job, physician/doctor, penitentiary/pen, bicycle/bike, cinema/movie, potato/spud, vomit/barf, journal/magazine.

epic. 1. A long narrative poem about a hero and his or her adventures. 2. By extension, a large work that deals with heroic subject matter. Thus, it is often said that *War and Peace* is an epic novel.

episode. One event in a narrative. In many novels, each chapter represents an episode, and on such television series as "Dallas," each show is an episode.

essay. A relatively brief prose discussion of a restricted topic. Examples from this book are "On Embalming," by F. Gonzalez-Crussi, "The Unforgettable Fire," by Lewis Thomas, and "Natural Selection and the Human Brain: Darwin *vs.* Wallace," by Stephen Jay Gould.

etymology. The history of a word's derivation. You can find etymologies in the standard desk dictionaries.

extended definition. A definition that goes beyond giving only the essentials of denotation that are normally found in a dictionary. The following extended definition gives the meaning and traces the history of *laid-back:*

> What is "laid-back" anyway?
> The term originated in and derives its only precise meaning from the drug culture. If one was high enough frequently enough, chances are one was not going to be in a state of tension or acceleration or even in a straight-up position but, rather, laid-back. Taking on a broader meaning, it began to describe a mood of being easygoing and convincingly unconcerned with the power-money-fame-success game. The laid-back style crystalized in southern California in the early Seventies. It has since spread across the country and put many young men in a brand-new bind, contending as they must with the new duality problem—of success or personal freedom—while putting themselves through the necessary contortions to hide the old ambition on their sleeves.
>
> —Gail Sheehy, "The Laid-Back Philosophy"

fable. A brief tale, the purpose of which is to point out a moral. Often the characters in fables are animals, as in the fable of the fox and the grapes.

fallacy. 1. A false belief or idea. 2. A logical inconsistency. For example, here is a fallacious argument: Each part of this machine is light; therefore, the machine is light. (Even though each part may be light, the total, when assembled, may be very heavy.)

fiction. Imaginative **narrative;** narrative not based on historical fact.

figurative language. Language that uses figures of speech.

figure of speech. Language that departs from the normal and everyday to achieve an effect. Some figures of speech come from structure, as when President John F. Kennedy used mirror-image clauses: "Ask not what your country can do for you; ask what you can do for your country." Some figures of speech arise from meaning, as in metaphor. "Life is but a day" does not literally mean that we live only twenty-four hours, but that life is very short. See **irony, metaphor, personification,** and **simile.**

form. The form of a text includes its organization, which can be represented by an outline or a table of contents, but form also includes coherence, which is the way a reader assembles the individual parts of a text so they add up and make sense. The main point, or thesis, of a text may not appear in the organization until the end, but in understanding the text, the reader relates all of the parts to the thesis, or main idea, so that a diagram of how the reader understands the text might look like a complex organizational chart with the main idea at the top. If the reader cannot determine what the main idea is and how the other ideas relate to it, the text is incoherent for that reader.

genre. A loose category of works that are similar in style or subject matter. The murder mystery is a genre, as are the epic poem, the personal essay, and so on.

gist. The main point of a piece of writing.

grammar. In popular usage, *grammar* refers to language standards and norms: in this sense, double negatives, verbs that don't agree with their subjects, and pronouns that don't refer clearly to antecedents are all bad grammar. In a technical sense, grammar is the description of the vocabulary, sound system, and structure of a language. By extension, we can speak of the grammar of film, the grammar of art, and so on.

historical present. Narrating past events in the present tense: "After conquering Gaul, Caesar goes to Egypt, where he falls in love with the young Cleopatra."

image. 1. A figure of speech, such as metaphor or simile. 2. A passage in a text that vividly portrays sense impressions: sights, sounds, smells, tastes, tactile experiences. See **metaphor, simile.**

irony. A figure of speech in which the literal and the figurative meanings of the language are at odds. Literally, "You're a real genius" would be praise, but it is ridicule (and hence ironic) when said of someone who has just made an obvious error.

jargon. The specialized language used by a group, as the jargon of physicians, lawyers, physicists, gamblers, truckers, teenagers, and so on. To those who are outside the group, the language often seems virtually unintelligible. *Jargon* is often used as a term to denote unnecessarily obscure language.

lyric. A relatively brief poem, characterized normally by its emotional content. Kenneth Burke defines *lyric* as "The dancing of an attitude"; hence, the editors of this book use *lyric* in referring to prose essays because they are largely the expression of authors' attitudes. The lyric, unlike the narrative, does not tell a story.

metaphor. A figure of speech in which one term is equated with another in such a way that the resulting statement could not convey the literal truth. "All the world's a stage, / And all the men and women merely players" is quite different from "All the world's either land or sea, and all the men and women Homo sapiens." The former sets up a comparison between the world and the theater and between ordinary human beings and actors; the latter merely sets forth information.

monologue. One person speaking, as opposed to dialogue, in which two or more persons speak.

myth. A story that explains the origins and beliefs of a people. The myth of Romulus and Remus tells of the founding of Rome, and Greek mythology is the stories of the gods. Myths, like folk tales, arise anonymously and cannot be traced back to definite authors or sources. Some myths, like that of the American cowboy, arise from collective sources and live independent of single works.

narrative. Writing that relates the details of actions and events in chronological sequence.

nonfiction novel. A narrative that uses novelistic techniques of storytelling to relate events that have a historical basis.

novel. An extended fictional narrative.

novella. A fictional narrative somewhat briefer than the novel.

organization. See **form.**

parable. A story that answers a question or makes a moral point, as in the parables of Christ.

personal essay. In the personal essay, the character and attitudes of the writer become a major focus; in the formal essay, on the other hand, the main focus is on the subject matter. Thus personal essays are likely to have a unique "voice," as we hear when Charles Lamb, William Hazlitt, Richard Selzer, or F. Gonzalez-Crussi "speak" about subjects that interest them.

personal narrative. Autobiographical writing. In personal narrative, writers tell about episodes in their own lives. Autobiography is, of course, personal narrative, and personal narrative is autobiographical.

picaresque novel. A tale about a rascal, usually of low birth, making his or her way by wit and agility.

romance. A type of narrative in which adventure and love-making play an important part. The romance novel is opposed to the realistic novel, which attempts to portray life as it is really lived in an era. Romance literature is often viewed as escapist—that is, people read it to get away from reality.

short story. A relatively brief fictional narrative.

simile. A metaphor in which the relationship between terms is expressed by *like* or *as*: My love is like a red, red rose.

style. The style of a text comes about through the author's choice of vocabulary, the sentence structures used, and the figures of speech employed. The following examples illustrate how style varies depending on these factors.
Vocabulary   At eleven, we got on the plane to start our trip back east.

At eleven o'clock, we boarded the airplane to begin our journey to the east coast.

Sentence Structure   We were hungry. We were tired. We wanted lunch. We wanted a nap.

Being hungry and tired, we wanted lunch and a nap.

Figurative Language   The food was barely edible, and the plane was so noisy we couldn't sleep.

We choked down our slops but then couldn't sleep in that raucous barnyard.

symbol. Something that stands for or suggests something else. The cross is the symbol of Christianity as the Star of David is the symbol of Judaism.

thesis. The main point of an argument; a proposition to be proved.

tone. The mood of a piece of writing. Thus, the tone of John Donne's meditations is somber, and the tone of Ogden Nash's verse is humorous or even flippant.

topic sentence. The main point of a text, expressed in one sentence.

Index